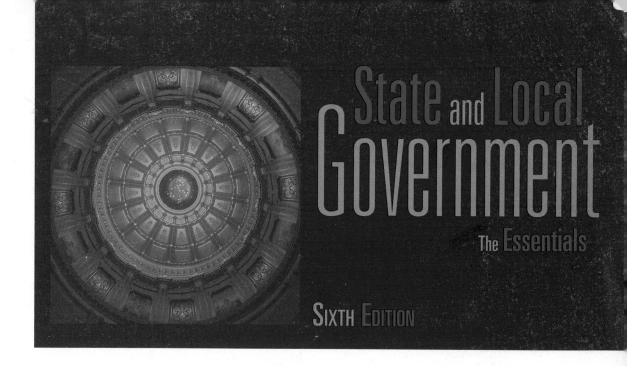

State and Local Government

The Essentials

SIXTH EDITION

Ann O'M. Bowman
Texas A&M University

Richard C. Kearney
North Carolina State University

CENGAGE
Learning

Australia • Brazil • Japan • Korea • Mexico • Singapore • Spain • United Kingdom • United States

**State and Local Government: The Essentials,
Sixth Edition**
Ann O'M. Bowman and Richard C. Kearney

Product Director: Suzanne Jeans

Product Manager: Carolyn Merrill

Content Developer: Lauren Athmer,
LEAP Publishing Services, Inc.

Content Coordinator: Jessica Wang

Product Assistant: Abigail Hess

Media Developer: Laura Hildebrand

Marketing Manager: Valerie Hartman

Rights Acquisitions Specialist: Jennifer
Meyer Dare

Manufacturing Planner: Fola Orekoya

Art and Design Direction, Production
Management, and Composition: Cenveo®
Publisher Services

Cover Image: Richard Cummins/Robert
Harding Picture Library/Age Fotostock

For product information and technology assistance, contact us at
Cengage Learning Customer & Sales Support, 1-800-354-9706
For permission to use material from this text or product, submit all requests online at **www.cengage.com/permissions.**
Further permissions questions can be emailed to
permissionrequest@cengage.com.

Library of Congress Control Number: 2013952681

ISBN-13: 978-1-285-73748-5

ISBN-10: 1-285-73748-2

Cengage Learning
200 First Stamford Place, 4th Floor
Stamford, CT 06902
USA

Cengage Learning is a leading provider of customized learning solutions with office locations around the globe, including Singapore, the United Kingdom, Australia, Mexico, Brazil and Japan. Locate your local office at **international.cengage.com/region**

Cengage Learning products are represented in Canada by Nelson Education, Ltd. For your course and learning solutions, visit **www.cengage.com**.

Purchase any of our products at your local college store or at our preferred online store **www.cengagebrain.com.**

Instructors: Please visit **login.cengage.com** and log in to access instructor-specific resources.

Printed in the United States of America
1 2 3 4 5 6 7 17 16 15 14 13

Brief Contents

Contents

Preface

The sixth edition of this book was written as states and localities began to rebound from the most profound national economic recession since the Great Depression. Even now, many parts of the country continue to deal with persistently high rates of unemployment and substantially reduced revenues for state and local governments. In many respects, it remains a difficult time.

Yet, the states and their localities are resilient. Many have been forced to cut critical services such as education and transportation to the bone, but they have done so proactively while ferreting out waste, furloughing and laying off thousands of workers, and conducting triage on the "extras" such as libraries, cultural events, and parks and recreation. Painful as the "Great Recession" was, it presented opportunities to use the crisis to make improvements in the way the business of government is done.

Despite the drumbeat of criticism of government and public officials in the mass media and by antigovernment talk show hosts, we like politics and public service, particularly at the state and local levels. We believe that government can be—and often is—a force for good in society. We do acknowledge some of the concerns voiced by critics of government. Yes, there continue to be inefficiencies, and sure, there are some politicians who, once elected, seem to forget the interests of the people back home, not to mention what their parents taught them. But by and large, state and local governments work well. On a daily basis, they tackle some of the toughest issues imaginable, designing and implementing creative and successful solutions to problems ranging from crime and corrections to education and the environment.

The full-length edition of *State and Local Government* will continue to appear at regular intervals. But some instructors prefer to assign a briefer paperback text to accommodate the demands of a quarter system, to leave time for other readings, and for many other reasons. In this sixth abbreviated edition of our text, we again attempt to capture the essentials of state and local government in all their immediacy and vitality. A major goal is to foster continuing student interest and involvement in state and local politics, policy, and public service. Many of the students who read this text will work in state and local government someday. Some will run successfully for public office. All will deal with state and local government throughout their lives. We want our readers to know that state and local governments are places where one person can "do good," make a difference, and serve a cause. For students who go on to graduate study in political science, public administration, public policy, or related fields, states and localities are fertile fields for research. And for those who are taking this course because they "have to" and who claim to dislike politics and government, we invite them to keep an open mind as they explore the fascinating world of politics at the grass roots.

THE THEME OF STATE AND LOCAL GOVERNMENT: THE ESSENTIALS

This book revolves around a central theme: The increased capacity and responsiveness of state and local governments. Our theme was tested during the Great Recession, and not found to be wanting. Despite their many challenges, state and local governments continue to be proactive, expanding their capacity to address effectively the myriad problems confronting their citizens. From Alabama to Wyoming, they are increasingly more responsive to their rapidly changing environment and to the demands of the citizens.

Our confidence in these governments does not blind us, however, to the varying capabilities of the fifty states and more than 89,000 units of local government. Some are better equipped to operate effectively than others. Many state and local governments benefit from talented leadership, a problem-solving focus, and an engaged citizenry. Others do not fare so well and their performance disappoints. Still, as a group, states and localities are the driving forces—the prime movers—in the U.S. federal system. Even those jurisdictions perennially clustered at the lower end of various ratings scales have made quantum leaps in their capability and responsiveness.

MAJOR CHANGES IN THE SIXTH EDITION

The political landscape of state and local government is forever changing. As a result, the sixth edition incorporates many new topics and emerging issues, without sacrificing the central theme of increased governmental capacity and responsiveness. Among the fresh items are the impact of population change and the continuation of "culture wars"; the most recent data on the 2012 and 2013 campaigns, elections, and ballot measures; states' reactions to the federal Affordable Care Act ("Obamacare"); a reexamination of states' rights arguments; the effect of new federal policies and new state laws; the latest round of legislative redistricting; and, of course, the impact of the Great Recession on states and localities. The growing threats to public employee unions and collective bargaining are covered, as is the increased incidence of conflict between local governments and their states. Moreover, the sixth edition contains the latest material on key court decisions and efforts to evaluate systematically judges' performance and legislative behavior. There are new discussions of innovative service delivery methods, intergovernmental finance, and the surprisingly large unfunded liabilities of retiree pensions and health care obligations. In exploring these topics and issues, we emphasize the differences across states and localities. In this sixth edition, coverage of local governments has been expanded and additional examples of policymaking have been included. Finally, we have made numerous updates to the tables and figures in the book, which yield opportunities for students to conduct their own Web-based research.

STRUCTURE AND CONTENT UPDATES

This book provides basic and up-to-date coverage of state and local institutions, processes, and policies. It can be used as a "stand-alone" text or in conjunction with supplementary readings.

In Chapter 1, we introduce the functions of nonnational governments and explore the theme of capacity and responsiveness. The central importance of federalism and intergovernmental relations is recognized in Chapter 2, which traces the twists and turns of the federal system from the scribblings of the framers to the Supreme Court's latest pronouncements on the Tenth Amendment. This chapter also includes a section on tribal governments and discussion of the current pause in devolution. The evolution and modern reform of the fundamental legal underpinnings of state governments—their constitutions—are discussed in Chapter 3. Chapter 4 explores citizen participation and elections, focusing on the increased access of citizens and the demands they are making on government. Featured in this edition are some of the innovative ways governments are engaging with citizens. Chapter 5, "Political Parties, Interest Groups, and Campaigns," includes essential material on party organization and interparty competition. Types and techniques of interest groups and the "new era" of political campaigns also receive attention.

Coverage of the three branches of government—legislative, executive, and judicial—incorporates changes resulting from the 2012 election outcomes. Legislative dynamics, behavior, processes, and capacity are presented in Chapter 6, with special attention paid to the impact of legislative professionalization and term limits. The roles, responsibilities, and powers of governors are examined in Chapter 7, with illustrations from today's chief executives. The so-called comeback governors—those who have returned to the office many years after they first occupied it—are showcased. Chapter 8 offers coverage of public administration, budgeting, and personnel policy, along with the politics of bureaucracy and the privatization, new public management, and e-government movements. In Chapter 9, judicial selection and decision making are considered within the context of judicial federalism and state court reform. New research on the role of money in judicial campaigns is presented.

Local governments are not treated as afterthoughts in this book. Most of the chapters provide a local dimension, whether political processes or governmental institutions. In addition, two chapters focus explicitly on the localities. Chapter 10 is devoted to state–local relations, including the distribution of authority between the two levels of government, and the all-important issues of urban sprawl and smart growth. Chapter 11 focuses on the multiple types and structures of local government and on leadership and governance in these jurisdictions. Finally, in Chapter 12, the principles and political economy of taxing and spending are explained, along with the fiscal unpleasantness of the Great Recession and the painful, as well as the innovative, ways that the states and localities are addressing the fiscal crisis, including the increased reliance by states on alternative revenues.

Throughout the text, policy examples are used to illustrate key concepts and critical points. Policymaking is, after all, a central function of government, regardless of level. Many of the examples highlight issues in education, criminal justice, economic development, social welfare, and environmental protection policy.

Those who prefer a more comprehensive and detailed treatment of state and local government, including separate policy chapters, are invited to examine the ninth edition of *State and Local Government* by the same authors (Cengage, ©2014, ISBN 978-1-4354-6268-7).

Much effort has been invested in making this book accessible to students. Examples throughout the chapters showcase the innovative, the unusual, and the insightful in state and local politics. New photographs offer visual images to bring the current world of state and local government to life for the reader. Maps, tables, and figures provide recent information in an engaging, colorful format. A glossary of key terms is located in the margins of the text. Each chapter opens with a chapter outline and a number of focus questions intended to highlight the chapter's most important issues and to spark discussion about the material. At the end of each chapter, major points are bulleted in a "Chapter Recap" section. References to websites, which can be accessed through the book's website, encourage student curiosity, engagement, and individual research.

TEACHING AND LEARNING AIDS

Online Instructor's Manual with Test Bank

ISBN 10: 1-285-73750-4 | ISBN 13: 978-1-2857-3750-8
A revised Instructor's Manual and Test Bank offers suggestions for class discussions, writing assignments, Internet and research projects, and exam questions to make course preparation easier. It is available at **login.cengage.com**.

Companion Website

ISBN 10: 1-285-73751-2 | ISBN 13: 978-1-2857-3751-5
Students will find open access to learning objectives, tutorial quizzes, chapter glossaries, flashcards, and crossword puzzles, all correlated by chapter. Instructors also have access to the Instructor's Manual. It is available at **login.cengage.com**.

ACKNOWLEDGMENTS

First, we thank our colleagues in the State Politics section and the Urban Politics section of the American Political Science Association for their ideas and comments on various editions of this book. And we thank as well researchers, too numerous to mention individually, for their insightful analyses that are published in scholarly journals and inform our latest edition. In addition, we thank our reviewers, who provided us with many thoughtful observations and examples:

Joe Gaziano, Lewis University
Lyle Stevens, Iowa Central Community College
Sandra Pavelka, Florida Gulf Coast University
Bruce Ransom, Clemson University
Steve Frank, St. Cloud State University
Paul Rozycki, Mott Community College, Flint, Michigan

We also extend our appreciation to our partners at Cengage Learning. Research assistance at Texas A&M University was provided by Sarina Rapini. At North Carolina State University, Lauren Hales assisted with various aspects of the book. Kathy Morgan compiled the user-friendly, comprehensive index. Finally, Carson, Blease, Kathy, Joel, and Laura contributed in many special ways to the final product, as usual. We assure them that they are not taken for granted.

A. O'M. B.

R. C. K.

About the Authors

Photo courtesy of Ann O'M. Bowman

Ann O'M. Bowman (Ph.D. University of Florida) is professor and holder of the Hazel Davis and Robert Kennedy Endowed Chair in the Bush School of Government and Public Service at Texas A&M University. She teaches courses in state and local politics and policy, intergovernmental relations, environmental policy and management, and public policy process. Her research interests revolve around questions of institutional change, policy adoption and implementation, and intergovernmental dynamics. She has published numerous books and articles on these topics over the years.

Photo courtesy of Richard C. Kearney

Richard C. Kearney (Ph.D. University of Oklahoma) is professor in the School of Public and International Affairs at North Carolina State University. He teaches courses in state and local politics, public policy process, and leadership. His research interests include comparative state politics and policy, labor relations, and human resource management policy. He has published prolifically on these and related topics.

New Directions for State and Local Governments

1

CHAPTER OUTLINE

- Studying State and Local Government in the Twenty-First Century
- The Capacity of States and Localities
- The People: Designers and Consumers of Government
- Linking Capacity to Results

FOCUS QUESTIONS

1. In what ways have state and local governments changed over the last three decades?
2. What are some of the challenges facing state and local governments today?
3. What qualities characterize state governments these days?

With appropriate oratorical flourishes, the Governor of New Hampshire, Maggie Hassan, delivered her 2013 State of the State message to the people of the Granite State. Although parts of the speech were specific to New Hampshire—such as the references to the Land and Community Heritage Investment program—many of the themes resonated beyond the state's borders. Balanced budgets, job creation, and educational reform were topics in countless gubernatorial addresses throughout the country. Governor Hassan's tone was determined: "I am ready to roll up my sleeves and work with you, because we have the opportunity and the capacity to build a bright economic future for our people."[1] And she urged the state legislators in attendance that day in the capitol to "lead the way and work together to build a stronger, more innovative New Hampshire." Spirited exhortations such as these were echoed in one state capitol after another in 2013. In New Hampshire and elsewhere, state and local governments are indeed tackling difficult issues and seeking innovative solutions to contemporary problems.

STUDYING STATE AND LOCAL GOVERNMENT IN THE TWENTY-FIRST CENTURY

The study of state and local government has typically received short shrift in the survey of U.S. politics.[2] Scholars and journalists tend to focus on glamorous imperial presidents, a rancorous and gridlocked Congress, and an independent and powerful Supreme Court. National and international issues capture the lion's share of media attention. Yet state and local politics are fascinating, precisely because they are up close and personal. True, a governor seldom gets involved in an international peace conference; state legislatures rarely debate the global narcotics trade. But the actors and institutions of states and localities are directly involved in our day-to-day lives. Education, welfare, health care, and crime are among the many concerns of state and local governments. These issues affect all of us. The sample of new state laws in Table 1.1 offers a glimpse into the world of state policymaking.

From Sewers to Science: The Functions of State and Local Governments

State and local governments are busy. They exist, in large measure, to make policy for and provide services to the public. This is no easy task. Nonnational governments must operate efficiently, effectively, and equitably, and they must do so

TABLE 1.1	A Sample of New State Laws Taking Effect in 2013
STATE	**DESCRIPTION OF THE LAW**
Alaska	Requires insurance coverage for autism spectrum disorders.
California	Prohibits the use of a vehicle or watercraft that has aquatic plants or animals on the exterior.
Florida	Revises the term "motor vehicle" to exclude swamp buggies.
Illinois	Permits those under 21 to consume alcohol if they are participating in a culinary program.
Maryland	Establishes the Civil Marriage Protection Act, becoming the ninth state to legalize same-sex marriage.
Michigan	Redefines the definition of a "pistol" from any firearm less than 30 inches in length to 26 inches. This definition also includes a firearm that by its construction and appearance conceals it as a firearm.
New Hampshire	Bans partial birth abortion except to save the life of the mother.
Oregon	Requires school districts to adopt a policy on teen dating violence and allocate funding for teen dating violence education.
Washington	Authorizes medical marijuana producers and dispensaries to ensure access to safe and adequate sources of marijuana for qualified patients.

SOURCE: National Conference of State Legislatures, "New Laws for a New Year: NCSL's Annual List of State Laws Going Into Effect on Jan. 1," http://www.ncsl.org/press-room/new-laws-for-a-new-year.aspx/ (December 20, 2012).

with limited financial resources. An efficient government is one that maximizes the output (services) from a given input (resources). A government performs effectively if it accomplishes what it sets out to do. Another expectation is that government function fairly—that its services be delivered in an equitable manner. It is no wonder, then, that state and local governments constantly experiment with new programs and new systems for delivering services, all the while seeking efficiency, effectiveness, and equity. For instance, the massive restructuring of Wyoming's state government a while back was intended, according to the governor, to produce "a better method of delivering services from the state government to the citizens."[3]

To promote the exchange of innovative approaches developed by state governments, the Council of State Governments (CSG), a national nonpartisan nonprofit organization, created a website called "Capitol Ideas." The intent is to showcase the different ways states address the myriad contemporary problems they face.[4] For example, in 2012, issues garnering attention at the Capitol Ideas site included home foreclosures, transportation finance, job growth, taxation of online purchases, and health insurance exchanges, among others. Although many of the innovations deal with public policies, some of the new ideas featured on the website are internal to government operations and are intended to make government function more effectively. These include the use of social media, the adoption of "budgeting for outcomes" approaches, the analysis of data with geographic information system technology, and the use of logic models to achieve desired program results. The unifying characteristic among these innovations is governmental willingness to try something new. And, good ideas tend to spread to other jurisdictions. Perhaps other cities will embrace the city of Houston's new web tool, "My Tax Dollars at Work." In an instant, a Houston homeowner can find out the proportion of her local property taxes going to various city departments such as public safety, trash and recycling pickup, parks and recreation services, land development, and city administration.

Our Approach

The argument of this book is that states and localities have the capacity to play central roles in the U.S. federal system. **Capacity** refers to a government's ability to respond effectively to change, make decisions efficiently and responsively, and manage conflict.[5] Capacity, then, is tied to governmental capability and performance. In short, states and communities with more capacity work better than those with less capacity.

But what factors make one government more capable than another? Governmental institutions such as the bureaucracy matter. The fiscal resources of a **jurisdiction** and the quality of its leadership make a difference. Much of the research on capacity has focused on the administrative dimension of government performance, evaluating items such as financial management, information technology, and strategic planning. In a 2008 study of state government performance, the highest overall scores went to Utah, Virginia, and Washington (each state received an A–) and Delaware, Georgia, Michigan, Missouri, and Texas (with grades of B+).[6] Earlier evaluations of forty large counties had

capacity
The ability of government to respond effectively to change, make decisions efficiently and responsively, and manage conflict.

jurisdiction
The territorial range of government authority; "jurisdiction" is sometimes used as a synonym for "city" or "town."

Fairfax, Virginia, and Maricopa, Arizona, earning the best grades. Among the thirty-five cities examined, Austin, Texas, and Phoenix, Arizona, were at the top of the list. Other things being equal, we would expect high-scoring states, counties, and cities to produce "better" government than low-scoring jurisdictions.

A survey in Iowa showed another side to governance. When asked about the characteristics of good government, Iowans put trustworthiness, ethics, financial responsibility, and accountability at the top of the list.[7] Residents of the Hawkeye State are not unusual; all of us want our institutions and leaders to govern honestly and wisely. As political scientist David Hedge reminds us, better government is found in jurisdictions that are responsible and democratic.[8] But states and localities face significant challenges as they govern. Complex, often contradictory forces test the most capable of governments. State and local governments need all the capacity they can muster and maybe even a little bit of luck to meet those challenges.

federalism

A system of government in which powers are divided between a central (national) government and regional (state) governments.

Federalism, with its overlapping spheres of authority, provides the context for state and local action. Intervention by the national government in the affairs of a state or local government is defensible, even desirable in some cases. For example, the environmental problems of the 1960s and 1970s exceeded state and local governments' ability to handle them, so corrective action by the national government was generally welcomed. However, some federal actions are greeted less enthusiastically. For instance, No Child Left Behind (NCLB), the education law promoted by President George W. Bush and enacted by the U.S. Congress in 2002, is considered too intrusive by many state leaders and school districts. Since its passage, state legislators throughout the country have debated resolutions challenging the authority of this federal law; and school districts have lamented the provisions related to student achievement and school accountability. In reaction, the U.S. Department of Education has granted a growing number of states waivers such that they can create their own programs to comply with the law.[9]

Our approach takes into account intergovernmental relations (that is, the relationships among the three levels of government)—particularly the possibilities for cooperation and conflict. Jurisdictions (national, state, or local) possess policymaking authority over specific, but sometimes overlapping, territory. They confront innumerable situations in which boundaries blur and they must work together to accomplish an objective. Cooperation in some cases, however, is countered by conflict in other instances. Each level of government tends to see problems from its own perspective and designs solutions accordingly. In sum, both cooperation and conflict define the U.S. federal system.

THE CAPACITY OF STATES AND LOCALITIES

With notable exceptions, states and their local governments in the 1950s and 1960s were havens of traditionalism and inactivity. Many states were characterized by unrepresentative legislatures, glad-handing governors, and a hodge-podge court system. Public policy tended to reflect the interests of the elite;

delivery of services was frequently inefficient and ineffective. According to former North Carolina governor Terry Sanford, the states "had lost their confidence, and people their faith in the states."[10] No wonder that, by comparison, the federal government appeared to be the answer, regardless of the question. In fact, political scientist Luther Gulick proclaimed, "It is a matter of brutal record. The American State is finished. I do not predict that the states will go, but affirm that they have gone."[11]

Those days are as outmoded as a black-and-white television set. States and their local governments have proved themselves capable of designing and implementing "an explosion of innovations and initiatives."[12] As a result, even many national leaders have embraced the roles of states and localities as laboratories for policy experimentation. A *New York Times* story with the headline, "As Congress Stalls, States Pursue Cloning Debate," is indicative of states pushing the policy envelope.[13]

The blossoming of state governments in the 1980s—their transformation from weak links in the federal chain to viable and progressive political units—resulted from several actions and circumstances, as discussed in the next section.[14] In turn, the resurgence of state governments has generated a host of positive outcomes. During the 1990s and early 2000s, states and localities honed their capacity and became **proactive** rather than reactive. They faced hard choices and creatively crafted new directions. A word of caution is necessary, however. The challenges of governance can be great, and not all states enjoy the same level of capacity. Furthermore, fiscal stresses such as those endured by state governments as the second decade of the twenty-first century began sorely tested the ability of even the most capable states to function effectively.

proactive
An anticipatory condition, as opposed to a reactive one.

How States and Localities Increased Their Capacity

Several factors contributed to the resurgence of the states. U.S. Supreme Court decisions in the 1960s on legislative apportionment made for more equitable representation; the extension of two-party competition in the 1970s to states formerly dominated by one party gave voters more choices. At the same time, states and localities expanded their lobbying presence in the nation's capital, exerting influence on the design and funding of intergovernmental programs.

Most important, state governments quietly and methodically reformed themselves by modernizing their constitutions and restructuring their institutions. Since the 1970s, more than three-quarters of the states have ratified new constitutions or substantially amended existing ones. Formerly thought of as the "drag anchors of state programs" and as "protectors of special interests,"[15] these documents have been streamlined and made more workable. Even in states without wide-ranging constitutional reform, tinkering with constitutions is almost endless, thanks to the amendment process. Almost every state general election finds constitutional issues on the ballot.

States have also undertaken various internal adjustments intended to improve the operations of state governments.[16] Modernized constitutions and statutory changes have strengthened the powers of governors by increasing appointment and removal powers and by allowing longer terms, consecutive succession, larger staffs, enhanced budget authority, and the power to reorganize the executive branch. Throughout the country, state agencies are staffed by skilled administrators. The bureaucracy itself is more and more demographically representative of the public. Annual rather than biennial sessions, more efficient rules and procedures, additional staff, and higher salaries have helped make reapportioned state legislatures more professional, capable, and effective. State judicial systems have also been the targets of reform; examples include the establishment of unified court systems, the hiring of court administrators, and the creation of additional layers of courts.

Increased Capacity and Improved Performance

The enhanced capacity enjoyed by state and local governments has generated a range of mostly positive results. The following five factors reinforce the performance of states and localities.

Improved Revenue Systems Economic downturns and limits on taxing and spending have caused states to implement new revenue-raising strategies to maintain acceptable service levels. States also granted local governments more flexibility in their revenue systems. South Carolina, for example, now allows counties the option of providing property-tax relief to residents in exchange for increasing the local sales tax.

As a rule, state governments prefer to increase user charges, gasoline taxes, and so-called sin taxes on alcohol and tobacco and only reluctantly raise sales and income taxes. Over time, revenue structures have been redesigned to make them more diversified and more equitable. State **rainy day funds**, legalized gambling through state-run lotteries and pari-mutuels, and extension of the sales tax to services are examples of diversification strategies. Exemptions of food and medicine from consumer sales taxes and the enactment of property-tax breaks for poor and elderly people characterize efforts at tax equity. These revamped revenue structures helped states deal with the budget crises they confronted during the Great Recession of 2008–2011.

States continue to tinker with their revenue-raising schemes. One successful foray into creative revenue raising has been the specialty license plate. Maryland, for example, has generated millions of dollars with its "Treasure the Chesapeake" plate. Monies generated by the plates are earmarked for special programs—in this case, water-quality monitoring and erosion control in the Chesapeake Bay. Nearly all states now offer specialty plates. In New York for instance, owners can equip their cars, for an extra fee, with license plates honoring their favorite professional sports team or NASCAR driver. A brand new approach to generating cash for states comes from the world of retail stores: the marketing of official gift cards. For example, both Kentucky and Ohio sell gift cards that can be used at state park locations for various park services and merchandise.

rainy day funds

Money set aside when a state's finances are healthy, for use when state revenues decline. Formally called "budget stabilization funds."

Another effort of enterprising localities is to sell merchandise. Los Angeles County has marketed coroner toe tags as key chains; Portland and Tampa rent the entire outside surfaces of their buses to advertisers. New York City, which loses thousands of street signs (Wall Street is especially popular) to souvenir-stealing tourists, now sells replicas. Tucson and several other Arizona cities operate an eBay-style online silent auction to sell surplus goods, such as unclaimed police evidence. But the revenue generated by those actions is dwarfed by Chicago, which has sold (actually, leased for ninety-nine years) four city-owned parking garages to an investment bank for a tidy sum of $563 million. As these examples show, states and localities are willing to experiment when it comes to revenue enhancement.

Expanding the Scope of State Operations State governments have taken on new roles and added new functions. In some instances, states are filling in the gap left by the national government's de-emphasis of an activity; in other cases, states are venturing into uncharted terrain. It was states that designed the first family leave legislation giving workers time off to care for newborn babies and ailing relatives, as well as the first Amber Alert systems to broadcast information about abducted children. The federal government eventually followed suit with a national family leave act and a national Amber Alert system. In addition, states have taken the initiative in ongoing intergovernmental programs by creatively using programmatic authority and resources. Prior to federal welfare reform in the mid-1990s, several states had established workfare programs and imposed time limits on the receipt of welfare benefits, provisions that were at the center of the subsequent federal legislation.

States persist in expanding their scope of operations, whether it is California's venture into stem-cell research or Florida's strides in bioterror readiness. Hawaii has begun construction of an extensive network of plug-in spots where electric cars can be recharged. New Mexico is a partner in a new commercial spaceport facility that it hopes will become the center for space tourism. In short, states are embracing their role as policy innovators and experimenters in the U.S. federal system.

Faster Diffusion of Innovations Among states, there have always been leaders and followers. The same is true for local governments. Now that states and localities have expanded their scope and are doing more policymaking, they are looking more frequently to their neighbors for advice, information, and models.[17] As a result, successful solutions spread from one jurisdiction to another. For example, Florida was the first state to create a way for consumers to stop telephone solicitations. By 1999, five more states had passed laws letting residents put their names on a "do-not-call" list for telemarketers. Seven additional states adopted similar legislation over the next two years before Congress enacted a national statute.[18] Another fast-moving innovation was a 2004 New York law that required cigarettes that were sold in the state to be self-extinguishing. Concerned over fire safety, California followed suit, and by 2007, nineteen other states had adopted the law.[19]

Local-level innovations spread rapidly, too. Education and environmental protection offer many examples of this phenomenon. When Miami-Dade County, Florida, hired a private company to run a public elementary school, other school districts hoping to improve quality and cut costs quickly followed suit. Initial experiments with privatization spawned other innovations such as charter schools. The issue of climate change was addressed at the local level in 2005 when the mayor of Seattle became the first local official to commit his city to a plan to reduce the emission of greenhouse gases. By 2013, more than 1,050 mayors of other U.S. cities had jumped on the climate change bandwagon.[20] It is worth noting, of course, that the diffusion of new ideas depends in large part on their fit and effectiveness.

Obviously, state and local governments learn from one another. Communication links, including social media such as Facebook and Twitter, are increasingly varied and frequently used. A state might turn to nearby states when searching for policy solutions. Regional consultation and emulation is logical: Similar problems often beset jurisdictions in the same region, a program used in a neighboring state may be politically more acceptable than one from a distant state, and organizational affiliations bring state and local administrators together with their colleagues from nearby areas. Research, however, has shown that states also borrow ideas from peer states, that is, states that are like them in important ways such as ideological leaning or economic base.[21] In the search for solutions, states and localities are increasingly inclusive.

Interjurisdictional Cooperation Accompanying the quickening flow of innovations has been an increase in interjurisdictional cooperation. States are choosing to confront and resolve their immediate problems jointly. A similar phenomenon has occurred at the local level with the creation of regional organizations to tackle area-wide problems collectively.

Interjurisdictional collaboration takes many forms, including informal consultations and agreements, interstate committees, legal contracts, reciprocal legislation, and interstate compacts. For example, all fifty states and the District of Columbia, Puerto Rico, and the U.S. Virgin Islands have a mutual agreement to aid one another when natural disasters such as hurricanes, earthquakes, and forest fires strike. Another illustration is the Streamlined Sales Tax Project, which led to an interstate agreement on the simplification of sales and use taxes. Twenty-four states were participating in the agreement as of 2013, the intent of which is to make it easier for states to collect taxes on items purchased online. In both the disaster-aid case and the tax project, the states worked together because they could see some benefit from cooperation.

States often cooperate when it comes to consumer protection litigation. Five states—Mississippi, Minnesota, West Virginia, Florida, and Massachusetts—were among the first to band together to share information and design tactics in their lawsuits against tobacco companies in the mid-1990s; by 1998, thirty-seven other states had joined in the effort to recover the Medicaid costs of treating tobacco-caused diseases.[22] In the same year, attorneys general in twenty states filed an antitrust lawsuit against Microsoft Corporation, claiming that the firm illegally stifled competition, harmed consumers, and undercut innovation in the computer software industry. In another illustration of inter-jurisdictional cooperation, two-thirds of the states joined together in a legal complaint against six computer chip manufacturers, alleging that they engaged in illegal price-fixing. The case was eventually settled out of court in 2010 for a tidy $173 million.[23]

Increased jurisdictional cooperation fosters a healthy climate for joint problem solving. In addition, when state and local governments solve their own problems, they protect their power and authority within the federal system. It appears that states are becoming more comfortable working with one another. The beginning of the twenty-first century was indeed historic. States were engaged in more cooperative interactions than ever before.[24]

Increased National-State Conflict An inevitable by-product of more capable state and local governments is intensified conflict with the national government. One source of this discord has been federal laws and grant requirements that supersede state policy; another is the movement of states onto the national government's turf. National-state conflict is primarily a cyclical phenomenon, but contention has increased in recent years. The issue of unfunded mandates—the costly requirements that federal legislation imposes on states and localities—has been particularly troublesome. In an effort to increase the visibility of the mandates issue, several national organizations of state and local officials sponsored a "National Unfunded Mandate Day" in the mid-1990s. Making a strong case against mandates, then-governor George Voinovich of Ohio stated: "Unfunded mandates devastate our budgets, inhibit flexibility and innovation in implementing new programs, preempt important state initiatives, and deprive states of their responsibility to set priorities."[25] Congress responded in 1995 by passing a mandate relief bill that requires cost-benefit analyses of proposed mandates; however, the law contains some loopholes that have weakened its impact.

Some of the disputes pit a single state against the national government, as in Nevada's fight to block the U.S. Energy Department's plan to build a nuclear fuel waste storage facility 100 miles northwest of Las Vegas. Another example is the effort by Texas to continue its use of a flexible permitting process to regulate industrial air pollution, a process that has been challenged repeatedly by the U.S. Environmental Protection Agency (EPA). In other conflicts, the national government finds itself besieged by a coordinated, multistate effort, for example, when ten states sued the U.S. EPA over the regulation of greenhouse gases or when twenty states challenged the federal health care reform law in 2010.[26]

National-state conflicts are resolved (and sometimes made worse) by the federal judicial system. Cases dealing with alleged violations of the U.S. Constitution by state and local governments are heard in federal courts and decided by federal judges. Sometimes the rulings take the federal government into spheres long considered the purview of state and local governments.

Challenges Facing State and Local Governments

Increased capacity does not mean that all state and local problems have been solved. Nonnational governments face three tough challenges today: fiscal stress, interjurisdictional conflict, and political corruption.

Fiscal Stress The most intractable problem for states and localities involves money. State and local finances are vulnerable to cyclical peaks and troughs in the national economy as well as occasional changes in public finance. The national economic recession of 2008–2011 hit states and localities hard—very hard—and the impact on governmental budgets was significant. Connecticut governor Jodi Rell did not mince words when she said, "These are the worst financial times any of us can remember . . . let's face it, it's scary."[27]

The fiscal impact of the Great Recession was deep and prolonged, with four consecutive years in which states faced significant mismatches between revenues and spending. During that time, state lawmakers scrambled to close budget gaps that, according to estimates by the National Conference of State Legislatures, totaled $510.5 billion.[28] State rainy day funds grew precariously drier as legislators looked to them for short-term relief. In an effort to save money, some prisons were closed in Colorado, Kansas, Michigan, North Carolina, and Washington; in some states funding for education was reduced and cash assistance for low-income families was cut; in others, state agencies were **downsized** and employee wages were frozen. State leaders sought new revenues also: Income tax rates were increased in California, Hawaii, and New York; sales tax increases were enacted in Arizona, California, and Massachusetts, among other states. Facing the largest deficit of any state, the governor of California battled with the legislature over several measures including "selling the Los Angeles Memorial Coliseum, San Quentin State Prison and other state property, eliminating welfare benefits for 500,000 families, terminating health coverage for nearly one million low-income children and closing 220 of the state's parks."[29]

Local governments felt the heat as well; Dallas, one of the country's largest cities, provides an example. To close a $190.2 million deficit in its budget, the city of Dallas made cuts in numerous city services including street repairs, arts funding, library hours, and park maintenance; in addition, nearly 800 city employees lost their jobs.[30] The story was much the same in many other localities: Reduce costs as painlessly as possible, and if necessary, increase fees. Some relief was provided when Congress passed the $787 billion American Recovery and Reinvestment Act, informally known as the federal stimulus plan, but many states and communities felt the fiscal pinch well into 2012. Cash-strapped states and localities are confronting a "**new normal**" in which they are expected to provide public services with fewer dollars at their disposal. If there were ever a time for innovation and fresh thinking, the aftermath of the Great Recession is it.

Increased Interjurisdictional Conflict Tension is inherent in a federal system because each of the entities has its own set of interests, as well as a share of the national interest. When one state's pursuit of its interests negatively affects

downsize
Reducing the size and cost of something, especially government.

new normal
An environment characterized by stagnant revenues and budget cuts, leading to changes in the provision of public services.

another state, conflict occurs. Such conflict can become destructive, threatening the continuation of state resurgence. In essence, states end up wasting their energies and resources on counterproductive battles among themselves.

Interjurisdictional conflict is particularly common in two policy areas very dear to state and local governments: natural resources and economic development. States rich in natural resources want to use these resources in a manner that will yield the greatest return. Oil-producing states, for instance, levy severance taxes that raise the price of oil. And states with abundant water supplies resist efforts by arid states to tap into the supply. The most serious disputes often occur among neighboring states. One illustration is the protracted dispute between California and six other western states over water allocations from the Colorado River. In short, the essential question revolves around a state's right to control a resource that occurs naturally and that is highly desired by other states. Resource-poor states argue that resources are in fact national and should rightfully be shared among states.

In the area of economic development, conflict is extensive because all jurisdictions want healthy economies. Toward this end, states try to make themselves attractive to business and industry often through tax breaks and regulatory relaxation. Conflict arises when states become involved in bidding wars—that is, when an enterprise is so highly valued that actions taken by one state are matched and exceeded by another. Suppose, for example, that an automobile manufacturer is considering shutting down an existing facility and relocating. States hungry for manufacturing activity will assemble a package of incentives such as below-cost land, tax concessions, and subsidized job training in an attempt to attract the manufacturer. The state that wants to keep the manufacturer will try to match these inducements. In the long run, economic activity is simply relocated from one state to another. The big winner is the manufacturer.

Political Corruption Corruption exists in government, which is no great surprise. Most political systems can tolerate the occasional corrupt official, but if corruption becomes commonplace, it undermines governmental capacity and destroys public trust. Public reaction ranges from cynicism and alienation (corruption as "politics as usual") to anger and action (corruption as a spur to reform). A survey found that the more extreme the corrupt act (a city clerk embezzling $100,000 versus a police officer accepting free food at a restaurant), the harsher the public's judgment.[31] Even so, mitigating motives or circumstances tend to reduce the public's outrage (for example, a public official taking a bribe but using the money to pay his sick child's hospital bills). But governmental scandals have been linked tentatively to another negative effect—a slowdown in economic growth. Research on states found that federal corruption convictions are associated with declines in job growth primarily because, from a business perspective, corruption creates uncertainty and inflates costs.[32]

States and localities have taken great precautions to reduce the amount of wrongdoing occurring in their midst. Government has much more **transparency** than ever before, with more openness and more rules. But the

transparency
A characteristic of a government that is open and understandable, one in which officials are accountable to the public.

statutes and policies are only as good as the people whose behavior they regulate. Examples of corrupt behavior are not hard to find. For instance, in 2008, flamboyant Illinois governor Rod Blagojevich was led away in handcuffs after federal officials arrested him in a "pay to play" scandal that involved his plan to sell a vacant U.S. Senate seat. He was later impeached and removed from office by the state legislature and in 2011 was convicted in federal court on eighteen corruption-related charges.

A pair of economists researching corruption in the states asked statehouse reporters—folks who are familiar with the goings-on in the capitol—to assess the overall level of corruption in their state compared to other states.[33] At the top of the list was Rhode Island, followed by Louisiana and New Mexico. States at the bottom of the comparative corruption list included the Dakotas, Colorado, and Maine. Others have speculated that capital cities isolated from major population centers tend to breed more corruption. At the local level, data on the number of federal convictions for public corruption over a thirty-five-year period showed the Chicago metropolitan area to be the most corrupt in the nation.[34] Although states and localities clearly are not corruption-free, the amount of corruption is relatively low, given the vast number of public officials serving in nonnational levels of government. Still, even a whiff of scandal can undermine public confidence in government and sap governmental capacity.

THE PEOPLE: DESIGNERS AND CONSUMERS OF GOVERNMENT

A book on state and local government is not only about places and governments; it is also about people—the public and assorted officeholders—and the institutions they create, the processes in which they engage, and the policies they adopt. Thus, this volume contains chapters on institutions, such as legislatures, and on processes, such as elections; and it discusses policies, such as those pertaining to education. But in each case, people are the ultimate focus: A legislature is composed of lawmakers and staff members who deal with constituents; elections involve candidates, campaign workers, and voters (as well as nonvoters); and education essentially involves students, teachers, administrators, parents, and taxpayers. In short, the word *people* encompasses an array of individuals and roles in the political system.

Ethnic-Racial Composition

More than 300 million people live in the United States. Some can trace their heritage back to the *Mayflower*, whereas others look back only as far as a recent naturalization ceremony. Very few can claim indigenous (native) American ancestry. Instead, most Americans owe their nationality to some forebear who came here in search of a better life or—in the case of a significant minority, the descendants of slaves—to ancestors who made the journey to this country not out of choice but because of physical coercion. The appeal of the United States to economic and political refugees from other countries continues, with Mexicans, Central Americans, and eastern Africans among the most recent arrivals.

The United States is a nation of immigrants. This gives it ethnic richness and cultural diversity. Official U.S. Census figures for 2010 put the Anglo population at 72 percent, the African American population at 13 percent, the Latino population at 16 percent, the Asian population at 5 percent, and the American Indian and Alaska Native population at 1 percent.[35] (The numbers total more than 100 percent because of some double-counting.) These figures vary, of course, from one jurisdiction to another. Approximately 38 million, or 13 percent, of the nation's population was born in another country, with 53 percent of the foreign born from Latin America, and another 28 percent from Asia.

One aspect of immigration—illegal immigration—is putting the words from the sonnet inscribed on the Statue of Liberty (containing the phrase "Give me your tired, your poor, your huddled masses") to a severe test. Although accurate numbers are hard to come by, one 2011 estimate by the U.S. Department of Homeland Security placed the number of illegal immigrants at approximately 11.5 million, of which approximately 59 percent were from Mexico.[36] The issue of illegal immigration has divided the American public into two camps. One camp argues that people who are in the United States illegally receive public benefits, take scarce jobs, and pay little in taxes. This group favors legislative proposals that clamp down on illegal immigration by requiring verification of workers' legal status and restricting the issuance of drivers' licenses to U.S. citizens and legal immigrants. The other camp contends that undocumented workers actually contribute more in taxes than they consume in public services; moreover they take on jobs that others do not want and therefore contribute to economic growth. This group tends to support legislation such as the "path to citizenship," a federal proposal that sets up a procedure for becoming a legal resident, and the "DREAM Act," which makes high school graduates and those who have served honorably in the military eligible for citizenship, despite their parents' illegal immigration status.

Arizona's tough new law, passed in 2010, requires immigrants to carry documents to prove they are in the United States legally and gives local police broad power to question and arrest anyone suspected of being in the country illegally.[37] Critics claim that the law is discriminatory and will lead to ethnic profiling. Upon enactment, the law unleashed a flurry of demonstrations, both supportive and oppositional, initially in Arizona, and eventually around the country. Some jurisdictions, such as Los Angeles, threatened to boycott the Grand Canyon State in retaliation for the law while several other states rallied around Arizona. Similarly tough laws were passed in 2011 in Alabama, Georgia, Indiana, South Carolina, and Utah. The federal government filed suit against the Arizona law in 2010, and parts of the law were struck down by the U.S. Supreme Court, although the major provision was sustained. Actions by state governments provoked the U.S. Congress into serious consideration in 2013 of national immigration reform.

Clearly, ethnicity and culture still matter, despite the image of America as a melting pot. Researchers have found that a state's racial and ethnic diversity goes a long way in explaining its politics and policies.[38] Looking toward the future, census projections for the year 2050 estimate a nation of approximately 440 million people, with the Anglo population dropping to 50 percent of the total, the African American population increasing slightly to 15 percent, the Latino population reaching 25 percent, and an Asian population at 8 percent.[39] If trends hold, state politics and policy in the mid-twenty-first century will be affected.

Population Growth and Migration

As a whole, the United States grew by an estimated 1.7 percent during the period 2010 to 2012. Disaggregating the data by state reveals several trends. Reflecting the pattern of the previous decade, high rates of growth occurred in western states; substantially slower growth rates characterized the Northeast and Midwest. (The map in Figure 1.1 displays the estimated percentage change in each state's population from 2010 to 2012.) North Dakota was the growth leader for the period, with an estimated 4 percent increase. Texas and Utah followed, growing at a 3.6 percent and 3.3 percent clip, respectively.[40] A strong labor market and an attractive, inexpensive lifestyle are among those states' features. The lowest rates of estimated population change were recorded in Rhode Island (-0.2 percent), Michigan (0 percent), and Vermont (0 percent).

Sunbelt

An unofficial region of the United States, generally comprising the South and the West.

For metropolitan areas, the population trends from 2010 to 2012 are equally compelling. On average, higher rates of growth are more prevalent in communities in the **Sunbelt** region than in communities of the **Frostbelt**. The growth leaders among metropolitan areas included places such as The Villages (8.8 percent), located in central Florida, and two Texas metro areas, Midland (7.1 percent) and Austin–Round Rock (6.9 percent).[41] Metro areas at the other end of the population change spectrum during the 2010 to 2012 period included Pine Bluff, Arkansas, which lost an estimated 2.8 percent of its population; Flint, Michigan, -1.7 percent; and Johnstown, Pennsylvania, -1.5 percent.

Frostbelt

An unofficial region of the United States, generally consisting of the Northeast and the Midwest.

Population changes carry economic and political consequences for state and local governments. As a general rule, power and influence follow population. A state's representation in the U.S. Congress and its votes in the Electoral College are at stake. As a result of the 2010 census, Texas picked up four seats in the U.S. House of Representatives, while Florida added two seats. Six other states (Arizona, Georgia, Nevada, South Carolina, Utah, and Washington) gained a single seat. This means, of course, that other states lost seats. New York and Ohio each lost two seats, with eight other states losing one apiece (Illinois, Iowa, Louisiana, Massachusetts, Michigan, Missouri, New Jersey, and Pennsylvania).The number of congressional districts in the rest of the states did not change. Population projections suggest that the electoral influence of Sunbelt states will continue to grow into the foreseeable future. The stakes are high for local governments, too. As a central city's population size is eclipsed by its suburban population, a loss in the city's political clout typically occurs.

State Population Change Estimates, 2010–2012

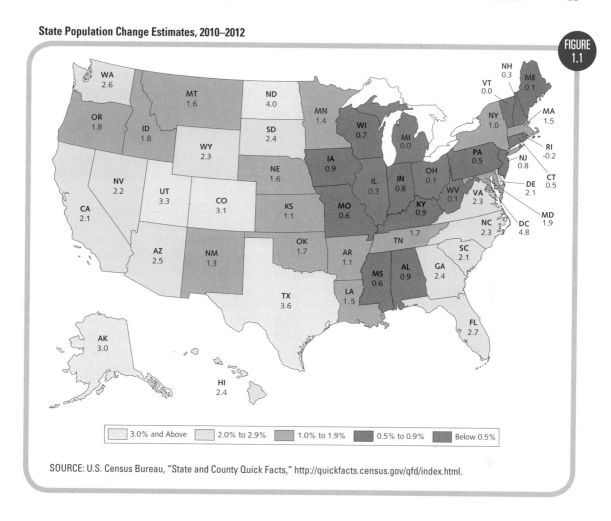

FIGURE 1.1

| 3.0% and Above | 2.0% to 2.9% | 1.0% to 1.9% | 0.5% to 0.9% | Below 0.5% |

SOURCE: U.S. Census Bureau, "State and County Quick Facts," http://quickfacts.census.gov/qfd/index.html.

Political Culture

One of the phrases that a new arrival in town may hear from longtime residents is "We don't do things that way here." **Political culture**—the attitudes, values, and beliefs that people hold toward government—is the conceptual equivalent of simply saying "It's *our* thing."[42] As developed by political scientist Daniel Elazar in the 1960s, the term refers to the way in which people think about their government and the manner in which the political system operates. Political culture is a soft concept—one that is difficult to measure—yet it has remained quite useful in explaining state politics and policy.

According to Elazar, the United States is an amalgam of three major political cultures, each of which has distinctive characteristics. In an *individualistic political culture*, politics is a kind of open marketplace in which people participate because of essentially private motivations. In a *moralistic political culture*, politics is an effort to establish a good and just society. Citizens are expected to

political culture

The attitudes, values, and beliefs that people hold toward government.

be active in public affairs. In a *traditionalistic political culture*, politics functions to maintain the existing order, and political participation is confined to social elites. These differing conceptions about the purpose of government and the role of politics lead to different behaviors.

Political culture is a factor in the differences (and similarities) in state policy. Research has found that moralistic states demonstrate the greatest tendency toward policy innovation, whereas traditionalistic states exhibit the least.[43] In economic development policy, for example, political culture has been shown to influence a state's willingness to offer tax breaks to businesses.[44] Other research has linked political culture to state environmental policy and successful state implementation of welfare reform.[45]

Today, few states are characterized by pure forms of these cultures. The mass media have had a homogenizing effect on cultural differences; migration has diversified cultural enclaves. This process of cultural erosion and synthesis has produced hybrid political cultures. For example, Florida, once considered a traditionalistic state, now has many areas in which an individualistic culture prevails, and even a moralistic community or two. In an effort to extend Elazar's pioneering work, researcher Joel Lieske has used race, ethnicity, and religion to identify contemporary subcultures.[46] With counties as the building blocks and statistical analysis as the method, he identified ten distinctive regional subcultures. A state like Pennsylvania, which Elazar characterized as individualistic, becomes a mix of "heartland," Germanic, ethnic, and rural/urban counties in Lieske's formulation. Very few states are dominated by a single subculture, as are Utah by a Mormon subculture and New Hampshire and Vermont by an Anglo-French subculture.

Political culture is not the only explanation for why states do what they do, of course. Socioeconomic characteristics (income and education levels, for example) and political structural factors (the amount of competition between political parties) also contribute to states' and communities' actions. In fact, sorting out the cause-and-effect relationships among these variables is a daunting job.[47] For example, why do some states pass more laws to regulate handguns than other states? Emily Van Dunk's study found that several factors were important, although the crime rate and partisanship, surprisingly, were not among them.[48] States with nontraditional political cultures adopt more handgun regulations, as do states with more women in the legislature and those with populations that are more urbanized and nonwhite. In general, political factors, socioeconomic characteristics, and the particulars of a specific problem combine to produce government action.

The variation among states makes for a nation that is highly diverse. One recent exercise in identifying the most typical state in the country, however, proved interesting. A study by political scientists Michael Lewis-Beck and Peverill Squire found Kansas to be the most representative state based on numerous social, economic, and political characteristics.[49] Rounding out the top five were Oregon, Delaware, Virginia, and North Carolina. The states least like the country as a whole were California, Mississippi, and New Mexico. Table 1.2 lists the forty-eight continental states from most to least typical. The numbers refer to a standardized score in which a zero would signify a state that is a microcosm of the nation.

How Typical Is Your State?			TABLE 1.2
STATE	**SCORE**	**STATE**	**SCORE**
1. Kansas	0.85	25. Kentucky	2.55
2. Oregon	0.95	26. Colorado	2.62
3. Delaware	1.02	27. New Hampshire	2.66
4. Virginia	1.04	28. Arkansas	2.68
5. North Carolina	1.46	29. Montana	2.73
6. Washington	1.50	30. Connecticut	2.73
7. Indiana	1.55	31. Idaho	2.75
8. Missouri	1.61	32. South Dakota	2.76
9. Oklahoma	1.80	33. Vermont	2.80
10. Rhode Island	1.88	34. Louisiana	2.80
11. Nebraska	1.88	35. Nevada	2.84
12. Iowa	1.92	36. Minnesota	2.87
13. Florida	1.97	37. Arizona	2.90
14. Georgia	1.97	38. Massachusetts	2.92
15. Illinois	2.02	39. Michigan	3.06
16. Maryland	2.07	40. Wyoming	3.07
17. Wisconsin	2.10	41. North Dakota	3.07
18. Tennessee	2.14	42. Utah	3.10
19. South Carolina	2.27	43. New Jersey	3.16
20. Pennsylvania	2.38	44. Texas	3.45
21. West Virginia	2.43	45. New York	3.89
22. Ohio	2.46	46. New Mexico	3.99
23. Alabama	2.51	47. Mississippi	4.01
24. Maine	2.54	48. California	4.78

SOURCE: Michael S. Lewis-Beck and Peverill Squire, "Iowa: The Most Representative State?" *PS: Political Science and Politics* 42 (January 2009), 41.

Culture Wars

In 2004, when San Francisco's mayor ordered city clerks to remove all references to gender on local marriage license applications, the action opened the door for same-sex marriages to take place in the city. As gay and lesbian activists and supporters celebrated, many politically conservative groups denounced the action and promised legal challenges and political repercussions for the mayor. This type of social conflict over morality issues is known informally as

culture wars

Political conflicts
that emerge from
deeply held moral
values.

culture wars, or "morality politics." And these culture wars are defining the politics of many communities and states. Besides gay rights, battlegrounds in the culture wars include abortion, pornography, and prayer in schools.

These issues tend to involve deeply held values, sometimes connected to religion, and they are less about economics than are many political issues. According to political scientist Elaine Sharp, culture wars have several distinctive features.[50] The issues are highly salient to people, eliciting passionate reactions; they mobilize people across different neighborhoods and racial and ethnic groups; and the ensuing political activism often takes unconventional forms, such as demonstrations. Throughout the country, battle lines have been drawn over issues such as more restrictive abortion laws and displaying the Ten Commandments in public buildings. But the most volatile culture war of the early 2000s involved same-sex marriage.

Generally, states bar gay and lesbian couples from marrying: More than thirty-five states have enacted defense of marriage acts (DOMAs), which define marriage as between a man and a woman; twenty-eight of these states took it one step further and put a definition of marriage in the state constitution. In California, San Francisco's precipitous action led to a 2008 state Supreme Court ruling that same-sex couples had the right to marry in the state. However, a ballot initiative, Proposition 8, which limited marriage to one man and one woman, was passed by the voters later that year. Legal action was necessary to sort out the contradictory policies. California courts upheld Proposition 8, but a federal district court, and later, a federal appeals court, ruled that it violated the U.S. Constitution. In 2013, the U.S. Supreme Court declined to rule in the matter, thereby affirming the lower federal courts' decisions. Same-sex marriage became legal in California again. At the same time, public opinion on the question of same-sex marriage had begun to shift in a more favorable direction. By mid-summer of that year, thirteen states and the District of Columbia had taken actions—through legislation, court decisions, and ballot measures—authorizing same-sex marriage. Yet even as receptivity to same-sex marriage increased, the issue continued to spark culture wars in some states and localities.

LINKING CAPACITY TO RESULTS

State and local governments have strengthened their position in the American federal system. On a regular basis, they tackle some of the most pressing problems facing the country. The interaction of three unique characteristics of our fifty-state system—diversity, competitiveness, and resiliency—both facilitates and complicates their task.[51] Consider the *diversity* of the United States. States and their communities have different fiscal capacities and different voter preferences for public services and taxes. As a result, citizens and businesses are offered real choices in taxation and expenditure policies across different jurisdictions.

Diversity is tempered, however, by the natural *competitiveness* of a federal system. No state can afford to be too far out of line with the prevailing thinking on appropriate levels of taxes and expenditures because citizens and business may opt to relocate. In essence, each jurisdiction is competing with every other jurisdiction. Such competition over the price and performance of government stabilizes the federal system.

The third characteristic, *resiliency*, captures the ability of state governments to recover from adversity. This feature was certainly put to the test during the economic downturn of 2008–2011. The stresses of that period compelled states to retrench and rethink; the fresh policy ideas that resulted were successful in some instances, unsuccessful in others. But the larger point is that state governments squared their shoulders to meet the challenges head on. Resiliency is the key.

As one astute observer of the U.S. governmental scene commented in 1998, "Over the past decade, without ever quite admitting it, we have ceased to rely on Congress (or the federal government, for that matter) to deal with our most serious public problems. . . . [T]he states have been accepting the challenge of dealing with problems that no other level of government is handling."[52] The 2007 comments of an Oregon legislator are apropos: "The states have become the petri dishes for new and evolving ideas."[53] Return to the first page of this chapter and reread Governor Hassan's inspiring words. The twenty-first century began full of challenges, but states and their local governments are taking charge. In the final analysis, that is what increased capacity is all about: results.

CHAPTER RECAP

- State and local governments are directly involved in our daily lives.

- The story of states and localities over the past three decades has been one of transformation. They have shed their backward ways, reformed their institutions, and emerged as capable and proactive.

- State resurgence is exemplified in improved revenue systems, the expanded scope of state operations, faster diffusion of innovations, more interjurisdictional cooperation, and increased national-state conflict.

- Several persistent challenges confront states and localities: Fiscal stress, inter-jurisdictional competition, and political corruption.

- The United States is becoming more racially and ethnically diverse. Sunbelt states tend to outpace the rest of the nation with their population growth.

- An outbreak of culture wars is redefining the politics of some communities and states.

- As a whole, the states are diverse, competitive, and resilient. Their increased capacity to govern effectively has been sorely tested in the first decade of the twenty-first century.

Key Terms

capacity *(p. 3)*

jurisdiction *(p. 3)*

federalism *(p. 4)*

proactive *(p. 5)*

rainy day funds *(p. 6)*

downsize *(p. 10)*

new normal *(p. 10)*

transparency *(p. 11)*

Sunbelt *(p. 14)*

Frostbelt *(p. 14)*

political culture *(p. 15)*

culture wars *(p. 18)*

Internet Resources

Nearly all states use the URL suffix **.gov** in their online addresses, such as **Ohio.gov** or **mt.gov**. Florida does something a little different with its URL: **www.myflorida.com**.

A website that offers a wealth of policy information about the states, especially policies and trends is **http://www.pewstates.org**, established by the Pew Charitable Trusts.

The website of *Governing* magazine, **www.governing.com**, contains up-to-date, in-depth discussions of issues in states and localities.

For a look at what is going on in state governments around the country, see the Council of State Governments, which can be found at **www.csg.org**.

At **www.census.gov**, the website of the U.S. Bureau of the Census, you can find historical, demographic data on states and localities.

The website for *State Politics and Policy Quarterly*, a scholarly journal that publishes research on important state-level questions is **spa.sagepub.com**. Also the journal *State and Local Government Review* contains the latest research on issues in the states and localities. Its URL is **slg.sagepub.com**.

Federalism and the States

2

CHAPTER OUTLINE

- The Concept of Federalism
- The History of U.S. Federalism
- Models of Federalism
- Intergovernmental Relations
- Federal Purse Strings
- The Future of Federalism

FOCUS QUESTIONS

1. What is the proper balance of power and responsibility between the national government and the states?
2. In what areas has there been a resurgence of state and local governments?
3. What models describe the power relationships among the three levels of government?
4. What is a key ingredient of federalism, particularly in financial interactions?
5. In what areas does the national government impose certain controversial requirements on state governments?

A single broad and enduring issue in American federalism transcends all others: What is the proper balance of power and responsibility between the national government and the states? The debate over this profound question, first joined by the Founders in preconstitutional days was argued between the Federalists and the Anti-Federalists. It continues today in the halls of Congress, the federal courts, and the state and local governments, over issues ranging from the mundane to the profound. For instance, which level of government should have the authority to regulate the sale and use of marijuana? Should Congress have the power to force people to purchase health insurance and to fine them if they do not? Which level of government has the power to combat illegal immigration?

Under federal law, growing, selling, possessing, or using marijuana is illegal. Marijuana is classified as a Schedule I controlled substance under the Controlled Substances Act (CSA). Yet eighteen states and the District of Columbia had legalized medical marijuana by mid-2013; and two states, Colorado and Washington, had legalized the recreational sale and use of it— all contrary to federal law. How can the states do that?

The Obama administration's signature—but highly controversial—health care law, officially labeled the Patient Protection and Affordable Care Act (and popularly known as "Obamacare") was signed into law in 2010. Under the Act, insurance companies are prohibited from refusing coverage to sick people or those with "preexisting conditions." The Act included various subsidies, tax credits, and mandates for employers to offer health care coverage and individuals to purchase it. Opponents challenged the law in the federal courts, as a number of states refused to participate. Several lower federal courts ruled on challenges to the Act's provisions, with mixed results. The U.S. Supreme Court finally held on June 28, 2012, that a provision that assessed a fine on individuals and firms who refused to participate in the health care insurance program was in fact a tax, and therefore constitutional under the federal government's power to tax. The Court also ruled, however, that Congress could not force people to purchase health insurance any more than it could force them to buy and eat broccoli.[1]

On April 23, 2010, Governor Jan Brewer (R) from Arizona signed the Support Our Law Enforcement and Safe Neighborhoods Act (SB 1070), making Arizona the first among many states to pass sweeping immigration reform that outraged many Constitutional scholars. Almost immediately after passage, the Obama administration expressed concerns about the bill and threatened to strike it down in federal court. One reason for the administration's dislike of the law was concern that it would hamper the federal government's ability to pursue terrorists, gang members, and other criminal immigrants.

What's all the fuss about? SB 1070 made Arizona the first state to require all aliens to carry immigration documents at all times. It also requires law enforcement officers to determine the status of a person and arrest him or her without probable cause if there is "reasonable suspicion" that the person could be in the country illegally. In addition, illegal aliens that work or seek jobs in Arizona could be charged with a crime. The basis for the lawsuit stemmed from a founding principle of our country: the right of the federal government to keep states from enacting laws that usurp its power. In this particular case, the federal government asserted that "a state may not establish its own immigration policy or enforce state laws in a manner that interferes with the federal immigration laws." The United States and Arizona duked it out in court over the proper balance of power between the federal government and the states.

Traditionally, the federal government has regulated immigration. But in the absence of comprehensive reform in the presence of a huge wave of illegal immigrants, Arizona argued that it was simply stepping in where the federal government had failed to do so. The Supreme Court did not buy into Arizona's main arguments. A split decision in June 2012 upheld Arizona's "show me your papers" requirement but declared invalid the other provisions. Thus, Indiana, South Carolina, and other states' "papers" requirements were accepted as constitutional as well.[2]

Highly politicized issues such as marijuana, health care reform, and immigration control tend to expose the soft underbelly of federalism. Every response is intergovernmentally complex with respective roles and responsibilities needing to be sorted out. Together, emotional issues such as Obamacare and illegal immigration have spawned a critical analysis of American federalism that has significant implications for all levels of government. These types of events and conflicts help define U.S. federalism. As a system for organizing government, federalism has important consequences that often affect our political and personal lives in ways both direct and hidden.

THE CONCEPT OF FEDERALISM

In a nation—a large group of people organized under a single, sovereign government and sharing historical, cultural, and other values—powers and responsibilities can be divided among different levels of government in three ways: through a unitary government, a confederacy, or a federal system. To understand our federal system, we must know how it differs from the other forms of government.

Unitary, Confederate, and Federal Systems

The great majority of countries (more than 90 percent) have a **unitary system** in which most, if not all, legal power is located in the central government. The central government may create or abolish regional or local governments as it sees fit. These subgovernments can exercise only those powers and responsibilities granted to them by the central government. In France, the United Kingdom, Chile, Japan, and the many other countries with unitary systems, the central government is strong and the regional or local jurisdictions are weak.

A **confederacy** is the opposite of a unitary system. In a confederacy, the central government is weak and regional governments are powerful. The regional jurisdictions establish a central government to deal with areas of mutual concern, such as national defense and a common currency, but they severely restrict the central government's authority in other areas. If they see fit, they may change or even abolish the central government. The United States

unitary system
One in which all authority is derived from a central authority.

confederacy
A league of sovereign states in which a limited central government exercises few independent powers.

began as a confederacy, and the southern states formed one following their secession in 1861.

federal system

A means of dividing the power and functions of government between a central government and a specified number of geographically defined regional jurisdictions.

A **federal system** falls somewhere between the unitary and confederate forms in the way it divides powers among levels of government. This system has a minimum of two governmental levels, each of which derives its powers directly from the people and can act directly on the people within its jurisdiction without permission from any other authority. Each level of government is supreme in the powers assigned to it, and each is protected by a constitution from being destroyed by the other. Thus, federalism divides the power and functions of government between a central government and a specified number of geographically defined regional jurisdictions. In effect, people hold dual citizenship, in the national government and in their regional government.

In the U.S. federal system, the regional governments are called states. In others, such as Canada, regional governments are known as provinces. Altogether there are approximately twenty federal systems in the world.

The Advantages and Disadvantages of Federalism

As it has evolved in the United States, federalism is a reasonably effective system of government. But it is not perfect, nor is it well suited to the circumstances of most other nations. Ironically, federalism's weaknesses are closely related to its strengths.

1. *A federal system helps manage social and political conflict.* It broadly disperses political power within and among governments, enabling national as well as regional and local concerns to reach the central government. Many places, or "democratic safety valves," exist for resolving conflicts before they reach the crisis stage. If such conflicts are not addressed satisfactorily, however, they can eventually lead to regional or ethnic conflict on a fearsome scale.
2. *Federalism promotes administrative efficiency.* The wide variety of services demanded by citizens are delivered more efficiently without a large central bureaucracy. From public elementary education to garbage collection, the government closest to the problem seems to work best in adapting public programs to local needs. Yet federalism presents problems in coordinating action across governments and boundaries. Picture trying to get some 90,000 squawking and flapping chickens to move in the same direction at once. The confusion and delays in responding to the BP oil spill illustrate this point.
3. *Federalism encourages innovation.* States and localities can customize their policies to accommodate diverse demands and needs—and, indeed, such heterogeneity flourishes. New policies are constantly being tested by the more than 90,000 government "laboratories" that exist throughout the country, thus further encouraging experimentation and flexibility. Yet federalism's many points of involvement can encourage obstruction and delay and result in ineffective national government programs and priorities. Duplication and confusion can be the result. Fifty sets of laws on banking and insurance practices, illegal immigration, firearms regulation, and marijuana use can make doing business across state lines an exercise in comparative public law.

4. *A federal system maximizes political participation in government.* Citizens have opportunities to participate at all three levels of government through elections, public hearings, and other means. The local and state governments fill almost 1 million offices in regular elections, serving as valuable political training camps for aspiring public leaders. The great majority of presidents and congressional representatives wet their feet in state or local politics. But such broad participation encourages local biases inimical to national interests. Problems in siting nuclear and hazardous waste disposal facilities readily illustrate this dilemma.

THE HISTORY OF U.S. FEDERALISM

The men who met in Philadelphia during the hot summer of 1787 to draw up the U.S. Constitution were not wild-eyed optimists, nor were they revolutionaries. In fact, as we will see in this section, they were consummate pragmatists whose beliefs shaped the new republic and created both the strengths and weaknesses of our federal system.

Early History

The Framers of the Constitution held to the belief of English political philosopher Thomas Hobbes that human beings are contentious and selfish. Some of them openly disdained the masses. Most of the Framers agreed that their goal in Philadelphia was to find a means of controlling lower forms of human behavior while still allowing citizens to have a voice in making the laws they were compelled to obey. The "philosopher of the Constitution," James Madison, formulated the problem in terms of **factions**, groups that pursue their own interests without concern for the interests of society as a whole. Political differences and self-interest, Madison felt, led to the formation of factions, and the Framers' duty was to identify "constitutional devices that would force various interests to check and control one another."[3]

factions
Any groups of citizens or interests united in a cause or action that can threaten the rights or interests of the larger community.

Three practical devices to control factions were placed in the U.S. Constitution. The first was a system of representative government in which citizens would elect individuals who would filter and refine the views of the masses. The second was the division of government into three branches: executive, legislative, and judicial. The legislative body was divided into two houses, each with a check on the activities of the other. Equal in power would be a strong chief executive with the authority to veto legislative acts, and an independent judiciary. Finally, the government was structured as a federal system in which the most dangerous faction of all—a majority—would be controlled by the sovereign states. Madison's ultimate hope was that the new Constitution would "check interest with interest, class with class, faction with faction, and one branch of government with another in a harmonious system of mutual frustration."[4]

Sometimes today there appears to be more frustration and factionalism than harmony, but Madison's dream did come true. The U.S. federal system is the longest-lived constitutional government on earth. Its dimensions and activities are vastly different from what the Framers envisioned, but it remains a dynamic, adaptable, responsive, and usually effective system for conducting the affairs of government.

The Move Toward Federalism

The drive for independence by the thirteen American colonies was, according to the Declaration of Independence, in large measure a reaction to "a history of repeated injuries and usurpations" and "absolute tyranny" under a British unitary system of government. The immediate struggle for independence left little time to develop a consensus on the form of government best suited to the future needs of American society. Hence the move toward federalism was gradual. The first independent government established in America was a confederacy; thus, Americans tested two types of government—unitary and confederate—before deciding permanently on the third, federalism.

The Articles of Confederation During the War for Independence, the colonies, now called states, agreed to establish a confederation. A unicameral (one-house) Congress was created to exercise the authority of the new national government. Its powers were limited to the authority to wage war, make peace, enter into treaties and alliances, appoint and receive ambassadors, regulate Indian affairs, and create a postal system. The states held all powers not expressly granted to the Congress. The governing document was the Articles of Confederation (effective from 1776 to 1787).

The inherent weaknesses of the confederacy quickly became apparent. The states had significant authority within their individual borders, but the central government was unable to carry out its basic responsibilities because it did not have the power to force the states to pay their share of the bill. Bankruptcy was a chronic concern. Furthermore, the lack of national authority to regulate either domestic or international commerce led to discriminatory trade practices by the states. These and many other defects were important concerns. But the key event that brought together representatives of the states to draft a constitution for a new type of government was Shays's Rebellion. Daniel Shays, a Revolutionary War officer, led an armed revolt of New England farmers who were fighting mad about debt and taxes. The weak central government had difficulty putting down the rebellion.

The Constitutional Convention How did the Framers create a long-lasting and successful system of government that seems to have the best features of both unitary and confederate forms? Above all they were pragmatists. Informed by political theory and their own colonial experiences,[5] they developed a practical compromise on the key issues of the day, including the proper role of the national government and the states. The reconciliation of the interests and powers of the states with the need for a strong national government is the United States' most distinctive political contribution.

Delegates from each of the states assembled at the constitutional convention. Here, the interests of large and small states diverged. The large states supported

Constitutional Distribution of Powers

FIGURE 2.1

National Government Powers:
- Coin money
- Regulate interstate and foreign commerce
- Tax imports and exports
- Make treaties
- Make all laws "necessary and proper" to fulfill responsibilities
- Make war
- Regulate postal system

Powers Denied:
- Tax state exports
- Change state boundaries
- Impose religious tests
- Pass laws that conflict with the Bill of Rights

Concurrent Powers:
- Tax
- Borrow money
- Charter banks and corporations
- Seize property (eminent domain)
- Make and enforce laws
- Administer a judiciary

State Government Powers:
- Conduct elections
- Regulate intrastate commerce
- Establish republican forms of state and local government
- Protect public health, safety, and morals
- All powers not delegated to the national government or denied to the state by the Constitution

Powers Denied:
- Tax imports and exports
- Coin money
- Enter into treaties
- Impair a legal contract
- Enter compacts with other states without congressional consent

SOURCE: © Cengage Learning

the Virginia Plan, which proposed a strong central government spearheaded by a powerful bicameral Congress. Because representation in both chambers was to be based on population, larger states would be favored. The smaller states countered with the New Jersey Plan, which put forward a one-house legislature composed of an equal number of representatives from each state.

The New Jersey Plan was defeated by a vote of 7 to 3, but the smaller states refused to give in. Finally, Connecticut moved that the lower house (the House of Representatives) be based on the population of each state and the upper house (the Senate) on equal state membership. This Great Compromise was approved, ensuring that a faction of large states would not dominate the small ones.

The Framers reached another important compromise by specifying the powers of the new central government. Those seventeen **enumerated (delegated) powers**, to be exercised through Congress, included taxation, regulation of commerce, operation of post offices, establishment of a national court system, declaration of war, conduct of foreign affairs, and administration of military forces. **Concurrent powers** would be exercised by both the state and national governments. The states would wield any residual powers under the Tenth Amendment. Figure 2.1 illustrates the constitutional distribution of powers.

enumerated (delegated) powers
Those powers expressly given to the national government, primarily in Article I, Section 8, of the Constitution.

concurrent powers
Those powers granted by the Constitution to both the national and the state governments.

State-Centered Federalism

nation-centered federalism

A theory holding that the national government is dominant over the states.

state-centered federalism

A theory holding that the national government represents a voluntary compact or agreement between the states, which retain a dominant position.

reserved powers

Those powers residing with the states by virtue of the Tenth Amendment.

Tenth Amendment

The amendment to the Constitution, ratified in 1791, reserving powers to the state.

compact theory

A theory of federalism that became the foundation for states' rights arguments.

Despite the fact that the new Constitution made the national government much stronger than it had been under the Articles of Confederation, the sovereign power of the states was still important.[6] As James Madison wrote, "The powers delegated by the proposed Constitution to the federal government are few and defined. Those which are to remain in the State governments are numerous and infinite."[7]

The first decades under the new Constitution witnessed a clash between profoundly different views on governing. George Washington, John Adams, Alexander Hamilton, and their fellow "Federalists" favored national supremacy, or **nation-centered federalism**. Opposed to them were Thomas Jefferson and the Republicans, who preferred **state-centered federalism**. Much of the debate then, as today, concerned the meaning of the **reserved powers** clause of the **Tenth Amendment** to the Constitution. Ratified in 1791, the Tenth Amendment gave support to the states by openly acknowledging that "the powers not delegated to the United States by the Constitution, nor prohibited by it to the States, are reserved to the States respectively, or to the people." But, in fact, the Tenth Amendment was an early omen of the eventual triumph of nation-centered federalism. As constitutional scholar Walter Berns pointed out, if the states were intended to be the dominant federal actors, they would not have needed the Tenth Amendment to remind them.[8]

Those who defended the power of the states under the Constitution—that is, state-centered federalism—saw the Constitution as a *compact*, an agreement among the sovereign states that maintained their sovereignty, or the right of self-governance. The powers of the national government listed in the Constitution—the enumerated (delegated) powers—were to be interpreted narrowly, and the states were obliged to resist any unconstitutional efforts by the national government to extend its authority.[9]

This **compact theory** of federalism became the foundation for states' rights arguments. In particular, it became central to the fight of the southern states against what they considered discrimination by the North. During the 1820s, a national tariff seriously damaged the economy of the southern states. The slave-based agricultural economy of the South had already begun a protracted period of decline while the North prospered. The tariff, which placed high taxes on imported manufactured goods from Europe, hit the South hard, for the South produced few manufactured goods. Rightly or wrongly, southern politicians blamed the "tariff of abominations" for many of their economic problems. They also, of course, staunchly resisted calls to abolish slavery.

When, in 2011, Virginia and several other states introduced "Repeal Amendments" to amend the U.S. Constitution to recognize states' rights to veto any Congressional enactment with which they disagreed, long-deceased Vice President John C. Calhoun must have arisen from his ancient grave and saluted. In 1828, Calhoun of South Carolina asserted that the United States was composed of sovereign states united in a central government through a compact. The powers of the national (central) government had been entrusted to it by the states, not permanently handed over. Calhoun claimed that a state thus had complete authority to reinterpret or even *nullify* (reject) the compact at any time, making it invalid within that state's borders. Most importantly, Calhoun declared that if a large majority of the states sided with the national government, the nullifying state had the right to *secede*, or withdraw from the Union.

In 1832, after an additional tariff was enacted by the national government, South Carolina nullified it. President Andrew Jackson and the Congress threatened military action to force the state to comply with the law, and Jackson even threatened to hang Calhoun, who by this time had resigned from the vice presidency.[10]

Ultimately, eleven southern states (led by South Carolina) did secede from the Union, at which point they formed the Confederate States of America. The long conflict between state sovereignty and national supremacy, and the slavery question as well, were definitively resolved by five years of carnage in such places as Antietam, Shiloh, and Gettysburg, followed by the eventual readmittance of the renegade states to the Union. The Civil War, often referred to in the South as The War Between the States, remains the single most violent episode in American history, resulting in more than 620,000 deaths (more than in all our other wars combined). Despite occasional calls for Texas to "be its own country," secession is not in the cards, and federal laws cannot be nullified by noncooperative states. Federal law may be flouted, as the marijuana issue shows, but it cannot be declared invalid.[11]

The Growth of National Power Through the Constitution and the Judiciary

After the Civil War, a nation-centered concept of federalism evolved. For the most part, the national government became the primary governing force, with the states and localities generally following its lead. Recently the states have been more inclined to act independently, but they are restrained by the history of the Supreme Court's interpretations of key sections of the Constitution.

The National Supremacy Clause Article III of the Constitution created the U.S. Supreme Court. The supremacy of national law and the Constitution is grounded in the **national supremacy clause** (Article VI), which provides that the national laws and the Constitution are the supreme laws of the land. Later decisions of the Supreme Court established the Court's role as arbitrator of any legal disputes between the national government and the states.

national supremacy clause
Article VI of the Constitution, which makes national laws superior to state laws.

The Necessary and Proper Clause The fourth chief justice of the United States, John Marshall, was the architect of the federal judiciary during his thirty-four years on the bench. Almost single-handedly, he made it a coequal branch of government. Several of his rulings laid the groundwork for the expansion of national governmental power. In the landmark case of *McCulloch v. Maryland* (1819), two issues were before the bench: the right of the national government to establish a national bank, and the right of the state of Maryland to tax that bank, once it was established.[12]

necessary and proper clause

Portion of Article I, Section 8, of the Constitution that authorizes Congress to enact all laws "necessary and proper" to carry out its responsibilities.

The crux of the issue was how to interpret the **necessary and proper clause**. The final power delegated to Congress under Article I, Section 8, is the power "to make all laws which shall be *necessary and proper* for carrying into execution the foregoing powers, and all other powers vested by this Constitution in the Government of the United States" (emphasis added). Thomas Jefferson argued that *necessary* meant "indispensable," whereas Alexander Hamilton asserted that it meant merely "convenient." Hamilton argued that in addition to the enumerated powers, Congress possessed **implied powers**. In the case of the national bank, valid congressional action was implied through the powers of taxation, borrowing, and making currency found in Article I, Section 8.

implied powers

Those powers that are not expressly granted by the Constitution but are inferred from the enumerated powers.

The bank dispute was eventually heard by Chief Justice Marshall. Marshall was persuaded by the Hamiltonian point of view. He pointed out that the Constitution nowhere stipulates that the only powers that may be carried out are those expressly described in Article I, Section 8. Thus, he ruled that Congress had the implied power to establish the bank and that Maryland had no right to tax it. Significantly, *McCulloch* v. *Maryland* meant that the national government had an almost unlimited right to decide how to exercise its delegated powers. Over the years, Congress has enacted a great many laws that are only vaguely, if at all, associated with the enumerated powers and that stretch the phrase *necessary and proper* beyond its logical limits.

The Commerce Clause Another important ruling of the Marshall Court extended national power through an expansive interpretation of the **commerce clause** of Article I, Section 8. The commerce clause gives Congress the power "to regulate commerce with foreign nations, and among the several states, and with the Indian tribes." In *Gibbons* v. *Ogden* (1824),[13] two important questions were addressed by Marshall: What is commerce? and How broadly should Congress's power to regulate commerce be interpreted?

commerce clause

Part of Article I, Section 8, of the U.S. Constitution, which gives Congress the power to regulate trade with foreign countries and among the states.

The United States was just developing a national economy as the Industrial Revolution expanded. National oversight was needed, along with regulation of emerging transportation networks and of state activities related to the passage of goods across state lines (interstate commerce). The immediate question was whether New York could grant a monopoly to run a steamship service between New York and New Jersey. Marshall's answer? No, it could not. He defined commerce very broadly and held that Congress's power to regulate commerce applied not only to traffic across state boundaries but, in some cases, also to traffic of goods, merchandise, and people *within* a state. The Court further expanded the meaning of "commerce" in rulings during the twentieth century, but the current Roberts court narrowed its scope in recent decisions.

general welfare clause

The portion of Article I, Section 8, of the Constitution that provides for the general welfare of the United States.

The General Welfare Clause The **general welfare clause** of Article I, Section 8, states that "the Congress shall have power to lay and collect taxes, duties, imposts, and excises to pay the debts and provide for the common defense and *general welfare* of the United States" (emphasis added). Before the Great Depression of the 1930s, it was believed that poor people were responsible for their own plight and that it was up to private charity and state and local governments to provide limited assistance. The Great Depression inflicted massive unemployment and poverty throughout the country and made necessary a major change in the national government's attitude. Despite their best efforts, the states and localities were staggered by the tremendous loss of tax revenues and by the need to help poor and displaced persons obtain food and shelter. Franklin D. Roosevelt, who won the presidency in 1932, set in motion numerous "New Deal" programs that completely redefined federal responsibility for the general welfare.

The Fourteenth Amendment Ratified by the states in 1868, the **Fourteenth Amendment** had the effect of granting former slaves official status as citizens of the United States and of the state in which they lived. It included two other very important principles as well—*due process* and *equal protection* of the laws. The federal courts have used the Fourteenth Amendment to increase national power over the states in several critical fields, especially with respect to civil rights, criminal law, and election practices.

> **Fourteenth Amendment**
> Enacted in 1868, this amendment contains citizenship rights, due process, and equal protection provisions that states must apply to all citizens.

The Growth of National Power Through Congress

The U.S. Supreme Court has not been the only force behind nation-centered federalism; Congress has worked hand in hand with the judiciary. The interstate commerce clause represents a good example. Given the simple authority to control or eliminate state barriers to trade across state lines, Congress now regulates commercial activities within a state's boundaries as well, as long as these activities purportedly have substantial national consequences (examples include banking and the movement of goods across state lines). Congress has also used the authority of the interstate commerce clause to expand national power into fields only vaguely related to commerce, such as protecting endangered species. The states have made hundreds of legal challenges to such exercise of the commerce power, but until recently (as shown in the Patient Protection and Affordable Care Act decision) almost all of these were resolved by the U.S. Supreme Court in favor of the national government.

Taxing and Spending Power Probably the most controversial source of the rise in national power in recent years has been the use of the *taxing and spending power* by Congress to extend its influence over the state and local governments. Under Article I, Section 8, Congress holds the power to tax and spend to provide for the common defense and general welfare. But the **Sixteenth Amendment**, which grants Congress the power to tax the income of individuals and corporations, moved the center of financial power from the states to Washington, D.C. Through the income tax, the national government raises vast sums of money. A portion of this money is sent to the states and localities as grants-in-aid. Because Congress insists on some sort of accountability in how state and local governments spend these funds, it attaches to federal grants a variety of conditions to which the recipients must adhere if they are to receive

> **Sixteenth Amendment**
> Enacted in 1913, an amendment that grants the national government the power to levy income taxes.

the money. The federal government also imposes mandates and regulations related to the purposes of the individual grant, such as forcing the states to adopt national standards on drivers' licenses and vehicle speed limits.

Federal Preemption The national government has also seized power through the process known as **federal preemption**. The legal basis for preemption is Article VI of the Constitution, the national supremacy clause. Whenever a state law conflicts with a national law, the national law is dominant.

federal preemption

The principle that national laws take precedence over state laws.

Congressional passage of a national law that supersedes existing state legislation is directly preemptive. An example is the Real ID Act of 2006, which imposed national requirements on how states must validate personal identification when issuing a driver's license. Designed to fight terrorism by imposing more strenuous requirements for obtaining a driver's license, Real ID was so unpopular that Washington, Montana, and nine other states refused to cooperate. A game of intergovernmental "chicken" ensued when the Department of Homeland Security (DHS) threatened to refuse to accept those states' drivers' licenses to board airplanes or enter federal buildings. For their part, states pointed out this unfunded mandate posed a threat to personal privacy and would require states to issue new, more costly licenses to all drivers to the tune of some $14.6 billion.[14] Finally, DHS blinked and granted all fifty states an extension to 2013 for compliance. Meanwhile, state officials sought and gained approval to adopt their own "Enhanced Driver's License" program at significantly lower cost. As of early 2013, only thirteen states were in compliance with Real ID.[15]

Smothering (Then Resuscitating) the Tenth Amendment Actions by Congress and the federal courts have gradually undermined the Tenth Amendment, which reserves to the states all powers not specifically granted to the national government or prohibited to the states. In fact, it is very difficult to identify any field of state activity not intruded on by the national government today.

The Supreme Court has sent mixed signals on the relevance of the Tenth Amendment. A good example of the Court's fickle federalism involves the Fair Labor Standards Act (FLSA). Following forty years of case law that essentially relegated the Tenth Amendment to the basement of federalism, the Court surprisingly ruled in favor of state and local governments in the 1976 case of *National League of Cities* v. *Usery*. At issue was the constitutionality under the interstate commerce clause of the 1974 amendments to the FLSA, which extended federal minimum wage and maximum hour requirements to state and local employees. In this case, the Court said that Congress did not have the constitutional right to impose wage and hour requirements on employees carrying out basic—or integral—functions, such as law enforcement or firefighting.[16]

But just nine years later, the Court reversed itself in *Garcia* v. *San Antonio Metropolitan Transit Authority*. A spate of litigation had not been able to resolve the issue of just which state and local activities are "integral." So the Court overturned its findings in *Usery* and once again applied federal wage and hour laws to nonnational governments—in this specific instance, to a mass transit system run by the city of San Antonio.[17] What really offended the states was the written opinion of the Court, in which it excused itself from such future controversies involving state claims against congressional power exercised under the commerce clause. Now Congress alone, with little or no judicial oversight, would be allowed to determine, through the political process, how extensively it would intrude on what had been state and local prerogatives. One dissenting Supreme Court justice wrote that "all that stands between the remaining essentials of state sovereignty and Congress is the latter's underdeveloped capacity for self-restraint."[18] In the view of some critics, the states were relegated to the status of any other special-interest group and the Tenth Amendment was irrelevant. Other critics more optimistically observed that the narrow 5-to-4 decision could be revisited by a more conservative Supreme Court at a later date.[19]

Sure enough, in 1995 the Court seemingly reaffirmed the Tenth Amendment in *U.S.* v. *Lopez* by recognizing a limit to Congress's power over interstate commerce. Ironically, this case also involved San Antonio, where a high school student, Alfonso Lopez, was arrested for bringing a handgun to school. He was charged with violating the Gun Free School Zones Act of 1990, which banned the possession of a firearm within 1,000 feet of a school. Here, the Court ruled that Congress had unconstitutionally extended its power to regulate interstate commerce because there was no connection between the gun law and interstate commerce.[20]

The Court continued to recalibrate the scales of power in favor of the states in a series of rulings beginning in 1997. First, the Court gave states the authority to incarcerate convicted sexual predators in mental institutions once their criminal sentences had been served.[21] Next, the Court ruled that Congress offended "the very principle of separate state sovereignty" by requiring local police to conduct background checks on people who want to purchase handguns.[22] More recently, the Court affirmed the right of state and local governments to seize private land for commercial development.[23] Recent rulings based on the Eleventh Amendment have revived the notion of the sovereign immunity of the states. According to this doctrine, which dates back to the Middle Ages, a king (the state) cannot be sued without his (its) consent (the Eleventh Amendment protects states from lawsuits by citizens of other states or foreign nations). Supreme Court decisions have upheld the sovereign immunity of the states from being sued in federal courts in cases involving lawsuits by Indian tribes,[24] patent infringement when a state ventures into commercial activities,[25] and discrimination against older or disabled employees.[26] The Court also protected the states against private complaints before federal agencies.[27]

The Supreme Court under Chief Justice William Rehnquist (1986–2005) positioned itself on the side of the states in most conflicts with the national government. However, the Supreme Court does not decide unilaterally in favor of the states in all cases, notwithstanding one justice's complaint that the majority has become "(a) mindless dragon that indiscriminately chews gaping holes in federal statutes."[28] For example, the Court limited the authority of the states to regulate tobacco advertising.[29] The Court's willingness to overturn the

Florida Supreme Court's decisions in issues concerning the ballot counting in the 2000 presidential race indicates that ideology and partisanship sometimes trump federalism.[30]

Federalism and the Courts Today The federalism feelings of current Chief Justice John Roberts and justices Samuel Alito, Sonia Sotomayor, and Elena Kagan are not yet clear. But the once narrow pro-state balance shows distinct signs of tilting in the opposite direction. For instance, on grounds of interference with interstate commerce, a 2011 ruling struck down state laws compelling coal-burning power plants to reduce their greenhouse gas emissions.[31] Also giving pause to federalism supporters was the Roberts Court's landmark decision that corporations, like individuals, have free political speech rights, which effectively abrogated states' rights to limit corporate and political action committee campaign contributions.[32]

Federal intrusions into the affairs of state and local governments continue to be burdensome and unwelcome, and the states are pushing back by resisting intrusive federal laws and regulations.[33] The Tenth and Eleventh Amendments have been useful weapons for fending off federal encroachments on the power of state and local officials, but their power can be shattered by a single justice's change of heart or by a new appointment to the bench.

MODELS OF FEDERALISM

Perceptions of the role of the states in the federal system have shifted from time to time throughout our history. Those who study the federal system have generally described these perceptions through various models or metaphors that attempt to present federalism's complexity in a readily understandable form. Such models have been used both to enhance understanding and, when opportunities arise, to pursue ideological and partisan objectives.

Dual Federalism (1787–1932)

dual federalism
A model of federalism in which the responsibilities and activities of the national and state governments are separate and distinct.

The model of **dual federalism** holds that the national and state governments are sovereign and equal within their respective spheres of authority as set forth in the Constitution. The national government exercises those powers specifically designated to it, and the remainder are reserved for the states. The metaphor is that of a layer cake, with two separate colored layers, one on top of the other.

Dual federalism, which has its roots in the compact theory, was dominant for the first 145 years of U.S. federalism, although the Civil War and other events led to substantial modifications of the model.[34] Until 1860, the functions of the national government remained largely restricted to the delegated powers. Federal financial assistance to the states was very limited. The states had the dominant influence on the everyday lives of their citizens. After the Civil

War shattered secession and dealt the compact theory of state-centered federalism a death blow, the nation-centered view became paramount.

Cooperative Federalism (1933–1964)

The selection of a specific date for the demise of dual federalism is rather subjective, but 1933, when Franklin D. Roosevelt became president, is a reasonable estimate. Roosevelt's New Deal buried dual federalism by expanding national authority over commerce, taxation, and the economy.

Cooperative federalism recognizes the sharing of responsibilities and financing by all levels of government. Beginning with the Great Depression, the national government increasingly cooperated with states and localities to provide jobs and social welfare, to develop the nation's infrastructure, and to promote economic development.

> **cooperative federalism**
> A model of federalism that stresses the linkages and joint arrangements among the three levels of government.

The cooperative aspects of this era were measured in governmental finances. The national government spent huge amounts of money to alleviate the ravages of the Great Depression and to get the U.S. economic machinery back into gear. (Comparisons are made with the federal response to combating the sharp national recession that began in 2008.) Total federal expenditures rose from 2.5 percent of the gross national product (GNP) in 1929 to 18.7 percent just thirty years later, far surpassing the growth in state and local spending during the same period. The number of federal grants-in-aid (programmatic transfers of federal dollars) rose from twelve in 1932, with a value of $193 million, to twenty-six in 1937, with a value of $2.66 billion. A substantial amount of the federal aid was sent directly to local governments, particularly counties and school districts. The variety of grant programs also exploded, with disbursements for maternal and child health care, aid to the blind, treatment of venereal disease, public housing, road and bridge construction, and wildlife conservation.

Contemporary Variations on Cooperative Federalism (Since 1964)

The broad theme of cooperative federalism has many variations. All of them stress intergovernmental sharing. Among these variations are creative federalism and new federalism.

> **creative federalism**
> A model of cooperative federalism in which many new grants-in-aid, including direct national-local financial arrangements, were made.

Creative federalism was devised by President Lyndon B. Johnson to promote his dream of a "Great Society." Johnson sought to build the Great Society through a massive, grant-funded attack on the most serious problems facing the nation: poverty, crime, poor health care, and inadequate education, among others. More than two hundred new grants were put into place during the Johnson presidency. Johnson's policy of vast government spending bypassed the states in distributing funds directly to cities and counties for some seventy of the new programs. Understandably, the states did not appreciate losing influence over how localities could spend their national dollars.

new federalism

A model that represents a return of powers and responsibilities to the states.

revenue sharing

A "no-strings" form of financial aid from one level of government to another.

New federalism is a model that has been employed with separate but related meanings in different presidencies. The new federalism initiated by Richard Nixon was intended to restore power to the states and localities and to improve intergovernmental arrangements for delivering services. Among the major policy changes were establishment of ten regional councils to coordinate national program administration across the country and implementation of **revenue sharing** to give states and localities greater flexibility in program spending and decision making.

Ronald Reagan's brand of new federalism, like Nixon's version, sought to give more power and program authority to states and localities, at least in theory. Reagan's main goal, however (to shrink the size of the national government), soon became obvious. Reagan's new-federalism initiative won congressional approval to merge fifty-seven categorical grants into nine new block grants and to eliminate another sixty categorical grants. The states got more authority, but the funding for the new block grants decreased almost 25 percent from the previous year's allocation for the separate categorical grants.[35]

Reagan and his congressional allies chipped away at other grant programs in an effort to reduce the size of government, and also terminated revenue sharing in 1986. Called *general revenue sharing* (GRS) when enacted during the Nixon administration, this program was highly popular with state and local officials. GRS provided funds to state and general-purpose local governments with no strings attached. It was discontinued largely because of the mounting national budget deficit and Congress's desire to exert greater control over, and take more credit for, how federal monies were spent. A new form of GRS, popularly known as the "stimulus plan," was adopted by Congress in 2009 to temporarily bail out the states' sinking economic ships, but expired in 2011.

In 1994, with the election of Republican majorities in the U.S. House and Senate as well as the election of many new Republican governors, new federalism came back in style with impressive force. The New Federalists, whose ranks included many Democrats, sought once again to sort out intergovernmental responsibilities. For the first time in recent memory, the states and localities were basically united and working together through a coalition of government interest groups, including the National Governors' Association and the National League of Cities, to

A patient identification card to legally obtain marijuana through the Arizona Medical Marijuana Program.
SOURCE: Norma Jean Gargasz/Alamy

design smaller, more efficient government with greater program and policy flexibility for the states and localities.

This planned delegating of power from the federal to state and local governments is termed **devolution**. The constellation of supporters for devolution is impressive. The governors, acting as individuals and through the National Governors' Association, found a sympathetic President Clinton and congressional majority, and a Supreme Court (at that time) likely to rule in favor of state authority. Moreover, public opinion is generally in favor of greater state and local government authority. Public opinion polls show that citizens believe state and local governments do a better job than the national government in spending money and delivering services.[36] Together, these powerful forces for devolution gradually reversed more than a century of centralizing tendencies in U.S. federalism. This trend was so striking that it has been called the "devolution revolution."

> **devolution**
> The delegating of power and programs from the federal to state and local governments.

Coercive Federalism The federalism views of President George W. Bush (2000–2008) were poorly articulated, but legislative initiatives of his administration and of Republican supporters in Congress sought to preempt state authority over school testing systems and right-to-die decisions, override state laws that guarantee patient rights, obstruct state laws that permit the medical use of marijuana, and impose new homeland security and accountability requirements on the states, among other preemptive acts. The predominance of business interests in Washington, D.C., appeared to have stanched devolution through what one writer calls "the law of political physics—that for every flurry of state and local business regulations, there is an equal and opposite" effort by business to counter it in the nation's capitol.[37] The centralizing policies of the "War on Terror" served as a convenient justification for many centralizing actions by the president and Congress,[38] including citizen surveillance, nationalization of the state National Guards, and various mandates that pulled power back into the White House.

By 2008, state dissatisfaction had reached such a peak that governors from both political parties denounced the "coercive federalism" of Washington, D.C., and increasingly pushed back by roundly criticizing some federal actions, ignoring others, and litigating still others.[39] Dissatisfaction persisted as President Obama and Congress took actions perceived to be coercive during 2008–2013.[40]

INTERGOVERNMENTAL RELATIONS

Cooperative federalism demands positive interactions among governments at all levels. Whatever the short-term trend of federal-state-local relations, cooperative activities are always in evidence. Relationships between the states and Indian tribes present an interesting example of both cooperative and coercive relationships.

Tribal Governments

With the arrival of the Europeans, the number of the estimated 7 to 10 million people who lived in what is now the ranks of the continental United States were soon severely depleted by warfare, disease, and famine. Hundreds of treaties, statutes, and other agreements notwithstanding, the Native Americans were eventually deprived of their traditional lands and isolated on reservations. Today, some 3.2 million people identify themselves as Native American, belonging to 564 recognized tribes. About one-third of them continue to live on tribal reservations, mostly in the western portion of the United States. The Navajo Nation, for instance, has a population of more than 250,000 and covers some 17 million acres, extending from northwest New Mexico to northeast Arizona and southeast Utah.

Tribes are semisovereign nations exercising self-government on their reservations. They are under the authority and supervision of Congress, and are subject to the authority of federal courts, but their legal relationship with the states is complex. Tribal governments are permitted to regulate their internal affairs, hold elections, and enforce their own laws under congressional supervision. States are prevented from taxing or regulating tribes, or extending judicial power over them. Off the reservation, however, Native Americans are subject to the same legalities as any other state residents. They enjoy voting rights in both federal and state elections.

Recently, the tribes and the states have adopted a cooperative relationship to pursue common interests, such as fishing and hunting rights, and regulation of gambling on reservations. The lucrative gaming enterprises of some tribes have advanced tribal interests and clout by enabling strong financial support to friendly politicians and other allies.[41] Many tribal governments have developed policy and lobbying expertise in support of gaming and other enterprise activities.[42]

Occasionally, however, interactions between tribal governments, the state, and nearby local governments are testy. Tribes seek to recover ancestral lands from present occupants. Actions concerning tribal land use may conflict with local zoning or state environmental policy. The tax-free sale of gasoline, alcohol, and tobacco products on the reservation diminishes sales tax revenues. And tribes sometimes offer casino games that are prohibited under state law. When conflicts arise, states and tribal governments may sort out their differences through compacts. Otherwise, Congress may be asked to enter the fray.

Interstate Cooperation

Cooperation Under the Constitution There are four formal provisions for cooperation among the states.

1. The *full faith and credit clause* of the Constitution binds every citizen of every state to the laws and policies of other states. Crossing a state boundary does not alter a legal obligation. The courts have interpreted full faith and credit to apply to contracts, wills, divorces, and many other legalities.

The clause does not, however, extend to criminal judgments. An interesting test of full faith and credit arises from civil union and gay marriage laws enacted in a growing number of states. Must Alabama recognize a relocated gay couple married in Vermont—now living in Birmingham? Thirty states outlaw same-sex marriage, but nine states have legalized it. State reciprocity on same-sex marriage is likely to be a subject of litigation in the federal courts in the next few years.

2. The *interstate rendition clause* begins where full faith and credit leaves off, covering persons convicted of criminal violations. Governors are required to extradite (return) fugitives to the state in which they were found guilty or are under indictment (although in certain cases they may refuse).

3. The *privileges and immunities clause* states that "the citizens of each state shall be entitled to all privileges and immunities of citizens in the several states." This clause was intended by the Framers to prevent any state from discriminating against citizens of another state who happen to be traveling or temporarily dwelling outside their own state's borders. Of course, states do discriminate against nonresidents in such matters as out-of-state tuition, hunting and fishing license fees, and residency requirements for voting. The Supreme Court has upheld these and other minor discrepancies, so long as the "fundamental rights" of nonresidents are not violated.

4. Finally, the *interstate compact clause* authorizes the states to negotiate compacts, which are binding agreements between two or more states that address important cross-boundary issues. Early interstate compacts were used to settle boundary disputes. About 215 are in effect today in a variety of areas, including rights to interstate water resources, pest control, riverboat gambling, and education.[43]

Informal Cooperation Among the States Interstate cooperation can be facilitated through a variety of informal methods. One example is the establishment of regional interstate commissions, such as the Appalachian Regional Commission (ARC), which was created by national legislation in 1965 to attack poverty in the states of Appalachia.

In addition, states have developed uniform laws to help manage common problems ranging from child support to welfare cheating. Interstate cooperation also occurs through information sharing among elected and appointed officials and the organizations to which they belong, such as the National Governors Association and the National Conference of State Legislatures. It may take place in legal actions, as demonstrated by the state attorneys general who united to file class-action lawsuits against tobacco companies and other corporate malefactors, and even against federal agencies. Or, one state may contract with another for a service, as Hawaii does with Arizona for a medical management information system. States have also marshaled their resources in cooperative efforts to reduce greenhouse gas emissions, establish common core standards in their schools, and protect interstate fisheries.

Intergovernmental Financial Relations

Revenues are the funds that governments have at their disposal. They are derived from taxes, fees and charges, and transfers from other levels of government. Expenditures are the ways in which governmental revenues are disbursed. Governments spend money to operate programs, build public facilities, and pay off debts.

The **grant-in-aid** is the primary mechanism for transferring money from the national to the state and local governments. The national government makes grants available for a number of reasons: to redistribute wealth, to establish minimum policy standards, and to achieve national goals. But grants (numbering more than 1,100 today) are primarily designed to help meet the needs of state and local governments, including environmental protection, transportation, community and regional development, education, and health care.

Discretion of Recipients There are two major variations in grants: the amount of discretion (independence) the recipient has in determining how to spend the money, and the conditions under which the grant is awarded. A **categorical grant** can be used by the recipient government only for a narrowly defined purpose, such as removing asbestos from school buildings or acquiring land for public use. A **block grant** is a *broad-based grant;* that is, it can be used anywhere within a functional area such as transportation or health care. The difference between categorical and block grants is that the recipient government decides how block grants will be spent. For instance, a local school system can decide whether the purchase of personal computers is more important than buying microscopes for the science laboratory. Today there are about 625 grants in existence, including 17 block grants. Block grants give nonnational governments considerable flexibility in responding to pressing needs and preferred goals. These grant mechanisms assume that state and local governments can make rational choices among competing claims.

Conditions for Grants Grants also vary in the manner in which they are awarded. A **formula grant** makes funding available automatically, based on state and local conditions such as poverty level or unemployment rate. A **project grant** is awarded to selected applicants, based on administrative assessments of the strength of competing proposals. Block grants are distributed on a formula basis; categorical grants can be either formula- or project-based.

Another factor also affects intergovernmental financial relations: the existence of *matching requirements*. Most federal grants require that the recipient government use its own resources to pay a certain percentage of program costs. This arrangement is designed to stimulate state and local spending on programs deemed to be in the national interest and to discourage nonnational governments from participating in a program simply because money is available.

---

grant-in-aid
An intergovernmental transfer of funds or other assets, subject to conditions.

categorical grant
A form of financial aid from one level of government to another to be used for a narrowly defined purpose.

block grant
A form of financial aid from one level of government to another for use in a broad, functional area.

formula grant
A funding mechanism that automatically allocates monies based on conditions in the recipient government.

project grant
A funding mechanism that awards monies based on the strength of an applicant government's proposal.

FEDERAL PURSE STRINGS

Federalism today turns less on theory and more on money. The distribution of intergovernmental monies and the conditions attached to them define the distribution of governmental power and authority. Federalism is a matter not only of which level of government will do what, but of which level will pay for it. Some have called this a period of "fend-for-yourself federalism," with each jurisdiction essentially on its own in a Darwinian struggle for financial survival.

The Importance of Federal Funds

Figure 2.2 provides a historical look at national grant-in-aid expenditures. The second set of bars in Figure 2.2 documents the growing proportion of national dollars in the expenditures of state and local governments. For the first time in history,

Historical Trends in Federal Grant-in-Aid Outlays

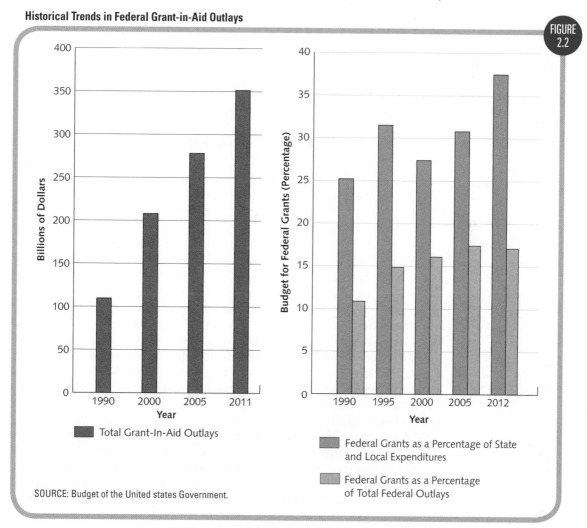

SOURCE: Budget of the United states Government.

federal aid has become the single largest source of total state and local revenues, as the national government pumped billions of new dollars into state and local coffers to stimulate the flagging national economy. Aid to states and localities, however, still consumes a relatively small share of the federal government's budget.

The Washington-funded portion of state and local expenditures is about 37.5 percent today, representing an important source of revenue for nonnational governments. But more than half the money is for health and human services programs that benefit individuals, including recipients of Medicaid, housing assistance, children's health insurance, and aid for needy families. The funds are not spread evenly across the country (see Table 2.1). In 2010, Alaska and Wyoming received the most per capita. Federal grants poured into these states at the rate of $4,682 and $4,180, respectively. In last place is Virginia, where federal grant monies averaged just $1,331 per person.

States battle in Congress over their share of grant allocations, which are affected by such factors as the poverty level and existence of military installations and other federal offices in the state. The states attempt to influence competitive project grant awards and lobby Congress to adjust the weighing of certain factors in formula grants in their favor. State and local influence is wielded by the representatives sitting in Congress and through various actions by elected state and local officials and their Washington lobbyists.

Here's the Check and Here's What to Do with It: Mandates, Preemptions, Set-Asides, and Cost Ceilings

Although many voices are shouting, "Let the states and localities do it," Congress continues to impose mandates and preempt the states. In addition, Congress includes set-asides and cost ceilings in block grants. Old habits die hard, and one of Congress's oldest habits is to place requirements and conditions on the states. Washington-based politicians of both major political parties may claim to support state power in principle, but when it conflicts with other priorities, devolution takes a back seat.

federal mandate

A requirement that a state or local government undertake a specific activity or provide a particular service as a condition of funding.

Federal mandates are especially burdensome when they are unfunded—that is, when the national government requires the states and localities to take action but does not pay for it. Who does pay? The states and localities must foot the bill. Recent federal mandates require the states to establish elaborate and expensive school testing programs, staff homeland security operations, standardize their drivers' licenses, and act as immigration police. The national health care reform bill of 2010 ("Obamacare") imposed an estimated $20 billion in new Medicaid costs on the states by requiring them to expand coverage and eligibility levels and to set up health insurance exchanges. Some twenty states sued to block the law, leading to a landmark U.S. Supreme Court decision in 2012 that freed them from mandatory expansion of coverage.[44]

The total cost of these "mandate millstones" hanging round the necks of states and localities has been estimated at up to $34 billion annually.[45] Mounting opposition to mandates without money finally convinced Congress to enact the Unfunded Mandate Reform Act of 1995 (UMRA), which provides that any

Federal Grants to State and Local Governments, 2010, in Rank Order

TABLE 2.1

STATE	GRANTS PER CAPITA	STATE	GRANTS PER CAPITA
District of Columbia	$16,523	Michigan	$1,988
Alaska	$4,682	Tennessee	$1,972
Wyoming	$4,180	Idaho	$1,950
Delaware	$3,703	Iowa	$1,927
New Mexico	$3,308	Wisconsin	$1,883
Vermont	$3,267	Maryland	$1,876
North Dakota	$3,225	New Jersey	$1,855
New York	$3,165	Hawaii	$1,852
Louisiana	$2,964	Illinois	$1,808
Mississippi	$2,902	Alabama	$1,801
Montana	$2,840	South Carolina	$1,793
Rhode Island	$2,797	New Hampshire	$1,789
Maine	$2,696	California	$1,787
South Dakota	$2,635	Washington	$1,776
West Virginia	$2,607	Kansas	$1,745
Massachusetts	$2,309	Texas	$1,739
Kentucky	$2,248	Nebraska	$1,709
Arkansas	$2,201	Georgia	$1,639
Connecticut	$2,147	North Carolina	$1,628
Oklahoma	$2,138	Indiana	$1,604
Missouri	$2,123	Utah	$1,524
Arizona	$2,092	Colorado	$1,521
Pennsylvania	$2,070	Florida	$1,475
Minnesota	$2,050	Nevada	$1,337
Oregon	$2,049	Virginia	$1,331
Ohio	$2,000		

SOURCE: U.S. Census Bureau, *Federal Aid to States 2010*; population data from U.S. Census Bureau, 2010.

bill imposing a mandate of more than $50 million (raised to $69 million in 2009) on a state or local government must include a cost estimate. If passed, the new legislation is supposed to include sufficient funds to pay for the mandate. Indications are that proposed laws containing unfunded mandates are facing tougher scrutiny in Congress than before and that Congress is taking a more consultative approach with state and local officials. UMRA, however, is riddled with loopholes, and members of Congress are always threatening to revert to their mandating ways.[46] They have done so on at least eleven occasions since 1995.[47]

As noted earlier, *preemption* represents another intrusion of the national government into the state sphere. It assumes two forms: *total* preemption, whereby the national government seizes all regulatory authority for a given function from states and localities; and *partial* preemption, whereby the national government establishes minimum national standards for state-implemented programs. Both forms prevent states from doing what they want. One example of a totally preemptive action is the Americans with Disabilities Act, which requires states and localities to make physical and occupational accommodation for disabled persons. More recent examples are federal litigation to strike down certain state immigration policies and restrictions on voting. Many partial preemptions involve environmental protection, whereby states may regulate pollution emissions so long as state standards are at least as stringent as those of the federal government.

Thus, when mandates and preemptions are taken into consideration, a less optimistic picture of intergovernmental relations emerges. To the states and localities it seems that the country has shifted from cooperative federalism to coercive federalism or, in the words of Ben Nelson, former governor of Nebraska, demoted states from significant policymakers to branch managers "of a behemoth central government."[48] The result has been an escalation of federal-state conflict that is now possibly at the highest level since the days leading to the Civil War.

THE FUTURE OF FEDERALISM

For the states and localities, national political gridlock has meant a golden opportunity to reverse more than a century of centralizing forces. They have taken up the slack in the federal system, busily innovating, developing, and implementing policies in a great variety of fields, from crime prevention and health care to greenhouse gas emissions and consumer protection. Public opinion polls consistently show that there is greater trust in state and local governments than in the federal government. As laboratories of democracy, state and local governments have designed and experimented with numerous policies that later have served as models for other states and for Congress. For instance, states have recently pioneered policy initiatives on prescription drug costs, immigration control, stem-cell research, nanotechnology, gay marriage, and global climate change, among many other fields. Lobbyists who once focused their attentions on Washington, D.C., are now spending hundreds of millions of dollars to woo state legislators. Hordes of lobbyists representing the health care and banking and insurance industries and other special interests have been attracted to state capitals like fleas to a dog.

Journalists and many citizens routinely refer "to 'the government' as if there were only one—the Big One."[49] But the United States is a nation of many governments, and Washington is not the best location for addressing all the nation's complex policy problems. Whereas centrally designing and implementing policies and programs is sometimes believed to be the best approach, it can also result in wasteful and ineffective one-size-fits-all government. The trend in government, as well as in business, is to decentralize decision making to the lowest feasible level of the organization. For the U.S. federal system, that means sending decision making to the states and localities and even, in some instances, to nonprofit organizations and citizens' groups.

But at the very time that the state and local governments are most needed as policy leaders and problem solvers, powerful social and economic forces seriously threaten state and local governments' capability. The collapse of financial and housing markets and the ensuing freefall in the U.S. economy in 2008–2011 produced frightening revenue declines in nearly all the states, putting at risk children, the poor, and the infirm. Ranks of Medicaid recipients climbed along with the homeless population. Following expiration of federal stimulus funds in 2013, record federal budget deficits and a "sequester," or large reduction in federal spending, severely constricted future federal funding for state and local grants-in-aid. Illegal drugs, gang activity, large numbers of chronically unemployed, and crumbling infrastructure present seemingly impossible challenges for the cities. Finally, the growing disparity of wealth and income is shrinking our great reservoir of political and social stability: the middle class.

For its part, the federal government provokes criticism for tying the hands of the states and localities with mandates, preemptions, and confused and conflicting policy directives. Most state and local governments *want* to become more creative, but they are also being *forced* to, so that they can figure out how to implement and pay for increasingly onerous federal mandates. This conflicted, coercive, and ambiguous federalism is something less than empowerment. When the president or Congress takes actions to squash innovative programs such as stem-cell research, assisted suicide, or carbon-reduction policy, they profess to do so for purposes of the national interest or high moral principles. But the issue is also about money and power and, perhaps at the most basic level, the need for a hopelessly divided and highly partisan Congress to justify its existence in an increasingly state and local policy world.

CHAPTER RECAP

- U.S. federalism is an ongoing experiment in governance.

- A fundamental question is: what is the proper balance of power and responsibility between the national government and the states?

- Actions of the courts, Congress, and the executive branch have expanded the powers of the national government.

- Until recently, the general trend has been in the direction of a stronger national government. But there has been a resurgence of the state and local governments as political and policy actors.

- The power relationships among the three levels of government are described by various models, including dual and cooperative federalism. The operative model is coercive federalism.

- A key ingredient of federalism is intergovernmental relations, particularly in financial interactions.

- The national government imposes certain controversial requirements on grants-in-aid, including mandates, preemptions, and set-asides.

Key Terms

unitary system *(p. 23)*
confederacy *(p. 23)*
federal system *(p. 24)*
factions *(p. 25)*
enumerated (delegated) powers *(p. 27)*
concurrent powers *(p. 27)*
nation-centered federalism *(p. 28)*
state-centered federalism *(p. 28)*
reserved powers *(p. 28)*
Tenth Amendment *(p. 28)*

compact theory *(p. 28)*
national supremacy clause *(p. 29)*
necessary and proper clause *(p. 30)*
implied powers *(p. 30)*
commerce clause *(p. 30)*
general welfare clause *(p. 30)*
Fourteenth Amendment *(p. 31)*
Sixteenth Amendment *(p. 31)*
federal preemption *(p. 32)*

dual federalism *(p. 34)*
cooperative federalism *(p. 35)*
creative federalism *(p. 35)*
new federalism *(p. 35)*
revenue sharing *(p. 36)*
devolution *(p. 37)*
grant-in-aid *(p. 40)*
categorical grant *(p. 40)*
block grant *(p. 40)*
formula grant *(p. 40)*
project grant *(p. 40)*
federal mandate *(p. 42)*

Internet Resources

Costs of unfunded mandates are tracked by NCSL in their "mandate monitor" at **www.ncsl.org/standcomm/scbudg/manmon.htm**. For additional information on unfunded mandates see **www.csg.org/policy/intergovernmentalaffairs.aspx**.

Federalism decisions of the U.S. Supreme Court and other federalism topics may be reviewed at the Council of State Governments' website at **www.csg.org**. Other websites that often feature federalism news and issues are **www.governing.com** and **www.stateline.org/live/**.

For current information on relationships among the three levels of government see **www.governing.com**.

The website **www.census.gov** has comparative data on the states and localities, particularly on state and local finances. It is not particularly user-friendly—you will have to dig around for what you seek.

Information on tribal governments and politics may be acquired at **www.tribal-institute.org** and **www.narf.org**.

State Constitutions

3

CHAPTER OUTLINE

- The Evolution of State Constitutions
- Weaknesses of Constitutions
- Constitutional Reform
- Methods for Constitutional Change
- State Responsiveness and Constitutional Reform

FOCUS QUESTIONS

1. What is the purpose of a state constitution?
2. How have state constitutions evolved?
3. How have state constitutions evolved to meet the challenges of modern governance?
4. What are the methods for changing state constitutions?

State constitutions are alike in many important respects, but they are decidedly different in others. Consider recent public votes on state constitutional changes. Nebraska voters decided to limit affirmative action as a criterion for filling public jobs and slots at public universities. Voters in Colorado and Washington legalized the sale of recreational marijuana. Oregon became the third state to allow assisted suicide for the terminally ill. Arizona and Connecticut joined the growing ranks of states legalizing medical marijuana. These actions demonstrate that constitutions are, in their essence, *political* documents—products of state history, culture, events, economics, and above all, the clash of interests.

All state constitutions both distribute and constrain political power among groups and regions. They set forth the basic framework and operating rules for government, allocate power to the three branches, establish the scope of state and local governmental authority, protect individual rights, and address various policy concerns.[1] Constitutions represent the **fundamental law** of a state, superior to statutory law. They provide a set of rules for the game of state government, and those who master the regulations and procedures have a distinct

> **fundamental law**
> The basic legal and political document of a state; it prescribes the rules through which government operates.

47

advantage over novices. Everything that a state government does and represents is rooted in its constitution. Constitutions do not describe the full reality of a political system, but they do provide a window through which to perceive its reality. Only the federal Constitution and federal statutes take priority over state constitutions. This is why the constitution is called the fundamental law.

To most people, however, constitutional law still means the federal document. State constitutions are often neglected in secondary school and college courses in history and political science. Astonishingly, one national survey discovered that 51 percent of Americans were not aware that their state had its own constitution.[2] Yet, state constitutions are distinctly different from the federal constitution in length, inclusion of policy provisions, and the relative ease of revising them.[3]

In the U.S. system of *dual constitutionalism*, in which there are both national and state constitutions, the national government is supreme within the spheres of authority specifically delegated to it in the U.S. Constitution. Powers granted to the national government are denied to the states. But the national Constitution is incomplete. It leaves many key constitutional issues to the states, including those pertaining to local finance, public education, and the organization of state and local government.[4] In theory, state constitutions are supreme for all matters not expressly within the national government's jurisdiction or preempted by federal constitutional or statutory law. In practice, however, congressional actions and federal court interpretations have expanded the powers of the national government and, in some cases, eroded the powers of the states. And, in reality, most concurrent powers, such as taxing, spending, and protecting citizens' health and safety, are shared by all three levels of government.

The earliest state constitutions were simple documents reflecting an agrarian economy, single-owner businesses, and horse-and-buggy transportation. As American society and the economy changed, the rules of state government also required transformation. Constitutional reform is a regular theme throughout our experiment in federalism. As a result, state constitutions "are a mine of instruction for the national history of democratic communities. They are distinctive in history, design, and underlying premises."[5]

Some reforms have reflected changing political fortunes: newly powerful groups have pressed to revise the state constitution to reflect their interests, or one or another political party has gained control of state government and sought to solidify its power. Constitutional reforms have promoted different views of politics and the public interest, as when Progressive reformers rallied for honest and efficient government in the late nineteenth and early twentieth centuries.[6] In more recent years, constitutional revisions have generally sought to make state government more efficient, effective, and responsive to shifting social and economic forces. The fact that constitutions are subject to change also recognizes that human judgment is not infallible, nor human understanding perfect.[7] Through constitutional reform, states can elevate their role as democratic laboratories by responding to the changing needs and opinions of citizens. This is in sharp contrast to the seldom-amended federal Constitution.

THE EVOLUTION OF STATE CONSTITUTIONS

When the states won their independence from Great Britain more than 235 years ago, there was no precedent for writing constitutions. A constitution of the Five Nations of the Iroquois called the Great Binding Law existed, but it was oral and not particularly relevant to the people in the colonies.[8] The thirteen colonial charters provided the foundation for the new state constitutions. These were brief documents (around five pages each) that the Crown had granted to trading companies and individuals to govern settlements in the new territories. As the settlements became full colonies, the charters were expanded to incorporate the "rights of Englishmen"—political and civil rights first enumerated by the Magna Carta in 1215. For distant territories too remote from their native country to be governed by its laws, these charters also laid down some basic principles of colonial government.[9]

In a sense, the existence of these documents helped fuel the fires of independence. In what was to become Connecticut, early settlers escaping the oppressive rule of the Massachusetts Bay Colony took matters of governance into their own hands. Under the leadership of Thomas Hooker, these ambitious farmers established an independent government free from references to the British Crown. The Fundamental Orders of 1639 contended that "the choice of the public magistrates belongs unto the people by God's own allowance. The privilege of election belongs to the people…it is in their power, also, to set the bounds and limitations of the power [of elected officials]."[10] Years later, a representative of King James II was sent to take possession of the Fundamental Orders and unite the New England colonies under the Crown. In a night meeting, as the Orders were laid out on a table before the king's men, the candles suddenly were extinguished. When they were rekindled, the document had disappeared. According to legend, a patriot had hidden it in a nearby hollow tree, later to be known as the Charter Oak. Infuriated, the king's men dissolved the colony's government and imposed autocratic rule that lasted many years. But they never found the Fundamental Orders, which essentially governed Connecticut until the Constitution of 1818 was adopted.[11]

The First State Constitutions

Following the War of Independence, the former colonies drafted their first constitutions in special revolutionary conventions or in legislative assemblies. With the exception of Massachusetts, the new states put their constitutions into effect

Connecticut's Charter Oak as depicted on the U.S. quarter.
SOURCE: United States Mint image.

immediately, without popular ratification. The making of the first state constitutions was not a simple affair. Issues of political philosophy were debated: how would citizens' "natural rights" be defined and protected? How would the principle of popular sovereignty be addressed in words and practice? Many practical questions also had to be answered in constitutional conventions, including the structure of the new government, how and when elections would be held, and how land once owned by the Crown would be distributed. Territorial integrity was not well defined. For example, in what is now known as Kentucky, people frustrated with Virginia's rule met in 1784 and petitioned the Congress for statehood. It took six years and nine constitutional conventions before Kentucky became a state. Complicating factors causing delay involved the "necessity of communicating across the mountains, the change from the Articles of Confederation to the Constitution of the United States, Indian attacks, [and] the revelation of a plot to have Kentucky secure independence and join Spain."[12]

In content, most of these documents simply extended the colonial charters, removing references to the king and inserting a bill of rights. All incorporated the principles of limited government: a weak executive branch, the separation of powers, checks and balances, a bill of rights to protect the people and their property from arbitrary government actions, and (except for Pennsylvania) a bicameral legislature.[13] The earliest constitutions were not truly democratic.

Essentially, they called for government by an aristocracy. Officeholding and voting, for instance, were restricted to white males of wealth and property.[14]

Only one of the thirteen original state constitutions (that of Massachusetts) survives, although it has been amended 120 times. It is the oldest functional constitution in the world. Its longevity can be attributed in large part to the foresight of its drafter, John Adams, who grounded the document in extensive research of governments that took him all the way back to the ancients. Even after many amendments, the Massachusetts constitution reflects a composite of the wisdom of the foremost political philosophers of the eighteenth century: John Locke, Jean-Jacques Rousseau, and the Baron de Montesquieu.[15] In this enduring document, Massachusetts establishes itself as a commonwealth (from the words *common weal*, meaning "general well-being"), on the principle that its citizens have a right to protect and manage their collective interests. (Kentucky, Pennsylvania, and Virginia are also commonwealths).[16] Rhode Island was established as "The State of Rhode Island and Providence Plantation."

Legislative Supremacy

The first state constitutions reflected their framers' fear and distrust of the executive—a result of their experiences with the colonial governors. The governors were not all tyrants; but because they represented the British Crown and Parliament, they became a symbol of oppression to the colonists. As a result, the guiding principle of the new constitutional governments was **legislative supremacy**, and the legislatures were given overwhelming power at the expense of governors. Most governors were to be elected by the legislature, not the people, and were restricted to a single term of office. State judiciaries also were limited in authorized powers; and judges, like governors, were to be elected by the legislature.

legislative supremacy
The legislature's dominance of the other two branches of government.

The Growth of Executive Power

Disillusionment with the legislatures soon developed, spreading rapidly through the states during the early 1800s. There were many reasons for disenchantment, including the legislatures' failure to address problems caused by rapid population growth and the Industrial Revolution; the growing amount of legislation that favored private interests; and a mounting load of state indebtedness, which led nine states to default on their bonds in a single two-year period.

Gradually the executive branch began to accumulate more power and stature through constitutional amendments that provided for popular election of governors, who were also given longer terms and the authority to veto legislative bills. As executive power grew, public confidence in state legislatures continued to erode. This circumstance was reflected in the process of constitutional revision. One delegate at Kentucky's 1890 constitutional convention proclaimed that "the principal, if not the sole purpose of this constitution which we are here to frame, is to restrain the legislature's will and restrict its authority."[17] Also affecting constitutional change were broader social and economic forces in the United States, such as the extension of suffrage and popular participation in government, the rise of a corporate economy, the Civil War and Reconstruction, the growth of industry and commerce, the process of urbanization, and a growing movement for government reform. States rapidly replaced and amended their constitutions from the early 1800s to 1920 in response to these and other forces. The decade of the Civil War saw the highest level of constitutional activity in U.S. history, much of it in the southern states; between 1860 and 1870, twenty-seven constitutions were replaced or thoroughly revised as Confederate states ratified new documents after secession, then redrew the documents after Union victory to incorporate certain conditions of readmission to the United States.

Constitutional change after Reconstruction was driven by the Populist and Progressive reform movements. During the late 1800s, the Populists championed the causes of the "little man," including farmers and laborers. They sought to open the political process to the people through such constitutional devices as the initiative, the referendum, and the recall (see Chapter 4). The Progressives, who made their mark during the 1890–1920 period, were kindred spirits whose favorite targets were concentrated wealth, inefficiencies in government, machine politics, corruption, and boss rule in the cities. Reformers in both groups successfully promoted constitutional reforms such as regulation of campaign spending and party activities, replacement of party conventions with direct primary elections, and selection of judges through nonpartisan elections.

WEAKNESSES OF CONSTITUTIONS

Despite the numerous constitutional amendments and replacements enacted during the nineteenth and early twentieth centuries, by 1950 the states were buffeted by a rising chorus criticizing their fundamental laws. Ironically, many states were victims of past constitutional change, which left them with documents that were extravagantly long, frustratingly inflexible, and distressingly detailed. In general, state constitutions still provided for a feeble executive branch, granting limited administrative authority to the governor, permitting the popular election of numerous other executive branch officials, and organizing the executive into a hodgepodge of semiautonomous agencies, boards, and commissions. State judiciaries remained uncoordinated and overly complex, whereas legislatures suffered from archaic structures and procedures. Statutory detail, out-of-date language, local amendments (those that apply only to designated local governments), and other problems contaminated the documents and straitjacketed state government.

Excessive Length

From the first constitutions, which averaged 5,000 words, state documents expanded into enormous tracts of verbiage averaging 27,000 words by 1967. (The U.S. Constitution contains 8,700 words). Some of this growth resulted from increasing social and economic complexity, as well as from a perceived need to be very specific about what the legislatures could and could not do. The states also delineated their residual powers (those powers not delegated to the national government), identified the scope of their responsibility, and defined the powers of local governments.

State constitutions are much easier to amend than the federal Constitution. But some constitutions went too far. Before a new constitution was adopted in 1982, Georgia's contained around 583,500 words, surpassing Tolstoy's *War and Peace* in length. Even today, the constitution of South Carolina limits local government indebtedness but then lists seventeen pages of exceptions. Maryland's constitution devotes an article to off-street parking in Baltimore. Oklahoma's sets the flash point for kerosene at 115 degrees for purposes of illumination,[18] and California's addresses a compelling issue of our time—the length of wrestling matches. A constitutional amendment in Florida prohibits "cruel and unusual confinement of pigs during pregnancy." The dubious prize for most verbose constitution goes to Alabama's 376,006-word document. Table 3.1 provides an overview of the fifty state constitutions, including each one's length.

Not surprisingly, lengthy state constitutions tend to be plagued by contradictions and meaningless clauses. Some even address problems that are no longer with us, such as the regulation of steamboats[19] or the need to teach livestock feeding. New Jersey's constitution employs archaic terms such as "bastardy" and provides that a woman forfeits her property rights to her husband if she has been willingly "ravished" by another man.

Verbose constitutions, such as those of Alabama, Oklahoma, and Colorado, fail to distinguish between fundamental law and issues that properly should be decided by the state legislature.[20] Excessive detail leads to litigation, as the courts must rule on conflicting provisions and challenges to constitutionality; hence the courts are often unnecessarily burdened with decisions that should more appropriately be made by the legislature.

Once incorporated into a constitution, a decision becomes as close to permanent as anything can be in politics. In contrast to a statute, which can be changed by a simple legislative majority, constitutional change requires an extraordinary majority, usually two-thirds or three-fourths of the legislature. This requirement hampers the legislature's ability to confront problems quickly and makes policy change more difficult. Of course, enshrining a principle in the constitution can be a deliberate strategy to protect special interests. Too many amendments may also deprive local governments of needed flexibility to cope with their own problems. Indeed, too much detail generates confusion, not only for legislatures and courts but also for the general public. It encourages political subterfuge to get around archaic or irrelevant provisions and breeds disrespect or even contempt for government.

State constitutions are political documents and, contrary to the admonitions of reformers, may sometimes be used to address some of the most controversial issues in politics, such as abortion rights, gun rights, gay marriage, and medical marijuana. Many detailed provisions explicitly favor or protect special interests, including public utilities, farmers, timber and mining companies, religious fundamentalists, and many others.

| TABLE 3.1 | State Constitutions 2011 |

STATE	NUMBER OF CONSTITUTIONS	EFFECTIVE DATE OF PRESENT CONSTITUTION	ESTIMATED NUMBER OF WORDS	NUMBER OF AMENDMENTS	
				SUBMITTED TO VOTERS	ADOPTED
Alabama	6	Nov. 28, 1901	367,000	1,179	854
Alaska	1	Jan. 3, 1959	13,479	42	29
Arizona	1	Feb. 14, 1912	47,306	266	147
Arkansas	5	Oct. 30, 1874	59,120	196	98
California	2	July 4, 1879	67,048	891	525
Colorado	1	Aug. 1, 1876	66,140	336	155
Connecticut	4	Dec. 30, 1965	16,401	31	30
Delaware	4	June 10, 1897	25,445	*	141
Florida	6	Jan. 7, 1969	56,705	154	118
Georgia	10	July 1, 1983	41,684	94	71
Hawaii	1	Aug. 21, 1959	21,498	131	110
Idaho	1	July 3, 1890	24,626	210	123
Illinois	4	July 1, 1971	16,401	18	12
Indiana	2	Nov. 1, 1851	11,476	79	47
Iowa	2	Sept. 3, 1857	11,089	59	54
Kansas	1	Jan. 29, 1861	14,097	125	95
Kentucky	4	Sept. 28, 1891	27,234	75	41
Louisiana	11	Jan. 1, 1975	69,876	233	164
Maine	1	March 15, 1820	16,276	204	171
Maryland	4	Oct. 5, 1867	43,198	261	225
Massachusetts	1	Oct. 25, 1780	45,283	148	120
Michigan	4	Jan. 1, 1964	31,010	68	30
Minnesota	1	May 11, 1858	11,734	215	120
Mississippi	4	Nov. 1, 1890	26,229	158	123
Missouri	4	March 30, 1945	69,394	175	114
Montana	2	July 1, 1973	12,790	56	31
Nebraska	2	Oct. 12, 1875	34,934	350	228
Nevada	1	Oct. 31, 1864	37,418	232	136
New Hampshire	2	June 2, 1784	13,060	287	145
New Jersey	3	Jan. 1, 1948	26,360	79	44

			NUMBER OF AMENDMENTS	
STATE	**NUMBER OF CONSTITUTIONS**	**EFFECTIVE DATE OF PRESENT CONSTITUTION**	**NUMBER OF WORDS**	**SUBMITTED TO VOTERS**	**ADOPTED**
New Mexico	1	Jan. 6, 1912	33,198	293	160
New York	4	Jan. 1, 1895	44,397	295	220
North Carolina	3	July 1, 1971	17,777	43	35
North Dakota	1	Nov. 2, 1889	18,746	265	150
Ohio	2	Sept. 1, 1851	52,995	284	171
Oklahoma	1	Nov. 16, 1907	81,666	354	187
Oregon	1	Feb. 14, 1859	49,016	490	249
Pennsylvania	5	April 23, 1968	26,078	36	30
Rhode Island	3	Dec. 4, 1986	11,407	12	10
South Carolina	7	Jan. 1, 1896	27,421	686	497
South Dakota	1	Nov. 2, 1889	27,774	229	215
Tennessee	3	Feb. 23, 1870	13,960	62	39
Texas	5	Feb. 15, 1876	86,936	642	467
Utah	1	Jan. 4, 1896	17,849	167	115
Vermont	3	July 9, 1793	8,565	212	54
Virginia	6	July 1, 1971	21,899	54	46
Washington	1	Nov. 11, 1889	32,578	176	103
West Virginia	2	April 9, 1872	33,324	121	71
Wisconsin	1	May 29, 1848	15,102	194	145
Wyoming	1	July 10, 1890	26,349	125	98

(continued)   TABLE 3.1

SOURCE: *Book of the States*, 2011, http://knowledgecenter.csg.org/drupal/content/book-states-2011-chapter-1-state-constitutions, Table 1.1.

There is enormous variance in the length of state constitutions (see Table 3.1). What accounts for such disparity? Studies by political scientists find, not surprisingly, that interest groups play an important role. In states with a single dominant political party, where legislative outcomes tend to be unpredictable because of dissension among members of the majority party, interest groups try to insulate their "pet" agencies and programs from uncertainty by seeking protective provisions for them in the constitution.[21] Also, research indicates that long, detailed documents tend to become even longer because their very complexity encourages further amendment, until they finally grow so cumbersome that political support develops for a simpler version. Finally, the easier it is to amend a constitution, the higher the amendment rate.[22]

Problems of Substance

In addition to the contradictions, anachronisms, wordiness, and grants of special privilege found in state constitutions, their *substance* has drawn criticism. Specific concerns voiced by reformers include the following:

- *The long ballot.* As elected executive branch officials are not beholden to the governor for their jobs, the governor has little or no formal influence on their decisions and activities. Reformers who seek to maximize the governor's powers would restrict the executive branch to only two elected leaders: the governor and the lieutenant governor.
- A *glut of executive boards and commissions.* This Jacksonian-era reform product was intended to expand opportunities for public participation in state government and to limit the powers of the governor. Today, it leads to fragmentation and a lack of policy coordination in the executive branch.
- A *swamp of local governments.* There are some 90,000 municipalities, counties, and special-purpose and school districts in the states. Sometimes they work at cross-purposes, and nearly always they suffer from overlapping responsibilities and an absence of coordination.
- *Restrictions on local government authority.* Localities in some states have to obtain explicit permission from the state legislature before providing a new service, tapping a new source of revenue, or exercising any other authority not specifically granted them by the state.
- *Unequal treatment of minorities and immigrants.* Even today, constitutional language sometimes discriminates against African Americans, Latinos, immigrants, and other groups by denying them certain rights guaranteed to white males.

CONSTITUTIONAL REFORM

Model State Constitution

An ideal of the structure and contents of a state constitution, emphasizing brevity and broad functions and responsibilities of government.

Shortly after World War II, problems of constitutional substance began to generate increasing commentary on the sorry condition of state constitutions. One of the most influential voices came in 1955 from the U.S. Advisory Commission on Intergovernmental Relations, popularly known as the Kestnbaum Commission. In its final report to the president, the Commission stated that the Constitution prepared by the Founding Fathers, with its broad grants of authority and avoidance of legislative detail, has withstood the test of time far better than the constitutions later adopted by the States. The Commission believes that most states would benefit from a fundamental review of their constitution to make sure that they provide for vigorous and responsible government, not forbid it.[23]

Another important voice for constitutional reform was the National Municipal League, which developed a **Model State Constitution** in 1921 that is now in its sixth version.[24]

Thomas Jefferson believed that each generation has the right to choose for itself its own form of government. He suggested that a new constitution every nineteen or twenty years would be appropriate. Between 1960 and 1980, it would appear that the states took his remarks to heart. Every state altered its fundamental law in some respect during this period, and new or substantially revised constitutions were put into operation in more than half the states. During the 1970s alone, ten states held conventions to consider changing or replacing their constitution. One of these was Louisiana, which set a record by adopting its eleventh constitution; Georgia is in second place with ten.

Two state constitutional traditions are evident today.[25] The **positive-law tradition** is represented by the detailed and lengthy documents of states such as Alabama, New York, and Texas. Detailed provisions tend to usurp the law-making powers of state legislatures by locking in rigid procedures and policies that typically favor strong political or economic interests. The original **higher-law tradition** is represented by the U.S. Constitution and the National Municipal League's Model State Constitution. It is embodied in brief documents that put forward basic, enduring principles and processes of government, and that view public policy choices as the proper responsibility of legislatures. Of course, no constitutional formula can be suitable for all the states because they differ too much in history, society, economics, and political culture. The best constitutions strike a balance between the need for stability and the requirement for enough flexibility to deal with emerging problems. Today, the higher-law tradition is once again in favor in those states whose constitutions have become briefer, more readable, and simple enough for the average citizen to understand. In others, however, conflicts between special interests are often resolved through constitutional change.

positive-law tradition

A state constitutional tradition based on detailed provisions and procedures.

higher-law tradition

A state constitutional tradition based on basic and enduring principles that reach beyond statutory law.

The Essential State Constitution

The Model State Constitution has twelve basic articles that are embodied to a greater or lesser extent in the various state constitutions in existence today. A brief description of each article and the ways in which its contents are changing follows.

Bill of Rights Individual rights and liberties were first protected in state constitutions. They closely resemble, and in some cases are identical to, those delineated in the first eight amendments to the U.S. Constitution. State constitutions and courts were the principal guardians of civil liberties until the U.S. Supreme Court's interpretation of the Fourteenth Amendment extended the protective umbrella of the national courts over the states in 1925.[26] U.S. Supreme Court rulings also applied the U.S. Bill of Rights to the states, especially during the Warren Court beginning in 1953. Some states had failed to uphold their trust, particularly those that perpetuated the unequal treatment of women and minorities.

In the 1980s, however, activist states began to reassert guarantees of individual rights under state constitutions. At a minimum, all state constitutions must protect and guarantee those rights found in the U.S. Bill of Rights. But state constitutional provisions may guarantee additional or more extensive

TABLE 3.2   Excerpts from State Bills of Rights

Alabama: "The legislature may hereafter, by general law, provide for an indemnification program to peanut farmers for losses incurred as a result of Aspergillus flavus and freeze damage in peanuts."

Alaska: "Public schooling shall always be conducted in English."

Illinois: "The equal protection of the laws shall not be denied or abridged on account of sex by the State or its units of local government."

Montana: "Human dignity is inviolable."

New York: "Every citizen may freely speak, write, and publish his sentiments on all subjects...."

North Carolina: "Secret political societies shall not be tolerated."

Pennsylvania: "The people have a right to clean air, pure water, and to the preservation of the natural, scenic, historic, and esthetic values of the environment. Pennsylvania's public natural resources are the common history of all the people, including generations yet to come...."

Rhode Island: "The power of the state and its municipalities to regulate and control the use of land and waters in the furtherance of the preservation, regeneration, and restoration of the natural environment, and ... of the rights of the people to enjoy and freely exercise the rights of fishery and the privileges of the shore ... shall be liberally construed, and shall not be deemed a public use of private property."

SOURCE: © Cengage Learning

rights to citizens. Twenty-two states now have equal rights amendments that guarantee sexual equality and prohibit sex-based discrimination. The U.S. Constitution does not guarantee a right to privacy, but ten states do so. And thirteen states give constitutional rights to crime victims. Some constitutional provisions border on the exotic. Residents of New Hampshire hold the right to revolution, and all Massachusetts citizens enjoy freedom from excessive noise. (See Table 3.2 for other rights provisions). In 2012, North Dakota became the first state to constitutionally enshrine the right to farm.

The major reason for the rebirth of state activism in protecting civil liberties and rights has been the conservatism of the U.S. Supreme Court. One commentator accused the Supreme Court of having abdicated its role as "keeper of the nation's 'conscience.'"[27] The states' power to write and interpret their constitutions differently from the U.S. Constitution's provisions in the area of protecting civil rights and liberties has been upheld by the Supreme Court, as long as the state provisions have "adequate and independent" grounds.[28] Increasingly, civil rights and liberties cases are being filed by plaintiffs in state rather than federal courts, based on state bills of rights protections.

Power of the State This very brief constitutional article states simply that the enumerated powers are not the only ones held by the state—that, indeed, the state has all powers not denied to it by the state or national constitutions.

Suffrage and Elections Voter registration and election procedures are specified here. Extensions—and retractions—of voting rights and alterations in election procedures have been made in response to U.S. Supreme Court decisions and to national constitutional and statutory changes. Some states have improved election administration; liberalized registration, voting, and officeholding requirements; and enhanced election technology and security. Very recently, other states have shortened early voting periods, imposed restrictive voter identification requirements, and taken other actions that supporters assert help prevent voter fraud, though opponents claim they are intended to discourage minorities and other traditional Democratic voters from participating in elections. Some states have amended this article in their own constitutions to provide for public financing of election campaigns; others have adopted provisions designed to count ballots more accurately.

The Legislative Branch This article sets forth the powers, procedures, and organizing principles of the legislature, including the apportionment of state legislatures on the basis of one person, one vote. District lines must be redrawn every ten years (most recently in 2012), after the national census has revealed population changes. Nineteen states have placed term limits on their elected officials in this article.

On the basis of this article, states have taken numerous actions to approach greater conformity with the Model State Constitution, including increasing the length and frequency of legislative sessions and streamlining rules and procedures. Instead of stipulating specific dollar amounts for legislators' pay and fringe benefits (which are soon rendered inappropriate by inflation), most state constitutions now establish a procedure to determine and occasionally adjust the compensation of legislators.

Interestingly, the model constitution for many years recommended a unicameral legislature as a means to overcome complexity, delay, and confusion. In its most recent revision, the National Municipal League tacitly recognized the refusal of the states to follow this suggestion (only Nebraska has a single-house general assembly) by providing recommendations appropriate for a bicameral body.

The Executive Branch The powers and organization of the executive branch, which are outlined in this article, have seen many notable modifications. Essentially, executive power continues to be centralized in the office of the governor. Governors have won longer terms and the right to run for reelection. Line-item vetoes, shorter ballots, the authority to make appointments within the executive branch, and the ability to reorganize the state bureaucracy have also increased gubernatorial powers. A number of states have opted for team election of the governor and lieutenant governor.

The Judicial Branch States have substantially revised not only their courts' organization and procedures but also the selection of judges. Most have unified their court systems under a single authority, usually the state supreme court. Many states now select judges through a merit plan rather than by gubernatorial appointment, legislative election, or popular election (see Chapter 9). The states have also established means to investigate charges against judges and to recommend discipline or removal from the bench when necessary.

Finance Taxation, debt, and expenditures for state and local government are the subject of this article. In many states, tax relief has been granted to senior citizens, veterans, and disabled people. In others, taxation and expenditure limits have been added.

Local Government Here, the authority of municipalities, counties, and other local governments is recognized. Most states have increased local authority through home rule provisions, which give localities more discretion in providing services. Local taxing authority has been extended. In addition, mechanisms for improved intergovernmental cooperation, such as consolidated city and county governments and regional districts to provide services, have been created.

Public Education On the basis of this article, the states establish and maintain free public schools for all children. Higher-education institutions, including technical schools, colleges, and universities, are commonly established in this section.

Civil Service The Model State Constitution sets forth a *merit system* of personnel administration for state government under which civil servants are to be hired, promoted, paid, evaluated, and retained on the basis of competence, fitness, and performance instead of political party affiliation or other such criteria (see Chapter 8).

Intergovernmental Relations As recommended by the Model State Constitution, some states stipulate specific devices for cooperation among various state entities, among local jurisdictions, or between a state and its localities. They may detail methods for sharing in the provision of certain services, or they may list cost-sharing mechanisms such as local option sales taxes.

Constitutional Revision The methods for revising, amending, and replacing the constitution are described. Generally, the trend has been to make it easier for the voters, the legislature, or both to change the constitution.

Constitutions Today

In general, state constitutions today conform more closely to the higher-law tradition and the Model State Constitution than did those of the past. They are shorter, more concise, and simpler, and they contain fewer errors, anachronisms, and contradictions. The latest states to enter the union, Alaska and Hawaii, have constitutional documents that follow the model constitution quite closely.

Work, however, always remains to be done. Some state constitutions are still riddled with unnecessary detail because new amendments have continually been added to the old documents, and obsolete provisions and other relics can still be found. But more important deficiencies demand the attention of legislators and citizens in states whose constitutions inhibit the operations of state government and obstruct the ability to adapt to change. In some jurisdictions, the governor's formal powers remain weak; a plethora of boards and commissions makes any thought of executive management and coordination a pipe dream; local governments chafe under the tight leash of state authority; and many other problems persist. Constitutional revision must be an ongoing process if the states are to cope with the changing contours of American society and stay in the vanguard of innovation and change.

METHODS FOR CONSTITUTIONAL CHANGE

There are only two methods for altering the U.S. Constitution. The first is the constitutional convention, wherein delegates representing the states assemble to consider modifying or replacing the Constitution. Despite periodic calls for a national constitutional convention, only one has taken place—in Philadelphia, more than two hundred years ago. Two-thirds of the states must agree to call a convention; three-fourths are required to ratify any changes in the Constitution.

The second means of amending the U.S. Constitution is through congressional initiative, wherein Congress, by a two-thirds vote of both houses, agrees to send one or more proposed changes to the states. Again, three-fourths of the states must ratify the proposals.

Since 1787, more than one thousand amendments have been submitted to the states by Congress. Only twenty-seven have been approved (the most recent one, in 1992, limits the ability of members of Congress to increase their pay), and the first ten of these were appended to the Constitution as a condition by several states for ratification. Note that neither method for amending the U.S. Constitution provides for popular participation by voters, in sharp contrast to the citizen-participation requirements for state constitutional change, as we shall see in the next section.

Informal Constitutional Change

In a letter to James Madison in 1789, Thomas Jefferson wrote the following: "The earth belongs to the living, and not to the dead … Every constitution, then, and every law, naturally expires at the end of 19 years. If it be enforced longer, it is an act of force and not of right."[29] Though Jefferson's admonitions are not followed literally, the states do frequently alter their constitutions. One informal and four formal methods for amending state constitutions exist. The informal route is **interpretation** of constitutional meaning by the state legislature, executive branch, courts, or attorneys general, or through usage and custom. Governors issue executive orders; courts and attorneys general issue advisory opinions on meanings of specific provisions; state agencies make decisions and implement policy. The force of habit can be a powerful influence, specific constitutional provisions notwithstanding. It is a good bet that one or more antiquated or unrealistic constitutional provisions are ignored in every state. A common example is the requirement that all bills be read, in their entirety, three times in each house for enactment. Another is the list of conditions for holding political office, such as a belief in God.

interpretation
An informal means of revising constitutions whereby members of the executive, legislative, or judicial branch apply constitutional principles and law to the everyday affairs of governing.

State supreme courts play the most direct role in changing constitutions through interpretation. In large measure, a constitution is what the judges say it is in their decisions from the bench. Judicial interpretation of constitutions may be based on a variety of standards, including strict attention to the express language of the document and to the original intent of the framers or authors of amendments, deference to legislative enactments or executive actions, precedent, policy considerations, and individual rights. The power of the state supreme courts to review executive actions, legislative actions, and decisions of lower courts is known as **judicial review**. This power evolved in the states much as it did on the national level—through the courts' own insistence that they hold this authority. During recent years, as the U.S. Supreme Court has become more conservative and activist in its interpretations of the law, some state courts have moved in the opposite direction and earned reputations as progressive judicial activists. On occasion, the U.S. Supreme Court strikes down state constitutional law, as it did in declaring an Arizona elections law unconstitutional in 2013.

judicial review

The power of the U.S. Supreme Court or state supreme courts to declare unconstitutional the actions of the executive and legislative branches as well as decisions of lower courts.

Formal Constitutional Change

The four formal procedures for constitutional change are legislative proposal, initiative, constitutional convention, and constitutional commission. All of them involve two basic steps: initiation and **ratification**. The state legislature, or in some cases the voters, propose (initiate) a constitutional change. Then the proposed amendment is submitted to the voters for approval (ratification).

ratification

The formal approval of a constitution or constitutional amendment by a majority of the voters of a state.

Legislative Proposal

The most common road taken to revision is **legislative proposal**; more than 90 percent of all changes in state constitutions have come through this method, which is permitted in all fifty states. The specifics of legislative proposal techniques vary, but most states require either two-thirds or three-fifths of the members of each house to approve a proposal before it is sent to the voters for ratification. Twelve states require two consecutive legislative sessions to consider and pass a proposed amendment. The procedure can become quite complicated. For instance, South Carolina's legislative proposal must be passed by two-thirds of the members of each house; it is then sent to the people during the next general election. If a majority of voters show approval, the proposal returns to the next legislative session, in which a majority of legislators have to concur.

legislative proposal

The most common means of amending a state constitution, wherein the legislature proposes a revision, usually by a two-thirds majority.

Almost all states accept a simple majority for voter ratification of a proposed revision. In New Hampshire, however, two-thirds of the voters must approve of the proposal. And Tennessee requires approval by a majority of the number of citizens who cast a vote for governor.

Legislative proposal is probably best suited to revisions that are relatively narrow in scope. Some legislatures, however, such as South Carolina's, have presented a series of proposals to the voters over a period of years and thereby have significantly revised the constitution. The disadvantage to such a strategy is that it tends to result in a patchwork of amendments that can conflict or overlap with

STATE	YEAR	NUMBER OF SIGNATURES REQUIRED ON INITIATIVE PETITION
		States Authorizing Constitutional Amendment by Citizen Initiative — TABLE 3.3
Arizona	1910	15% of total votes cast for all candidates for governor at last election.
Arkansas	1909	10% of voters for governor at last election.
California	1911	8% of total voters for all candidates for governor at last election.
Colorado	1910	5% of total legal votes for all candidates for secretary of state at last general election.
Florida	1972	8% of total votes cast in the state in the last election for presidential electors.
Illinois	1970	8% of total votes cast for candidates for governor at last election.
Massachusetts	1918	3% of total votes cast for governor at preceding biennial state election (not fewer than 25,000 qualified voters).
Michigan	1908	10% of total voters for all candidates at the gubernatorial election.
Mississippi	1992	12% of total votes for all candidates for governor at last election.
Missouri	1906	8% of legal voters for all candidates for governor at last election.
Montana	1904	10% of qualified electors, the number of qualified electors to be determined by number of votes cast for governor in preceding general election.
Nebraska	1912	10% of total votes for governor at last election.
Nevada	1904	10% of voters who voted in entire state in last general election.
North Dakota	1914	4% of population of the state.
Ohio	1912	10% of total number of electors who voted for governor in last election.
Oklahoma	1907	15% of legal voters for state office receiving highest number of voters at last general state election.
Oregon	1902	8% of total votes for all candidates for governor at last election of which governor was elected for four-year term.
South Dakota	1898	10% of total votes for governor in last election.

SOURCE: Adapted from *The Book of States*, 2012, Table 1.3 Vol. Reprinted by permission of The Council of State Governments.

other constitutional provisions. Moreover, if many complex amendments are inflicted on the voters at one time, they might reject all of them out of frustration, as Florida voters seemed to do in 2012.[30]

Initiative

Eighteen states permit their citizens to initiate and ratify changes in the constitution on their own, bypassing the legislature (see Table 3.3). Only five of these initiative states are east of the Mississippi River, reflecting the fact that the initiative was a product of the Progressive reform movement of the early 1900s. Most of the territories admitted as states during this period chose to permit

initiative

A proposed law or constitutional amendment that is placed on the ballot by citizen petition.

direct initiative

A procedure by which the voters of a jurisdiction propose the passage of constitutional amendments, state laws, or local ordinances, bypassing the legislative body.

indirect initiative

Similar to the direct initiative, except that the voter-initiated proposal must be submitted to the legislature before going on the ballot for voter approval.

constitutional convention

An assembly of delegates chosen by popular election or appointed by the legislature or the governor to revise an existing constitution or to create a new one.

the **initiative** (known as constitutional initiative in some states). Twenty-three states also authorize the initiative for enacting statutory change.

The number of signatures needed for the initiative petition to be valid varies widely: Arizona requires 15 percent of total votes cast in the last gubernatorial election, whereas Massachusetts requires merely 3 percent.[31] Moreover, to ensure that an initiative favoring one region does not become embodied in the constitution, eight states specify that the petition signatures must be collected widely throughout the state.

In general, a petition for constitutional amendment is sent to the office of the secretary of state for verification that the required number of registered voters have signed their names. Then the question is placed on a statewide ballot in the next general election. Ratification requires a majority vote of the people in most states.

It is usually easy enough to collect the required number of signatures to place a proposed amendment on a statewide ballot (firms are happy to perform this service for a fee). But actual passage of the initiative is much more difficult once it receives a close public examination and opposing interests proclaim their objections. If the legislature is circumvented altogether and propositions are placed directly on the general-election ballot by citizens, the procedure is called a **direct initiative**. If a legislature participates by voting on the citizen proposal, as in Massachusetts and Mississippi, the procedure is known as an **indirect initiative**.

The initiative is useful in making limited changes to the state constitution and, in recent years, has addressed some controversial issues that state legislatures have been loath to confront. Voters in several states have recently addressed same-sex marriage, immigration policy, property rights, school vouchers, and the right to carry firearms.

A major advantage of the initiative is that the people's will can counter a despotic or inertia-ridden legislature. For instance, Illinois voters in 1978 reduced the size of the House of Representatives from 177 to 118 after the legislature voted itself a huge pay raise during a period of economic hardship. Another advantage is that this method appears to enhance citizen interest and participation in government.

The initiative, however, can also be abused by special-interest groups with selfish motives who seek to gain privileges, and under crisis conditions it can result in ill-conceived, radical changes to the constitution. Indeed, the initiative can result in just the kind of excessive detail and poorly drafted verbiage that is so widely condemned by constitutional scholars and reformers. It can also make doing routine business extremely difficult. In Colorado, for example, initiatives appear to require simultaneous tax cuts and spending increases.[32]

Constitutional Convention

Legislative proposals and initiatives are quite specific about the type of constitutional change that is sought. Only those questions that actually appear on the ballot are considered. In contrast, a **constitutional convention** assembles delegates who suggest revisions or even an entirely new document; the proposed changes are then submitted to the voters for ratification. The convention is especially well suited for considering far-reaching constitutional changes or a new fundamental law, but none has convened since 1992 in Louisiana.

The convention is the oldest method for constitutional change in the states and is available in all fifty of them. The process begins when the electorate or the legislature decides to call for a constitutional convention. In fourteen states, the question of calling a convention must be regularly voted on by the electorate, but all convention calls have been routinely rejected since Rhode Island's was approved in 1986. Alaskans and Iowans hold an "automatic convention call" every ten years; in New York and Maryland, the convention issue is submitted to the voters every twenty years. Except in Delaware, where the legislature can take direct action, proposals emerging from the convention must be ratified by the voters before they become part of the constitution.

Delegates to a convention are usually elected on a nonpartisan ballot by the voters from state house or senate districts. Conventions are usually dominated by lawyers, educators, and businesspeople. The characteristics of a delegate pool are important for several reasons. First, the delegates need knowledge of and experience in state government and politics if they are to contribute meaningfully to the debate and drafting of proposed amendments. It is usually not too difficult to attract qualified people for service; the experience is important and unique, and many consider it a privilege. Second, the delegates should represent a cross-section of the state's population insofar as possible. If the delegate pool does not reflect gender, racial, regional, ethnic, and other salient characteristics of the population, the fruit of its labor may lack legitimacy in the eyes of substantial numbers of voters. Finally, partisanship should be avoided when possible. Partisan differences can wreck consensus on major issues and destroy the prospects for voter ratification of suggested amendments that emerge from the convention.

Voter approval of convention proposals is problematic. If partisan, racial, regional, religious, or other disagreements dominate media reports on the convention, voter approval is difficult to obtain. People naturally tend to be skeptical of suggestions for sweeping, unbounded changes in the basic structures and procedures of government. Conventions have greater likelihood of winning voter approval when specific changes are to be considered.[33]

Once a convention is approved and convened, delegates usually understand these dynamics and are sensitive to how their proposed changes may affect the general public. They must, for example, carefully consider how to present the proposed amendments for ratification. There are two choices: the all-or-nothing strategy of consolidating all changes in a single vote, and the piecemeal strategy of offering each proposal as a separate ballot decision. Voters tend to reject inclusive packages. Each suggested change is certain to offend some minority, and when all the offended minorities coalesce, they may well constitute a majority of voters.

Constitutional Commission

**constitutional
commission**

A meeting of
delegates appointed
by the governor
or legislature to
study constitutional
problems and
propose solutions.

Often called a *study commission*, the **constitutional commission** is usually established to examine the existing document and to recommend changes to the legislature or to the voters. Depending on the mandate, the constitutional commission may examine the entire constitution with a view toward replacement or change, focus on one or more specific articles or provisions, or be given the freedom to decide its own scope of activity. Commission recommendations are only advisory, thus helping to account for this method's popularity with elected officials, who sometimes prefer to study a problem to death rather than engage it head on. Some or all of the recommendations may be submitted to the voters; others may be completely ignored. Only in Florida can a commission send its proposals directly to voters.

Constitutional commissions were operating in Alabama and Ohio in 2013, and Utah's revision commission functions permanently. Service on a constitutional commission can be a thankless task, because legislators sometimes ignore the commission's recommendations or employ them as a symbolic device for relieving political pressure. For example, Kentucky's 1987–1988 Revision Commission recommended seventy-seven changes to the constitution, but only one was referred by the legislature to the voters as a proposed amendment.[34] When used properly, however, commissions can furnish high-quality research both inexpensively and relatively quickly.

STATE RESPONSIVENESS AND CONSTITUTIONAL REFORM

Each state's constitution is designed specifically to meet the needs of that state. The rich political culture, history, economics, values, and ideals of the state's community are reflected in state constitutional language. Through their constitutions, the states experiment with different governmental institutions and processes. As avid patriot Thomas Paine observed some 225 years ago, "It is in the interest of all the states, that the constitution of each should be somewhat diversified from each other. We are a people founded upon experiments, and have the happy opportunity of trying variety in order to discover the 'best.'"[35]

State constitutions were the original guardians of individual rights and liberties, with their own bills of rights preceding that of the U.S. Constitution by many years. They have generally reassumed that responsibility during the past several decades. Yet few tasks in government are more difficult than modernizing a constitution. The process requires "sustained, dedicated, organized effort; vigorous, aggressive and imaginative leadership; bipartisan political support; education of the electorate on the issues; judicious selection of the means; and seemingly endless 'patience.'"[36] In the words of constitutional scholar W. Brooke Graves, "The advocate of constitutional reform in an American state should be endowed with the patience of Job and the sense of time of a geologist."[37] The solemn duty of framing the original state constitutions, so effectively discharged by our predecessors, must be matched by the continuous oversight of present and future generations. Changes are necessary to adjust state governments to the vagaries of the future.

The constitutional changes enacted in the states since the Kestnbaum Commission report have generally resulted in documents in the higher-law tradition, documents that "are shorter, more clearly written, modernized, less encumbered with restrictions, more basic in content and have more reasonable amending processes. They also establish improved governmental structures and contain substantive provisions assuring greater openness, accountability and equity."[38] The states have made a great deal of progress in modernizing their governments. As state constitutional scholar Richard Leach has put it, "There are not many constitutional horrors left."[39]

Recent constitutional amendments have responded to, and indeed caused, profound changes in state government and politics. Since the genesis of modern reform in the mid-1960s, some forty states have adopted new constitutions or substantially amended existing ones. Problems persist, and future constitutional tinkering and replacements will be necessary. But in most states, the constitutional landscape is much cleaner and more functional than it was a generation ago.

CHAPTER RECAP

- The constitution is the fundamental law of a state, superior to statutory law.

- State constitutions evolved from the original colonial charters. Shifting from an original basis of legislative supremacy, they have gradually increased executive power.

- Some constitutions continue to suffer from excessive length and substantive problems.

- Constitutional reform has modernized the documents and made them conform more closely to present challenges of governance.

- Methods for changing constitutions include interpretation, judicial review, legislative proposal, initiative, constitutional convention, and constitutional commission.

Key Terms

fundamental law *(p. 47)*
legislative supremacy *(p. 51)*
Model State Constitution
(p. 56)
positive-law tradition *(p. 57)*
higher-law tradition *(p. 57)*

interpretation *(p. 61)*
judicial review *(p. 62)*
ratification *(p. 62)*
legislative proposal *(p. 62)*
initiative *(p. 64)*
direct initiative *(p. 64)*

indirect initiative *(p. 64)*
constitutional convention
(p. 64)
constitutional commission
(p. 66)

Internet Resources

For full texts of state statutes and constitutions, see individual state websites (for example, **www.state.fl.us**.

State constitutions can also be accessed through **www.findlaw.com/11stategov/indexconst.html**, or **www.constitution.org**.

The Alaska constitution draws heavily on the Model State Constitution. It is located in the state of Alaska Documents Library at **www.law.state.ak.us**.

A helpful site is the Center for State Constitutional Studies at **www.camlaw.rutgers.edu/statecon**.

The most recent data on state constitutions can be accessed at **www.csg.org**.

Citizen Participation and Elections

4

CHAPTER OUTLINE

- Participation
- Elections
- Direct Democracy
- Citizen Access to Government
- The Effects of Citizen Participation

FOCUS QUESTIONS

1. What are some of the reasons that voter participation varies from state to state?
2. Which ballot-based process, available to voters in many states, has emerged as an important policymaking tool?
3. In addition to voting, what are some ways in which citizens can participate in their state and local government?
4. What are some innovations and programs that states and localities can use to increase civic participation in government?

The city of Takoma Park, Maryland, a suburb of Washington, D.C., made history in 2013 when it granted sixteen- and seventeen-year-olds the right to vote in city elections. Why take such an unprecedented step? Simple: City leaders believed that lowering the voting age would help local residents develop a lifelong habit of participation in government. Sure, there were naysayers who claimed that teenagers are too immature to handle the responsibility. But in the end, the desire to engage local teens in the most basic right of citizenship prevailed. After all, as one of the newly enfranchised high school students said, "We cultivate interest in democracy by giving people opportunities to participate."[1] It remains to be seen whether other cities will emulate Takoma Park's bold action and grant their sixteen- and seventeen-year-old residents the right to vote in municipal elections.

PARTICIPATION

participation

Actions through which ordinary members of a political system attempt to influence outcomes.

Democracy assumes citizen **participation**—acting to influence government. In contemporary America, there is persistent evidence that citizens are not much interested in participation. We have grown accustomed to reports of low voter turnout and public hearings that few attend. In his influential book, *Bowling Alone*, political scientist Robert Putnam documented this gradual disengagement of people from all sorts of community activities and organizations.[2]

On the surface, government works just fine with limited participation: the interests of the active become translated into public policy, and those who are inactive can be safely ignored because they do not vote.[3] If, however, some traditional nonvoters (such as low-income, less-educated citizens) went to the polls, then vote-seeking candidates would be forced to pay more attention to their interests, and public policy might be nudged in a different direction. In this light, it is important to understand both why many people do participate and why others do not. This chapter addresses individual citizen involvement in government; Chapter 5 takes up collective participation (that is, participation by political parties and interest groups).

Why and How People Participate

In a representative democracy, voting is the most common form of participation. For many citizens, it is a matter of civic responsibility. It is a fundamental facet of citizenship—after all, it is called "the right to vote." Citizens go to the polls to elect the officials who will govern them. But there are other methods of participation. Consider the citizen who is unhappy because the property taxes on her home have increased substantially from one year to the next. What options are available to her besides voting against incumbent officeholders at the next election? As shown in Figure 4.1, she can be either active or passive; and her actions, either constructive or destructive. Basically, she has four potential responses: loyalty, voice, exit, and neglect.[4]

According to this formulation, voting is an example of *loyalty*, a passive but constructive response to government action. Specifically, this response reflects the irate taxpayer's underlying support for her community despite her displeasure with particular tax policies. An active constructive response is *voice*: The aggrieved property owner could contact officials, work in the campaign of a candidate who promises to lower tax assessments, or (assuming that others in the community share her sentiments) participate in anti-tax groups and organize demonstrations. Research has shown that emotions, especially anger, can be a powerful stimulant to citizen participation.[5]

Destructive responses (those that undermine the citizen-government relationship) are similarly passive or active. If the citizen simply shrugs and concludes that "you can't fight city hall," she is exhibiting a response termed *neglect*. She has nearly given up on the community and does not participate. A more active version of giving up is to *exit*—that is, to leave the community altogether (a response often referred to as "voting with your feet"). The

Possible Responses to Dissatisfaction in the Community

SOURCE: From "The Organization of Political Space and Citizen Responses to Dissatisfaction in Urban Communities: An Integrated Model," William E. Lyons and David Lowery, *Journal of Politics* 48, no. 2 (1986): 321–45, Figure 1. Reprinted with permission from Blackwell Publishers.

unhappy citizen will relocate in a community that is more in line with her tax preferences.

Every citizen confronts these participatory options. It is much healthier for the political system if citizens engage in the constructive responses, but some individuals are likely to conclude that constructive participation is of little value to them and opt for neglect or, in more extreme cases, exit.

Nonparticipation

What motivates citizens who choose neglect as their best option? One explanation for nonparticipation in politics is socioeconomic status. Individuals with lower levels of income and education tend to participate less than wealthier, more educated individuals.[6] Tied closely to income and education levels is occupational status. Unskilled workers and hourly wage earners do not participate in politics to the same degree as white-collar workers and professionals. Individuals of lower socioeconomic status may not have the time, resources, or civic skills required to become actively involved in politics.

Other explanations for nonparticipation have included age (younger people have participated less than middle-aged individuals), race (blacks have participated less than whites), and gender (women have participated less than men). Of these factors, however, only age continues to affect political activity levels. African American political participation actually surpasses that of whites when socioeconomic status is taken into consideration,[7] and the gender gap in the types and levels of political participation has disappeared.[8] America's youth, however, remain less likely to frequent polling places. The upsurge in voting among the eighteen- to twenty-four-year-olds in the 2008 presidential election was thought by many to signal a new trend in youthful participation, but turnout in that age group dropped in 2012. Groups such as Kids Voting USA have developed programs to socialize children about political affairs, surmising that children who get into the habit of citizen participation at an early age will be more politically active as adults.[9] For older youth, websites such as the MTV-sponsored Rock the Vote encourage active participation in politics and government.

Another factor that exerts an independent effect on participation is where one lives. Big-city dwellers (those who live in places with a population of 1 million or more) are less likely than people in small communities (less than 5,000 inhabitants) to participate in various civic activities, including contacting local officials, attending community meetings, and voting in local elections.[10] In a recent survey asking nonvoters why they did not participate in an election, the top two explanations were "didn't like choices (of candidates)" and "too busy."[11] The explanation for nonparticipation does not rest solely with the individual. Institutional features—the way the political system is designed—may suppress participation. For example, local governments that have instituted nonpartisan elections in which candidates run without political party affiliation have removed an important mobilizing factor for voters. Voter turnout tends to be lower in these elections than in partisan contests. City council meetings scheduled at 10:00 a.m. put a tremendous strain on workers who must take time off from their jobs if they want to attend; consequently, attendance is low. And localities in which it is difficult for citizens to contact the appropriate official with a service request or complaint are not doing much to facilitate participation. Features like these play an often unrecognized role in dampening participation.

The Struggle for the Right to Vote

State constitutions in the eighteenth and early nineteenth centuries entrusted only propertied white males with the vote. They did not encourage public involvement in government, and the eventual softening of restrictions on suffrage did not occur without a struggle. Restrictions based on property ownership and wealth eventually were dropped, but women, blacks, and Native Americans were still denied the right to vote.

In an effort to attract women to its rugged territory, Wyoming enfranchised women in 1869. The suffragists—women who were actively fighting for the right to vote—scored a victory when Colorado extended the vote to women in 1893. Gradually, other states began enfranchising women, and in 1920 the

Nineteenth Amendment to the U.S. Constitution, forbidding states to deny the right to vote "on account of sex," was ratified.

Even after the Fifteenth Amendment (1870) extended the vote to blacks, some southern states clung defiantly to traditional ways that denied blacks and poor people their rights. Poll taxes, literacy tests, and white primaries were among the barriers erected by segregationists. U.S. Supreme Court decisions such as *Smith* v. *Allwright* (1944), which outlawed white primaries, and federal actions such as the Civil Rights Act of 1964 and the Twenty-Fourth Amendment (1964), which made poll taxes unconstitutional, helped blacks gain access to the polls. But in some jurisdictions, informal methods designed to discourage participation by African Americans continued.

The **Voting Rights Act of 1965** (VRA) finally broke the back of the segregationists' efforts. Under its provisions, federal poll watchers and registrars were dispatched to particular counties to investigate voter discrimination. Counties covered under the Voting Rights Act (all of nine southern states and parts of seven other states) had to submit to the U.S. Department of Justice any changes in election laws, such as new precinct lines or new polling places, well in advance of the election. This is known as the *preclearance* provision. During the ensuing decades, the VRA has been revised and extended several times by Congress. One of the most important modifications of the law has been the substitution of an effects test for the original intent test. In other words, if a governmental action has the effect of discouraging minority voting, whether intentionally or not, the action must be rejected. Civil rights activists welcomed this change because proving the intent of an action is much more difficult than demonstrating its effect. A dramatic change occurred in 2013 when the U.S. Supreme Court, arguing that times had changed, ruled that the formula used to determine which jurisdictions were covered under the VRA was flawed, thereby eliminating the preclearance requirement.

Voting Rights Act of 1965
The law that effectively enfranchised racial minorities by giving the national government the power to decide whether individuals are qualified to vote and to intercede in state and local electoral operations when necessary.

Voting Patterns

Voter turnout is affected by several things. First, it varies according to the type of election. A presidential race usually attracts a higher proportion of eligible voters than does a state or local election. In 2012, with a presidential race underway, voter turnout was approximately 55 percent of the **voting-age population**; in 2010, when there was no presidential election on the ballot—but many governors' races—turnout was only 40 percent. Second, popular candidates running a close race seem to increase voter interest. When each candidate has a chance to win, voters sense that their vote will matter more than in a race with a sure winner. Third, not only partisan competition but party ideology affects voter turnout.[12] When candidates take distinctive ideological stances in competitive elections, the incentive for party-identifiers to vote increases. Finally, based on new research, it appears that media hand-wringing about low voter turnout may have a quite unintended effect: rather than stimulating turnout it may actually depress it.[13]

voting-age population
Adults eighteen years of age and older.

Nationally, voter registration stands at approximately 76 percent of the voting-age population. Not everyone who is of voting age is actually eligible to vote, however. Noncitizens cannot vote (although they can in school board elections in a few localities), and most states have laws barring convicted felons and the mentally incompetent from participating. When you remove the ineligible population from consideration, registration among the **voting-eligible population** stood at approximately 88 percent in 2012. Registration matters because people who are registered tend to vote, and votes translate into political power. Thus, groups anxious to increase their electoral clout will launch registration drives among their membership.

voting-eligible population
The voting-age population excluding those who are noncitizens, convicted felons, or mentally incompetent, depending on state law.

Registering to vote has gotten easier. Passage of the National Voter Registration Act in 1993 means that individuals can register to vote when they apply for a driver's license, welfare benefits, or unemployment compensation, or when they register their automobile. States allow voters to register by mail, and some states, such as Florida, have taken another step by allowing online voter registration; any computer terminal with an Internet connection can be a registration site. Many states have moved the closing date for registration nearer to the actual date of the election, giving potential voters more time to register. This factor is important because campaigns tend to heighten the public's interest in the election.[14] Most states now close their registration books fewer than thirty days before an election, and California, Connecticut, Iowa, Maine, Minnesota, New Hampshire, Wisconsin, and Wyoming allow registration on Election Day.[15] North Dakota is the only state in the nation that does not require voter registration.

States can be differentiated according to voter turnout rates (see Figure 4.2). In 2012, the highest turnout rates were recorded in Minnesota, where 75.7 percent of the voting-eligible population voted, and Wisconsin, where 72.5 percent voted. Hawaii, with 44.2 percent voting, garnered the dubious distinction of being the state with the lowest voter turnout in 2012, with West Virginia a close second (46.3 percent).[16] States with moralistic political cultures typically experience higher voter turnout than do states with traditionalistic political cultures. States with competitive political parties (as opposed to states where one party dominates) tend to have elections with a higher proportion of voters participating; each party needs to mobilize individuals who identify with it in order to win. Finally, states can affect turnout by the way in which they administer the elections: Is voting a convenient exercise, or is it an arduous task marked by hard-to-find precinct locations, long lines at polling places, a requirement to show a government-issued photo ID card (a provision that many states adopted in 2012), and confusing ballots once inside the voting booth?

Many states give their citizens the choice to cast their votes before the day of the election. The list below outlines the options:

- Thirty-two states and the District of Columbia allow "no-excuse" early voting, at a county courthouse or satellite voting locations, on average, beginning nineteen days before Election Day (e.g., California and Texas).
- States have procedures for regular absentee voting by mail, twenty-one states require an excuse (e.g., out of town on Election Day, disabled), and twenty-seven do not require an excuse.

State Voter Turnout, 2012

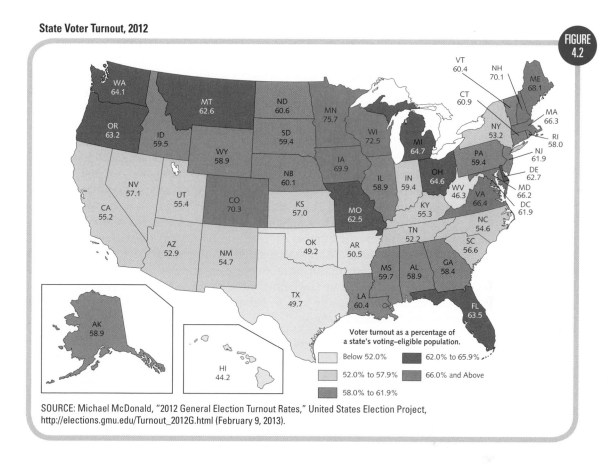

FIGURE 4.2

SOURCE: Michael McDonald, "2012 General Election Turnout Rates," United States Election Project, http://elections.gmu.edu/Turnout_2012G.html (February 9, 2013).

- Two states have set up a vote-by-mail system for their elections (a ballot is automatically mailed to every eligible voter) and do not operate traditional polling places (Oregon and Washington).[17]

Does making voting easier matter? The findings of new research on conveniently located Election Day vote centers—alternatives to precinct-based polling places—suggest that it does, especially among people who tend to be infrequent voters.[18] Moreover, analysis of Oregon's vote-by-mail system showed that the turnout rate increased in some types of elections.[19] More voters are choosing to cast their ballots early, upward of 60 percent in some states. As more states loosen the restrictions on early voting, the notion of Election *Day* is gradually giving way.

ELECTIONS

Elections are central to a representative democracy. Voters choose governors and legislators, and in most states, lieutenant governors, attorneys general, secretaries of state, and state treasurers. In some states they also choose the heads of the agriculture and education departments, judges, and the public utility commissioners. At the local level, the list of elected officials includes mayors and council members, county commissioners, county judges, sheriffs, tax assessors, and school board members. If state and local governments are to function effectively, elections must provide talented, capable leaders. But elections are not just about outcomes; they are also about the process itself. Florida's troubles with ballot design, voting machines, and recount rules in the 2000 presidential election underscored the need for elections to be administered fairly and transparently.

Significant changes in election management and especially in voting technology have occurred during the past few years. Lever-operated voting machines and punch card devices have lost favor, while electronic voting machines and optical scan ballots are being used more widely. This is an important trend because improvements in voting technology have been shown to lead to a significant decline in the number of "lost" or uncounted votes, which are referred to as **residual votes**.[20] Although electronic voting machines (akin to automatic teller machines) are becoming more popular, concerns over their accuracy and security remain. At issue is whether these systems should provide a VVPAT, or voter-verified paper audit trail, to supplement the record of the count in the electronic machine's memory.

residual votes
The number of uncounted, unmarked, and spoiled ballots in an election.

Primaries

For a party to choose a nominee for the general-election ballot, potential candidates must be winnowed. In the pre-Jacksonian era, party nominees were chosen by a legislative caucus—that is, a conference of the party's legislators. Caucuses gave way to the mechanism of state party conventions, which were similar to national presidential nomination conventions but without most of the spectacle; popularly elected delegates from across a state convened to select the party's nominees. Then the Progressive movement sought to open up the nomination process and make it more democratic. Political parties adopted the **primary system,** whereby voters directly choose from among several candidates to select the party's nominees for the general election. The use of primaries has effectively diminished the organizational power of political parties.

Thirteen states still allow for party conventions in particular instances, such as nominations for lieutenant governor and attorney general (Michigan) and selection of a slate of nominees by third parties (Kansas). Connecticut, the last state to adopt primaries, operates a challenge system whereby party nominees for various state offices are selected at a convention; but if a contest develops at the convention and a second candidate receives as much as 15 percent of the votes, the convention's nominee and the challenger square off in a primary.[21]

primary system
The electoral mechanism for selecting party nominees to compete in the general election.

closed primary
A primary in which only voters registered in the party are allowed to participate.

open primary
Voters decide which party's primary they will participate in.

Primary Types Primaries can be divided into two types: closed and open. The only voters who can participate in a **closed primary** for a particular party are those who are registered in that party; an **open primary** does not require party membership. Even this basic distinction, however, lends itself to some variation. States differ, for example, in terms of the ease with which voters can change party affiliation and participate in the closed primary of the other party. In eleven closed primary states, a voter is an enrolled member of one party (or is an Independent and may or may not be eligible to vote in either party's primary, depending on state law) and can change that affiliation only well in advance of the primary election. Democrats vote in the Democratic Party primary, Republicans vote in the GOP primary. Eleven states operate open primaries in which a voter secretly selects the ballot of the party in which he or she wishes to participate. Voters unaffiliated with either of the major parties may vote in open primaries. Obviously this system allows people who consider themselves Republicans to vote in a Democratic primary if they wish, and vice-versa. The other 28 states have primary systems that are neither completely closed nor open.[22] Table 4.1 groups the states by the types of primaries they operate.

The "hybrid" category in Table 4.1 reflects significant variation across states, not only in whether they lean toward closed or open primaries, but also in how much leeway they give political parties to alter their rules. Some of the twenty-four hybrid states hold "semiclosed" primaries, in which voters register as members of a party but are allowed to change that affiliation on the day of the primary election. Still other hybrid states operate "semiopen" primaries, in which voters can select either party's ballot but must do so publicly at the polling place.

Louisiana and a handful of other states do something completely different: The Pelican State uses a single nonpartisan primary for its statewide and congressional races. Candidates, regardless of party affiliation, appear on the same ballot, and voters are free to choose from among them. If a candidate receives a majority of votes in the first round of voting, he or she is elected to office; if he or she does not, the top two vote-getters face each other in a **runoff election.** In 2010, California voters, dissatisfied with the level of partisan rancor in the Golden State, approved a constitutional amendment that provides a similar nonpartisan primary system there, starting with the 2012 elections. Washington, which historically had allowed voters to cross over from one party to another in a single election, adopted its own variation on the top-two primary scheme. Finally, Nebraska uses a top-two primary for its nonpartisan legislative races and for some statewide races.

runoff election
A second election pitting the top two vote-getters from a first election in which no candidate received a majority of the votes cast.

Primary Runoff Elections A runoff election is held in some states if no one candidate for an office receives a majority of votes in the primary. Primary runoff elections are used by parties in eight states: Alabama, Arkansas, Georgia, Mississippi, North Carolina, Oklahoma, South Carolina, and Texas. (Kentucky and South Dakota use primary runoffs but only in certain instances; Florida abolished primary runoffs in 2005.) In the past, these eight states were one-party (Democratic) states, so the greatest amount of competition for an office occurred in the Democratic Party's primaries, in which as many as ten candidates might enter a race. When many candidates compete, it is quite probable that no one will receive a majority of the votes, so the top two vote-getters face

TABLE 4.1	State Use of Different Types of Primary Elections		
CLOSED	**OPEN**	**HYBRID**	**TOP-TWO**
Delaware	Alabama	Alaska	California
Florida	Arkansas	Arizona	Louisiana
Kansas	Georgia	Colorado	Nebraska*
Kentucky	Hawaii	Connecticut	Washington
Maine	Michigan	Idaho	
Nevada	Minnesota	Illinois	
New Jersey	Missouri	Indiana	
New Mexico	Montana	Iowa	
New York	North Dakota	Maryland	
Pennsylvania	Vermont	Massachusetts	
Wyoming	Wisconsin	Mississippi	
		New Hampshire	
		North Carolina	
		Ohio	
		Oklahoma	
		Oregon	
		Rhode Island	
		South Carolina	
		South Dakota	
		Tennessee	
		Texas	
		Utah	
		Virginia	
		West Virginia	
(11)	(11)	(24)	(4)

*In Nebraska, the top-two primary is used for the state's nonpartisan legislative races and for some statewide elections.

SOURCE: "State Primary Elections Types," National Conference of State Legislatures, www.ncsl.org/legislatures-elections/elections/st ate-primary-election-systems.aspx, September 28, 2011.

each other in a runoff. This process ensures that the party's nominee is preferred by a majority of the primary voters.

Theoretically, the rationale for the runoff primary is majority rule. But political circumstances have changed since several southern states adopted the runoff primary system in the 1920s, and the Democratic Party no longer dominates the region. In fact, in many southern states the two parties are competitive, and in some the Republican Party has overtaken the Democrats. This raises an important question: has the runoff primary outlived its usefulness? It is often difficult for a party to mobilize its voters for the primary runoff election, and voter participation in the runoff drops, on average, by one-third.[23] And they are costly to operate: Kentucky estimated the administrative cost of holding a statewide gubernatorial runoff primary to be approximately $5.4 million.[24] One solution to this problem for parties might be the ranked choice or **instant runoff** that San Francisco, California, Minneapolis, Minnesota, and Burlington, Vermont, and a few other cities have begun using in their municipal elections.[25] In an instant runoff, voters rank the primary candidates in their order of preference. If no candidate receives a majority of first choices, the candidate with the fewest is eliminated, and voters who ranked the eliminated candidate first now have their ballots counted for their second choice. The process continues until one candidate has a majority; a runoff primary election is avoided.

instant runoff
Voters use preference rankings to select candidates at a single election.

General Elections

Primaries culminate in the general election through which winning candidates become officeholders. When the general election pits candidates of the two major parties against one another, the winner is the candidate who receives a majority of the votes cast. In a race where more than two candidates compete (which occurs when an Independent or a third-party candidate enters a race), the leading vote-getter may not receive a majority of the votes cast, but instead receives a **plurality**. A few states allow candidates to run under the label of more than one party, which is called **fusion**. In New York in 2010, for example, Andrew Cuomo was the candidate for governor of the Democratic and Independence parties.

plurality
The number of votes (though not necessarily a majority) cast for the winning candidate in an election with more than two candidates.

Political parties have traditionally been active in general elections, mobilizing voters in support of their candidates. Their role has diminished over time, however, because general-election campaigns have become more candidate-centered and geared to the candidate's own organization. One new twist in the past two decades has been the emergence of legislative party caucuses as major factors in general elections. In large states with professionalized legislatures, the funds distributed to their party's nominees by legislative party caucuses run into the millions of dollars. In addition to funding, legislative party caucuses provide other types of election assistance, such as seminars on issues and on campaign management, making these organizations powerful players in some states' politics.

fusion
A state-election provision that allows candidates to run on more than one party ticket.

Most states schedule their gubernatorial elections in "off-years"—that is, years in which no presidential election is held. Only eleven states elected governors during the presidential election year of 2012; forty-one held their statewide races in other years. (The number sums to fifty-two because New Hampshire and Vermont limit their governors to two-year terms, thereby holding gubernatorial elections in both off- and on-years.) Among those forty-one off-year states, five—Kentucky, Louisiana, Mississippi, New Jersey, and Virginia—have elections that take place in odd-numbered years. Off-year elections prevent the presidential race from diverting attention from state races and also minimize the possible **coattail effect**, by which a presidential candidate can affect the fortunes of state candidates of the same party. With elections held in off-years, races for governor may serve instead as referenda on the sitting president's performance in office. Generally, however, the health of a state's economy is a critical issue in gubernatorial elections.[26]

coattail effect
The tendency of a winning (or losing) presidential candidate to carry state candidates of the same party into (or out of) office.

Recent State Elections

The off-off year elections in 2011 did not hold much partisan drama: the incumbent Democratic governor of Kentucky was reelected, while the Republicans held onto the Louisiana and Mississippi governorships. On the legislative side, 434 seats were in contention in four states (Louisiana, Mississippi, New Jersey, and Virginia). The elections resulted in a gain for Republicans as they wrested control of the Mississippi House from the Democrats for the first time in 150 years and were able to create a partisan split (20-20) in the formerly Democratic-controlled Virginia Senate.

With a presidential campaign garnering the lion's share of media attention in 2012, eleven states held elections for the governorship and other statewide offices; forty-three states had legislative elections on tap. In most states, the 2012 elections were the first to be held after legislative district boundaries had been redrawn, which occurs after each decennial census. (See the discussion of legislative redistricting in Chapter 6.)

In terms of partisanship, the eleven gubernatorial elections of 2012 produced little change: in only one state (North Carolina) was the opposition party (the GOP) successful in winning the seat. In the other ten gubernatorial races, Democrats retained control of the office in seven states, Republicans in three states. All six of the incumbent governors seeking reelection won. In state legislatures, the level of change was somewhat higher, with the Democratic Party enjoying greater success than the Republican Party. Democrats added 150 seats overall and regained majority control of eight chambers they had lost in 2010. In four legislative chambers, Republicans took control from Democrats, including both houses of the Arkansas legislature—something that had not happened since 1874. Receiving a lot of attention in the 2012 elections were ballot questions in three states to legalize the recreational use of marijuana for adults. The measure passed in Colorado and Washington; it failed in Oregon.

State elections in 2013 were limited to gubernatorial and legislative races in New Jersey and Virginia. Although Governor Chris Christie was an odds-on favorite to win reelection in New Jersey, the race in Virginia, where there was no incumbent running, was a hotly contested battle between Attorney General Ken Cuccinelli, a Republican, and former chair of the Democratic National

Committee, Terry McAuliffe. Predominant topics in the Virginia gubernatorial campaign included tax reform, job creation, ethics, and social issues.

Nonpartisan Elections

A **nonpartisan election** removes the political party identification from candidates in an effort to depoliticize the electoral campaign. Elections that have been made nonpartisan include those for many judicial offices and local-level positions. The special task of judges—adjudicating guilt or innocence, determining right and wrong—does not lend itself to partisan interpretation. The job of local governments—delivering public services—has also traditionally been considered nonideological. Nonpartisan local elections are likely to be found in municipalities, as well as in school districts and special districts.

Under a nonpartisan election system, all candidates for an office compete in a first election and, if there's no majority winner, the top two vote-getters run in a second election (runoff). Although approximately three-quarters of cities use nonpartisan elections, some regional variation exists in their usage. The prevalence of nonpartisanship is somewhat lower in the Northeast and Midwest than it is in western cities.

Most studies have concluded that nonpartisanship depresses turnout in municipal elections that are held independent of state and national elections. The figures are not dramatic, but in what are already low-turnout elections, the difference can run as high as 10 percent of municipal voters.[27] Studies have shown that lower turnout results in lessened representation of Latinos and Asian Americans on city councils and in the mayor's office.[28] Nonpartisan elections seem to produce a city council that is somewhat well-to-do by socioeconomic standards and a greater number of officeholders who consider themselves Republicans.

What does it take to get elected? In the absence of political parties, candidates are forced to create their own organizations in order to run for office. They raise and spend money (much of it their own), and they seek the support of business and citizen groups. Money matters; and according to studies of city elections in Atlanta and St. Louis, so do incumbency and newspaper endorsements.[29] In some communities, **slating groups** function as unofficial parties by recruiting candidates and financing their campaigns; citizens' groups can also be an important factor in local elections.[30]

nonpartisan election
An election without party labels.

slating groups
Nonpartisan political organizations that endorse and promote a slate of candidates.

DIRECT DEMOCRACY

What happens when the government does not respond to the messages that the people are sending? More and more frequently, the answer is to transform the messages into ballot propositions and let the citizens make their own laws. As explained in Chapter 3, *initiatives* are proposed laws or constitutional amendments that are placed on the ballot by citizen petition, to be approved

popular referendum

A special type of referendum whereby citizens can petition to vote on actions taken by legislative bodies.

referendum

A procedure whereby a governing body submits proposed laws, constitutional amendments, or bond issues to the voters for ratification.

recall

A procedure that allows citizens to vote elected officials out of office before their term has expired.

or rejected by popular vote. An initiative lets citizens enact their own laws, bypassing the state legislature. This mechanism for legislation by popular vote was one of several reforms of the Progressive era, which lasted roughly from 1890 to 1920.

Other Progressive reforms included the popular referendum and the recall. The **popular referendum** allows citizens to petition to vote on actions taken by legislative bodies. It provides a means by which the public can overturn a legislative enactment. (A popular referendum is different from a general **referendum**—a proposition put on the ballot by the legislature that requires voter approval before it can take effect. Constitutional amendments and bond issues are examples of general referenda.) The **recall** election, another citizen-initiated process, requires elected officials to stand for a vote on their removal before their term has expired. Recall provides the public with an opportunity to force an official out of office.

The key characteristic shared by initiative, popular referendum, and recall is that they are actions begun by citizens. The Progressives advocated these mechanisms to expand the role of citizens and to restrict the power of intermediary institutions such as legislatures, political parties, and elected officials.[31] Their efforts were particularly successful in the western part of the United States, probably owing to the difficulty of amending existing state constitutions in the East and to an elitist fear of the working class (namely, the industrialized immigrants in the Northeast and the rural black sharecroppers in the South). The newer western states, in contrast, were quite open, both procedurally and socially. In 1898, South Dakota became the first state to adopt the initiative process. And the initiative was actually used for the first time in Oregon in 1902, when citizens successfully petitioned for ballot questions on mandatory political party primaries and local-option liquor sales. Both of the initiatives were approved.

Today, twenty-four states allow the initiative for constitutional amendments, statutes, or both; Mississippi is the most recent addition, having adopted it in 1992. A few of the twenty-four states use the indirect initiative, which gives the legislature an opportunity to consider the proposed measure. Popular referendum is provided for in twenty-four states, and recall of state officials in nineteen. These figures understate the use of such mechanisms throughout the country, however, because many states without statewide initiative, popular referendum, and recall allow their use at the local government level. Table 4.2 lists some of the states that give their citizens all three of the direct democracy options and some of the states with none of them.

The Initiative

The first step in the initiative process is the petition. A draft of the proposed law (or constitutional amendment) is circulated along with a petition for citizens to sign. The petition signature requirement varies by state but usually falls between 5 and 10 percent of the number of votes cast in the preceding statewide election. To ensure that a matter is of statewide concern and that signatures have

Five States That Do, Five States That Don't		TABLE 4.2
ALL THREE DIRECT DEMOCRACY OPTIONS	**NONE OF THE DIRECT DEMOCRACY OPTIONS**
Arizona	Connecticut
California	Iowa
Colorado	North Carolina
North Dakota	Vermont
Wyoming	Virginia
SOURCE: Initiative and Referendum Institute, www.iandrinstitute.org/statewide_i%26r.htm (July 20, 2010).	

been gathered beyond a single area, some states set geographic distributional requirements. In Montana, for example, signature requirements must be met in at least one-third of the legislative districts; in Nebraska, in two-fifths of the counties. Signatures can be gathered by door-to-door canvassing, buttonholing people at shopping malls and sporting events, posting downloadable petition forms on the Internet, and sending forms to a preselected list of likely signers.

The Popularity of Initiatives One of the most influential modern initiatives was California's Proposition 13 (1978), which rolled back property taxes in the state and spawned an immediate wave of tax-reduction propositions across the land. The increased popularity of initiatives has at least two explanations: (1) Some observers believe that wavering public confidence in government has led citizens to take matters into their own hands. The attitude seems to be "if government can't be trusted to do the right thing, we'll do it ourselves." (2) New methods of signature collection have brought the initiative process within the reach of virtually any well-financed group with a grievance or concern. An example from Massachusetts makes the point. When then-governor Paul Cellucci could not get the legislature to pass his tax-cut proposals, he took the issue straight to the voters. Using donations from supporters, he paid a company to collect sufficient signatures on petitions, and he got his issue on the ballot.[32] Massachusetts voters approved it.

Recent Initiatives If ballot questions are any indication of the public's mood, then the public has had quite an attitude lately. Here is a sampling of initiatives on 2012 ballots in particular states and the outcomes:

- Arkansas, a proposal to permit the medical use of marijuana (failed).
- California, a proposal to increase the criminal penalties for human trafficking (passed).
- Maine, a proposal to legalize same-sex marriage (passed).
- Massachusetts, a proposal to legalize physician-assisted suicide (failed).
- Oregon, a proposal to eliminate estate and inheritance taxes (failed).

- South Dakota, a proposal to increase the sales tax rate from 4% to 5% and split the proceeds between education and Medicaid (failed).
- Washington, a proposal to authorize the creation of forty charter schools (passed).[33]

Questions About the Initiative Is the initiative process appropriate for resolving tough public problems? Seldom are issues so simple that a yes-or-no ballot question can adequately reflect appropriate options and alternatives. A legislative setting, in contrast, fosters the negotiation and compromise that produce workable solutions. Also, is the public sufficiently informed to make intelligent choices and avoid susceptibility to emotional appeals? Ballot questions are considered low-information elections: Facing little information or conflicting claims, voters respond to readily available cues that may be misleading or erroneous. And finally, do ballot initiatives place citizens in an adversarial relationship with their government? There is some evidence that, despite stimulating greater participation, initiatives tend to spur distrust of public officials.[34]

Legislators are of two minds when it comes to direct citizen involvement in policymaking. On the one hand, having the public decide a controversial issue such as abortion or school prayer helps legislators out of tight spots. On the other hand, increased citizen law-making intrudes on the central function of the legislature and usurps legislative power. Given the popularity of initiatives, legislators must proceed cautiously with actions that would make them more difficult to use. So far, efforts to increase the signature requirements or to limit the kinds of topics an initiative may address have been unsuccessful. A citizenry accustomed to the initiative process does not look kindly on its dismantling. A survey of Oregon citizens found 81 percent agreeing with this statement: "Ballot initiatives enhance the democratic process in Oregon by allowing voters to decide important policy issues."[35]

Still, direct democracy enthusiasts should heed the words of political scientist Valentina Bali, who studied local compliance with a California initiative intended to dismantle bilingual education programs: "the large number of constraints suggests that the final policy outcome of an initiative can be quite limited after the initiative's implementation."[36] Initiative sponsors have learned that if they want their initiative to have the desired impact, they have to keep the pressure on, even after the measure has been approved.

The Recall

Recalls, too, were once a little-used mechanism in state and local governments. Only nineteen states provide for recall of state officials; and in seven of them, judicial officers are exempt. City and county government charters, even in states without recall provisions, often include a process for recalling local elected officials. In fact, the first known recall was aimed at a Los Angeles city council member in 1904. Recalls have a much higher petition signature requirement than do initiatives; it is common to require a signature minimum of 25 percent of the votes cast in the last election for the office of the official sought to be recalled. (Kansas, for example, requires a 40 percent minimum.)

Recall efforts usually involve a public perception of official misconduct. On occasion, however, simply running afoul of citizen preferences is enough to trigger a recall, as former California governor Gray Davis discovered in 2003. Californians unhappy with Davis's leadership in resolving the state's budget crunch and its problems with energy deregulation collected sufficient signatures (a total of 986,874) to force a recall election. Governor Davis was recalled from office by a 55-to-45 percent margin. What can only be described as "recall fever" hit Wisconsin in 2011 as nine state senators (six Republicans and three Democrats) faced recall elections as a result of controversy surrounding Governor Scott Walker's efforts to eliminate most collective bargaining for public employees. Two Republican senators who had supported the governor's proposal in the legislature were recalled from office. And in 2012, as public discontent continued, recall elections were held for governor, lieutenant governor, and four Republican state senators in the Badger State. Except for one state senator, these officials survived their recall elections and continued in office.

The rationale for the recall process is straightforward: Public officials should be subject to continuous voter control. Not surprisingly, the power to recall public officials is valued by the public. But it can be a costly process, not only for the groups organizing the recall petition process and for the candidates, but for state and local governments also. Wisconsin estimated the price tag for the nine state Senate recall elections it held in 2011 at about $2.1 million, with projections for a statewide gubernatorial recall in 2012 reaching the $9 million mark.[37]

Initiatives and recalls have helped open up state and local government to the public. Yet ironically, increased citizen participation can also jam up the machinery of government, thus making its operation more cumbersome. Advocates of greater citizen activism, however, would gladly trade a little efficiency to achieve their goal.

CITIZEN ACCESS TO GOVERNMENT

As we saw in Figure 4.1, citizens have opportunities to participate in government in many nonelectoral ways. Because state and local governments have undertaken extensive measures to open themselves to public scrutiny and stimulate public input, citizen access to government has been increased. Many of these measures are directly connected with the policymaking process. At minimum, they enable government and the citizenry to exchange information, and thus they contribute to the growing capacity of state and local governments. At most, they may alter political power patterns and resource allocations.

Opening Up Government

Many of the accessibility measures adopted by state and local governments are the direct result of public demands that government be more accountable. Others have resulted from an official effort to involve the public in the ongoing work of government.

open meeting laws

Statutes that open the meetings of government bodies to the public.

Open Meeting Laws Florida's 1967 "sunshine law" is credited with sparking a surge of interest in openness in government, and today **open meeting laws** are on the books in all fifty states. These laws do just what the name implies: they open meetings of government bodies to the public, or, in Florida's parlance, they bring government "into the sunshine." Open meeting laws apply to both the state and local levels and affect the executive branch as well as the legislative branch. Basic open meeting laws have been supplemented by additional requirements in many states. Advance public notice of meetings is required in all states; most insist that minutes be kept, levy penalties against officials who violate the law, and void actions taken in meetings held contrary to sunshine provisions. New technology is playing a role; for example, many state agencies broadcast their meetings via the Internet.

Although some states might prefer to resist the sun's rays, the trend is toward more openness and transparency in government. But this is complicated by the fact that most states' sunshine laws were written for a world of paper-based records stored in metal filing cabinets. Colorado was one of the first states to make the archived email files of the state's politicians open to the public. Now forty states require that governmental e-mails be subject to their open-records laws, and twelve treat text messages the same way.[38] Table 4.3 groups states according to their transparency grades, which reflect how informative and user-friendly state government websites are. As the numeric scores show, the states earning "A's" are performing substantially better opening up government to public scrutiny than the states with "F's."

administrative procedure acts

Acts that standardize administrative agency operations as a means of safeguarding clients and the general public.

Administrative Procedure Acts After state legislation is passed or a local ordinance is adopted, an administrative agency typically is responsible for implementation. This process involves the establishment of rules and regulations and, hence, constitutes powerful responsibility. In practice, agencies often have wide latitude in translating legislative intent into action. For example, if a new state law creates annual automobile safety inspections, it is the responsibility of the state's Department of Motor Vehicles to make it work. Unless the law specifies the details, bureaucrats will determine the items to be covered in the safety inspection, the number and location of inspection stations, and the fee to be charged. These decisions are just as important as the original enactment.

To ensure public access to this critical rule-making process, states have adopted **administrative procedure acts**, which require public notice of the proposed rule and an opportunity for citizen comment. All states provide for this "notification and comment" process, as it is known. These provisions offer the public and various political actors a way to influence the content of agency

State Government Transparency Grades

TABLE 4.3

STATE	GRADE	POINT TOTAL	STATE	GRADE	POINT TOTAL
Texas	A	96	New York	C	73
Massachusetts	A	93	South Carolina	C	73
Florida	A	92	Tennessee	C	73
Illinois	A	92	Idaho	C	72
Kentucky	A	92	Louisiana	C	71
Michigan	A	91	Minnesota	C	71
Oklahoma	A	91	New Jersey	C	71
Oregon	B+	89	South Dakota	C	70
Utah	B+	88.5	Arkansas	C−	69
Nebraska	B+	88	Delaware	C−	69
Arizona	B	86	Kansas	C−	68
Iowa	B	85	Maine	C−	68
Pennsylvania	B	85	Alabama	C−	66
Washington	B−	81	Alaska	D+	64.5
New Hampshire	B−	80.5	Nevada	D+	62
Virginia	B−	80.5	Ohio	D+	61
Georgia	C+	77	Colorado	D+	60
Vermont	C+	77	North Carolina	D	58
Connecticut	C+	76	Montana	D	57
Indiana	C+	75	Rhode Island	D−	54
Missouri	C	74.5	Wyoming	F	48
West Virginia	C	74	Wisconsin	F	47
Maryland	C	73	Hawaii	F	39
Mississippi	C	73	California	F	37
New Mexico	C	73	North Dakota	F	31

SOURCE: U.S. PIRG Education Fund, "Transparency 2.0," http://pennpirgedfund.org/sites/pirg/files/reports/PA_Following_the_Money_screen_final_0.pdf (May 15, 2013).

rules.[39] In addition, some states give citizens the right to petition an administrative agency for an adjustment in the rules.

Advisory Committees Another arena for citizen participation that is popular in state and especially local governments is the **advisory committee**, in the form of citizen task forces, commissions, and panels. Regardless of name, these organizations are designed to study a problem and to offer advice, usually in the form of recommendations. People chosen to serve on an advisory committee tend to

advisory committee

An organization created by government to involve members of the public in studying and recommending solutions to public problems.

have expertise as well as interest in the issue and, in most cases, political connections. These days, the **focus group** plays a similar role by providing a small group setting for intense discussion and debate about public issues.[40]

Citizen advisory committees provide a formal structure for citizen input. If officials heed public preferences, citizen advice can become the basis for public policy. Citizen advisory organizations also provide elected officials with a "safe" course of action. In a politically explosive situation, a governor can say, "I've appointed a citizen task force to study the issue and report back to me with recommendations for action." The governor thus buys time, with the hope that the issue will gradually cool down. Another benefit of these organizations is that they ease citizen acceptance of subsequent policy decisions, since the governor can note that an action "was recommended by an impartial panel of citizens." This is not to suggest that citizen advisory committees are merely tools for manipulation by politicians, but they do have uses beyond citizen participation.

E-Government

The Internet has brought state and local government into citizens' homes in a way earlier technology could not. States and localities of all sizes have incorporated electronic communications into their daily operations. Websites abound; emails proliferate. State governments have created elaborate websites that link the user to vast databases and information resources. People can click on a city's homepage and find an array of useful information, such as the agenda for the next city council meeting, the minutes of previous council sessions, the city budget, the comprehensive plan, and the like. Some elected officials use blogs as a way to stay in touch with their constituents—and bypass conventional media. Facebook and Twitter offer more ways for politicians to connect with the public.

Now states and localities are expanding their use of the Internet and social media in dealing with the public. It started with the downloading of public reports and generic forms and has moved into more highly individualized interaction such as filing of taxes, applying for licenses and permits, and accessing personal information. Although some have touted the use of the Internet in voting, worries over security and accuracy have slowed the move to the Internet as a virtual polling place.

The Internet also offers an efficient way for government to gauge public opinion and preferences. This aspect of e-government was put to good use recently when many states were struggling to balance their budgets. Several states developed online simulations to engage the public in budget-balancing exercises. For instance, in Colorado's "backseat budgeter," players have the option to expand or shrink state programs, as well as to increase or decrease various revenue sources, all in an effort to keep the budget in balance.[41] As players quickly learn, balancing budgets is a task more easily said than done, especially because constitutional provisions limit the range of options. Still, the engaging online format acquaints the public with the budget process, and policymakers with the public's preferences.

One of the major concerns as the push toward e-government grows is that the so-called technology have-nots will be left behind. Low-income Americans lag far behind middle- and upper-income groups in their access to the Internet. This digital divide has led many communities to install personal computers in libraries, as well as in government information kiosks located in shopping malls and transit stations. Some rural areas have found it difficult to attract start-up businesses and related investment because high-speed Internet is not available. To combat this, New York created a $25 million fund to expand broadband Internet access to rural and underserved urban areas of the Empire State. Other e-government concerns involve security and privacy. Fear that hackers might break into government computers (as they did in 2012 at South Carolina's Department of Revenue) or that personal information might be misused tempers some public enthusiasm for e-government.

Volunteerism

Voluntary action is another constructive participatory activity unrelated to the ballot box. People and organizations donate their time and talents to supplement or even replace government activity. **Volunteerism** is a means of bringing fresh ideas and energy, whether physical or financial, into government while relieving some of the service burden. Washington created the first statewide volunteerism office in 1969, and within twenty years all states had volunteer programs in place.

volunteerism
A form of participation in which individuals or groups donate time or money to a public purpose.

One highly visible example of volunteerism is the "Adopt a Highway" program, which is active in forty-nine states and Puerto Rico. The program grew out of a successful antilittering effort in Texas, dubbed "Don't Mess With Texas." Over the past twenty years, the number of local businesses and civic clubs willing to pick up litter along designated stretches of state highways has skyrocketed. You have probably noticed the "Adopt a Highway" road signs with the names of volunteering groups listed underneath. The state saves money, the roadsides stay cleaner, and the volunteering groups have good feelings and free advertising to go along with their sore backs.

Successful volunteer programs such as Adopt a Highway are emblematic of the concept of **social capital**, that is, networks of reciprocal social relations among people. Stephen Knack's study showed a positive relationship between several indicators of social capital, especially the percentage of the public engaged in volunteerism, and state governmental quality.[42] States with a greater propensity toward volunteerism scored higher on several government performance measures, including financial management, capital management, and information technology.

social capital
A dense network of reciprocal social relations that promotes greater civic engagement.

Local governments use volunteers in various ways. Generally, volunteerism is most successful when citizens can develop the required job skills quickly or participate in activities they enjoy, such as library work, recreation programs, or fire protection. In addition to providing services to others, volunteers can be utilized for self-help; that is, they can engage in activities in which they are the primary beneficiaries. For example, some New York City neighborhoods take responsibility for the safety and maintenance of nearby parks. Residential crime-watch programs are another variety of self-help. In both of these instances, the volunteers and their neighborhoods benefit. Overall, studies show, volunteerism is especially successful in rural areas and small towns.[43]

Important supplements to government volunteer programs are those of the nonprofit sector. Members of local faith-based groups and civic organizations, for example, often volunteer their time in support of community improvement projects such as Habitat for Humanity, Meals on Wheels, and Sistercare. Sometimes volunteerism has a political agenda, as did the Minutemen Civil Defense Corps, a group of volunteers who in 2005 launched a border watch program that remained active until 2010. Periodically, they massed along stretches of the border with Mexico to monitor illegal entry into the United States. Their actions added fuel to the firestorm of debate over illegal immigration.

THE EFFECTS OF CITIZEN PARTICIPATION

Consider again the four quadrants of Figure 4.1. Constructive participatory behaviors, whether active or passive, invigorate government. The capacity of state and local governments depends on several factors, one of which is citizen participation. Underlying this argument is the implicit but strongly held belief shared by most observers of democracies that an accessible, responsive government is a legitimate government. Some commentators held out hope that new media technologies such as cable television and the Internet would stimulate interest in politics and move more people into the constructive quadrants. However, recent research indicates that this has not happened. Instead, politically interested individuals use these technologies to become better informed while the politically uninterested opt for entertainment programming.[44]

An active public, one that chooses the *voice* option in Figure 4.1, has the potential to generate widespread change in a community. Public policy tends to reflect the interests of active citizens. The mobilization of lower-class voters, for instance, is linked to more generous state welfare policies.[45] From the perspective of government officials and institutions, citizen participation can be a nuisance because it may disrupt established routines. The challenge is to incorporate citizen participation into ongoing operations. Some places are trying to do just that. Durham, North Carolina, has posted a clever YouTube video inviting its residents to join the city council for coffee and conversation about the city's budget priorities.[46] Citizen involvement may not always be easy or efficient, but, in a democracy, it is the ultimate test of the legitimacy of that government.

CHAPTER RECAP

- Citizen participation in the community can be active or passive, constructive or destructive. Local governments have devoted much time and energy to encouraging active, constructive participation among the citizenry.

- Voter turnout rates vary dramatically from one state to another and the reasons have to do with the political culture of the state, the competitiveness of the political parties, and the way elections are administered.

- As a result of the 2012 elections, Republicans control more governorships (29) than Democrats (20) do.

- Almost half of the states have an initiative process, and in those that do, it has become an important tool for policymaking.

- Although it is difficult to mobilize the public in support of a statewide recall of an elected official, it happened in California in 2003 when Governor Gray Davis was recalled from office.

- E-government is on the rise, with states and localities adopting more and more high-tech ways of interacting with citizens. This trend holds tremendous potential for increasing citizen participation in government.

- Volunteerism is a way of bringing fresh ideas and energy into government and helps connect citizens to their community.

- State and localities continue to encourage their citizens in meaningful participation.

Key Terms

participation *(p. 70)*
Voting Rights Act of 1965 *(p. 73)*
voting-age population *(p. 73)*
voting-eligible population *(p. 74)*
residual votes *(p. 76)*
primary system *(p. 76)*
closed primary *(p. 76)*

open primary *(p. 76)*
runoff election *(p. 78)*
instant runoff *(p. 79)*
plurality *(p. 79)*
fusion *(p. 79)*
coattail effect *(p. 80)*
nonpartisan election *(p. 81)*
slating groups *(p. 81)*
popular referendum *(p. 82)*
referendum *(p. 82)*

recall *(p. 82)*
open meeting laws *(p. 86)*
administrative procedure acts *(p. 86)*
advisory committee *(p. 87)*
focus group *(p. 88)*
volunteerism *(p. 89)*
social capital *(p. 89)*

Internet Resources

The website of the Federal Election Commission, **www.fec.gov**, contains information about U.S. elections, including laws, voter turnout, and results. To learn more about various state laws on elections, visit each state's home page or see the website of the National Association of Secretaries of State at **www.nass.org**.

The League of Women Voters, a well-respected organization that encourages informed and active participation of citizens in government, maintains a website at **www.lwv.org**.

A nonpartisan, nonadvocacy website providing up-to-the-minute news and analysis on election reform can be found at **www.electionline.org**.

MTV's Rock the Vote, an effort to boost political participation among young voters, is at **www.rockthevote.com**.

The websites **www.iandrinstitute.org** and **www.ballotpedia.org** provide a wealth of historical data and current information on ballot measures. The Ballotpedia website also includes comparative information about local government transparency.

Political Parties, Interest Groups, and Campaigns

5

FOCUS QUESTIONS

- How have political parties evolved in the face of weakened voter loyalty?
- What are some of the consequences of increased interparty competition?
- What types of interest groups are influential in state politics and what kinds of techniques do they use?
- What new methods are being employed in political campaigns and how are states dealing with campaign financing?

Dale Peterson came in third in the Republican primary election for Alabama's Agriculture Commissioner in 2010, but he became a minor celebrity in the process. The reason for his fame was a video produced by his campaign and posted on the Web. In the video, an intense, rifle-toting Peterson rides up on a horse, looks viewers squarely in the eyes, and shouts: "Listen up! Alabama Agriculture Commissioner is one of the most powerful positions in Alabama. Responsible for five billion dollars. Bet you didn't know that. You know why? Thugs and criminals." He goes on to call his opponent a "dummy," who doesn't "give a rip about Alabama." He accuses people of stealing his yard signs and claims that immigrants are being "bused in by the thousands."[1] In an era of prepackaged and predictable political advertisements, it did not take long for the Peterson video to go viral on YouTube. It just goes to show that political campaigns are not what they used to be.

POLITICAL PARTIES

political parties
Organizations that nominate candidates to compete in elections and promote policy ideas.

The two major **political parties**—the Democratic Party and the Republican Party—offer slates of candidates to lead us. Candidates campaign hard for the high-profile jobs of governor, state legislator, mayor, and various other state and local positions. In some states, even candidates for judicial positions compete in partisan races. But party involvement in our system of government does not end on Election Day—the institutions of government themselves have a partisan tone. Legislatures are organized along party lines; governors offer Republican or Democratic agendas for their states; county commissioners of different ideological stripes fight over the best way to provide services to local residents. Through the actions of their elected officials, political parties play a major role in the operation of government.

The Condition of Political Parties

The condition of contemporary American political parties has been described with words such as *decline*, *decay*, and *demise*. In some ways, the description is accurate, but in other ways, it is overstated. True, the number of people who identify themselves as members of one of the two major parties is about 55 percent of the electorate, while the number of people calling themselves independents is nearly 40 percent.[2] Furthermore, campaigns are increasingly candidate-centered rather than party-centered, and they rely on personal organizations and political consultants. But at the same time, the party organization has become more professionalized, taking on new tasks and playing new roles in politics and governance. Parties have more financial and technological resources at their disposal.[3] Thus, to some observers, political parties are enjoying a period of *revitalization* and *rejuvenation*. While the debate over the condition of political parties continues, it seems clear that they have undergone a *transformation* during the past thirty years and that they have proven to be quite adaptable.

American political parties are composed of three interacting parts: the party organization (party committees, party leaders, and activists), the party in government (candidates and officeholders), and the party in the electorate (citizens who identify with the party).[4] These parts interact to do many things, but among their central tasks are nominating and electing candidates, educating (some might say, propagandizing) citizens, and once in office, governing.

Parties in the United States function as umbrella organizations that shelter loose coalitions of relatively like-minded individuals. In terms of **ideology**, Republicans tend to be more conservative, favoring a limited role for government; Democrats tend to be more liberal, preferring a more activist government. A general image for each party is discernible: the Republicans typically have been considered the party of big business, the Democrats the party of workers. On many of the social issues of the day—gay rights, abortion, pornography, and prayer in schools—the two parties tend to take different positions. In foreign

ideology
Core beliefs about the form and role of the political system.

Party Identification in the United States, 2004–2012

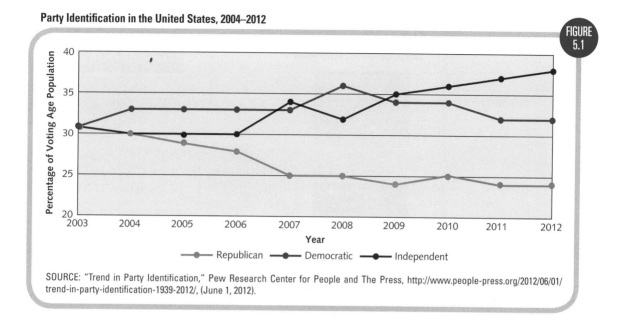

SOURCE: "Trend in Party Identification," Pew Research Center for People and The Press, http://www.people-press.org/2012/06/01/trend-in-party-identification-1939-2012/, (June 1, 2012).

FIGURE 5.1

affairs, Republicans favor a much more assertive U.S. policy than do Democrats. By 2012, approximately 32 percent of the voting-age population considered themselves Democrats, while Republican identifiers slipped to 24 percent and the Independent segment climbed to 38 percent.[5] Note, however, that typically about one-third to one-half of those who identify themselves as independents lean toward one of the two major parties. (See Figure 5.1, which tracks party identification during the recent past.)

The geographical distribution of partisan loyalties has produced some interesting patterns. The South, where conservative political attitudes predominate, is no longer the Democratic stronghold it was forty years ago. In fact, it has become a region of so-called red states, that is, states that vote Republican in presidential elections. Other red states are found in the plains region and the Rocky Mountain west. States that are more reliably Democratic in presidential elections—usually the Northeastern region, the Pacific Coast, and the upper Midwest—are designated "blue" states. (The labels "red" and "blue" refer to the color-coded maps that television broadcasters use to show election returns.) States with greater partisan diversity have been called "purple" by some pollsters. It is important not to overgeneralize from these colorful, but simple, descriptors of state-level partisanship. Within an individual state, various partisan configurations exist, as research on presidential voting at the county level has shown.[6]

Voters display a remarkable penchant for **ticket splitting**—that is, voting for a Democrat for one office and a Republican for another in the same election. Many voters are fond of saying that they "vote for the person, not the party."

ticket splitting
Voting for candidates of different political parties in a general election.

Typical State Party Organization

FIGURE 5.2

SOURCE: © Cengage Learning

Party Organization

Political parties are decentralized organizations, with fifty state Republican parties and fifty state Democratic parties. Each state also has local party organizations, most typically at the county level. Although they interact, each of these units is autonomous—a situation that promotes independence but is not so helpful to party discipline. Specialized partisan groups, including the College Democrats, the Young Republicans, Democratic Women's Clubs, Black Republican Councils, and so on, have been accorded official recognition. Party organizations are further decentralized into precinct-level clusters, which bear the ultimate responsibility for turning out the party's voters on Election Day. Figure 5.2 shows a typical state party organization.

State Parties State governments vary in how closely and vigorously they regulate political parties. In states with few laws, parties have more discretion in their organization and functions.[7] Regardless, each state party has a charter or bylaws to govern its operation. The decision-making body is the state committee, sometimes called a central committee, which is headed by a chairperson and is composed of members elected in party primaries or at state party conventions. State party organizations differ in their organizational vitality and resources. In nonelection years, the parties operate with limited staff and revenue. In election years, however, their employment and their funds increase dramatically. Republican organizations generally outstrip Democratic ones in these measures of organizational strength.

State parties, officially at least, lead their party's push to capture statewide elected offices. Although they may formulate platforms and launch party-centered fund-raising appeals, their value to candidates is in the services they provide.[8] In many states, parties host seminars for party nominees on how to campaign effectively; the parties also conduct research into the public's mood and advertise on behalf of their candidates. To a candidate, one of the most valuable services the state party can provide is access to its database of party voters.[9] Although partisan volunteers still canvass neighborhoods, knocking on doors and talking to would-be voters, these activities are increasingly supplemented by web-based and email appeals for funds and votes.

Local Parties County party organizations are composed of committee members chosen at the precinct level. Local parties are less professionally organized than state parties. Although many local organizations maintain campaign headquarters during an election period, few operate year-round offices. County chairpersons report devoting a lot of time to the party in the months before the election, but otherwise the post does not take much of their time. Most chairpersons lead organizations without any full-time staff, and vacancies in precinct offices are common.

Local party workers are volunteers whose primary reward is the satisfaction of being involved in politics. But the work is rarely glamorous. Party workers are the people who conduct voter registration drives, drop off the lawn signs for residents' front yards, and organize candidate forums. On behalf of the party's candidates, they distribute campaign literature, contribute money, make calls to voters, and run newspaper advertisements. But what impact do these activities have on the campaign? State legislative candidates report that local parties are most helpful when providing traditional grassroots services such as rounding up volunteer workers and getting voters to the polls on Election Day.[10]

Factions Political parties frequently develop *factions*—that is, identifiable subsets. These may be ideologically based, as exemplified by the struggle between moderates and liberals for control of state Democratic parties. They may be organized around particular political leaders, or they may reflect sectional divisions within a state. When factions endure, they make it difficult for a party to come together on behalf of candidates and in support of policy.[11] Persistent intraparty factions create opportunities for the opposing party.

Ohio offers a relevant example. Claiming that the leadership of the state's GOP was "out of touch with its base," conservative Christians launched the Ohio Restoration Project in 2005, an effort "to register half a million new voters, enlist activists, train candidates and endorse conservative causes."[12] The group's "patriot pastors" had plans to develop voter guides, hold rallies, set up e-prayer networks on the Internet, and raise funds to donate to selected candidates. Leaders of the Ohio Republican Party cast a wary eye on the project, contending that if the party moved too far to the right on the ideological spectrum, its electoral success could be jeopardized. Another challenge facing the GOP in many states has come from the **Tea Party**, a conservative grassroots movement that developed in 2009. Favoring budget cuts and less government, Tea Party candidates took on establishment Republican candidates in gubernatorial and legislative primaries in several states in 2010 and 2012.

Tea Party
A conservative grassroots political movement whose supporters favor smaller government.

The Two-Party System

General elections in the United States are typically contests between candidates representing the two major political parties. Such has been the case for the past century and a half. The Democratic Party has been in existence since the 1830s, when it emerged from the Jacksonian wing of the Jeffersonian Party. The Republican Party, despite its label as the "Grand Old Party," is newer; it developed out of the sectional conflict over slavery of the 1850s.

Why Just Two There are numerous reasons for the institutionalization of two-party politics. Explanations that emphasize sectional dualism, such as East versus West or North versus South, have given way to those that focus on the structure of the electoral system. Parties compete in elections in which there can be only one winner. Most legislative races, for example, take place in single-member districts in which only the candidate with the most votes wins; there is no reward for finishing second or third. Hence the development of radical or noncentrist parties is discouraged. In addition, laws regulating access to the ballot and receipt of public funds contribute to two-partyism by creating high start-up costs for third parties. Another plausible explanation has to do with tradition. Americans are accustomed to a political system composed of two parties, and that is how we understand politics.

Third Parties The assessment of former Alabama governor George Wallace that "there ain't a dime's worth of difference between Democrats and Republicans," although exaggerated, raises questions about the need for alternative parties. Third parties (also called nonmajor or minor parties) are a persistent phenomenon in U.S. politics. The Greens, Libertarians, Socialists, and the Constitution Party are some examples of third parties currently active in some states. The two major parties may not differ substantially, but for the most part their positions reflect the public mood. Third parties suffer because the two established parties have vast reserves of money and resources at their disposal; new parties can rarely amass the finances or assemble the organization necessary to make significant inroads into the system. Further, third parties typically receive scant attention from the news media, and without it, credibility wanes.

Public interest in partisan alternatives may be increasing. Two third parties that have enjoyed some success in local races in recent times are the Libertarian

Party, which seeks to reduce the government's size, and the Green Party, which grew out of the environmental movement. By 2013, Libertarians held elective office in 140 local jurisdictions in twenty-nine states, with their numbers highest in California and Pennsylvania. That same year, there were 133 Greens holding local offices in twenty-four states, including city council positions in cities such as Cleveland, Minneapolis, and Oklahoma City.[13]

Interparty Competition These days, most states exhibit meaningful two-party electoral competition. In other words, when you look at a general-election ballot, you will find both the Democrats and the Republicans offering credible candidates for state offices. The extension of interparty competition to states that lacked it in the past is a healthy development in American politics. Citizens who are dissatisfied with the performance of the party in power have another choice.

Another way of thinking about interparty competition is to examine which party controls the major policymaking institutions in the state—the governor's office and the state legislature. Generally, there is a link between the partisan composition of the electorate and partisan control of a state's institutions. For instance, in Utah in 2012, the Republican Party had a voter registration advantage over the Democratic Party of more than 2 to 1. Not surprisingly, in the Utah legislature, Republicans outnumbered Democrats by a 3-to-1 margin, and a Republican occupied the governor's office. When the governorship and both legislative chambers are controlled by the same party, the result is **unified government**. But the electorate-institution relationship is not a simple one. Sometimes control of policymaking institutions is split between the two parties and the result is called **divided government**.

In 2013, the Republican Party controlled the governor's office and both houses of the legislature in twenty-four states; the Democratic Party had institutional control of twelve states. Although these thirty-six states had unified government, in thirteen states, divided government prevailed. (Nebraska with its nonpartisan legislature is not counted in these numbers.) It is important to remember that even with unified partisan control of state institutions, the governor and the legislature may still be at odds, jockeying for political power.

Two-party competition has spread at a time when states are becoming the battleground for the resolution of difficult policy issues. Undoubtedly, as governors set their agendas and legislatures outline their preferences, cries of "partisan politics" will be heard. But in a positive sense, such cries symbolize the maturation of state institutions. Partisan politics will likely encourage a wider search for policy alternatives and result in innovative solutions.

In the view of many, two parties are better than one. Heated partisan competition turns a dull campaign into a lively contest, sparking citizen interest and increasing voter turnout. In governance, however, many believe that unified government is preferable to divided government. When competitive elections produce unified party control of government institutions, it is easier for the public to hold the party accountable for what it does—or does not do—while in office.

unified government
Both houses of the legislature and the governor's office are controlled by the same party.

divided government
A situation in which one party controls the governor's office and the other party controls the legislature.

Is the Party Over?

Have political parties, as we know them, outlived their usefulness? Will they be cast aside as new forms of political organization and communication emerge? As some have argued, a more educated populace that can readily acquire political information via the Internet is likely to be less reliant on party cues.[14] Today's generation is less loyal to political parties than its grandparents were and is not so likely to vote along party lines. The trend toward **dealignment**, or weakening of individual partisan attachments, slowed for a period but has begun to pick up again. According to one consultant, "a large group of the electorate tends to be socially tolerant and more receptive to fiscally conservative methods. They don't have a home in either party."[15] This trend is not good news for the two major parties. Neither are the conclusions of a recent study showing that in states with an initiative process, political parties find it difficult to shape public policy.[16]

> **dealignment**
> The weakening of an individual's attachment to political parties.

The two major political parties are not sitting idly by as their function in the political system is challenged. Party organizations are making their operations more professional and have more money to spend and more staff to spend it. They are actively seeking to make their organizations more meaningful to younger voters, using various new technologies to engage the millennial generation. The past several years have seen the development of party-centered advertising campaigns and a renewed commitment to get-out-the-vote drives. All in all, parties are doing their best to adapt to the changing environment.

INTEREST GROUPS

> **interest groups**
> Organizations of like-minded individuals who desire to influence government.

Interest groups have become powerful players in our democratic system. Joining a group is a way for individuals to communicate their preferences—their interests—to government. Interest groups attempt to influence governmental decisions and actions by pressuring decision-making bodies to, for example, put more guidance counselors in public schools, restrict coastal development, keep a proposed new prison out of a neighborhood, or strengthen state licensing of family therapists. Success is defined in terms of getting the group's preferences enacted—or blocking actions that are detrimental to the group's interests. In certain states, interest groups actually dominate the policymaking process.

In considering the role of groups in the political system, we must remember that people join groups for reasons other than politics. For instance, a teacher may be a member of a politically active state education association because the group offers a tangible benefit such as low-cost life insurance, but he may not be interested in or may even disagree with some of the political positions taken by the organization. In general, then, motivations for group membership are individually determined.

Types of Interest Groups

Interest groups come in all types and sizes. If you were to visit the lobby of the state capitol when the legislature was in session, you might find the director of the state school boards association conversing with the chairperson of the education committee, or the lobbyist hired by the state hotel-motel association exchanging notes with the representative of the state's restaurateurs. If a legislator were to venture into the lobby, she would probably receive at least a friendly greeting from the lobbyists and at most a serious heart-to-heart talk about the merits of a bill. You would be witnessing efforts to influence public policy. Interest groups want state government to enact policies that are in their interest or, conversely, not to enact policies at odds with their preferences.

The interests represented in the capitol lobby are as varied as the states themselves. One that is well represented and powerful is business. Whether a lobbyist represents a single large corporation or a consortium of businesses, when he talks, state legislators listen. From the perspective of business groups (and other economically oriented groups), legislative actions can cost or save their members money. Therefore, the Chamber of Commerce, industry groups, trade associations, financial institutions, and regulated utilities maintain a visible presence in the state capitol during the legislative session. It is important to remember, however, that business interests are not monolithic; occasionally they may find themselves on opposite sides of a bill.

Other interests converge on the capitol. Representatives of labor, both established AFL-CIO unions and professional associations such as the state optometrists' group or sheriffs' association, frequent the hallways and committee meeting rooms to see that the legislature makes the "right" decision on the bills before it. For example, if a legislature were considering a bill to change the licensing procedures for optometrists, you could expect to find the optometrists' interest group immersed in the debate. Another workers' group, schoolteachers, has banded together to form one of the most effective state-level groups. In fact, schoolteachers' organizations are ranked among the most influential interest groups in thirty-one states.[17]

Many other interest groups are active (but not necessarily influential) in state government, and a large number of them are ideological in nature. In other words, their political activity is oriented toward some higher good, such as clean air or fairer tax systems or consumer protection. Members of these groups do not have a direct economic or professional interest in the outcome of a legislative decision. Instead, their lobbyists argue that the public as a whole benefits from their involvement in the legislative process. Penn PIRG, for instance, describes itself as a nonprofit, nonpartisan watchdog group working on behalf of consumers, the environment, and responsive government in Pennsylvania. The group's motto, and that of other PIRGs (public interest research groups), is "Standing Up to Powerful Interests."

Local-Level Interest Groups

Interest groups also function at the local level. Because so much of local government involves the delivery of services, local interest groups devote a great deal of their attention to administrative agencies and departments. Groups are involved in local elections and in community issues, to be sure, but their major focus is on the *actions* of government: policy implementation and service delivery. According to surveys of local officials in small cities, the two functional areas in which interest groups have the greatest influence are economic development and parks and recreation.[18]

As in states, business groups are influential in local government. Business-related interests, such as the local chamber of commerce or a downtown merchants' association, and developers usually wield power in the community. An increasingly important group at the local level is the neighborhood-based organization, which in some communities rivals business interests in influence. Other groups active at the local level include faith-based organizations, public employee unions, and ethnic minority groups.[19] Thus far, however, these groups have not achieved the degree of influence accorded to business and neighborhood groups.

Neighborhood organizations deserve a closer look. Some have arisen out of issues that directly affect neighborhood residents—a local school that is scheduled to close, a wave of violent crime, a proposed freeway route that will destroy homes and businesses. Members of these groups devote much of their time to networking, to building relationships with policymakers, and to recruiting more individuals to their cause.[20] Others have been formed by government itself as a way of channeling citizen participation, such as the neighborhood councils created in Los Angeles. Neighborhood groups, as well as others lacking a bankroll but possessing enthusiasm and dedication, may resort to tactics such as **direct action**, which might involve protest marches at the county courthouse or human blockades of bulldozers clearing land for a new highway. Direct action is usually designed to attract attention to a cause; it tends to be a last resort, a tactic employed when other efforts at influencing government policy have failed. A study of citizen groups in seven large cities found that 34 percent of the groups engaged in protests or demonstrations at least occasionally.[21]

direct action

A form of participation designed to draw attention to a cause.

Techniques Used by Interest Groups

Interest groups want to have a good public image. It helps a group when its preferences can be equated with what is "good for the state" (or the community). Organizations use slogans such as "The timber industry benefits Oregon" or "Schoolteachers have the interests of New York City at heart." Some groups have taken on the label "public interest groups" to designate their main interest as that of the public at large. Groups, then, invest resources in creating a positive image.

Being successful in the state capitol or at city hall, however, involves more than a good public image. For example, interest groups have become effective at organizing networks that exert pressure on legislators. If a teacher pay-raise bill is in jeopardy in the senate, for instance, schoolteachers throughout the state may be asked by the education association to contact their senators to urge them to vote favorably on the legislation. To maximize their strength, groups with common interests often establish coalitions.

Sometimes, related groups carve out their own niches to avoid direct competition for members and support.[22] For example, gay and lesbian groups, relatively new to state politics, focus on narrow issues such as ending prohibitions against same-sex marriages rather than on broad concerns.[23] This targeting strategy allows more groups to flourish. Interest groups also hire representatives who can effectively promote their cause. To ensure that legislators will be receptive to their pressures, groups try to influence the outcome of elections by supporting candidates who reflect their interests.

Several factors affect the relative power of an interest group. Twelve characteristics are said to give some groups more political clout than others:

- the degree of necessity of group services and resources to public officials;
- whether the group's lobbying focus is primarily defensive or offensive;
- the extent and strength of group opposition;
- potential for the group to enter into coalitions;
- group financial resources;
- size and geographical distribution of group membership;
- political cohesiveness of the membership;
- political, organizational, and managerial skills of group leaders;
- timing and the political climate;
- lobbyist-policymaker relations;
- legitimacy of the group and its demands—how these are perceived by the public and public officials;
- extent of group autonomy in political strategizing.[24]

No single interest group is at the high end of all twelve of these characteristics all of the time. An indispensable group armed with ample resources, a cohesive membership, and skilled leaders, when the timing is right, can wield enormous influence in the state capitol. This is especially true when the group has taken a defensive posture—that is, when it wants to block proposed legislation. On the other hand, victory comes less easily to a group lacking these characteristics.

Lobbying **Lobbying** is the attempt to influence government decision makers. States have developed official definitions to determine who is a lobbyist and who is not. A common definition is "anyone receiving compensation to influence legislative action." A few states, such as Nevada, North Dakota, and Washington, require everyone who attempts to influence legislation to register as a lobbyist (even those who are not being paid), but most states exclude from this definition public officials, members of the media, and people who speak only before committees or boards. Because of definitional differences, comparing the number of interests represented by lobbyists across states creates the

lobbying
The process by which groups and individuals attempt to influence policymakers.

proverbial apples-and-oranges problem. But with that in mind, some cautious comparisons can be made. Table 5.1 shows the number of clients (businesses, associations, organizations) represented by lobbyists in each state in 2011, from a low of 137 in Wyoming to a high of 5,140 in Florida. In Colorado, for instance, among the 1,270 lobbyist clients are MillerCoors, the Denver Broncos Football Club, the Mobile Home Park Owners Association, the Sierra Club, and the University of Colorado System.

TABLE 5.1	Number of Clients Represented by Lobbyists, 2011		
STATE	**TOTAL LOBBYIST CLIENTS**	**STATE**	**TOTAL LOBBYIST CLIENTS**
Alabama	837	Montana	452
Alaska	361	Nebraska	621
Arizona	1,737	Nevada	1,186
Arkansas	659	New Hampshire	511
California	3,382	New Jersey	457
Colorado	1,270	New Mexico	811
Connecticut	991	New York	4,484
Delaware	507	North Carolina	990
Florida	5,140	North Dakota	432
Georgia	1,819	Ohio	1,725
Hawaii	295	Oklahoma	839
Idaho	557	Oregon	923
Illinois	1,862	Pennsylvania	2,208
Indiana	828	Rhode Island	467
Iowa	611	South Carolina	537
Kansas	754	South Dakota	549
Kentucky	650	Tennessee	746
Louisiana	1,602	Texas	3,785
Maine	398	Utah	447
Maryland	1,051	Vermont	357
Massachusetts	1,491	Virginia	850
Michigan	1,462	Washington	1,232
Minnesota	1,353	West Virginia	440
Mississippi	689	Wisconsin	708
Missouri	2,170	Wyoming	137

SOURCE: National Institute on Money in State Politics, "Total Lobbyist Clients for 2011," www. followthemoney.org/database/graphs/lobbyistlink/lobbymap.phtml?p=1&y=2011&l=0 (May 1, 2013).

As state government has expanded and taken on more functions, the number of interests represented at the statehouse has exploded. The increase in the number of lobbyists has a very simple, but important, cause: Interests that are affected by state government cannot afford to be without representation. An anecdote from Florida makes the point. A few years ago, legislators supported a new urban development program that Florida cities had lobbied for but for which they could not agree on a funding source. After much debate, they found one: a sales tax on dry cleaning. Because the dry-cleaning industry did not have a lobbyist in Tallahassee, there was no one to speak out on its behalf. Indeed, because their views were not represented in the debate over funding sources, dry cleaners were an easy target.[25] (The dry-cleaning industry learned its lesson and hired a lobbyist a few days after the tax was enacted.)

In most states, lobbyists are required to file reports indicating how and on whom they spent money. Concern that lobbyists would exert undue influence on the legislative process spurred states to beef up reporting requirements and to impose tougher penalties for their violation. Maine and New Jersey, for instance, require lobbyists to report their sources of income, total and categorized expenditures, the names of the individual officials who received their monies or gifts, and the legislation they supported or opposed.

Disclosure requirements offer one way of dealing with the problem of undue influence; another approach is to limit gifts from lobbyists to public officials. In Arizona, lobbyists may not give a public official a gift with a total value of more than ten dollars, unless the official donates the higher-value gift to charity within fifteen days. In Minnesota, a lobbyist is prohibited from giving a legislator any gift except trinkets or mementos of insignificant value.[26] There is evidence that these laws produce the desired effect. In a fifty-state study, political scientist Joshua Ozymy found that when states increase the number of formal lobbying regulations, the influence of interest groups in the legislative process declines.[27]

Lobbyists are spending money; many of them are spending a lot of money. For example, in New Jersey, lobbyist spending exceeded $73 million in 2011, an 11 percent increase over the preceding year. Table 5.2 compares lobbyist spending in Minnesota and New Jersey in 2011. In both states, business groups are at or near the top; in New Jersey, it is the state education association that far outstrips other groups' spending. It is important to remember that these spending amounts reflect more than just lobbying the legislature—they may include campaign contributions and media advertising on behalf of the group's policy preferences. Also keep in mind that many registered lobbyists spend less than $500 per year.

To win over legislators in their decision making, lobbyists need access, so they cultivate good relationships with lawmakers. In other words, they want connections; they want an "in." There are many ways of establishing connections, such as contributing to campaigns, gift giving (if allowed), and entertaining. For example, during the 2012 legislative session in Georgia, the Savannah Chamber of Commerce spent $88,000 to host a seafood festival for lawmakers.[28] The relaxed venue offered Chamber members an opportunity to

TABLE 5.2	Lobbyist Spending in Two States	
NEW JERSEY	**MINNESOTA**	
Five Highest Spending Groups	**Five Highest Spending Groups**	
New Jersey Education Association: $11.3 million	Xcel Energy: $2.4 million	
Verizon New Jersey: $1.2 million	Minnesota Chamber of Commerce: $2.1 million	
AFL-CIO: $794,000	Minnesota Business Partnership: $980,000	
Public Service Enterprise Group (public utilities): $774,000	Minneapolis Radiation Oncology Physicians: $900,000	
New Jersey Hospital Association: $771,000	Minnesota Vikings: $840,000	
Total for All Lobbyist Spending: $73 million	**Total for All Lobbyist Spending: $59 million**	

SOURCE: Matt Friedman, "N.J. Lobbyist Spending Hits New High at $73M; Teachers Union Tops List Again," NJ.Com, www.nj.com/news/index.ssf/2012/03/ (March 7, 2012); Megan Boldt, "Minnesota: Lobbyists Spend $59 Million to Influence State," TwinCities.com, www.twincities.com/news/ci_20206836/ (March 20, 2012).

build goodwill with legislators who would be taking up bills of particular interest to the Chamber and the Savannah area.

Social lobbying—wining and dining legislators—still goes on, but it is being supplemented by another technique: the provision of information. Lawmakers want to know how a proposed bill might affect the different interests throughout the state and especially in their legislative districts and what it is expected to achieve. Lobbyists are only too happy to provide that information. A new breed of lobbyists has emerged, trained as attorneys and public relations specialists, skilled in media presentation and information packaging.

An analysis of the lobbying environment in three states—Colorado, Ohio, and West Virginia—identified the kinds of techniques that lobbyists rely on. Table 5.3 lists the techniques that more than 75 percent of the 376 lobbyists surveyed said they used. Making contacts with key actors in the policymaking process—legislators, legislative and gubernatorial staff, and agency officials—are at the top of a lobbyist's "to-do" list.[29] Moreover, a substantial 92 percent of the lobbyists indicated that they helped draft legislation, which makes them key actors as well. Notice that lobbying is not confined to the legislative process. Lobbyists regularly attempt to shape the implementation of policies after they are enacted.

A not-so-new tactic that is enjoying a resurgence is **grassroots lobbying**, in which groups use their members to communicate with legislators (translation: bombard with mail, email, faxes, and telephone calls) on behalf of the group's issue. Grassroots lobbying is not just a technique for outsiders. Citizen groups, unions, religious/charitable groups, corporations, and trade

grassroots lobbying

Group mobilization of citizens to contact public officials on behalf of shared public policy views.

The Most Popular Techniques Used by Lobbyists	TABLE 5.3
1.	Meeting personally with state legislators
2.	Meeting personally with state legislative staff
3.	Entering into coalitions with other organizations
4.	Helping to draft legislation
5.	Meeting personally with executive agency personnel
6.	Testifying at legislative committee hearings
7.	Meeting personally with members of the governor's staff
8.	Talking with people from the media
9.	Inspiring letter-writing, telephone, or e-mail campaigns to state legislators
10.	Submitting written testimony to legislative committees
11.	Submitting written comments on proposed rules/regulations
12.	Helping to draft regulations, rules, or guidelines

SOURCE: Anthony J. Nownes and Krissy Walker DeAlejandro, "Lobbying in the New Millennium: Evidence of Continuity and Change in Three States," *State Politics and Policy Quarterly* 9 (Winter 2009): 429–55.

and professional associations all use grassroots techniques.[30] Are they effective? A recent study reached this unequivocal conclusion: "Grassroots lobbying by e-mail has a substantial influence on legislative voting behavior."[31]

Political Action Committees Political action committees (PACs) have become a regular feature of state politics since the 1980s. Narrowly focused subsets of interest groups, PACs are political organizations that collect funds and distribute them to candidates. PACs serve as the campaign-financing arm of corporations, labor unions, trade associations, and even political parties. They grew out of long-standing federal laws that made it illegal for corporations and labor unions to contribute directly to a candidate. Barred from direct contributions, these organizations set up "political action" subsidiaries to allow them legal entry into campaign finance.

The impact of PACs on state politics is potentially far-reaching. Some Michigan legislators, for example, consider PACs a potentially dangerous influence on state politics because their money "buys a lot of access that others can't get."[32] And access usually means influence. Analysis of tobacco-industry PACs suggests that their campaign contributions affect legislative behavior: "As legislators [in California, Colorado, Massachusetts, Pennsylvania, and Washington] received more tobacco industry campaign contributions...legislators were more likely to be pro-tobacco industry"[33] Similarly, in Florida, campaign contributions from teacher union PACs were shown to have influenced legislators' votes on a school vouchers bill.[34]

political action committee (PAC)
An organization that raises and distributes campaign funds to candidates for elective office.

States have responded to the proliferation of PACs by increasing their regulation. In New Jersey, for instance, PACs are required to register and to provide information regarding their controlling interests. One likely possibility is that an independent interstate network of groups with money to spend could emerge as a real threat to political parties as a recruiter of candidates and financier of campaigns. As a harbinger of tighter regulation of PACs, Alaska and Washington enacted a law that restricts contributions from out-of-state PACs.

Most states have acted to limit the amount of PAC contributions, although the content of the laws varies. For example, Tennessee restricts the proportion of PAC contributions to fifty percent of a candidate's total contribution amount; Colorado allows "small donor" PACs to contribute more than "regular" PACs.[35] Some states such as Nevada and New Mexico have set absolute dollar amount ceilings on PAC contributions ($5,000 per candidate per election campaign); others differentiate by office and set lower amounts for legislative races than for statewide campaigns. States with extremely low allowable contribution levels include Florida ($500 per candidate per election) and Rhode Island ($1,000 per candidate per election year). Thirteen states (Alabama, Indiana, Iowa, Mississippi, Missouri, North Dakota, Oregon, Pennsylvania, South Dakota, Texas, Utah, Virginia, and Wyoming) have taken a completely different approach and allow unlimited contributions from PACs to candidates.

POLITICAL CAMPAIGNS

Political parties and interest groups bump into each other all the time, especially in political campaigns. Like so many things these days, political campaigns aren't what they used to be. But despite changes in campaign styles and technologies, the goal remains the same: attracting enough voters to win the election. Figure 5.3 diagrams the voting configuration in a hypothetical election district. This district typically splits its vote evenly between Democrats and Republicans. Thus, in any given election, each party can count on about 25 percent of the vote (labeled the "base" in the diagram), with another 17 percent that is fairly likely to vote for the party's candidate (the "soft" partisan vote). That leaves about 16 percent of the vote up for grabs (the toss-up vote).[36] The toss-up vote and the soft partisan vote comprise what is typically referred to as the swing vote. Candidates target their energies on the swing vote, the size of which varies with the distribution of the partisan base vote. It is important to remember that most districts are not so evenly divided in their partisan loyalties.

A New Era of Campaigns

In the new era of campaigns, direct contact with potential voters still matters, of course. Candidates for state legislative seats, for example, devote time to door-to-door canvassing, telephone calls, neighborhood drop-ins, and public forums. New studies reaffirm the value of these types of contacts in mobilizing voter turnout,

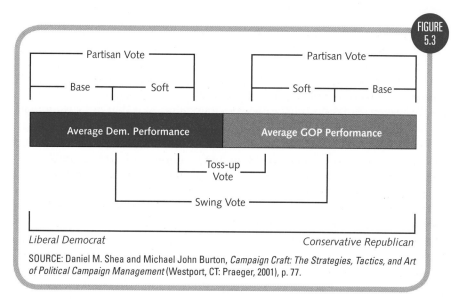

SOURCE: Daniel M. Shea and Michael John Burton, *Campaign Craft: The Strategies, Tactics, and Art of Political Campaign Management* (Westport, CT: Praeger, 2001), p. 77.

FIGURE 5.3

The Voting Configuration of a Hypothetical Election District
Candidates rely on their partisan base and compete for the swing vote.

especially among folks who are considered "occasional voters."[37] Yet more and more, campaigns rely on direct mail and electronic media to deliver their messages to voters and on political consultants to help them craft the message.

Using Old and New Media The mass media, especially television, are intrinsic aspects of modern statewide campaigns. Even candidates for legislative and local offices are increasingly using the mass media to transmit their messages. Campaigns can either buy air time and newspaper space for advertising or get it free by arranging events that reporters are likely to cover. These events range from serious (a candidate's major policy statement) to gimmicky (a candidate climbing into the ring with a professional wrestler to demonstrate his "toughness"); either way, they are cleverly planned to capture media attention. A candidate seeking free media attention needs to create visual events, be quotable, and relentlessly attack opponents or targeted problems. Televised debates offer another opportunity for free media time.

Free media time is seldom sufficient. Candidates, particularly those running for higher-level state offices and for positions in large cities, rely on paid advertisements to reach the public. Paid media advertisements these days seem to be of two distinct varieties: generic and negative. Generic advertisements include:

1. the *sainthood spot*, which glorifies the candidate and her accomplishments;
2. the *testimonial spot*, in which other people (celebrities, average citizens) attest to the candidate's abilities;
3. the *bumper-sticker policy spot*, which emphasizes the campaign's popular and noncontroversial themes (good schools, lower taxes, more jobs); and
4. the *feel-good spot*, which identifies and capitalizes on the spirit of a place and its people (for example, "Vermont's a special place" or "Nobody can do it better than Pennsylvania").[38]

Media advertising is important because it is frequently the only contact a potential voter has with a candidate. A candidate's personal characteristics and style—important considerations to an evaluating public—are easily transmitted via the airwaves. And, indeed, advances in communications technology offer new options to enterprising candidates.

The Internet has become a powerful campaign tool that can disseminate the candidate's message to far-flung audiences, mobilize potential supporters, and serve as a vehicle for attracting contributions. Nearly all major candidates for state and local offices routinely maintain campaign websites, some rudimentary, others much more elaborate. Several statewide candidates pioneered the use of campaign e-cards (the electronic equivalent of chain letters) so that supporters could contact people in their e-mail address books about the candidate. One of the keys for the future is the creation of interactive websites that engage Web surfers and keep them coming back. By 2008, the advent of YouTube provided opportunities for candidates and for their opponents as videos of campaign high points—and low moments—made their way to the website. YouTube is easy to use, cost-effective for campaigns, and increasingly popular. Social networking sites such as Facebook and Twitter hold tremendous potential for generating a fan base for candidates and for raising money. Running for mayor of Houston in 2009, Annise Parker took to the Internet to ask supporters to click the "submit" box and send her at least five dollars. Within four months, she had raised $304,000 from 1,099 online donors.[39]

Negative Campaigning Negative campaign advertising comes in three flavors: fair, false, and deceptive. A fair ad might emphasize some embarrassing aspect of an opponent's voting record or some long-forgotten indiscretion. A false ad, as the label implies, contains untrue statements. More problematic are deceptive advertisements, which distort the truth about an opponent. The task for states is to regulate negative campaign advertising without violating the free-speech guarantees of the U.S. Constitution. False advertising that is done with actual malice can be prohibited by a state, but deceptive ads, replete with accusation and innuendo, are more difficult to regulate.[40]

Most states have enacted laws prohibiting false campaign statements; candidates who use false ads against their opponents can be fined. One of the problems with these laws is that the damage is done long before the remedy can be applied. Fining a candidate after the election is akin to latching the barn door after the horse has fled. Some states, such as California and Nevada, have adopted a fair campaign practices code. These codes typically contain broad guidelines such as "do not misrepresent the facts" or "do not make appeals to prejudice based on race or sex." The limitation of the codes is that compliance is voluntary rather than mandatory.

In addition to government action, many newspapers and websites have begun to report regularly on the content, presentation, and relative accuracy of campaign advertising. "Ad watches" or "truth boxes," as they are often called, occasionally have led to the retraction or redesign of ads. Despite the efforts of government and the media, however, negative campaign advertising persists because many candidates believe that, if done cleverly, it can benefit their campaigns. Research by political scientist Ted Braden has confirmed that negative messages, accompanied by fear-evoking music and images, trigger strong reactions in viewers.[41] People may not like negative ads, but they certainly seem to remember them.

Political Consultants An occupational specialty that sprang up during the 1970s and 1980s is clearly here to stay: political consulting. Individuals with expertise in polling, direct mail, fund-raising, advertising, and campaign management put their talents to work in political campaigns. These consultants form the core of the professional campaign management team assembled by candidates for state offices. They identify and target likely voters, both those who are already in the candidate's camp but need to be reminded to vote *and* those who can be persuaded to vote for the candidate. Consultants use survey research and focus groups to find out what the public is thinking. They carefully craft messages to appeal to specific subsets of voters, such as the elderly, homeowners, and environmentalists. Advertising on cable television stations, radio, and through direct mail are popular means of getting a candidate's message to targeted segments of the voting public. In fact, recent research has found that much of the public actually prefers narrowcast messages, tailored to their interests.[42]

Any number of factors can influence the result of an election, such as the presence of an incumbent in a race and the amount of funds a challenger has accumulated, but one significant factor is the ability to frame or define the issues during the campaign. Even in a quietly contested state legislative race, district residents are likely to receive mailings that outline the candidate's issue positions, solicit funds, and perhaps comment unfavorably on the opposition. The candidate who has an effective political consultant to help set the campaign agenda and thereby put her opponent on the defensive is that much closer to victory. A study of legislative elections indicates that the use of campaign professionals is especially valuable to challengers who are hoping to unseat incumbents.[43]

Campaign Finance

To campaign for public office is to spend money—a lot of money. For instance, in Missouri, gubernatorial candidates spent a total of $28 million competing for an open seat; in Washington, the figure topped $25 million. Table 5.4 displays contributions and candidates' expenditures in the twelve states holding elections for governor in 2012. Winning an election takes money, either the candidate's or someone else's. If the latter, it may come with a string or two attached. And as noted earlier, that is the real concern: To what extent do campaign contributions buy access and influence for the contributor?

Recent research has confirmed several long-standing truths about the costs of campaigning.[44] For instance, close elections cost more than elections in which one candidate is sure to win, since uncertainty regarding the outcome

TABLE 5.4	Campaign Costs in Gubernatorial Races, 2012			
STATE	EXPENDITURE TOTAL (ALL GUBERNATORIAL CANDIDATES) ($)	CONTRIBUTIONS TO DEMOCRATS ($)	CONTRIBUTIONS TO REPUBLICANS ($)	CONTRIBUTIONS TO THIRD PARTIES/ NONPARTISAN ($)
Delaware	2,660,095	2,459,838	199,905	352
Indiana	22,268,936	6,895,581	15,292,634	80,721
Missouri	28,398,006	15,172,165	13,185,124	40,716
Montana	5,438,469	1,892,245	3,540,689	5,535
New Hampshire	4,472,517	2,264,919	2,207,598	0
North Carolina	19,841,258	5,526,334	14,168,570	146,354
North Dakota	4,251,632	651,284	3,593,179	7,169
Utah	4,243,883	364,606	3,877,233	2,044
Vermont	1,752,421	1,314,186	438,235	0
Washington	25,425,192	12,138,229	13,276,705	10,258
West Virginia	6,412,688	3,451,931	2,959,678	1,080

SOURCE: "National Overview Map," National Institute on Money in State Politics, http://followthemoney.org/database/nationalview.phtml?l=0&f=G&y=2012&abbr=0 (April 9, 2013).

is a spur to spending. A candidate quickly learns that it is easier to get money from potential contributors when the polls show that she has a chance of winning. Also, elections that produce change—that is, in which an incumbent is unseated or the out-party gains the office—typically cost more. Taking on an existing officeholder is a risky strategy that drives up election costs. An open race in which there is no incumbent represents an opportunity for the party out of office to capture the seat, thus triggering similar spending by the in-party in an effort to protect the seat. It is no wonder that campaign costs are exploding. But there may be a side benefit to more campaign spending: an increase in voter turnout. A study of state legislative elections revealed a link between expenditure levels and turnout.[45]

527 groups

Named after a section in the U.S. tax code, these groups spend money to influence the outcome of elections, but they do not contribute directly to candidates.

In addition to PACs, another type of political organization has sprung up: **527 groups**. These groups are not connected to candidates but spend money to influence the outcome of elections. For instance, in West Virginia in 2004, a 527 group called "For the Sake of the Kids" spent $3.6 million in a massive advertising campaign to defeat an incumbent state Supreme Court justice. West Virginia's limits on campaign contributions did not apply because it was a 527 group that was spending the money on an issue (ostensibly, the future for the Mountain State's children), not a candidate. That same year in Washington, a 527 group called the Voters Education Committee spent nearly $1.5 million to defeat a candidate for state attorney general. As it turned out, in both

West Virginia and Washington, the 527 groups were funded by the U.S. Chamber of Commerce, which disagreed with the candidates' positions on issues related to the regulation of business.[46] The spending of 527 groups has not diminished. In the 2012 election cycle, 527 groups spent $290 million in support of (or opposition to) state and local candidates and ballot issues.[47] Expenditures by 527 groups weaken a state's campaign finance laws. They skew spending upward, and circumvent disclosure provisions.

State Efforts at Campaign Reform Concern over escalating costs and the influence of deep-pocketed special interests in campaigns has led reform groups such as Common Cause to call for improved state laws to provide comprehensive and timely disclosure of campaign finances, impose limitations on contributions by individuals and groups, create a combined public-private financing mechanism for primaries and general elections, and establish an independent commission to enforce tough sanctions on violators of campaign finance laws.

States have performed impressively on the first of these recommendations; in fact, all states have some sort of campaign-financing reporting procedure. Most states make information on campaign contributions available online in a searchable database; many states provide similar access to campaign expenditure data. In response to the fourth recommendation, more than half of the states have established independent commissions, such as California's Fair Political Practices Commission, to oversee the conduct of campaigns, although they have found it somewhat difficult to enforce the law and punish violators. The other recommendations have proved more troublesome. States have grappled with the issue of costly campaigns but have made only modest progress in controlling costs. A 1976 decision by the U.S. Supreme Court in *Buckley* v. *Valeo* made these efforts more difficult: The Court ruled that governments cannot limit a person's right to spend money in order to spread his views on particular issues and candidates. In essence, then, a candidate has unlimited power to spend his own money on his own behalf, and other individuals may spend to their hearts' content to promote their own opinions on election-related issues. The U.S. Supreme Court extended this logic to corporations and labor unions, ruling in 2010 in *Citizens United* v. *Federal Election Commission* that these entities have a constitutional right to advertise on issues and influence elections. In 1996, in a lawsuit from Colorado, the Court decided that independent spending by political parties, so-called **soft money** could not be limited, either. What the Court let stand, however, were state limits on an individual's contributions to candidates and parties; it also ruled that if a candidate accepts public funds, he is then bound by whatever limitations the state may impose. The 2002 federal Bipartisan Campaign Reform Act aims at controlling the flow of soft money, but reports from subsequent election cycles suggest that loopholes remain.

Some states have established specific limits on the amount of money that organizations and individuals can contribute to a political race. In New York, for example, corporations are limited to a contribution maximum of $5,000 per

soft money
Unregulated funds contributed to national political parties and nonparty political groups.

calendar year, and individuals (other than official candidates) are restricted to $41,000 in a gubernatorial election, and $10,300 and $4,100 in general elections for senate and house seats, respectively. Florida's approach is straightforward: individuals (other than the candidate herself), political parties, corporations, labor unions, and PACs are allowed to contribute a maximum of $500 per candidate per election. Some states, such as Alaska, Iowa, Kentucky, Massachusetts, Minnesota, Rhode Island, South Dakota, Wisconsin, and Wyoming, have gone even further by prohibiting direct contributions from corporations and labor unions.[48] But a totally different philosophy pervades the politics of several states that continue to operate their election systems without any limitations on contributions. In Missouri, Oregon, Utah, and Virginia organizations and individuals can contribute as much as they wish.

States have also considered the other side of the campaign-financing equation: expenditures. All states require candidates and political committees to file reports documenting the expenditure of campaign funds. A few states tried to impose limits on a candidate's total expenditures, but a 2006 U.S. Supreme Court ruling that Vermont's spending limits were too low to allow candidates to compete effectively has complicated that approach. Many have followed Hawaii's lead and set voluntary spending limits. Colorado, for example, has adopted a nonbinding $2.5 million spending cap for gubernatorial candidates. Michigan takes a different approach: Candidates who accept public funds (governor and lieutenant governor) are restricted to $2 million per election, with additional spending allowable in certain circumstances. Florida has a similar system in place for candidates receiving public funds.

Public Funding as a Solution One-third of the states have adopted some sort of public funding of campaigns, although in most of these states, public financing supplements the private contributions candidates receive. As a condition of accepting public money, whether it is a matching grant (as in Florida and Hawaii) or a fixed subsidy (as in Minnesota), candidates must abide by state-imposed spending limits. In states that have adopted a fully funded "clean elections" system of campaign finance (Arizona, Connecticut, Maine, New Mexico, North Carolina, and Vermont), a candidate who wishes to participate must first demonstrate her viability by getting signatures on a petition and/or collecting a certain number of small dollar contributions. Once in the program, she may spend only public funds.[49] Not all elective offices in these states are covered by public funding, however. For instance, Arizona's and Connecticut's program covers statewide offices and the legislature, Maine's applies to the governor and the legislature, New Mexico's affects the Public Regulation Commission and statewide judicial offices, North Carolina's program covers several statewide offices and judges, while Vermont's applies to the governor and lieutenant governor. It is worth noting that in 2012, West Virginia launched a pilot program for public funding of supreme court races—the same state where expenditures by 527 groups shook up a state supreme court campaign eight years earlier.

States' public financing systems are fairly easy to administer and are relatively transparent for citizens. In most of the public funding states, citizens can use their state income tax form to earmark a portion (a dollar or two) of their tax liability for the fund. A check-off system of this sort does not directly increase taxpayers' tax burden. (Iowa, Kentucky, and Utah are among the eight states in which a taxpayer can specify that a political party be the recipient of the check-off amount.) In a few states, the public fund is amassed through a voluntary surcharge, or additional tax (usually $1 or $5). In addition to check-offs and surcharges, some of the public-funding states, including Arkansas and Virginia, offer taxpayers a tax credit (usually a percentage of the contribution, up to a specific maximum) when they contribute to political campaigns. Another option is a state tax deduction for campaign contributions, an approach used in Oklahoma. In addition to taxpayer contributions some states also allocate money from specific sources, such as Arizona's traffic and criminal fine surcharges.

Public campaign financing is supposed to rid the election process of some of its evils. Proponents argue that it will democratize the contribution process by freeing candidates from excessive reliance on special-interest money. Other possible advantages include expanding the pool of potential candidates, allowing candidates to compete on a more equal basis, and reducing the cost of campaigning. Not everyone has embraced public funding, however. Obviously, it represents a cost to taxpayers, and some contend that incumbents will benefit from limits on campaign spending and that nonserious candidates will be able to use public funds as their own personal treasury. In Arizona in 2002, Janet Napolitano became the first governor to be elected with full public financing of her campaign. In the next election cycle, 60 percent of state legislative candidates ran with public money and 93 percent of them were elected. Research on Arizona and Maine shows that clean elections programs deliver on the promise of increased competition.[50] A U.S. Supreme Court ruling in 2011, however, weakened some aspects of Arizona's law.

Although more research needs to be done, studies suggest that public financing produces at least some of the benefits its supporters claim. For instance, an analysis of gubernatorial campaigns indicated that the use of public funds by incumbents and challengers holds down overall spending. It also narrows the expenditure gap between them.[51] North Carolina recently adopted its version of clean elections, the "Voter-Owned Elections Act," amid high expectations. This following excerpt from the language of the act sets out the lofty purpose of the law:

> The purpose of this Article is to ensure the vitality and fairness of democratic elections in North Carolina to the end that any eligible citizen of this State can realistically choose to seek and run for public office. It is also the purpose of this Article to protect the constitutional rights of voters and candidates from the detrimental effects of increasingly large amounts of money being raised and spent in North Carolina to influence the outcome of elections.[52]

Public financing continues to be an important weapon in the state struggle to reform and control the influence of money in campaigns.

CHAPTER RECAP

- Even though voter loyalties have weakened, political parties have proved remarkably resilient and have taken on new roles in politics and governance.

- The Democratic Party can claim just over 32 percent of the voting-age public for itself; the Republican Party, around 24 percent. Approximately 38 percent of the electorate considers itself independents (although they might lean toward one of the major parties), with a small fraction affiliated with third parties.

- Interparty competition has increased over time. One result has been a rise in divided government.

- Interest groups exert a powerful force in state government, with business lobbyists and teachers' groups the most influential in the majority of states.

- The state interest group system is changing: A more diverse set of interests lobbies at the statehouse; meanwhile, state governments have tightened their regulation of lobbyists.

- Groups are involved in local elections and in community issues, but their major focus is on the *actions* of government: policy implementation and service delivery.

- Campaigns for state office still involve door-to-door canvassing, neighborhood drop-ins, and public forums, but they increasingly use direct mail, various electronic media, and political consultants.

- Running for public office can be an expensive proposition. To try to level the playing field and diminish the role of private money, most states limit contributions and some provide public financing.

Key Terms

political parties *(p. 94)*
ideology *(p. 94)*
ticket splitting *(p. 95)*
Tea Party *(p. 98)*
unified government *(p. 99)*

divided government *(p. 99)*
dealignment *(p. 100)*
interest groups *(p. 100)*
direct action *(p. 102)*
lobbying *(p. 103)*

grassroots lobbying *(p. 106)*
political action committee (PAC) *(p. 107)*
527 groups *(p. 112)*
soft money *(p. 113)*

Internet Resources

The major political parties have official websites: **www.democrats.org and www.gop.org.** At the state level, illustrative websites are Hawaii's at **www.hawaiidemocrats.org** and Ohio's at **www.ohiogop.org**. An interesting state-level, third-party website, **www.cagreens.org**, is the site for the Green Party of California.

The websites for the chambers of commerce for Florida and Illinois are **www.flchamber.com** and **www.ilchamber.org**, respectively. Other state chambers use similar URLs.

The Texas State Teachers' Association at **www.tsta.org** is an example of a state school-teachers' organization. A different but related perspective is provided by the Oregon Congress of Parents and Teachers Associations at **www.oregonpta.org**.

Other examples of state-level interest groups include the West Virginia Association of Realtors at **www.wvrealtors.com** and the Arizona Hospital and Healthcare Association at **www.azhha.org**.

On its website, **www.commoncause.org**, the reform group Common Cause tracks the activities of its thirty-six state offices and the progress of campaign finance reform.

Another group devoted to cleaning up elections is Public Campaign. Their website is **www.publicampaign.org**. Another group with a reform focus is the Center for Public Integrity at **www.publicintegrity.org**.

To chart campaign contributions and expenditures in the states, see the site of the National Institute on Money in State Politics at **www.followthemoney.org/index.phtml**.

6

State Legislatures

CHAPTER OUTLINE

- The Essence of Legislatures
- Legislative Dynamics
- Legislative Behavior
- How a Bill Becomes Law (or Not)
- Legislative Reform and Capacity
- Relationship with the Executive Branch
- Legislatures and Capacity

FOCUS QUESTIONS

1. What are the three principal functions of legislatures?
2. How would you characterize the lawmaking process?
3. In making policy for the state, what powers can legislatures exercise in their competition with governors?
4. The initiative process and term limits present what problems and risks for legislatures?
5. What should a new era of legislative reform entail?

The Alaska legislature took a big technological step when it developed a smart phone app in 2012. Those who download the free app can track bills, access committee material, keep up with the House and Senate calendars, and get contact information for legislators, all on an iPhone or Android device. Committee hearings are streamed so that users can watch the proceedings in real time. Legislatures in eighteen states have created websites optimized for mobile devices, but Alaska, along with the New York Senate, the North Carolina General Assembly, and a Texas Senate committee, has taken it one step further with downloadable apps.[1] This is just the latest example of using technology to make the work of the legislature more accessible to the public. These days it is not uncommon to follow various legislative entities (e.g., Michigan House Democrats, New Jersey Senate Republicans) on Facebook or Twitter; and several legislatures have created channels on YouTube, where they regularly upload videos. Finding out what is happening in the legislature no longer requires a trip to the state capitol.

THE ESSENCE OF LEGISLATURES

The New Year dawns quietly in Boise, Idaho; Jefferson City, Missouri; and Harrisburg, Pennsylvania. But it does not remain quiet for long: State legislators are ready to converge on their state capitols. Every January (or February or March in a few states; every other January in some others), state legislatures reconvene in session to do the public's business. More than 7,000 legislators hammer out solutions to intricate and often intransigent public problems. They do so in an institution that is steeped in tradition and governed by layers of formal rules and informal norms.

Legislatures engage in three principal functions: *policymaking, representation*, and *oversight*. The first, policymaking, includes enacting laws and allocating funds. The start of the second decade of the twenty-first century found legislators debating such issues as budget shortfalls, health care, higher education, and alternative energy sources. These deliberations resulted in the revision of old laws, the passage of new laws, and changes in spending, which is what policymaking is all about. Legislatures do not have sole control of the state policymaking function; governors, courts, and agencies also determine policy, through executive orders, judicial decisions, and administrative regulations, respectively. But legislatures are the dominant policymaking institutions in state government. Table 6.1 lists issues that attracted legislative attention in 2013.

In their second function, legislators are expected to represent their constituents—the people who live in their district—in two ways. At least in theory, they are expected to speak for their constituents in the legislative chamber—to do the will of the public in designing policy solutions. This is not easy. On quiet issues, a legislator seldom has much of a clue about public opinion. Moreover, on noisy issues, constituents' will is rarely unanimous. Individuals and organized groups with different perspectives may write to or visit their legislator to urge her to vote a certain way on a pending bill. In another representative function, legislators act as their constituents' facilitators in state government. For example, they may help a citizen deal with an unresponsive state agency. This kind of constituency service, or **casework**, as it is often called, may pay dividends at reelection time because voters tend to look favorably on a legislator who has helped them.[2]

casework
Legislative assistance on behalf of a constituent, usually with the bureaucracy.

The third function, oversight, is different from the policymaking and representation functions. Concerned that the laws they passed and the funds they allocated frequently did not produce the intended effect, lawmakers began to pay more attention to the performance of the state bureaucracy. Legislatures have adopted a number of methods for checking up on agency implementation and spending. Their oversight role takes legislatures into the administrative realm of

TABLE 6.1	Popular Legislative Issues in 2013	
ISSUE	**WHAT IT'S ALL ABOUT**	
Expanding Medicaid	Deciding whether to expand Medicaid; opening health insurance exchanges; developing state-run exchanges	
Revenue	Recovering from the recession and refunding key areas	
Federal Deficit	Lobbying to protect state and local budgets from the federal deficit reduction	
K-12 Education	Implementing Common Core State Standards; starting summer professional development programs	
Veterans	Reintegrating veterans into the work force and ensuring mental health for veterans	
Funding Infrastructure	Finding new ways to fund and improve infrastructure; authorizing public-private partnerships; increasing vehicle registration fees	
Legislating Marijuana	Establishing legal markets for marijuana while still keeping it a Schedule 1 controlled substance	
Pensions	Continuing to modify and reform pension programs to cut costs	
Citizens United Ruling	Creating transparency in campaign financing; advocating for a public financial system	
Section 5 of the Voting Rights Act	Ruling on whether Section 5, which requires federal approval for changes made to voting practices, is unconstitutional	

SOURCE: Dylan Scott et al., "Top 10 Legislative Issues to Watch in 2013," *Governing*, www.governing.com/topics/finance/gov-top-10-legislative-issues-2013.html (January 2013).

state government. Not surprisingly, agencies rarely welcome this role, although legislatures see it as a logical extension of their policymaking function.

LEGISLATIVE DYNAMICS

State legislative bodies are typically referred to as the legislature, but their formal titles vary. In Colorado, the General Assembly meets every year; in Massachusetts, the General Court; and in Oregon, the Legislative Assembly. The legislatures of forty-six states meet annually; in only four states (Montana, Nevada, North Dakota, and Texas) they meet every other year. (Arkansas and Oregon had been among the biennial sessions group until 2008 and 2010, respectively, when voters approved a switch to annual legislative sessions.) The length of the legislative session varies widely. For example, the Utah General Assembly convened in Salt Lake City on January 28, 2013, and adjourned on March 14, 2013, for a total of 45 calendar days in session. In contrast, in states like Massachusetts and New York legislative sessions run nearly year round.

The length of a state's legislative session can be a sensitive issue. In 1997, the Nevada legislature met for 169 days—the longest, most expensive session in its history.[3] Nevadans showed their displeasure the following year when they passed a measure limiting future legislative sessions to 120 days. Voters in the Silver State apparently believe that it should not take more than four months—every two years—to conduct their state's business.

The Senate and the House

Forty-nine state legislatures are bicameral, that is, they have two houses or chambers, similar to those of the U.S. Congress. (As noted in Chapter 3, the exception is Nebraska, which in 1934 established a nonpartisan unicameral legislature.) Bicameralism is a legacy of the postcolonial era, when an upper house represented the interests of the propertied class, and a lower house represented everyone else. Even after this distinction was eliminated, states stuck with the bicameral structure, ostensibly because of its contribution to the concept of checks and balances. It is much tougher to pass bills when they have to survive the scrutiny of two legislative houses. Having a bicameral structure, then, reinforces the status quo. Unicameralism might improve the efficiency of the legislature, but efficiency has never been a primary goal of the consensus-building deliberative process.

In the forty-nine bicameral states, the upper house is called the Senate; the lower house is usually called the House of Representatives. The average size of a state senate is 40 members; houses typically average about 100 members. As with many aspects of state legislatures, chamber size varies substantially—from the Alaska senate with 20 members to the New Hampshire house with 400 representatives. Chamber size seldom changes, but in 2003, a voter mandate forced Rhode Island to reduce the size of its 150-member legislature by one-fourth.

For senators, the term of office is usually four years; approximately one-quarter of the states use a two-year senate term. In many states, the election of senators is staggered. House members serve two-year terms, except in Alabama, Louisiana, Maryland, Mississippi, and North Dakota, where four-year terms prevail. The 2013 state legislative sessions found Republicans in control of both chambers in twenty-six states, the Democratic Party controlling both houses in nineteen states, and four states in which legislative power was split: Each party controlled one chamber, or the chamber was evenly divided between the two parties.

There are 7,382 state legislators in this country: 1,971 senators and 5,411 representatives. As of 2013, the proportion of Democrats and Republicans was 45 percent and 54 percent, respectively; men outnumbered women 76.3 to 23.7 percent. (Colorado and Vermont led in terms of the percentage of women in the legislature: 42 percent and 41 percent, respectively.) Legislatures are becoming more racially and ethnically diverse. African Americans occupy 9 percent of all legislative seats, Latinos 3 percent, Asian Americans 1 percent, and Native Americans 1 percent. Yet even these small proportions of women and racial and ethnic minorities represent a substantial increase, relative to their near absence from most legislatures before the 1970s. The average age of legislators is 56, but an occasional "Gen Y'er" can be found amid the lawmakers. In terms of occupations, full-time legislators make up the single largest category (16.4 percent), overtaking attorneys (15.2 percent), which historically had been the dominant occupation. These two groups are followed by retirees (11.7 percent), business owners (9.2 percent), and business executives/ managers (8.7 percent).[4]

Legislative Districts

Legislators are elected from geographically based districts, with each district in a state containing approximately the same number of inhabitants. Most legislative districts are single-member districts (SMDs), that is, one legislator represents the district. In Nebraska, for instance, each member of the unicameral legislature represents 37,273 people, more or less. Dividing or apportioning a state into districts is an intensely political process that affects the balance of power in a state. In the 1960s, for example, Florida's legislative districts were drawn such that the less populated panhandle area was overrepresented in the legislature at the expense of the heavily populated southern areas of the state. The balance of power lay with the northern rural regions. Therefore, despite Florida's rapid urbanization during that period, public policy continued to reflect the interests of a rurally based minority of the population.

multimember district (MMD)
A legislative district that contains more than one seat.

Eight states, including Minnesota and the Dakotas, continue to use **multimember districts (MMDs)** containing more than one lower house seat. (Usually, it is a two-member district and the number of people residing in the MMD is approximately double that of an SMD.) There are two main types of MMDs. In the first type, all candidates compete against one another and the two candidates with the most votes are elected. In the other type, candidates have to declare which of the district's two seats they are seeking. In both types, voters in the district vote in as many races as there are seats in the district. Once elected, the legislators represent the entire MMD area. Is there any difference between legislators elected in multimember districts and those in single-member districts? The answer is a cautious "yes" if research on the Arizona legislature can be extended to other states. Researchers found that lawmakers in the MMD House of Representatives tended to be more ideologically extreme than lawmakers in the SMD Senate.[5]

malapportion-ment
Skewed allocation of legislative districts that violate the "one person, one vote" ideal.

Malapportionment Unequal representation, or **malapportionment**, has characterized many legislative bodies. In the past, for example, some states allocated an equal number of senators to each county. (This system calls to mind the U.S. Senate, which has two senators per state.) Because counties vary in population size, some senators were representing ten or twenty times as many constituents as their colleagues. New Jersey offered one of the most extreme cases. In 1962, one county contained 49,000 residents and another had 924,000; yet each county was allotted one senator, and each senator had one vote in the senate. This kind of imbalance meant that a small group of people had the same institutional power as a group that was nineteen times larger. Such disproportionate power is inherently at odds with representative democracy, in which each person's vote carries the same weight.

Until the 1960s, federal courts ignored the issue of legislative malapportionment. It was not until 1962, in a Tennessee case in which the malapportionment was especially egregious (house district populations ranged from 2,340 to 42,298), that the courts stepped in. In *Baker* v. *Carr*, the U.S. Supreme Court ruled that the Fourteenth Amendment guarantee of equal protection applies to state legislative apportionment. With this decision as a wedge, the Court ruled that state legislatures should be apportioned on the basis of population. Two years later, in *Reynolds* v. *Sims* (1964), which extended the principle of equal representation to state senates, Chief Justice Earl Warren summed up the apportionment ideal by saying, "Legislators represent people, not trees or acres."[6] Accordingly, districts should reflect population equality: one person, one vote. In the aftermath of this decision, which overturned the apportionment practices of six states, a **reapportionment** fever swept the country, and district lines were redrawn in every state.

Reapportionment provided an immediate benefit to previously underrepresented urban areas, and increased urban representation led to a growing responsiveness in state legislatures to the problems and interests of cities and suburbs. Where reapportionment had a partisan effect, it generally benefited Republicans in the South and Democrats in the North. Other impacts of reapportionment have included the election of younger, better educated legislators and, especially in southern states, better representation of African Americans. All in all, reapportionment is widely credited with improving the representativeness of American state legislatures.

reapportionment
The reallocation of seats in a legislative assembly.

Redrawing District Lines State legislatures are reapportioned following the U.S. census, which is taken every ten years. Reapportionment allows population fluctuations—growth in some areas, decline in others—to be reflected in redrawn district lines. Twenty-six legislatures **redistrict** themselves; by contrast, thirteen states attempt to depoliticize the process by using impartial commissions to develop their redistricting plans.[7] In the remaining states, the redistricting task involves the legislature and either a commission or another political institution such as the governor (Maryland) or the state Supreme Court (Florida). A state's decision to use a less politicized approach such as a commission often comes about after a well-publicized redistricting controversy that creates a climate for reform of the process.[8]

redistrict
The redrawing of legislative district lines to conform to the one person, one vote ideal.

In states where the legislature redistricts itself (and the state's congressional districts), the party controlling the legislature controls the redistricting process. District lines have traditionally been redrawn to maximize the strength of the party in power. The art of drawing district lines creatively was popularized in Massachusetts in 1812, when a political cartoonist for the *Boston Gazette* dubbed one of Governor Elbridge Gerry's district creations a **gerrymander** because the district, carefully configured to reflect partisan objectives, was shaped like a

gerrymander
The process of creatively designing a legislative district to enhance the electoral fortunes of the party in power.

salamander. Two hundred years later, gerrymandering has not disappeared and neither has the partisan politics surrounding the process.

Amid the politics, redistricting has become a sophisticated operation in which statisticians and geographers use computer mapping to assist the legislature in designing an optimal districting scheme. Although "one person, one vote" is the official standard, some unofficial guidelines are also taken into consideration. Ideally, districts should be geographically compact and unbroken. Those who draw the lines pay close attention to traditional political boundaries such as counties and, as noted, to the fortunes of political parties and incumbents. As long as districts adhere fairly closely to the population equality standard (if a multimember district contains three seats, it must have three times the population of a single-member district), federal courts tolerate the achievement of unofficial objectives. But redistricting can produce some oddly shaped districts resembling lobsters, spiders, and earmuffs. Carving Montgomery County, Maryland, into eight legislative districts after the 2010 census produced the shapes displayed in Figure 6.1.

FIGURE 6.1

State Legislative Districts in Montgomery Country, Maryland

Source: Courtesy Montgomery County, Md., Planning Department.

Legislatures have to pay attention to the effects of their redistricting schemes on the voting strength of racial minorities. In fact, amendments to the Voting Rights Act and subsequent court rulings instructed affected states to create some districts in which racial minorities would have majority status. The intentional creation of majority minority districts more favorable to the election of African Americans had a partisan consequence. African Americans are more likely to be Democrats than Republicans; therefore, clustering black voters into specific districts diluted the potential Democratic vote of adjacent districts. This increased the likelihood that Republican candidates would win in those nearby districts.

The courts have not spoken with crystal clarity on the question of reapportionment. Yes, the racial composition of districts should be taken into account, but no, racial considerations should not be the sole criterion. In *Vieth* v. *Jubelirer* (2004), the U.S. Supreme Court ruled that reliance on partisan considerations remains an appropriate redistricting option. As one expert, political scientist Ronald Weber, put it, the strategy for line drawers is "to determine the best way to waste the vote of the partisans of the other party."[9] Deals are made, interests are protected, and coalitions are built, all in an effort to craft an acceptable map, one that the legislature will adopt and the courts will uphold.

Legislative Compensation

Legislative compensation has increased handsomely in the past two decades, again with some notable exceptions. Before the modernization of legislatures, salary and per diem (money for daily expenses) levels were set in the state constitution, and thus were impossible to adjust without a constitutional amendment. The lifting of these limits put legislatures, as the policymaking branch of state government, in the curious position of setting their own compensation levels. Recognizing that this power is a double-edged sword (legislators can vote themselves pay raises, while the public can turn around and vote them out of office for doing so), almost half of the states have established compensation commissions or advisory groups to make recommendations on legislative remuneration. Arizona carries it one step further by requiring that a commission-recommended pay raise for legislators be submitted to the voters for approval—or rejection.

As of 2013, annual salaries of legislators (excluding **per diem**, which is a payment to cover expenses while the legislature is in session) ranged from a low of $100 in New Hampshire to a high of $90,526 in California.[10] (California legislators had topped the $115,000 mark just a few years ago, but a state commission reduced legislative salaries by 18 percent in 2009 and another 5 percent in 2012). Other states at the top of the legislative compensation list include Pennsylvania ($82,026), New York ($79,500), Michigan ($71,650), Illinois ($67,836), Massachusetts ($61,133), and Ohio ($60,584). Eleven states pay their lawmakers between $30,000 and $50,000 annually. Compare these figures with the more modest pay levels of legislators in Georgia ($17,342), Idaho ($16,116), Nebraska ($12,000), Texas ($7,200), and South Dakota ($6,000). (These figures do not include per diem, which can increase overall compensation, depending on the state's rules for documenting expenses.)

per diem
Literally, "per day." The payment a legislator receives to cover expenses during the session.

As a general rule, states paying generous compensation typically demand more of a legislator's time than do low-paying states. And in most states, legislative leadership positions such as speaker of the house come with additional pay; in a few states, the chairs of major committees get a salary supplement. New Mexico legislators certainly cannot be accused of seeking elective office for the money. There, legislators receive no salary. What is their financial reward for legislative service? One hundred fifty-nine dollars per day for living expenses while in Santa Fe during the session, plus a travel allowance.

Legislative pay is but a small fraction of the cost of operating a legislature. Legislative staff salaries consume a large chunk of the expenditures, as do building maintenance and technological improvements.

Legislative Leadership

Legislatures need leaders, both formal and informal. Each chamber usually has four formal leadership positions. In the senate, a president and a president pro tempore (who presides in the absence of the president) are in charge of the chamber; in the house, the comparable leaders are the speaker and the speaker pro tempore. These legislative officials are chosen by the members, with voting following party lines. (In twenty-six states, the post of senate president is occupied by the lieutenant governor, but the role is ceremonial in most of these states.[11]) Both houses have two political party leadership positions: a majority leader and a minority leader.

The leaders are responsible for making the legislature, which is a relatively decentralized system, run smoothly and for seeing that it accomplishes its tasks. In a typical chamber, the presiding officer appoints committee members, names committee chairs, controls the activity on the floor, allocates office space and committee budgets, and, in some states, selects the majority leader and the holders of other majority party posts.[12] The actual influence of the leadership varies from one chamber to another. One factor that affects leaders' power is whether the positions are rotated or retained. Leaders who have the option of retaining their position can build power bases. In the case of rotation, however, one set of leaders is replaced with another on a regular basis, so the leaders are **lame ducks** when they assume the posts.

lame duck
An elected official who cannot serve beyond the current term of office.

On average, today's leaders are different from the caricatured wheeler-dealers of the past. For one thing, in 2011, three women were senate presidents; three women served as speakers of the house.[13] New Hampshire scored two historic firsts in 2009: the first state with a female majority in a legislative chamber (the Senate: 54 percent women) and the first state to have women occupy both the house speakership and the senate presidency. More evidence that legislative leadership has changed comes from Colorado, where, in 2009, it became the first state in which African Americans led both chambers of the legislature at the same time. Another indicator of change has less to do with diversity and more to do with process: rank-and-file members of the legislature are not as reluctant as they used to be to challenge their leaders on both procedural and policy matters.

As political parties become more competitive in the states, legislative behavior and decisions take on a more partisan cast, that is, the legislature becomes more "procedurally partisan."[14] As noted, voting to fill leadership posts follows party lines. There are Democratic and Republican sides of the chamber, and Democratic and Republican positions on bills. Each party meets in a caucus to design its legislative strategy and generate camaraderie. In states where one political party continues to dominate, partisanship is less important; however, in these one-party settings, the dominant party typically develops splits or factions at the expense of party unity. But when the vastly outnumbered minority party begins to gain strength, the majority party usually becomes more cohesive.

In many states, legislative leaders have embraced a new function: fundraising. Leaders tap interest groups and lobbyists for money and divide it among their party's candidates for legislative seats. California has led the way with multimillion dollar **war chests**. The amount of money raised is not as great in other states, of course, but it has become a significant source of campaign funding. Lobbyists find it difficult to say "no" to a request for funds from the leadership. The leaders then allocate the funds to the neediest candidates—those in close races. If these candidates are victorious, their loyalty to party leaders pays legislative dividends.

war chest
A stash of funds accumulated in advance of a campaign.

The Committee System

The workhorse of the legislature is the committee. Under normal circumstances, a committee's primary function is to consider bills—that is, to hear testimony, perhaps amend the bills, and ultimately approve or reject them. Committee action on a bill precedes debate in the house or senate. Along with the leadership, committees provide a structure for organizing the process of making laws.

All legislative chambers are divided into committees, and most committees have created subcommittees. Committees can be of several types. A *standing committee* regularly considers legislation during the session. A *joint committee* is made up of members of both houses. Some joint committees are standing; others are temporary (sometimes called ad hoc or select committees) and are convened for a specific purpose, such as investigating a troubled agency or solving a particularly vexing public policy problem. A *conference committee* is a special type of joint committee that is assembled to iron out differences between house- and senate-passed versions of a bill. To get a head start on an upcoming session, most states use *interim committees* during the period when the legislature is not in session. The number of committees varies, but most senates and houses have standing committees on the issues listed in Table 6.2. Most of these committees, in turn, have professional staffs assigned to them.

A substantive standing committee tends to be made up of legislators who have expertise and interest in that committee's subject matter.[15] Thus, farmers would be assigned to the agriculture committee, teachers to the education committee, small business owners to the commerce committee, lawyers to the judiciary committee, and so on. These legislators bring knowledge and commitment to their committees; they also bring a certain bias because they tend to function as advocates for their career interests. Note, too, that every chamber

TABLE 6.2	**Standing Committees of the Legislature**

BOTH HOUSES OF STATE LEGISLATURES TYPICALLY HAVE STANDING COMMITTEES DEALING WITH THESE SUBSTANTIVE ISSUES:

Agriculture	Government operations
Banking/financial institutions	Health
Business and commerce	Insurance
Communications	Judiciary and criminal justice
Education	Local affairs
Elections	Public employees
Energy	Rules
Environment and natural resources	Social/human services
Ethics	Transportation

IN ADDITION, BOTH HOUSES HAVE STANDING COMMITTEES THAT ADDRESS THE RAISING AND ALLOCATING OF STATE FUNDS. THESE COMMITTEES MAY HAVE DIFFERENT NAMES IN DIFFERENT CHAMBERS:

Appropriations
Finance and Taxation
Ways and Means

SOURCE: © Cengage Learning

has at least one undesirable committee (usually defined as one whose substance is boring) to which few legislators want to be assigned.[16]

The central concern of a standing committee is its floor success—getting the full chamber to accede to its recommendations on a bill. Several plausible explanations exist for a committee's floor success.[17] A committee whose ideological composition is similar to that of the whole chamber is likely to be more successful than one whose members are at odds with the chamber. The leadership takes this situation into account when it makes committee assignments; thus, very few committees are ideological outliers.[18] Also, committees full of legislatively experienced members generally have more floor success than committees composed of legislative novices. And committees that have a reputation for being tough have more floor success with their bills than committees that pass everything that comes before them.

LEGISLATIVE BEHAVIOR

Legislatures have their own dynamics, their own way of doing things. Senate and house rule books spell out what can and cannot be done, in the same way that an organization's bylaws do. Legislatures are self-regulating institutions, for the most part; it is especially important, therefore, that participants know what is expected of them. To make certain that the chamber's rules are understood, most legislatures conduct orientation sessions for new members.

Norms of the Institution

An understanding of the legislature involves not only knowledge of formal structures and written rules but also awareness of informal norms and unwritten policies. For example, nowhere in a state's legislative rules does it say that a freshman legislator is prohibited from playing a leadership role, but the unwritten rules of most legislatures place a premium on seniority. A primary rule of legislative bodies is that "you gotta go along to get along," a phrase that emphasizes teamwork and paying your dues. Legislators who are on opposite sides of a bill to regulate horse racing might find themselves on the same side of a bill to lower the cost of prescription drugs. Yesterday's opponent is today's partner. For this reason, no one can afford to make bitter enemies in the legislature and expect to flourish.

Those who aspire to rise from rank-and-file legislator to committee chairperson and perhaps to party leader or presiding officer find consensus-building skills quite useful. These skills come in handy because many norms are intended to reduce the potential for conflict in what is inherently a setting full of conflict. For instance, a freshman legislator is expected to defer to a senior colleague. Although an energetic new legislator might chafe under such a restriction, one day he will have gained seniority and will take comfort in the rule. Moreover, legislators are expected to honor commitments made to each other, thus encouraging reciprocity: "If you support me on my favorite bill, I will be with you on yours." A legislator cannot be too unyielding. Compromises, which are sometimes principled but more often political, are the backbone of the legislative process. Few bills are passed by both houses and sent to the governor in exactly the same form as when they were introduced.

Informal rules are designed to make the legislative process flow more smoothly. Legislators who cannot abide by the rules, those who refuse to go along, find it difficult to get along. They are subjected to not-so-subtle efforts at behavior modification, such as powerful social sanctions (ostracism and ridicule) and legislative punishment (the bottling up of their bill in committee or their assignment to an unpopular committee), that promote adherence to norms.

Legislative Cue Taking and Decision Making

Much has been written about how legislators make public policy decisions, and a number of explanations are plausible. Legislators may adopt the policy positions espoused by their political party. They may follow the dictates of their conscience—that is, do what they think is right. They may yield to the pressures of organized interest groups. They may be persuaded by the arguments of other legislators, such as a committee chairperson who is knowledgeable about the policy area, or a trusted colleague who is considered to be savvy; or they may succumb to the entreaties of the governor, who has made a particular piece of legislation the focus of her administration. Of course, legislators may also attempt to respond to the wishes of their constituents. On a significant issue—one that has received substantial media attention—they are likely to be subjected to tremendous cross pressures.

Assuming that legislators are concerned about how a vote will be received back home, it seems logical that they would be particularly solicitous of public opinion. In actuality, state legislators frequently hold opinions at odds with those of their constituents. They occasionally misperceive what the public is thinking; at such times it is difficult for them to act as mere **delegates** and simply fulfill the public's will. To improve the communications link, some lawmakers use questionnaires to poll constituents about their views; others hold town meetings at various places in the district to assess the public's mood.

It is quite probable that first-term legislators feel more vulnerable to the whims of the public than legislative veterans do. Hence the new legislator devotes more time to determining what the people want, whereas the experienced legislator "knows" what they want (or perhaps knows what they need) and thus functions as a **trustee**—someone who follows his or her own best judgment. Because the vast majority of legislators are returned to office election after election, it appears that there is some validity to this argument. In fact, a study of lawmakers in eight states found that the members' personal opinions were consistently important in their decision choices.[19]

In the final analysis, the determining factor in how legislators make decisions depends on the issue itself. On the one hand, "when legislators are deeply involved with an issue, they appear to be more concerned with policy consequences" than with constituency preferences.[20] In this situation, the legislators are focused on a goal other than reelection. On the other hand, if lawmakers are not particularly engaged in an issue and it is important to their constituents, they will follow their constituents' preference. In that sense, they act as **politicos**, adjusting as the issues and cues change.

delegate
A legislator who functions as a conduit for constituency opinion.

trustee
A legislator who votes according to his or her conscience and best judgment.

politico
A legislator who functions as either a delegate or a trustee, depending on the circumstances.

HOW A BILL BECOMES LAW (OR NOT)

A legislative bill starts as an idea and travels a long, complex path before it emerges as law. It is no wonder that of the 4,282 bills introduced in the Tennessee legislature in 2011, only 542 had become law by the end of the regular session.[21] A legislative session has a rhythm to it. Minor bills and symbolic issues tend to be resolved early, whereas major, potentially divisive issues take a much longer time to wend their way through the legislative labyrinth. The budget or appropriations bill typically generates several rounds of contentious debate among legislators. And if legislatures cannot get their work completed, they may end up back in the state capitol at a later date in a special session. In 2011, for example, twenty-two states convened special legislative sessions; some held more than one. Lawmakers in Arizona returned to Phoenix for four special sessions that year; West Virginia legislators revisited the capitol in Charleston four times.[22]

The lawmaking process has been described in many ways: a zoo, a circus, a marketplace. Perhaps the most apt description is "casino," because there are winners and losers, the outcome is never final, and there is always a new game ahead.[23] Lawmaking is a dynamic and exciting process; it can be an arduous process as well. Ideas for bills are everywhere: with constituents, interest groups, and state agencies. Legislators may turn to their staffs for ideas or to other states. **Policy entrepreneurs**, people who are knowledgeable about certain issues and are willing to promote them, abound. Introducing a bill—"putting it in the hopper," in legislative parlance—is just the beginning. A bill can get sidetracked at many points, and even derailed altogether. Subcommittee and committee hearings may pose a challenge, and even if the committee does approve the bill, getting it scheduled for floor debate can be another hurdle. Assuming successful passage in the first chamber, a bill goes through the same steps in the second chamber. Even if it is successful there, a conference committee may be needed to resolve any differences between the two passed versions. And the clock is ticking—most legislatures impose deadlines for the completion of the various steps.

Clearly, a bill does not make it through the legislative process without a lot of effort and even a little luck. A bill's chances of passage rise as more legislators sign on as cosponsors, and if the cosponsors are legislative leaders, even better. Assignment of the bill to a favorable committee improves the likelihood that the bill will be scheduled for a hearing in a timely manner. (Many bills get bottled up in committee and never receive a hearing.) Strong support from key interest groups is a powerful advantage, as is the emergence of only weak opposition to the bill. Sometimes, bill passage is a matter of fortuitous timing. For example, a spectacular prison break from an overcrowded state penitentiary might garner support for passage of a prison construction bill.

Controversial issues such as abortion raise the stakes. The former speaker of the Wisconsin Assembly, Tom Loftus, described abortion politics in his state as trench warfare in which compromise was virtually impossible. Leadership on the issue came from legislators who felt strongly about the matter and who held safe seats. (In this instance, "safe" meant that taking a position was not likely to cost them too many votes or generate too many serious challengers when they ran for reelection.) As antiabortion bills were introduced, battle lines were drawn. According to the speaker:

> The pro choice side, which included the Democratic leadership, tried to keep the bill bottled up in committee, and the pro life side, through political pressure on the Republicans and conservative Democrats, tried to pull it out so the whole Assembly could vote on it on the floor of the chamber. If the pro life people could get the bill to the floor for a vote, they would win. To accomplish this end, they needed to gain supporters from the pivotal middle group of legislators, usually moderates of both parties from marginal districts.[24]

policy entrepreneur
A person who brings new ideas to a policymaking body.

The powerful antiabortion group Wisconsin Citizens Concerned for Life pressured vulnerable legislators. These legislators were in a tough position because they knew that "regardless of how you voted, you were going to make a slew of single issue voters mad."[25] Their strategy became one of parliamentary maneuvering and delay.

Even if a bill is successful in one chamber, potential hurdles await in the other chamber. Representatives and senators may see the same issue in very different terms. In Ohio a few years back, everyone agreed that the state's system for funding public education needed reform. (The Ohio Supreme Court had found the state's school funding system unconstitutional and had given the legislature one year to devise a new system.) But initial efforts derailed when the House and Senate could not agree on a plan. The Senate approved a funding package that would have increased the sales tax, provided debt financing, and allowed local school boards to propose property tax increases.[26] The House, dominated by Republicans who had signed an anti-tax pledge the preceding year, approved a bill that did not include tax hikes. Each chamber rejected the other's plan. Hammering out a compromise agreeable to both chambers took a long time, even with the court's order as a spur to action.

Once conference or concurrence committees resolve differences and agreement is secured in both chambers, then the bill is enrolled (certified and signed) and sent to the governor. The governor may do one of three things: (1) sign the act (once passed, a bill is called an act) into law, (2) veto it (in which case the legislature has a chance to have the last word by overriding the veto), or (3) take no action. If the governor does not take action and the session has ended, then in most states the act will become law without the governor's signature. Why not simply sign it if it is going to become law anyway? Sometimes it is a matter of political symbolism for the governor. In approximately one-third of the states, if the governor does not sign or veto the act and the legislature has adjourned, the act dies (an outcome known as a pocket veto).

During its 2011 regular session, the Tennessee legislature passed only 13 percent of the bills that were introduced. Is this a sign of success or failure? Tennessee's figures are lower than those of most states—20 to 25 percent is a common passage rate—but not necessarily a cause for alarm. Not all bills are good ones, and the inability to generate sufficient consensus among legislators may reflect that condition.

LEGISLATIVE REFORM AND CAPACITY

During the 1970s, fundamental reforms occurred throughout the country as legislatures sought to increase their capacity and to become more professional. And even though these reforms have had a substantial impact, the institutional modernization process never really ends.

The Ideal Legislature

In the late 1960s, the Citizens' Conference on State Legislatures (CCSL) studied legislative performance and identified five characteristics critical to legislative improvement.[27] Ideally, a legislature should be functional, accountable, informed, independent, and representative; the acronym is FAIIR.

The *functional* legislature has almost unrestricted time to conduct its business. It is assisted by adequate staff and facilities, and has effective rules and procedures that facilitate the flow of legislation. The *accountable* legislature's operations are open and comprehensible to the public. The *informed* legislature manages its workload through an effective committee structure, legislative activities between sessions, and a professional staff; it also conducts regular budgetary review of executive branch activities. The *independent* legislature runs its own affairs independently of the executive branch. It exercises oversight of agencies, regulates lobbyists, manages conflicts of interest, and provides adequate compensation for its members. Finally, the *representative* legislature has a diverse membership that effectively represents the social, economic, ethnic, and other characteristics of the constituencies.

The fifty state legislatures were evaluated and scored by CCSL according to the FAIIR criteria. For the first time ever, the rankings offered a relatively scientific means of comparing one state legislature with another. Overall, the "best" state legislatures were found in California, New York, Illinois, Florida, and Wisconsin. The "worst," in the assessment of CCSL, were those in Alabama, Wyoming, Delaware, North Carolina, and Arkansas.

The CCSL report triggered extensive self-evaluation by legislatures around the country. Most states launched ambitious efforts to reform their legislatures. The results are readily apparent. In terms of the CCSL criteria, states have made tremendous strides in legislative institution building. The evidence of increased professionalism includes more staff support, higher legislative compensation, longer sessions, and better facilities. Many legislatures revamped their committee systems, altered their rules and procedures, and tightened their ethics regulations. The consequences of these actions are state legislatures that are far more FAIIR now than they were found to be in the late 1960s. Analysts at the National Conference of State Legislatures sum it up this way: "Legislatures became more muscular, agile, intelligent and independent than at any other time in American history."[28]

The Effects of Reform

Today's legislative institutions are different, but are they better? Although many observers would answer in the affirmative, the legislative reform picture is not unequivocally rosy. Political scientist Alan Rosenthal, who has closely observed legislative reform, warns that "the legislature's recent success in enhancing its capacity and improving its performance may place it in greater jeopardy than before."[29] Rosenthal's argument is that a constellation of demands pulls legislators away from the legislative core. That is, the new breed of legislator gets caught up in the demands of reelection, constituent service, interest groups, and political careerism, and thus neglects institutional matters such as structure, procedure, staff, image, and community. The legislature as an institution suffers because it is not receiving the necessary care and attention from its members. For example, California's highly reformed legislature performed poorly in the early 2000s, mired in a period of bitter partisanship and gridlock. Some observers blame reform for some of the Golden State's legislative troubles.

Consider the idea of a citizen-legislator, someone for whom service in the legislature is a part-time endeavor. Since the onset of reform, the proportion of legislators who are lawyers, business owners, or insurance or real estate executives has dropped, and the number of full-time legislators has risen. In states such as California and Pennsylvania, roughly three-quarters of the lawmakers identify themselves as legislators with no other occupation. The critical issue is whether the decline of the citizen-legislator is a desirable aspect of modernization. Should a state legislature represent a broad spectrum of vocations, or should it be composed of career politicians? One perspective is this: "If I'm sick, I want professional help. I feel the same way about public affairs. I want legislators who are knowledgeable and professional."[30] Another view is represented by a Michigan legislator who believes that his careerist colleagues have lost touch with their constituents: "When you spend all your time in Lansing, you're more influenced by the lobbyists than by your constituents."[31]

In effect, state legislatures are becoming more like the U.S. Congress. In many states, legislators are staying in the legislature in record numbers. Modernization has made the institution more attractive to its members, so turnover rates are declining. But do we really want fifty mini-Congresses scattered across the land? Today's legislatures are more FAIIR than in the past, but reform has also brought greater professionalization of the legislative career, increased polarization of the legislative process, and more fragmentation of the legislative institution.[32] Figure 6.2 shows the pattern of citizen (17 states), professional (10 states), and "hybrid" (23 states) state legislatures. The categories are derived from an index developed by the National Conference of State Legislatures that reflects legislator salary and benefits, the time demands of legislative service, and the staff resources available to the legislature.[33] Lawmakers in the most professionalized legislatures are paid more, devote more time to the job, and have far greater staff resources at their disposal than their counterparts in citizen legislatures. States categorized as hybrids fall between professional and citizen on these characteristics.

To some analysts, the reforms of the past decades have produced a legislative monster. Richard Nathan, a veteran observer of the states, argues that the key to increased government productivity is the empowerment of the governor.[34] Nathan advocates term limits, unicameral legislative bodies, rotation of committee memberships, and reduction of legislative staff and sessions as a means of reining in the legislature vis-à-vis the governor. If adopted, Nathan's recommendations would undo thirty-five years of legislative reform. And the governor's political power would be significantly strengthened. This helps explain why, in 2007, Pennsylvania's governor Ed Rendell proposed a far-reaching plan

Legislative Professionalization

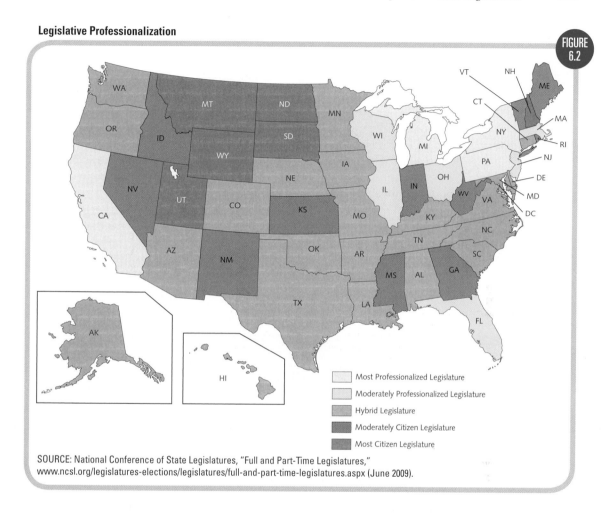

SOURCE: National Conference of State Legislatures, "Full and Part-Time Legislatures," www.ncsl.org/legislatures-elections/legislatures/full-and-part-time-legislatures.aspx (June 2009).

to trim the size of the Keystone State's General Assembly, limit legislative terms, and change the redistricting process.[35] As you might imagine, Governor Rendell's plan fell on deaf ears in the legislative branch. The legislative-gubernatorial nexus receives further analysis in a later section of this chapter.

Term Limits

In September 1990, Oklahoma voters sent state legislatures reeling. Oklahomans overwhelmingly approved a ballot measure limiting the tenure of state legislators and statewide officers. As it turned out, limiting terms was not just a Sooner thing. Within two months, voters in California and Colorado had followed suit. With a close defeat in Washington slowing it only slightly, the term-limits movement swept the country. In Oregon, a group called LIMITS (Let Incumbents Mosey Into the Sunset) grew out of a tax-limitation organization. In Wisconsin, a coalition known as "Badgers Back in Charge" took up the cause of term limitation. And political activists of many stripes—populists, conservatives, and libertarians—found a home in the term-limitation movements in Florida, Michigan, and Texas.[36] In time, twenty-one states slapped limits on legislative terms, although in six of these states, term limits were repealed by state courts or the legislature itself. All told, approximately one-fourth of state legislative seats are subject to term limits. The term-limits laws eventually bore the intended fruit: By 2010, more than 2,200 state legislators had been barred from seeking reelection.[37] Table 6.3 compares the term-limits provisions of the fifteen states where legislative term limits remain in force. Note that Nebraska voters had approved term limits three times prior to the 2000 initiative, but the courts had invalidated the measures.

In most states, the measure limits service in each chamber separately. In Maine, for example, a legislator is limited to eight years in the house and eight years in the senate. It is quite possible, then, that an individual could serve a total of sixteen years in the legislature under this plan. In a few states, the restriction is on total legislative service. In Oklahoma, for instance, the limitation is twelve years, whether in the house, in the senate, or in a combination of

TABLE 6.3   Term Limits in the States

STATE	YEAR ADOPTED	SENATE	HOUSE	YEAR LAW TOOK EFFECT	REFERENDUM VOTE	BALLOT STATUS
Arizona	1992	8	8	2000	74 to 26	Initiative
Arkansas	1992	8	6	2000/1998	60 to 40	Initiative
California	1990	8	6	1998/1996	52 to 48	Initiative
Colorado	1990	8	8	1998	71 to 29	Initiative
Florida	1992	8	8	2000	77 to 23	Initiative
Louisiana	1995	12	12	2007	76 to 24	Referendum
Maine	1993	8	8	1996	67 to 33	Indirect Initiative
Michigan	1992	8	6	2002/1998	59 to 41	Initiative
Missouri	1992	8	8	2002	74 to 26	Initiative
Montana	1992	8	8	2000	67 to 33	Initiative
Nebraska	2000	8	—	2006	56 to 44	Initiative
Nevada	1994	12	12	2006	70 to 30	Initiative
Ohio	1992	8	8	2000	66 to 34	Initiative
Oklahoma	1990	12	12	2002	67 to 33	Initiative
South Dakota	1992	8	8	2000	63 to 37	Initiative

SOURCE: National Conference of State Legislatures, "The Term Limited States," www.ncsl.org/Default.aspx?TabId=14844 (June 2009); updated by the authors.

the two. Some term limits are for a lifetime (as in Arkansas and Nevada); others simply limit the number of consecutive terms (as in Ohio and South Dakota).

Limiting legislative terms captured the fancy of a public angry with entrenched politicians. The measure offers voters a chance to strike back at an institution perceived as self-serving and out of touch. But not everyone favors limiting legislative terms. Opponents offer several arguments against them. On a theoretical level, they argue that term limits rob voters of their fundamental right to choose their representatives. In a related vein, they contend that these measures unfairly disqualify a subset of the population—legislators—from seeking office. And, finally, they claim that term limits are unnecessary, that sufficient legislative turnover occurs without them. Term limits were expected to produce several consequences:

- Ending the domination of a chamber by powerful, entrenched veteran legislators;
- Increasing the proportion of first-term legislators in any given session;
- Increasing representation by groups underrepresented in the legislature, especially women and minorities, because of the guarantee of open seats;[38]
- Shifting power from the legislature to the governor and to lobbyists.

Three of the four expected consequences have indeed come to pass. The exodus of veteran legislators and the influx of inexperienced members have some observers shaking their heads in dismay. For instance, twenty-nine of Michigan's thirty-eight senators (76 percent) could not seek reelection in 2010 due to term limits.[39] Not surprisingly, data from term-limit states reflect procedural difficulties, a slower-working institution, less deliberation in committees, and less complex legislation.[40] As for shifting power to other actors, consensus seems to exist among researchers that governors, agency heads, legislative staff, and interest groups have benefited at the expense of the term-limited legislature.[41]

The expectation that terms limits would produce greater representation of underrepresented groups has not been borne out—at least not yet. The number of women in term-limited legislatures has actually decreased slightly, and the increase in racial and ethnic minorities may be due more to their increased voting strength rather than to term limits.[42] Term limit devotees who wanted to strike back at an out-of-touch institution would be surprised to learn that term-limited legislators actually become less beholden to their constituents.[43] Moreover, a recent study found that term-limited legislatures appear to be less able to develop effective fiscal policy for their states.[44] In sum, limiting the terms of legislators has consequences beyond simply forcing incumbents out of office.

Regardless of the effects, term limits remain popular with the public.[45] In 2008, South Dakota legislators asked voters if they wanted to repeal legislative term limits; the answer was a resounding "no"—76 to 22 percent. But the term-limit movement is losing steam. Citizen initiatives are the primary vehicle through which the term-limits question has been placed before the voters. And the issue has just about run the gamut of states that allow initiatives. (The Utah legislature imposed term limits on itself in 1994, but it had a change of heart and repealed the law in 2003.) Court challenges have undone legislative term limits in Massachusetts, Oregon, Washington, and Wyoming. And in a surprising move, the Idaho legislature, bowing to an array of political pressures, repealed the term-limits law that was adopted via the initiative process in 1994.[46] Angry Idahoans gathered a sufficient number of signatures to place a question on the 2002 ballot asking whether the legislature's action should be upheld. After a heated campaign, the Repeal the Repeal question was defeated, thus ending term limits in Idaho before they took effect.

RELATIONSHIP WITH THE EXECUTIVE BRANCH

In Chapter 7, you will read about strong governors boldly leading American states in the twenty-first century. In this chapter, you have read about strong legislatures charting a course for that same century. Do these institutions ever collide in their policymaking? You bet they do. Conflict between the legislature and the governor is inevitable, but it is not necessarily destructive. It is inevitable because both governors and legislators think that they know what is best for the state. It is not necessarily destructive because, during the posturing, bargaining, and negotiating that produces consensus, governors and legislators may actually arrive at an optimal solution.

Dealing with the Governor

The increased institutional strength of the legislature and its accompanying assertiveness have made for strained relations with a governor accustomed to being the political star. Institutional conflict is exacerbated under conditions of divided government, that is, when a legislature is controlled by one party and the governor is of the other party. The result of divided government is often gridlock, accompanied by finger pointing and blame-gaming. As the Republican governor of Mississippi, Haley Barbour, said to the Democratic-controlled legislature in his first State of the State address, "As Governor of Mississippi you have two choices...you can work with the Legislature, or you can fail. Well, I'm not into failure, so I look forward to working with each of you to make sure we all succeed."[47] As Governor Barbour quickly learned, that is much easier said than done.

A governor and a legislature controlled by the same party do not necessarily make for easy interbranch relations either. Especially in states where the two parties are competitive, legislators are expected to support the policy initiatives of their party's governor. Yet the governor's proposals may not mesh with individual legislators' attitudes, ambitions, or agendas. South Carolina offers an illustration. In 2012, the Republican governor and the overwhelmingly Republican legislature battled long and hard over issues as diverse as comprehensive tax reform and dredging at a state port. Despite their partisan affinity, they saw these and many other issues very differently.

Governors have a media advantage over deliberative bodies such as a legislature. The governor is the visible symbol of state government and, as a single individual, fits into a media world of thirty-second sound bites. By contrast, media images of the legislature often portray deal making, pork barrel politics, and general silliness. To be sure, those images can be quite accurate at times. "Gotcha" journalism, the term for media efforts to catch public officials in seemingly questionable situations, certainly complicates legislative life.

The legislature is not without its weapons. If the legislature can muster the votes, it can override a gubernatorial veto. In fact, new research shows that in states with term limited legislatures, the incidence of veto overrides is actually higher than it is in states that do not limit legislative terms.[48] Legislatures have also enacted other measures designed to enhance their control and to reduce the governor's flexibility in budgetary matters. For example, some states now require the governor to get legislative approval of budget cutbacks in the event of a revenue shortfall. Professional legislatures with their longer sessions and higher paid members can hold their own in budget battles with the governor.[49] Other states have limited the governor's power to initiate transfers of funds among executive branch agencies. These actions reflect the continuing evolution of legislative–executive relations.

Overseeing the Bureaucracy

Legislative involvement with the executive branch does not end with the governor. State legislatures are increasingly venturing into the world of state agencies and bureaucrats, with the attitude that after authorizing a program and allocating funds for it, they should check on what has happened to it. Legislative oversight involves four activities: policy and program evaluation, legislative review of administrative rules and regulations, sunset legislation, and review and control of federal funds received by the state.

Policy and Program Evaluation Legislatures select auditors to keep an eye on state agencies and departments. (In a few states, auditors are independently elected officials.) Auditors are more than super-accountants; their job is to evaluate the performance of state programs as to their efficiency and effectiveness, a task sometimes known as the postaudit function. Specifically, they conduct periodic performance audits to measure goal achievement and other indicators of progress in satisfying legislative intent, a process that has been credited with both saving money and improving program performance. Virginia's Joint Legislative Audit and Review Commission (JLARC) is regarded as a model for the rest of the country. Throughout its thirty-five-year history, JLARC has conducted hundreds of evaluations of state programs and saved the state millions of dollars. The key to a useful auditing function is strong legislative support (even in the face of audits that turn up controversial findings) and, at the same time, a guarantee of a certain degree of independence from legislative interference.

Legislative Review of Administrative Rules Forty-seven state legislatures conduct reviews of administrative rules and regulations, but they vary in their methods. They may assign the review function to a special committee (such as a rule review committee) or to a specific legislative agency, or they may incorporate the review function in the budgetary process. In this role, the legislature acts as a gatekeeper, striving to keep agency rules in line with legislative preferences.[50]

Legislative review is a mechanism through which administrative abuses of discretion can be corrected. Legislative bills frequently contain language to the effect that "the Department of Youth Services shall develop the necessary rules and regulations to implement the provisions of this act." Such language gives the agency wide latitude in establishing procedures and policies. The legislature wants to be certain that in the process, the agency does not overstep its bounds or violate legislative intent. If it is found to have done so, then the legislature can overturn the offending rules and regulations through modification, suspension, or veto—depending on the state.

This issue is a true gray area of legislative–executive relations, and court rulings at both the national and state levels have found the most powerful of these actions, the **legislative veto**, to be an unconstitutional violation of the separation of powers. For example, in 1997 the Missouri Supreme Court declared that the legislature's rule-review process was an unconstitutional intrusion into the functions of the executive branch. Legislatures continue to use the budgetary process to review (and sanction) agency behavior. Increasingly, legislatures are requiring state agencies to furnish extensive data to justify their budget requests, and they can use their appropriations power to indicate their displeasure with agency rules and regulations.

legislative veto
An action whereby the legislature overturns a state agency's rules or regulations.

Sunset Legislation Half the states have established **sunset laws** that set automatic expiration dates for specified agencies and other organizational structures in the executive branch. An agency can be saved from termination only through an overt renewal action in the legislature. Review occurs anywhere from every four years to every twelve years, depending on individual state statute, and is conducted by the standing committee that authorized the agency or by a committee established for sunset-review purposes (such as a government operations committee). The reviews evaluate the agency's performance and its progress toward achieving its goals.

During the 1970s, sunset legislation was widely hailed as an effective tool for asserting legislative dominion over the executive branch; but more than thirty years' experience with the technique has produced mixed results, and some states have repealed their sunset laws. Agency reviews tend to be time-consuming and costly. And the process has become highly politicized in many states, involving not only agencies and legislators but lobbyists as well. On the positive side, sunset reviews are said to increase agency compliance with legislative intent. Statistics show that nationwide, only about 13 percent of the agencies reviewed are eventually terminated, thus making termination more of a threat than an objective reality.[51]

sunset laws
Statutes that set automatic expiration dates for specified agencies and other organizations.

Review and Control of Federal Funds Since the early 1980s, legislatures have played a more active role in directing the flow of federal funds once they have reached the state. Before this time, the sheer magnitude of federal funds and their potential to upset legislatively established priorities caused great consternation among legislators. The executive branch controlled the disposition of these grant funds by designating the recipient agency and program. In some cases, federal money was used to fund programs that the state legislature did not support. Federal dollars were simply absorbed into the budget without debate and discussion, and legislators were cut out of the loop. By making federal fund disbursement part of the formal appropriations process, however, legislators have redesigned the loop.

If legislatures are to do a decent job in forecasting state priorities, some control of federal funds is necessary. In the face of reduced federal aid to states, it is critical for legislators to understand the role that federal dollars have played in program operation. When funding for a specific program dries up, it is the legislature's responsibility to decide whether to replace it with state money.

How effectively are legislatures overseeing state bureaucracies? As with so many questions, the answer depends on who is asked. From the perspective of legislators, their controls increase administrative accountability. A survey of legislators in eight states found legislative oversight committees, the postaudit function, and sunset laws to be among the most effective bureaucratic controls available.[52] Another effective device, and one that legislatures use in special circumstances, is legislative investigation of an agency, an administrator, or a program. But from the perspective of the governor, many forms of legislative oversight are simply meddling and, as such, they undermine the separation of powers.[53]

LEGISLATURES AND CAPACITY

State legislatures are fascinating institutions. Although they share numerous traits, each maintains some uniqueness. Houses and senates have different traditions and styles, even in the same state. And across states, the variation in legislative systems is notable. As Alan Rosenthal writes, "Legislatures are interwoven in the fabric of their states."[54] As institutions, legislatures are dynamic; amid layers of traditions and rules, they change and evolve.

The demands placed on state legislatures are unrelenting. Challenges abound. In these times, the ability of legislatures to function effectively depends on institutional adaptation. The extensive modernization that almost all legislatures underwent in the 1970s is evidence of institutional renewal. Structural reforms and a new breed of legislator have altered state legislatures and made them more capable. How ironic then, with all their institutional improvement, legislatures continue to struggle with their public image. Figure 6.3 arrays the states on two dimensions: public approval of the institution and the degree of legislative professionalization. As is evident, in the vast majority of states,

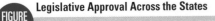

Legislative Approval Across the States

FIGURE
6.3

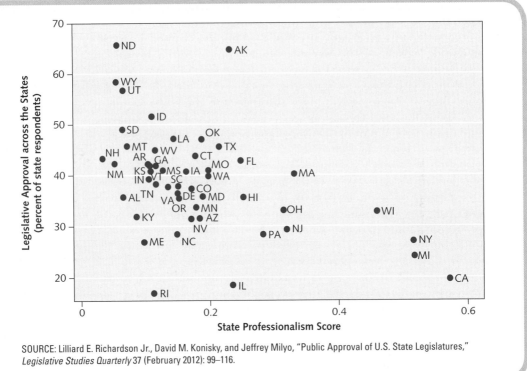

SOURCE: Lilliard E. Richardson Jr., David M. Konisky, and Jeffrey Milyo, "Public Approval of U.S. State Legislatures,"
Legislative Studies Quarterly 37 (February 2012): 99–116.

public approval falls below the 50 percent mark. This is especially the case with the more professional legislatures. Research has shown that it is among ideological conservatives that the negative relationship between professionalization and approval is greatest.[55]

Other stressors remain. Another real concern is that the legislatures of some states are being marginalized through a citizen-empowering mechanism, the initiative, and an institution-weakening mechanism, term limits. No wonder then that the National Conference of State Legislatures has encouraged its members to develop "a process that clarifies the current problems, what changes are needed and how to put those remedies into place."[56] Perhaps a new and different era of legislative reform is upon us.

CHAPTER RECAP

- The three principal functions of legislatures are policymaking, representation, and oversight.

- Redistricting is a battleground for state legislatures because drawing district lines is a partisan process.

- Legislatures operate with their own formal and informal rules. Violations of institutional norms result in sanctions.

- The lawmaking process is a complex one with multiple opportunities for delay and obstruction. Most bills never make it through, and those that do seldom look as they did when they were introduced.

- Although legislatures perform more effectively than they used to, in 2013, fifteen states had legislative term limits in effect. Term limits create open seats and thus increase competition for legislative seats. But when legislative terms are limited, other institutional actors such as the governor gain power.

- Legislators vie with governors in the policymaking process. Governors have the power to veto, but legislators have the power to override a gubernatorial veto. In addition, the legislature plays several oversight roles with regard to the bureaucracy.

- Legislative capacity has increased but, at the same time, legislatures risk becoming marginalized in states with the initiative process and term limits.

Key Terms

casework *(p. 119)*
multimember district (MMD) *(p. 122)*
malapportionment *(p. 122)*
reapportionment *(p. 123)*
redistrict *(p. 123)*

gerrymander *(p. 123)*
per diem *(p. 125)*
lame duck *(p. 126)*
war chest *(p. 127)*
delegate *(p. 130)*
trustee *(p. 130)*

politico *(p. 130)*
policy entrepreneur *(p. 131)*
legislative veto *(p. 140)*
sunset laws *(p. 140)*

Internet Resources

To find out what's up in state legislatures, visit the website of the National Conference of State Legislatures at **www.ncsl.org**.

Most states have websites that allow citizens to follow the progress of legislation during the session. See, for example, the legislative sites for Iowa and Minnesota at **www.legis.iowa.gov** and **www.leg.state.mn.us**, respectively.

The website **www.votesmart.org** tracks the performance of political leaders, including state legislators.

To learn about model state laws, see the National Conference of Commissioners on Uniform State Laws at **http://uniformlaws.org**.

An advocacy website, **www.termlimits.org** provides up-to-date coverage of the term-limits issue.

An avowedly conservative organization that drafts model legislation on various topics and reviews legislative activities across the states maintains a website at **www.alec.org**.

7

Governors

CHAPTER OUTLINE

- The Office of Governor
- The Roles of the Governor: Duties and Responsibilities
- Formal Powers of the Governor
- Informal Powers
- Leaving Office
- Other Executive Branch Officials
- The Capability of U.S. Governors

FOCUS QUESTIONS

1. How has the institution of governor changed from the early days of state governments to contemporary times?
2. What are some of the common duties and powers (formal and informal) that governors exercise?
3. What are some of the other offices typically found in the executive branch?

Problems of biblical proportions sometimes come crashing down on governors and the people of their states. Earthquakes, fires, tornados, floods, and hurricanes can ravage a state and devastate many of its residents. When such catastrophic events occur, people may first think of calling for help from the president of the United States, but it is often the governor who takes charge. The governor's actions may draw praise or castigation—or both—from the afflicted and other citizens.

Identify a natural or man-made catastrophe and you will also find a governor gathering and providing state resources. A governor will quickly visit the scene; demonstrate personal concern; reallocate money and personnel; call out the National Guard; coordinate the response of the Federal Emergency Management Agency (FEMA), state agencies, local governments, and non-government agencies; and appeal to Congress, the president, and neighboring states for assistance.

If a governor does not perform up to expectations, she suffers the consequences, as shown by the example of Louisiana Governor Kathleen Babineaux Blanco. When Hurricane Katrina devastated New Orleans and South Louisiana in 2005, Blanco seemed hesitant and uncertain during the first days following the storm and the subsequent floods. Considering the more than one thousand fatalities, tens of thousands of stranded flood victims, and massive destruction, perhaps any governor would have appeared stunned. But Blanco's public support declined significantly.

Hurricane Sandy ripped through the Northeast in October 2012, killing seventy-two people; flooding large areas of coastal New York, New Jersey, and Delaware; and wreaking an estimated $70 billion in damages. New Jersey Governor Chris Christie quickly emerged as a strong, confident, and compassionate leader in the aftermath of "The Storm of the Century." As a result, Christie's favorability ratings jumped nineteen points in the following month.[1] Today, governors speak with voices of authority on important national and even international policy issues. Although they do not always agree on what they want, the governors are influencing the Congress and president as never before in our history.

Asserting themselves as a righteous third force and speaking through the National Governors Association (NGA), the governors have helped shape federal welfare, education, and health care reform, and even global warming policy. And while Congress continually feuds along partisan lines over virtually all significant issues, the governors preach—and often practice—partisan peacemaking to reach common policy ground with their own legislatures and to promote positive national policy changes. The challenges of conciliation are complicated by a voting public with no stomach for raising taxes, and tight state budgets, in which some three-quarters of expenditures are earmarked to education, Medicaid, and local government. But the governors must make tough choices. Some bravely advance tax hikes despite the possible electoral consequences. Others impose brutal spending cuts on prisons, Medicaid, and higher education. Still others champion controversial issues such as gay marriage, abortion restrictions, or climate change policy.

The governors are newly challenged by the divisive partisan politics that have infected the national government and that are threatening to sicken the states as well, at the expense of their collaborative, "can-do" spirit. The governors' contributions to national policy and politics have been a tribute to their policymaking capacity and responsiveness to common—and uncommon—problems affecting the citizens of their respective states. Their prominence in the U.S. federal system depends substantially on their ability to set aside divisive partisan differences and work collaboratively to tackle shared problems.

THE OFFICE OF GOVERNOR

It has been said that the American governorship was "conceived in mistrust and born in a straitjacket." Indeed, because the excesses of some colonial governors appointed by the English Crown created strong dislike and distrust of executive power by the early American settlers, the first state constitutions concentrated political power in the legislative branch.

History of the Office

Early governors were typically elected by the legislature rather than by the voters, were restricted to a single one-year term of office, and had little authority. Two states, Pennsylvania and Georgia, even established a plural (multimember) executive. Slowly, the governorships became stronger through longer terms, popular election, and use of the veto; but power did not come easily. The movement for popular democracy during the Jacksonian era led to the election of other executive branch officials, and reaction to the excesses of Jacksonian democracy resulted in numerous independent boards and commissions in the executive branch. Although governors did gain some power, they could not exercise independent authority over these executive boards and commissions.

In the early 1900s, along with their efforts to democratize national politics and clean up the corrupt city political machines, Progressive reformers launched a campaign to reform state government. Their principal target was the weak executive branch. Efforts to improve the state executive branch continued throughout the twentieth century. The essential goal has been to increase the governors' powers to make them more commensurate with the office's increased duties and responsibilities. As a result, constitutional and statutory changes have strengthened the office of the chief executive, reorganized the executive branch, and streamlined the structure and processes of the bureaucracy. The capacity of governors and the executive branch to apply state resources to the solution of emerging problems has thus been greatly enhanced.[2] And, as observed at the beginning of this chapter, the governors have become prominent players in national policymaking.

Today's Governors

Today, being governor is a high-pressure, physically demanding, emotionally draining job. As political scientist Larry Sabato states, "Governors must possess many skills to be successful. They are expected to be adroit administrators, dexterous executives, expert judges of people, combative yet sensitive and inspiring politicians, decorous chiefs of state, shrewd party tacticians, and polished public relations managers."[3] The job is also hard on the governor's private life. It consumes an enormous amount of waking hours at the expense of family activities, hobbies, and, in some cases, more significant money-making opportunities in law, consulting, or business.

Fortunately, governorships are attracting well-qualified chief executives, most of whom are a far cry from the figureheads of the eighteenth and nineteenth centuries and the stereotypical back-slapping, cigar-smoking, wheeler-dealers of the first half of the twentieth century. Today's governors are better educated and better prepared for the job than their predecessors. Many recent governors hold law or other graduate degrees. Most of today's governors paid their political dues in state legislatures, gaining an understanding of important issues confronting the state, a working familiarity with influential figures in government and the private sector, and a practical knowledge of the legislative process and other inner secrets of state government. About one-third served previously as elected state executive branch officials, including lieutenant governor and attorney general. Several are former mayors. Although previous elected experience is a great advantage in winning a governorship, a number have come straight from the private sector. The attractiveness of the governorship is evident in the fact that several current chief executives left a congressional seat to take office. Why would someone desert the glamour of the nation's capital for the statehouse? For political power and the opportunity to make a difference in one's own state. Simply put, being a state chief executive is just more rewarding and greater fun. It is, according to current and former chief executives, "the best job in politics."[4]

Although still predominantly white males, today's governors are more representative of population characteristics than former chief executives. Two Latinos serve as governors: Susana Martinez of New Mexico and Brian Sandoval of Nevada. Three African Americans have served: L. Douglas Wilder of Virginia (1990–1994); Deval Patrick of Massachusetts (2007–2014), and David Patterson (2008–2010), who assumed office in New York when Eliot Spitzer resigned in the aftermath of a prostitution scandal. The first Asian American governor not from Hawaii, Gary Locke served in Washington; today, there are two, Bobby Jindal in Louisiana

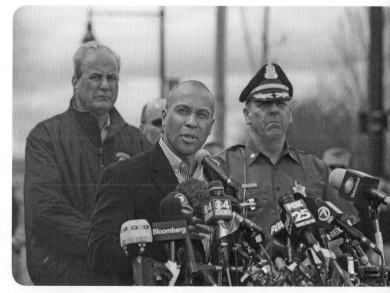

Massachusetts Governor Deval Patrick speaks to the media on April 19, 2013, following the Boston Marathon bombing, which killed 3 and injured over 200.
SOURCE: Jeremiah Robinson/ZUMA Press/Newscom

TABLE 7.1	Female Governors, 2013				
NAME	STATE	PARTY	YEAR ELECTED	AGE FIRST ELECTED	PREVIOUS PUBLIC SERVICE
Nikki Haley	SC	Democrat	2010	39	State legislature
Mary Fallin	OK	Republican	2010	56	U.S. Congress, state legislature, lieutenant governor
Jan Brewer	AZ	Republican	2009*	64	Secretary of state, state legislature
Maggie Hassan	NH	Democrat	2013	55	State legislature
Susana Martinez	NM	Republican	2006	51	District attorney

*Brewer first assumed the governorship in 2009, when Governor Janet Napolitano became secretary of the U.S. Department of Homeland Security.

SOURCE: © Cengage Learning 2015

and Nikki Haley in South Carolina. In early years, several women succeeded their husbands as governor, but many have recently won governorships on their own, including five sitting governors in 2013 (see Table 7.1).

Getting There: Gubernatorial Campaigns

The lure of the governorship must be weighed against the financial costs. Campaigning for the office has become hugely expensive. Because candidates no longer rely on their political party to support them, they must continuously solicit great sums of money from donors to pay for the campaigning costs—political consultants, opinion polls, air travel, media advertisements, telephone banks, direct mailings, websites, and interactive video links.

Until 2010, the most expensive governor's race was the 2002 election in New York, in which the loser, Thomas Golisano, invested $76.3 million; the winner, George Pataki, spent "only" $44.2 million. But candidate Meg Whitman spent $141.5 million of her own money, and $160 million in total, only to lose in the 2010 California election! The official figures do not include in-kind donations such as free transportation, telephones, door-to-door canvassing, and other contributions from supporters. Generally, elections tend to cost more when they are close, held in a nonpresidential election year, involve a partisan shift (that is, when a Democrat succeeds a Republican, or vice versa), and are held in highly populated and geographically large states (for example, Florida, Texas, California, and New York).[5] Campaign cost-per-vote received in recent gubernatorial elections ranged from $34 in West Virginia to 41 cents in Missouri.[6]

Money has a profound influence on gubernatorial election results, but it isn't the only important factor. As one veteran of political campaigns has reflected, "Everyone knows that half the money spent in a political campaign is wasted. The trouble is that nobody knows which half."[7] Other factors are also important in candidate success, such as incumbency and the strength of the candidate's political party in the state electorate, and prevailing levels of unemployment and other economic conditions.[8] High-profile candidates stand a solid chance of being elected because they possess campaign skills, political experience, and other characteristics that help them raise the campaign funds needed to get their message and persona across to the electorate.[9] Of course, being independently wealthy doesn't hurt either.

Incumbency is a particularly important aspect of a candidate's profile. An incumbent governor running for reelection stands an excellent chance of victory; about three-quarters of incumbents have retained their seats since 1970. Incumbents enjoy a number of important advantages, including the opportunity while in office to cultivate both popularity with the voters and campaign donations from interest groups. Reelection, however, is no sure thing. Budget and tax woes can lead voters to toss chief executives out of office, particularly those who as candidates pledge not to raise taxes but then do so after election.[10]

THE ROLES OF THE GOVERNOR: DUTIES AND RESPONSIBILITIES

In performing the duties of the office, the governor wears the hats of top policy-maker, chief legislator, chief administrator, ceremonial leader, intergovernmental coordinator, economic development promoter, and political party leader. Sometimes several of these hats must be balanced atop the governor's head at once. All things considered, these roles make the governorship one of the most difficult and challenging, yet potentially most rewarding, jobs in the world.

Developing and Making Public Policy

A governor is the leading formulator and initiator of public policy in his state, from his first pronouncements as a gubernatorial candidate until his final days in office. The governor's role as chief policymaker involves many other players, including actors in the legislature, bureaucracy, courts, interest groups, and voting public. Most major policies that are enacted are initiated by the governor, and success or failure depends largely on how competently the governor designs and frames policy proposals and develops public support for them. The governor is also responsible for following through to see that adopted policies are put into effect as originally intended.

Some issues are by nature transitory, appearing on the agenda of state government and disappearing after appropriate actions are taken. These issues are often created by external events, such as a federal court decision that mandates a reduction in prison overcrowding, a new national law requiring a state response, or an act of nature or man such as a tornado, flood, forest fire, or hurricane.

Most policy issues, however, do not emerge suddenly out of the mists. Perennial concerns face the governor each year: education, taxing and spending issues, and economic development. Cyclical issues also appear, periodically increasing in intensity and then slowly fading away. Examples of the latter are consumer protection, ethics in government, reapportionment, and budget shortfalls. Of course, national policy issues sometimes absorb the governor's time as well, such as preparing for and addressing economic downturns, coping with the flow of illegal immigrants, abortion rights, gun control, and health care. Several factors have contributed to stronger policy leadership from the chief executives in recent years, including larger and more able staffs that are knowledgeable in important policy fields; a more integrated executive branch with department heads appointed by the governor; strengthened formal powers of the office, such as longer terms and the veto and budget powers; and the assistance of the National Governors Association, which offers ideas for policy and program development.

Marshaling Legislative Action

The gubernatorial role of marshaling action is closely related to that of policymaker because legislative action is required for most of the chief executive's policies to be put into effect. In fact, the governor cannot directly introduce bills; party leaders and policy supporters in the house and senate must actually put the bills in the hopper. Dealing with legislators is a demanding role for a governor, consuming more time than any other role, and representing for many the single most difficult aspect of the job.

Executive-Legislative Tensions Developing a positive relationship with the legislature requires great expenditures of a governor's time, energy, and resources. Several factors hinder smooth relations between the chief executive and the legislature, including partisanship and personality clashes. Even the different natures of the two branches can cause conflict. Governors are elected by a statewide constituency and therefore tend to take a broad, comprehensive, long-range view of issues, whereas legislators, who represent relatively small geographical areas and groups of voters, are more likely to take a piecemeal, parochial approach to policymaking.

According to one study, the amount of strife between the two branches is influenced by three factors: the size of the majority and minority parties, the personalities of the governor and legislative leaders, and the nearness of an election year.[11] Following the 2012 elections, there were nineteen Democratic governors, thirty Republican governors, and one Independent. In fourteen states today, the governor has to deal with a one- or two-house majority from the opposing political party. When the opposition party is strong, the governor must seek bipartisan support to get favored legislation passed. Often, a governor facing a large legislative majority from the opposing party has only the veto and the possibility of mobilizing public support as weapons against the legislature. Independent governors do not even have a minority party to count on, but this does not preclude success. Former Maine Independent governor King observed "I have no automatic friends in the legislature, but I have no automatic enemies. I have 186 skeptics."[12]

A governor who ignores or alienates members of the opposing political party can quickly find himself in the desert without a drink of water. Arizona Governor Janet Napolitano, a Democrat, assumed a combative posture with her majority Republican legislature. She vetoed more than 100 bills during her first term (2002–2006) but won favor with the voters and was reelected to a second term in 2006. New York Governor David Patterson compared legislators to "bloodsuckers…who cater to special interests during the day and go home without taking…action."[13] New Jersey's Governor Chris Christie entered office as a Republican with tough talk and a brusque manner. He "never found a battle he didn't want to pick or a position he was willing to compromise."[14] He fought with the democratic legislature over judicial appointments, taxes, employee pensions, education funding, and many other issues. Soon, however, even Christie learned the value of the occasional legislative compromise.

Even in states where the governor's own party enjoys a large majority in both houses of the legislature, factions are certain to develop along ideological, rural–urban, geographical, institutional, or other divisions. Ironically, a very large legislative majority can create the greatest problems with factionalism, primarily because there is no sizable opposition to unite the majority party. The stronger the numbers of the majority party, the more likely it is to degenerate into intraparty rivalries beyond the governor's control. As one Democratic governor lamented in the face of a 4-to-1 majority of his own party in the legislature, "You've got Democrats, you've got moderate Democrats, you've got suburban Democrats, you've got urban Democrats, you've got rural Democrats."[15]

Executive Influence on the Legislative Agenda Despite the difficulties in dealing with the legislature, most governors dominate the policy agenda, usually by working hand in hand with legislative leaders. The governor's influence begins with the State of the State address, which kicks off each new legislative session, and strong influence continues with the annual budget message. In 2013, the governors stressed jobs, health care policy, gun control, and education.

During the session, the governor might publicly threaten to veto a proposed bill or appeal directly to a particular legislator's constituency. Most of the drama, however, takes place behind the scenes. The governor might promise high-level executive branch jobs or judgeships, either for certain legislators or for their friends, to influence legislative votes. Kentucky Governor Steve Beshear, a Democrat, appointed two Republican legislators to posts in the executive branch to gain the majority needed to pass a bill expanding betting on horse races.[16] Or, a governor might offer some sort of **pork barrel** reward, such as funding a highway project in a legislator's district or approving an appropriation for the local Strawberry Festival. Private meetings or breakfasts in the governor's mansion flatter and enlist support from small groups or individual legislators. Successful governors are usually able to relate to representatives and senators on a personal level. Many are former members of the state legislature, so they can rely on their personal connections and experiences to win over key supporters.

pork barrel
Favoritism, by a governor or other elected official, in distributing government monies or other resources to a particular program, jurisdiction, or individual.

In addition, all governors have legislative liaisons who are assigned to lobby for the administration's programs. Members of the governor's staff testify at legislative hearings, consult with committees and individuals on proposed bills, and even write floor speeches for friends in the legislature. Some governors designate a floor leader to steer their priorities through the legislature.

Most governors, however, are careful not to be perceived as unduly interfering in the internal affairs of the legislature. Too much meddling in legislative affairs can provoke a political backlash that undermines a governor's policy program. The role of chief legislator, then, requires a balancing act that ultimately determines the success or failure of the governor's agenda.

Governors and the Courts

Sometimes the best laid plans of governors are squelched by the courts, either state or federal. Florida Governor Rick Scott's aggressive and controversial actions to compel drug testing of all state employees and job applicants, restrict the right of physicians to ask patients about guns in their houses, retract 3 percent of state worker salaries, and censor K-12 textbooks spawned a tornado of lawsuits aimed at overturning his actions.[17] Nevada Governor Brian Sandoval's "No-Tax Pledge" resulted in a proposed state budget that, among other things, raided local government accounts to balance the state accounts. With less than two weeks left in the legislative session, the Nevada Supreme Court ruled that such local funds transfers were unconstitutional. Sandoval was forced to release a revised budget that included an increase in the personal income tax.[18] In New Mexico, the state supreme court ruled against Governor Susana Martinez's freeze on publication of new pollution control measures by a state government agency. Finally, federal judges threatened to hold California Governor Jerry Brown in contempt of court if he did not quickly produce a plan for removing convicts from overcrowded prisons.

Administering the Executive Branch

As chief executive of the state, the governor is (in name, at least) in charge of the operations of numerous agencies, departments, boards, and commissions. In the view of many voters, the governor is directly responsible not only for pivotal matters such as the condition of the state's economy but also for mundane concerns such as clearing snow off state highways in a timely manner. Most governors are sensitive to their chief administrative responsibilities and spend a great amount of time and energy attending to them. Constitutional and statutory reforms, including the concentration of executive power in the office of the governor and the consolidation of numerous state agencies, have considerably strengthened the governor's capacity to manage the state. (See Chapter 8 for further discussion of public administration.) If governors are diligent in expeditiously appointing talented and responsive people to policymaking posts, they should feel no compulsion to micromanage the state's day-to-day affairs.

Instead, they can focus their energies on leadership activities such as identifying goals, marshaling resources, and achieving results.

In many respects, the governor's job is comparable to that of the chief executive officer of a large corporation. Governors must manage tens of thousands of workers, staggering sums of money, and complex organizational systems. They must establish priorities, manage crises, and balance contending interests. But there are important differences as well. For one, governors are not paid comparably for their responsibilities. In terms of expenditures and employees, most states are as big as or bigger than *Fortune* 500 companies, whose chief executive officers typically earn tens of millions of dollars a year in salary and other forms of remuneration. Yet the fifty governors average only $130,595 annually, and Maine's earns but $70,000.[19] Moreover, governors confront several unique factors that constrain their ability to manage, a topic to which we now turn.

Restraints on Management Reforms of the executive branch have allowed for more active and influential management, but significant restraints still remain. For example, the separation-of-powers principle dictates that the governor share his authority with the legislature and the courts, either or both of which may be politically or philosophically opposed to any given action. Changes in state agency programs, priorities, or organization typically require legislative approval, and the legality of such changes may be tested in the courts.

The governor's ability to hire, fire, motivate, and punish is severely restricted by the courts, merit-system rules and regulations, collective bargaining contracts, independent boards and commissions with their own personnel systems, and other elected executive branch officials pursuing their own administrative and political agendas. Thus, most employees in the executive branch are outside the governor's formal sphere of authority and may challenge that authority almost at will. Career bureaucrats—who have established their own policy direction and momentum over many years, and who see governors come and go—usually march to their own tune. In sum, governors must manage through third parties and networks in the three branches of government as well as in the private and nonprofit sectors. They have very little unilateral authority.

Governors as Managers Some governors minimize their managerial responsibilities, preferring to delegate them to trusted staff persons and agency heads. Others provide strong administrative and policy leadership in state government. Virginia Governor Tim Kaine (2006–2010) enjoyed unusual success by using a collaborative decision-making style to earn a national award for Virginia as "Best Managed State." The honor went to North Dakota in 2012, as the state (and Governor Jack Dalrymple) enjoyed the proceeds of a huge oil and gas boom.

But the constraints on the governor's managerial activities are not likely to lessen, nor are the potential political liabilities. The governors who courageously wade into the bureaucratic fray must invest a great deal of time and scarce political resources, yet they risk embarrassing defeats that can drag their administrations into debilitation and disrepute. After all, "Reorganized the State Bureaucracy" hardly resonates as a campaign slogan. Meanwhile, in the face of social and economic changes, the management of state government has become increasingly complex and the need for active managerial governors more critical than ever before.

Master of Ceremonies

Some governors thrive on ceremony, and others detest it, but all spend a large portion of their time on it because it helps garner reelection votes. Former governors remember ceremonial duties as the second-most-demanding of the gubernatorial roles, just behind working with the legislature.[20] Cutting the ribbon for a new highway, celebrating the arrival of a new business, welcoming potential foreign business investors, receiving the queen of the Collard Green Festival, announcing "Respect Your Parents Week," opening the state fair, and handing out diplomas are the kind of ceremonial duties that take a governor all over the state and often consume a larger portion of their workweek than any other role. Even a seemingly pleasant task can have its personal horrors. George A. Aiken, the late governor of Vermont, dreaded having to pin the ribbon on the winner of the Miss Vermont contest because he could not figure out how to put the pin in without getting under the bathing suit.

Coordinating Intergovernmental Relations

Governors serve as the major points of contact between their states and the president, Congress, and national agencies. Everything from emergency response to settling disputes over cross-boundary water pollution issues are carried out through the governor's office. At the local level, governors are involved in allocating grants-in-aid, promoting cooperation and coordination in economic development activities, and various other matters. Governors also provide leadership in resolving disputes with Indian tribes involving casino gambling and related issues.

The role of intergovernmental coordinator is most visible at the national level, where governors are aided by the National Governors Association (NGA) and the state's Washington office. The NGA meets two times a year in full session to adopt policy positions, and to discuss governors' problems and "best practice" policy solutions. (C-SPAN covers national meetings of the governors.) The NGA's staff analyzes important issues, distributes its analyses to the states, offers practical and technical assistance to governors, and holds a valuable seminar for new governors. The NGA, however, has come under fire from conservative Republicans, who object to the organization's perceived "tax and spend" agenda even if it benefits their own states. In fact, Republican governors of Florida, Idaho, Maine, Ohio, and Texas recently withdrew from the NGA over this and related issues. Increasingly, the Democratic Governors Association and Republican Governors Association are becoming the first-choice coordinating bodies. Like so many other features of contemporary American politics, the NGA has not escaped partisan and ideological disputes.

Most states have established Washington offices to fight for their interests in Congress, the White House, and, perhaps most important, the many federal agencies that interact with states on a daily basis. A governor's official inquiry can help speed up the progress of federal grant-in-aid funds or gain special consideration for a new federal facility. Washington offices are often assisted by major law and lobbying firms under contract to individual states.

The governor's role as intergovernmental coordinator is highly important. It reflects the elevated position of the states in the scheme of American federalism and their increasing importance in national and international affairs. It also is a reaction to provocations and intrusions from the national government. Acting together and as individuals, the governors have exercised national policy leadership on critical issues such as taxation of Internet sales, climate change, and education and health care reform. Frequently, when the national government confronts a policy problem, it turns to the states for solutions.

Promoting Economic Development

As promoter of economic development, a governor works to recruit business and tourists from out of state and to encourage economic growth from sources within the state (see Chapter 12). Governors attend trade fairs, visit headquarters of firms interested in locating in the state, telephone and email promising business contacts, and welcome business leaders. The role may take the governor and the state economic development team to Mexico, China, Germany, or other countries, as well as to other states. Governors also work hard to promote tourism. But mostly, economic development entails making the state's climate "good for business" by improving infrastructure, arranging tax and other incentive deals, and engaging in other strategies to entice out-of-state firms into relocating and to encourage in-state businesses to expand or at least stay put.

When a state enjoys success in economic development, the governor claims a major portion of the credit. Sometimes, the personal touch of a governor can mean the difference between an industrial plum and economic stagnation. Success stories are proudly heralded. Are incumbent governors punished in a reelection attempt when economic growth lags? Research findings on this question are mixed.[21]

Leading the Political Party

By claiming the top elected post in the state, the governor becomes the highest-ranking member of his or her political party. This role is not as significant as it was several decades ago, when the governor controlled the state's party apparatus and legislative leadership, and had strong influence over party nominations for seats in the state legislature and executive branch offices. The widespread adoption of primaries, which have replaced party conventions, has put nominations largely in the hands of the voters. And legislative leaders are a much more independent breed than before. Still, some governors get involved in legislative elections through campaign aid, endorsements, or other actions. If the governor's choice wins, he or she may feel a special debt to the governor and support the governor on important legislation.

The political party remains at least marginally useful to the governor for three principal reasons.[22] First, legislators from the governor's own party are more likely to support the chief executive's programs. Second, communication lines to the president and national cabinet members are more likely to be open when the president and the governor are members of the same party. Finally, the party remains the most convenient means through which to win nomination to the governor's office.

When a state has two competitive parties, a governor finds that he must work with the opposition if his legislative programs are to pass. For Independent governors, a special challenge exists: how to govern without a party behind them to organize votes and otherwise push proposed laws through the convoluted legislative process. The recent record has been mixed. Maine's Independent governor, Angus King, demonstrated a talent for working successfully with shifting legislative coalitions on a variety of issues, as has current Rhode Island governor Lincoln Chafee.

FORMAL POWERS OF THE GOVERNOR

formal powers
Powers of the governor derived from the state constitution or statute.

informal powers
Powers of the governor not derived from constitutional or statutory law.

A variety of powers are attached to the governor's office. A governor's **formal powers** include the tenure of the office, the power of appointment, the power to veto legislation, the responsibility for preparing the budget, the authority to reorganize the executive branch, and the right to hire professional staff in the governor's office. These powers give governors the *potential* to carry out the duties of office as they see fit. The formal powers vary considerably, however, from state to state. Some governors' offices (Illinois, New York) are considered strong and others (Alabama, Georgia) weak. Also, the fact that these powers are available does not mean that they are used effectively. Equally important are the **informal powers** that governors have at their disposal. These are potentially empowering features of the job or the person that are not expressly provided for by law. Many of the informal powers are associated with personal traits on which the chief executive relies to carry out the duties and responsibilities of the office. They are especially helpful in relations with the legislature.

Both sets of powers have increased over the past several decades. Governors are more influential than ever before, primarily because of their enhanced formal powers; charisma, however, remains as important as ever. The most successful governors are those who employ their informal powers to maximize the formal powers. The term for this concept is *synergism*, a condition in which the total effect of two distinct sets of attributes working together is greater than the sum of their effects when acting independently. An influential governor, then, is one who skillfully combines formal and informal powers to maximum effectiveness.

Tenure

The governor's tenure power has two components: the duration (number of years) of a term of office and the number of terms that an individual may serve as governor. Both have slowly but steadily expanded over the past two centuries. From the onerous restriction of a single one-year term of office placed on ten of the first thirteen governors, the duration has evolved to today's standard of two or more four-year terms (only New Hampshire and Vermont restrict their governors to two-year terms). In addition, gubernatorial elections have become distinct from national elections now that thirty-nine states hold them in non-presidential election years. This system encourages the voters to focus their attention on issues important to the state instead of allowing national politics to contaminate state election outcomes.

The importance of longer consecutive terms of office is readily apparent. A two-year governorship condemns the incumbent to a perpetual reelection campaign. As soon as the winner takes office, planning and fund-raising must begin for the next election. For any new governor, the initial year in office is typically spent settling into the job. In addition, the first-term, first-year chief executive must live with the budget priorities adopted by his predecessor. A two-year governorship, therefore, does not encourage success in matters of legislation or policy. Nor does it enable the governor to have much effect on the bureaucracy, whose old hands are likely to treat the governor as a mere bird of passage, making her virtually a lame duck when her term begins.

In truth, two four-year terms are needed for a governor to design new programs properly, acquire the necessary legislative support to put them into place, and get a handle on the bureaucracy by appointing competent political supporters to top posts. A duration of eight years in office also enhances the governor's intergovernmental role, particularly by giving him sufficient time to develop and nurture relationships with other governors and to win leadership positions in organizations such as the National Governors Association. The record of an eight-year chief executive stands on its own, untainted by the successes or failures of the office's previous inhabitant.

The average time actually served by governors has grown with fewer restrictions on tenure. The first gubernatorial graybeard was Illinois Governor Jim Thompson, who stepped down after serving his fourth consecutive term in 1990—a twentieth-century record. (North Carolina's Jim Hunt served four nonconsecutive four-year terms [1977–1985 and 1993–2001].) Three "comeback governors" were elected in 2010: Jerry Brown, California (1975–1983), Iowa's Terry Branstad (1983–1999), and Oregon Governor John Kitzhaber (1995–2003). Long periods in office strengthen the governor's position as policy leader, chief legislator, chief administrator, and intergovernmental coordinator, as shown by the policy legacy left in Illinois by Thompson and in North Carolina by Hunt.[23] Another sort of gubernatorial record was set by Cecil H. Underwood, who in 1956 became West Virginia's youngest governor at the age of thirty-four. He was reelected for a second term in 1996 as the state's *oldest* governor at seventy-four years of age.

There is resistance to unlimited tenure. More than one reelection creates fears of political machines and possible abuses of office. And, pragmatically speaking, a long period of "safe governorship" can result in stagnation and loss of vigor in the office. Even in states that do not restrict governors to two consecutive terms, the informal custom is to refrain from seeking a third term.

Appointment Power

Surveys of past governors indicate that they consider appointment power to be the most important weapon in their arsenal for managing the state bureaucracy. The ability to appoint one's own people to top positions in the executive branch also enhances the policy management role. When individuals who share the governor's basic philosophy and feel loyal to the chief executive and her programs direct the operations of state government, the governor's policies are more likely to be successful. Strong appointment authority can even help the governor's legislative role. The actual or implicit promise of important administrative and especially judicial positions can generate a surprising amount of support from ambitious lawmakers.

plural executive
A system in which more than one member of the executive branch is popularly elected on a statewide ballot.

Unfortunately for today's governors, Jacksonian democracy lives on in the **plural executive**. Most states continue to provide for popular election of numerous officials in the executive branch, including insurance commissioners, public utility commissioners, and secretaries of agriculture. Proponents of popular election claim that these officials make political decisions and therefore should be directly responsible to the electorate. Opponents contend that governors and legislators can make appointment decisions more effectively, based on the recommendations of appointed executive branch professionals who are not beholden to special interests.

Should appointment authority depend on the office under consideration? Those offices that tend to cater to special interests, such as agriculture, insurance, and education, probably should be appointive. Less substantive offices such as secretary of state or treasurer probably should be appointive as well. It makes sense, however, to *elect* an auditor and an attorney general because they require some independence in carrying out their responsibilities. (The auditor oversees the management and spending of state monies; the attorney general is concerned with the legality of executive and legislative branch activities.)

Many governors are weakened by their inability to appoint directly the heads of major state agencies, boards, and commissions. These high-ranking officials make policy decisions in the executive branch, but if they owe their jobs in whole or in part to popular election or legislative appointment, the governor's authority as chief executive is diminished significantly. Although nominally in charge of these executive branch agencies, the governor is severely constrained in her ability to manage. Such an arrangement would be unthinkable in a corporation.

The fragmented nature of power in the executive branch diminishes accountability and frustrates governors. Former Oregon Governor Tom McCall once lamented that "we have run our state like a pick-up orchestra, where the members meet at a dance, shake hands with each other, and start to play."[24]

Separately Elected State Officials	TABLE 7.2
OFFICE	**NUMBER OF STATES ELECTING**
Governor	50
Lieutenant governor	43
Attorney general	43
Treasurer	36
Secretary of state	35
Auditor	23
Education superintendent	14
Secretary of agriculture	13
Insurance commissioner	12
Controller	11

SOURCE: Adapted from *The Book of the States 2012*, vol. 43 (Lexington, KY: Council of State Governments, 2012), Table 4.10. Reprinted by permission of The Council of State Governments.

When the assorted performers are not selected by the chief conductor, their performance may lack harmony, to say the least. And elected statewide offices provide convenient platforms for aspiring governors to criticize the incumbent.

Most reformers interested in "good government" agree on the need to consolidate power in the governor's office by reducing the number of statewide elected officials and increasing the power of appointment to policy-related posts in the executive branch. Most states have expanded the number of policymaking, or "unclassified," positions in the governor's staff and in top agency line and staff positions. But the number of elected branch officials has remained virtually the same since the 1970s. Table 7.2 shows the range and number of separately elected officials. North Dakota has the greatest number, with twelve statewide offices filled through elections. At the bottom of the list are the reformer's ideal states, Maine, New Hampshire, New Jersey, and Tennessee, which elect only the governor. The average number of elected officials is about eight.

Why has it been so difficult to abolish multiple statewide offices? The best answer is that incumbent education superintendents, agricultural commissioners, and others have strong supporters in the electorate and elsewhere. Special-interest groups, such as the insurance industry, benefit from having an elected official—the insurance commissioner—representing their concerns at the highest level of state government. Such groups fiercely resist proposals to make the office appointive. Additional resistance may be credited to the fact that many citizens simply like having an opportunity to vote on a large number of executive branch officials.

Professional Jobs in State Government The vast majority of jobs in the states are filled through objective civil service (merit-system) rules and processes. Governors are generally quite content to avoid meddling with civil service positions, and a few have actually sought to transfer many **patronage** appointments—those based on personal or party loyalty—to an independent, merit-based civil service (see Chapter 8). Gubernatorial sacrifice of patronage power is comprehensible in view of the time and headaches associated with naming political supporters to jobs in the bureaucracy. There is always the possibility of embarrassment or scandal if the governor accidentally appoints a person with a criminal record, a clear conflict of interest, or a propensity for sexual harassment or other inappropriate behavior; or someone who causes harm through simple incompetence. Moreover, those who are denied coveted appointments may become angry. One governor, just as he was about to name a new member of a state commission, is quoted as saying, "I now have twenty-three good friends who want on the Racing Commission. [Soon] I'll have twenty-two enemies and one ingrate."[25] A governor benefits from a stable, competent civil service that hires, pays, and promotes on the basis of knowledge, job-related skills, and abilities rather than party affiliation or personal friendship with a legislator or other politician.

> **patronage**
>
> The informal power of a governor (or other officeholder) to make appointments on the basis of party membership and to dispense contracts or other favors to political supporters.

The Power to Fire The power of the governor to hire is not necessarily accompanied by the power to fire. Except in cases of extreme misbehavior or corruption, it is very difficult to remove a subordinate from office, even if such action is constitutionally permitted. For instance, if a governor attempts to dismiss the secretary of agriculture, he can anticipate an orchestrated roar of outrage from legislators, bureaucrats, and farm groups. The upshot is that the political costs of dismissing an appointee can be greater than the pain of simply living with the problem.

Several U.S. Supreme Court rulings have greatly restricted the governor's power to dismiss or remove from office the political appointees of previous governors. In the precedent-setting case of *Rutan et al.* v. *Republican Party of Illinois* (1990), the Court found that failure to hire, retain, or promote an individual because of his or her political or party affiliation violates that person's First Amendment right.[26]

A good appointment to a top agency post is the best way for a governor to influence the bureaucracy. By carefully choosing a competent and loyal agency head, the governor can more readily bring about significant changes in the programs and operations of that agency. Where appointment powers are circumscribed, the chief executive must muster his or her informal powers to influence activities of the state bureaucracy or rely on the seasoned judgment of professional civil servants.

Veto Power

As we noted in Chapter 6, the power to veto bills passed by the legislature bolsters the governor as chief policymaker and chief administrator. A veto also can punish an offending state agency by eliminating a favorite program or cutting the budget. Often the mere threat of a veto is enough to persuade a recalcitrant legislature to see the governor's point of view and compromise on the language of a bill. Vetoes are not easy to override. Most states require a majority of three-fifths or two-thirds of the legislature.

Types of Vetoes The veto can take several forms. The **package veto**, for instance, is the governor's rejection of a bill in its entirety. All governors hold package veto authority. The **line-item veto** allows the governor to strike out one or more objectionable sections of a bill, permitting the remaining provisions to become law. Only Nevada, Maine, and six other states forbid this gubernatorial power. Several states permit a hybrid form of line-item veto in which the governor may choose to reduce the dollar amount of a proposed item for purposes of holding down state expenditures or cutting back support for a particular program. In some states, the line-item veto is permitted only in appropriation bills.

The **pocket veto**, which is available in fourteen states, allows the governor to reject a bill by refusing to sign it after the legislature has adjourned. In two states (Hawaii and Utah) the legislature can reconvene to vote on a pocket veto; otherwise, the bill dies. A governor might use the pocket veto to avoid giving the legislature a chance to override a formal veto or to abstain from going on record against a proposed piece of controversial legislation.

A fourth type of veto is the **executive amendment**, formally provided for in fifteen states and informally used in several others. With this amendatory power, a governor may veto a bill, recommend changes that would make the bill acceptable, and then send it back to the legislature for reconsideration. If the legislature concurs with the suggestions, the governor signs the bill into law.

Use of the Veto The actual use of the veto varies by time, state, and issue. Some states, such as California and New York, often record high numbers of vetoes, whereas others, like Virginia, report few. On average, governors veto around 4 percent of the bills that reach their desks.[27] The variation among states reflects the tensions and conflicts that exist between the governor and the legislature. The largest number of vetoes typically occurs in states with divided party control of the executive and legislative branches.

Governors cast vetoes for many different reasons, including philosophical opposition to policies and budget items, or to make a powerful symbolic statement about an issue. Occasionally, the governor stands as the last line of defense against a flawed bill backed by the legislature because of powerful interest groups. It is not unknown for legislators to secretly ask the governor to veto a questionable bill they have just passed because the bill's contents, although undesirable, are politically popular.

Although the overall rate of veto utilization has not grown significantly, the proportion of successful legislative overrides has increased in the past two decades. This is an indication of the growing strength and assertiveness of state legislatures, the increase in conflict between the executive and legislative branches, and the prevalence of split-party government. Differences in party

package veto
The governor's formal power to veto a bill in its entirety.

line-item veto
The governor's formal power to veto separate items in a bill instead of the entire piece of proposed legislation.

pocket veto
The governor's power to withhold approval or disapproval of a bill after the legislature has adjourned for the session, thus vetoing the measure.

executive amendment
A type of veto used by the governor to reject a bill and also to recommend changes that would cause the governor to reconsider the bill's approval.

affiliation between the governor and the legislative majority probably provoke more vetoes than any other situation, especially when party ideology and platforms openly clash. New York Governor David Patterson vetoed some 6,700 budget items during a single week in 2010. Conversely, when mutual respect and cooperation prevail between the two branches, the governor rarely needs to threaten or actually use the veto. Most governors interact with the legislature throughout the bill-adoption process. Before rejecting a bill, the governor will request comments from key legislators, affected state agencies, and concerned interest groups. She may ask the attorney general for a legal opinion. And before actually vetoing proposed legislation, the governor usually provides advance notification to legislative leaders, along with a final opportunity to make amendments.

The veto can be a powerful offensive weapon to obtain a legislator's support for a different bill dear to the governor's heart, particularly near the end of the legislative session. The governor may, for instance, hold one bill hostage to a veto until the legislature enacts another bill that he favors. California governor Arnold Schwarzenegger did just that in 2008 when he began vetoing all bills sent to his desk until the legislature approved a budget bill; all told, he vetoed 35 percent of the bills sent to him that session.[28] Wisconsin's storied history includes the "Vanna White Veto" and the "Frankenstein Veto." The first, abolished in 1990, permitted the governor to delete individual letters and numbers to change a bill's content. The second, which took a stake to the heart in a 2008 voter referendum, allowed the governor to strike out some words and piece together others to alter a bill's content. For instance, Governor Jim Doyle (2003–2011) used the Frankenstein Veto to delete 752 words from a bill, which effectively shifted $427 million from transportation to education.[29]

Budgetary Power

The governor's budget effectively sets the legislative agenda at the beginning of each session. By framing the important policy issues and attaching price tags to them, the governor can determine the scope and direction of budgetary debates in the legislature and ensure that they reflect his overall philosophy on taxing and spending. All but a handful of governors have the authority to appoint (and remove) the budget director and to formulate and submit the executive budget to the legislature. In Mississippi and Texas, budget authority is shared with the legislature or with other elected executive branch officials. And in these two states, two budgets are prepared each year: one by the governor and one by a legislative budget board.

Because primary budgetary authority is normally housed in the office of the chief executive, the governor not only drives the budgetary process in the legislature but also enjoys a source of important leverage in the bureaucracy. The executive budget can be used to influence programs, spending, and other activities of state agencies. For example, uncooperative administrators may discover that their agency's slice of the budget pie is smaller than expected, whereas those who are attentive to the concerns of the governor may receive strong financial support. Rational, objective criteria may determine departmental budget allocations, but a subtle threat from the governor's office does wonders to instill a cooperative agency attitude.

The governor's budget requests are rarely, if ever, enacted exactly as put forward. Rather, they are usually argued and debated thoroughly in both houses of the legislature. A legislature dominated by the opposing political party is nearly certain to scorn and disparage the governor's budget. Ultimately, "the governor proposes, but the legislature disposes." In fact, no monies may be appropriated without formal action by the legislature. Which branch is most powerful budgetarily speaking: the governor or the legislature? Research is inconclusive.[30] (The budget process is discussed further in Chapter 8.)

During state budget crises, governors find themselves in an extremely vulnerable political position, particularly if they signed a "no new taxes" pledge when running for office. To balance the budget, a governor may cut spending, seek higher taxes, or both. None of these actions is likely to please many voters.

Reorganization Power

The phrase *reorganization power* refers to the governor's ability to create and abolish state agencies, departments, and other offices and to reallocate administrative responsibilities among them. Reorganizations are usually aimed at the upper levels of the bureaucracy to streamline the executive branch and thereby make it work more efficiently and effectively. The basic premise is that the governor, as chief manager of the bureaucracy, needs the authority to alter administrative structures and processes to meet changing political, economic, and citizen demands. For instance, serious and recurring problems in coordinating the delivery of social services among several existing state agencies may call for a consolidated human services department with expanded powers. A governor with strong reorganization power can bring about such a department without approval of the legislature.

Traditionally, legislatures have been responsible for organization of state government; and in the absence of a constitutional amendment to the contrary or a statutory grant of reorganization power to the governor, they still are. But today, more than twenty states specifically authorize their chief executive to reorganize the bureaucracy through **executive order**, through which the governor can make needed administrative changes when she deems it necessary. All governors are permitted through constitution, statute, or custom to issue directives to the executive branch in times of emergency, such as during natural disasters or civil unrest.

Administrative reorganization today takes place under the assumption that streamlined government improves bureaucratic performance and saves money by cutting down on duplication, waste, and inefficiency. Achieving a more efficient and user-friendly government is a top priority of governors. Initiatives to reinvent and reinvigorate government aim to make the bureaucracy more flexible and responsive by changing incentive systems for state employees, privatizing certain operations, reducing layers of bureaucracy, implementing e-government, and decentralizing human resource management agency activities.

executive order
A rule, regulation, or policy issued unilaterally by the governor to affect executive branch operations or activities.

Executive branch reorganization is widely practiced, but its actual benefits may be ephemeral. Reorganization typically achieves modest financial savings, if any at all, and it can produce delays, bureaucratic infighting, unexpected financial costs, and widespread confusion.[31] Such actions are not a cure for state fiscal ills. Executive branch reorganization, however, may help to provide a clearer focus on a particular problem, such as the needs of children, or help to contain administrative costs; it can eliminate unnecessary boards, commissions, and task forces; and it may serve political purposes, such as rationalizing the pain of employee layoffs.[32]

The Politics of Reorganization Reorganization is a politically charged process. Mere talk of it sounds alarms in the halls of the legislature, in the honeycombs of state office buildings, and in the offices of interest groups. Reorganization attempts usually spawn bitter controversy and conflict, both inside and outside state government, as assorted vested interests fight for favorite programs and organizational turf. Accordingly, reorganization proposals are frequently defeated or amended in the legislature, or abandoned by discouraged chief executives. One study of proposed state reorganizations discovered that almost 70 percent resulted in rejection of the plan either in part or in entirety.[33] Even when adopted, reorganizations may generate fierce opposition from entrenched interests in the bureaucracy and, in the final analysis, be judged a failure. In the memorable words of former Kansas governor Robert F. Bennett:

> In the abstract, [reorganization] is, without a doubt, one of the finest and one of the most palatable theories ever espoused by a modern-day politician. But in practice it becomes the loss of a job for your brother or your sister, your uncle or your aunt. It becomes the closing of an office on which you have learned to depend. So there in many instances may be more agony than anything else in this reorganization process.[34]

Most governors who have fought the battle for reorganization would concur. Perhaps such predictable opposition helps explain the rarity of far-reaching executive branch restructuring in the past several years and the preferences for small, incremental steps to reorganize and streamline state agencies.[35]

Staffing Power

The governor relies on staff to provide policy analyses and advice, serve as liaisons with the legislature, assist in managing the bureaucracy, and provide constituent services. Professional staff members are a significant component of the governor's team, composing a corps of political loyalists who help the governor cope with the multiple roles of the office. From the handful of political cronies and secretaries of several decades ago, the staff of the governor's office has grown in number, quality, and diversity. Today the average number of professional and clerical staff members is approximately sixty-two. In the larger, more highly populated states staff members number well over one hundred. The principal staff positions of the governor's office include those of chief of staff, legislative liaison, budget director, policy director, legal counsel, scheduler, press secretary, and intergovernmental coordinator.

A question of serious concern, especially in the states whose governors have large staffs, is whether too much power and influence are being placed in the hands of nonelected officials. Clearly, professional staff members have been highly influential in developing and promoting policies for the governor in some states, particularly in states where the governor lacks a coherent set of priorities and lets the staff have free rein. In other states, the chief executive is very much in charge, relying on staff primarily for drafting bills and providing technical information. Given their physical and intellectual proximity to the governor, staff members are in a highly advantageous position to influence their boss. In their role as the major funnel for policy information and advice, they can affect the governor's decisions by controlling the flow of information and individuals into his office.

The Relevance of the Formal Powers

In Table 7.3, the states are scored as to the strength of the governor's formal powers of office. As noted, governors have won stronger powers during the past three decades. But how helpful are the formal powers? Despite the major transformation of the governor's office, governors remain relatively weak because of the setting of state government. They must function in a highly complex and politically charged environment with formal authority that is quite circumscribed by the legislature, the courts, and constitutional and statutory law. Owing to the nature of our federal system, the national government effectively strips them of control over many policy and administrative concerns. Moreover, the business of state government is carried out in a fishbowl, open to regular scrutiny by the media, interest groups, talk-show hosts, bloggers, and other interested parties. Notwithstanding the continued constraints on the exercise of their authority, however, today's governors as a group are probably more effective than their predecessors were in carrying out their varied responsibilities. The formal powers of the office are substantially strengthened, and, in general, qualified people are serving as chief executives.

In theory, governors with strong formal powers, such as the governors in Alaska, New Jersey, and Massachusetts, should be more effective than their counterparts in Vermont and Rhode Island. In practice, that tends to be true—but not always. The potential for power and influence must not be confused with action. A governor with strong formal powers enjoys the capacity to lead and serve effectively but he may choose not to do so or, for various reasons, be unable to utilize the formal powers properly. Alternatively, a governor with weak formal powers can nonetheless be an effective, strong chief executive if she actively and skillfully applies the levers of power available in the constitution and in statutes.

TABLE 7.3	Relative Power of the Offices of Governor																		
2.5	2.6	2.7	2.8	2.9	3.0	3.1	3.2	3.3	3.4	3.5	3.6	3.7	3.8	3.9	4.0	4.1	4.2	4.3
VT	RI		AL	IN	NV	WY	CA	ID	AZ	DE	AR	NM	IL	CO	UT	AK		MA
			OK	MS	SC		GA	KS	HI	MT	CT		IA	ND		MD		
				NC	SD		NH	KY	LA	OR	FL		NE			NJ		
							TX		WI	ME			PA			NY		
							VA			MI			TN			WV		
										MN								
										MO								
										OH								
U.S. Average: 3.5										WA								

NOTE: The scale is measured from 2.5 to 4.3. The measures of power are SEP (separately elected executive branch officials), TP (tenure potential of governors), AP (governor's appointment in six functional areas: corrections, K-12 education, health, highways/transportation, public utilities regulation, and welfare), BP (budget power), VP (veto power), and PC (gubernatorial party control).

SOURCE: Adapted from Thad Beyle, http://www.unc.edu/~beyle/gubnewpwr.html (accessed May 15, 2009).

INFORMAL POWERS

No doubt a governor with strong formal powers has an advantage over one without them. But at least equally important for a successful governorship is the exploitation of the informal powers of the office. These powers carry authority and influence that are not directly attached to the governorship through statute or constitution but, rather, are associated with the human being who happens to occupy the governor's mansion. Governors who can master these powers can be highly effective, even in the absence of strong formal powers.

The informal powers help transform the capacity for action into effective action. They react in synergy with the formal powers to create a successful governorship. An incumbent chief executive in the strong governor state of Massachusetts will be hopelessly weak unless he also uses his personal assets in performing the multiple roles of the office. Alternatively, a chief executive in a weak governor state such as Oklahoma can be remarkably successful if she fully employs her informal powers to excel in persuading the state to adopt new ideas. The informal powers are not as easy to specify as the formal powers are. However, they generally include such tools of persuasion and leadership as popular support, prestige of the office, previous elected experience, public relations and media skills, negotiating and bargaining skills, pork barrel and patronage; and personal characteristics such as ambition, experience, and energy.

Tools of Persuasion and Leadership

Popular support refers to public identification with and support for the governor and her program. It may be measured in terms of the margin of victory in the primary and general elections or in terms of the results of public opinion polls. Governors with large victory margins and high levels of public support can lay claim to a popular mandate, channeling the pressures of public opinion to their legislative advantage.

Prestige of the office helps the governor open doors all over the world that would be closed to an ordinary citizen. National officials, big-city mayors, corporate executives, foreign officials, and even the president of the United States recognize that the governor sits at the pinnacle of political power in the state, and they treat him accordingly. Governors of California, New York, and Texas—the largest states—almost automatically assume national and even international prominence. Within the state, the governor typically makes use of the prestige of the office by inviting important individuals for an official audience, or perhaps to a special meal or celebration at the mansion.

Previous electoral experience is a valuable asset. Those who have made their way up the state's political ambition ladder by serving in the state legislature or as attorney general or lieutenant governor, have learned how to find their way through political briar patches and avoid tar pits.[36] They can also take advantage of political friends and allies they cultivated along the way. Arkansas Governor Mike Beebe used the experiences of twenty years of service in the state senate and four years as attorney general to get just about everything he asked for from the legislature.[37]

Other informal powers may be defined in terms of leadership skills. Public relations and media skills help the governor command the "big mike": the captive attention of the press, radio, and television. Any governor can call a press conference at a moment's notice and get a substantial turnout of the state's major media representatives, an advantage enjoyed by precious few legislators. Some chief executives appear regularly on television to explain their policy positions and initiatives to the people. Nearly all governors use forms of social media, such as blogs, Facebook, and Twitter, for the same purpose. Frequent public appearances, staged events, telephone calls, YouTube clips, and "public interest" advertisements delivered through the mass media are tools in the governors' media kits.

Effective governors, knowing instinctively that the media can be a strong ally in carrying out their programs and responsibilities, cultivate the press like a flower garden. But media relations are a two-way street. The media expect the governor to be honest, forthright, and available. If she instills respect and cooperation, the governor's media relations can be "of incalculable value in his contest for the public eye and ear."[38] After all, most or all of what the public knows about the governor comes from the media.

But popular support may erode when governors' actions alienate the voters. Nevada Governor Jim Gibbons's support dropped to just 28 percent within six months of taking office. Gibbons had made several poorly thought-out policy proposals (e.g., to sell water rights under state highways) and endured an FBI investigation into helping a friend secure lucrative military contracts.[39] Gibbons lost significant female support when he compared his wife (who had filed for divorce on grounds of infidelity) to an "enraged ferret."[40] Former South Carolina Governor Mark Sanford's lies and peccadilloes concerning a "foreign affair" with an Argentinian woman depressed his popular support below that of used car salesmen. (In a striking example of voters' willingness to forgive and forget, Sanford was recently elected to a vacant seat in the U.S. House of Representatives.)

Negotiating and bargaining skills are leadership tools that help the governor to convince legislators, administrators, interest groups, and national and local officials to accept his point of view on whatever issue is at hand. These skills are of tremendous assistance in building voting blocs in the legislature, particularly in divided-power settings where hyperpluralism—such as exists in national politics—must be avoided. They also help persuade new businesses to locate in the state and effectively represent a state's interests before the national government. Governor Beebe used his persuasive powers in Arkansas to accomplish far-reaching policy changes in tax reform.[41]

Pork barrel and patronage are aspects of the seamier side of state politics. Although they are utilized much less frequently now than they were before the civil service reforms of the first half of the twentieth century, governors are still known to promise jobs, contracts, new roads, special policy consideration, electoral assistance, and other favors to influential citizens, legislators, donors, and others in return for their support. All governors have discretionary funds with which to help a special friend who has constituents in need. And although patronage appointments are severely limited in most jurisdictions, a personal telephone call from the governor can open the door to an employment opportunity in state government.

Characteristics of a Successful Governor

The personal characteristics of an effective governor are nearly impossible to measure. Leadership, however, is generally agreed to be a very important quality. Leadership traits are difficult to define, but former Utah Governor Scott Matheson identified the best governors as "men and women who have the right combination of values for quality public service—the courage to stick to their convictions, even when in the minority, integrity by instinct, compassion by nature, leadership by perception, and the character to admit wrong and, when necessary, to accept defeat."[42]

A successful governor blends these qualities with the formal and informal powers of office in order to achieve her objectives. For example, following the political campaign to win the election, the governor must conduct a "never-ending campaign" to win the loyalty and support of her cabinet, state employees, the legislature, and the people, if she is to be effective.[43] Sixteen-hour days and 100-hour workweeks are not uncommon.

Realizing that not all things are possible, governors focus on a few critical issues at a time and marshal their formal and informal resources behind them. Eventually, the determined governor can wear down opponents. But more important, the successful governor exercises leadership by convincing the public that he is the person to pursue their vision and their interests. He prevails in the legislature by applying the pressure of public opinion and by building winning blocs of votes, and he leads the bureaucracy by personal example. Above all else, the successful governor must be persuasive.

In short, the formal powers of the office are important to any governor, but even strong formal powers do not guarantee success. As noted earlier, they must be combined with the informal powers to be effective. Whatever approach the governor chooses as chief executive, his individual skills are probably more important than formal powers.[44] Evidence of this conclusion is provided by governors who have won and held their state's top job and successfully pursued their policy agendas in the face of significant opposition. A notable example in Indiana is Governor Mitch Daniels, whose leadership led to dramatic improvements in the performance of state agencies, successful privatization of activities in highways and public welfare, and even the legislature's reluctant approval of the Hoosier state finally adopting Daylight Savings Time.[45]

LEAVING OFFICE

Upon leaving office, the vast majority of governors simply continue their public service in another venue. Four of the past five presidents were former governors. The experience of serving as a state's chief executive is widely believed to be excellent training for the top job in the nation. Others choose different paths to public service. Former California governor Jerry Brown was elected mayor of Oakland, then state attorney general, and in 2010, he once again successfully became governor. At least seven former governors are serving in the U.S. Senate.

Because state chief executives are held to higher standards today than ever before and are constantly under the microscope of the media and watchdog groups, illegal actions or conflicts of interest are likely to be found out and prosecuted. Recently, this has occurred with alarming frequency.

All states but one provide for the impeachment of the governor and other elected officials. (In Oregon, they are tried as regular criminal offenders.) Impeachment proceedings are usually initiated in the state house of representatives, and the impeachment trial is held in the senate. A two-thirds vote is necessary for conviction and removal of the governor in most states.

Of the more than 2,100 governors who have held office, only twenty-three have been either impeached and removed from office, or resigned under a cloud of legal problems. Besieged governors are much more likely to resign than face a lengthy public scourging through impeachment and legislative trial.

The most recent governors to leave office in disgrace were James McGreevey of New Jersey, Eliot Spitzer of New York, and Rod Blagojevich of Illinois.

McGreevey resigned after a homosexual affair with an appointed agency head was revealed. Spitzer stepped down after getting snared in a federal prostitution sting operation. His dramatic rise and fall as attorney general and then governor of the Empire State shocked people across the nation. The Blagojevich saga involved a host of federal criminal charges, including trying to sell the U.S. Senate seat that was vacated when Barack Obama assumed the presidency. It concluded with convictions on eighteen corruption counts and a sentence of fourteen years in prison.

But these fallen governors are the gubernatorial black sheep, political throwbacks who spawn media feeding frenzies. They deflect proper attention from the vast majority of hardworking, capable, and honest chief executives who typify the American state governorship today.

OTHER EXECUTIVE BRANCH OFFICIALS

The states elect more than 300 officials to key offices in their executive branches, not counting the fifty governors, ranging from attorneys general and treasurers to railroad commissioners. The four most important statewide offices are described here.

Lieutenant Governor

This office was originally created by the states for two major reasons: to provide for orderly succession to a governor who is unable to complete a term owing to death or other reasons, and to provide for an official to assume the responsibilities of the governor when the incumbent is temporarily incapacitated or out of the state. Five states do not see a need for the office: Arizona, Maine, New Hampshire, Oregon, and Wyoming. Tennessee and West Virginia designate the president of the senate as lieutenant governor. Other states attach little importance to the office, as indicated by a very low salary or the absence of official responsibilities. The historical reputation of the lieutenant governor was that of a corpse at a funeral—you are needed for the ceremony but no one is expecting much from you. When the sitting Florida lieutenant governor resigned in the wake of a gambling investigation in 2013, Governor Rick Scott simply shut down the office.

Lieutenant governors have risen to occupy the executive office because of deaths, impeachments, or resignations. In fourteen states today, the lieutenant governorship was a springboard to election to the state's top office. The lieutenant governorship in the majority of states has become a more visible, demanding, and responsible position. This trend is likely to continue as state governance grows increasingly complex and as additional states adopt the team election of governor and lieutenant governor. Many lieutenant governors hold important powers in the state senate, including serving as presiding officer, making bill assignments to committees, and casting tie-breaking votes in the senate. They are official members of the cabinet or of the governor's top advisory body in twenty-three states.[46] And virtually all lieutenant governors accept special assignments from the chief executive, some of which are quite visible and important. For example, Indiana's lieutenant governor acts as the state's commissioner of agriculture and discharges another forty-one statutory duties, and Utah's heads up the state's homeland security efforts, and several act as agency heads. In general, lieutenant governors' salaries, budget allocations, and staff have grown markedly.

A lingering problem is that eighteen states continue to elect the governor and lieutenant governor independently. This system can result in conflict and controversy when, for example, the chief executive is out of the state and the two officeholders are political rivals or members of opposing political parties. On several recent occasions, a lieutenant governor, assuming command, has proceeded to make judicial appointments, veto legislation, convene special sessions of the legislature, and take other actions at odds with the governor's wishes.

To avoid partisan bickering and politicking in the top two executive branch offices, twenty-five states now require team election. In addition to avoiding embarrassing factionalism, team election has the advantages of promoting party accountability in the executive branch, making continuity of policy more likely in the event of gubernatorial death or disability, and ensuring a measure of compatibility and trust between the two state leaders.

Attorney General

The attorney general (AG) is the state's chief legal counsel. The AG renders formal written opinions on legal issues such as the constitutionality of a statute, administrative rule, or regulation when requested to do so by the governor, agency heads, legislators, or other public officials. In most states, the attorney general's opinions have the force of law unless they are successfully challenged in the courtroom. Many high-profile AGs have successfully positioned themselves for the governor's mansion. In 2012, eight governors had served previously as AG.

The attorney general represents the state in litigation in which the state government is a legal party in federal and state courts. The AG can initiate civil and criminal proceedings in most states. More active today than ever before, attorneys general have recently contested national health care reform, various unfunded mandates, and administrative activities in controversial fields such as education reform and business regulation. Activist AGs have taken steps to protect consumers against cybercrime, Medicaid fraud, misleading advertisements by pharmaceutical companies, and other white-collar crimes, and portions of the "Obamacare" health care law.

AGs often work together through the National Association of Attorneys General to assert and protect the authority of the states in the federal system. Quite recently, some AGs have refused to defend state laws that they consider to be unconstitutional. For example, in 2013 Pennsylvania's AG, Kathleen Kane, declined to defend a ban on same-sex marriage. Predictably, AG activism has produced corporate and partisan backlash and intense interest and participation in AG elections.

Treasurer

The treasurer is the official trustee and manager of state funds and the state's chief financial officer. He or she collects revenues and makes disbursements of state monies. (The treasurer's signature is on the paycheck of all state employees and on citizens' state tax refunds.) Another important duty is to invest more than $3.0 trillion in state funds, including state employee pension monies. The failure to make profitable investments can cost the treasurer his job. West Virginia Treasurer A. James Manchin was impeached for losing $279 million in state funds through bad investments. Other treasurers have been criticized for leaving midterm for lucrative private-sector jobs (Connecticut, New Jersey), accepting gifts or kickbacks from financial firms (Massachusetts, Arkansas), and using their post to raise large sums of campaign money from investment companies.

Secretary of State

In the past, the duties of this office were rather perfunctory, entailing record-keeping and election responsibilities. But voting system reforms, e-government, and other changes have substantially elevated the position's responsibilities. Secretaries of state typically register corporations, securities, and trademarks, and also commission people to be notaries public. In their election-related responsibilities, they determine the ballot eligibility of political parties and candidates, verify initiative and referendum petitions, supply election ballots to local officials, file the expense papers and other campaign reports of candidates, and maintain voter registration rolls to deter voter fraud. The typical secretary of state also maintains state archives, files agency rules and regulations, publishes statutes and copies of the state constitution, and registers lobbyists. An indication of the office's rising importance is the secretaries of state's efforts to prevent voter fraud and protect citizen's privacy rights.[47]

THE CAPABILITY OF U.S. GOVERNORS

The states have reformed their executive branches to enhance the capability of the governor as chief executive and to make the office more efficient, effective, accountable, and responsive. In general, the reforms discussed in this chapter not only have extended the formal powers and capacity of the office but also have improved the contemporary governor's performance in his many demanding roles.

In addition, today's governors are better educated, more experienced in state government, and generally more competent than their predecessors. Unfortunate exceptions notwithstanding, their strength and policy influence impresses. They are better able to employ the informal powers of their office in meeting multiple and complex responsibilities. In sum, the governorships display more capability and vigor than perhaps ever before.

Unfortunately, severe national political divisions over such issues as abortion, gun control "Obamacare," Medicaid, gay marriage, and immigration threaten to conscript today's governors into bitter and dysfunctional partisan warfare. This is a very recent development that raises concern, and bears close attention.[48]

CHAPTER RECAP

- The American governorship was historically institutionally weak, with very limited formal powers.

- Today's governors are better qualified, educated, and prepared for the office than governors of the past. But winning the office is increasingly expensive.

- The duties of a governor include making policy, marshaling legislative action, administering the executive branch, serving as master of ceremonies, coordinating intergovernmental relations, promoting economic development, and leading their political party.

- Formal powers of the office, which have strengthened over time, are tenure, appointment, veto, budgeting, reorganizing the executive branch, and staffing.

- To be successful, a governor must master the informal powers of the office and integrate them with the formal powers. Among the informal sources of power are tools of leadership and persuasion, such as public relations skills and negotiations and bargaining skills.

- Governors who violate the law may be removed from office through impeachment.

- Other key executive branch officials are the attorney general, lieutenant governor, treasurer, and secretary of state.

Key Terms

pork barrel *(p. 151)*
formal powers *(p. 156)*
informal powers *(p. 156)*
plural executive *(p. 158)*

patronage *(p. 160)*
package veto *(p. 161)*
line-item veto *(p. 161)*
pocket veto *(p. 161)*

executive amendment *(p. 161)*
executive order *(p. 163)*

Internet Resources

Each state's governor has his or her own website, which can be located through the state homepage or from links at **www.nga.org**, the NGA's website. It features, among other items, governors' biographies, the latest State of the State addresses, and a subject index on various state and local issues, including welfare reform.

For information about the individual attorneys general, see **www.naag.org**.

State treasurers can be audited at **www.nast.org**, and lieutenant governors at **www.nlga.us**. Secretaries of state have a national organization as well: see **www.nass.org/**

8

Public Administration: Budgeting and Service Delivery

CHAPTER OUTLINE

- Public Employees in State and Local Government: Who They Are, What They Do
- Budgeting in State and Local Government
- Human Resource Policy in State and Local Government: From Patronage to Merit
- The Politics of Bureaucracy
- New Public Management
- The Quality of Public Administration

FOCUS QUESTIONS

1. What are the key trends that characterize public administration in state and local government?
2. Who are the key actors in state budgetary processes?
3. What are some of the public administration challenges facing state and local governments?
4. As state and local governments continue to evolve, what are the implications for the quality of state administration?

bureaucracy

The administrative branch of government, consisting of all executive offices and their workers.

Bureaucracy is a paradox. On the one hand, bureaucracy and public employees are sometimes portrayed as "the problem" with U.S. government at all levels. From the ponderous department of social services to the dilatory department of motor vehicles, to the county tax assessor's office, bureaucracy is depicted as all-powerful and out of control, inefficient, wasteful, and drowning in red tape. Public employees (bureaucrats) are often portrayed as insensitive and uncaring, yet stay in their jobs forever. Nearly everyone, from elected officials—presidents, governors, mayors, and legislators at all levels—to bloggers, talk-show commentators, and even product advertisers have stridently bashed the bureaucrats, blaming them for all imaginable sins of omission and commission (and all too often for their *own* personal shortcomings as well). The answer to the problem is no less than bureaucratic liposuction to "get the fat out" and surgery to "get the government off our backs."

On the other hand, bureaucracy can be beautiful.[1] Bureaucratic organization is indispensable to public administration. Legislative bodies and chief executives enact public policies through vague laws, relying on a variety of state and local agencies to deal with the specifics, such as operationally defining key components of the policies and putting the policies into effect. Some bureaucracies make our lives more difficult, but others help the quality of our lives by enforcing the laws and punishing the criminals, putting out the fires, repairing and maintaining the roads, and helping the poor and disadvantaged among us.

A theme of this chapter is that state agencies and local departments (the public administration) should not be treated as scapegoats for all the social, economic, and political maladies that befall society. Rather, public employees should be treated with respect—not rebukes. The quality and capacity of public administration have improved markedly in the country's states, municipalities, and counties in terms of the characteristics of employees and the efficiency, effectiveness, and professionalism with which they perform their duties. In fact, studies comparing public employees with cohort groups in the private sector find few important differences between them. Government workers are just as motivated, competent, and ethical as private-sector workers. Moreover, public employees tend to be more sensitive to other human beings, more highly educated than their counterparts in business and industry, and they are imbued with a "public service ethos" that motivates them[2] (see Table 8.1). State and local employees are responding to citizens' demands by providing a wider range of services in greater quantities to more people than ever before; and publicly provided services are perceived to be just as good as the same services provided by private firms.[3]

Contrary to popular opinion, government work does not consist of pay without labor. Public employees perform some of the most unpleasant and dangerous (but necessary) tasks imaginable, from taking abused or threatened children away from their parents to caring for the mentally ill and guarding prisoners who hurl feces at them. They expend considerable quantities of "emotional labor."[4] When governments fail to perform effectively, blame can occasionally be laid at the feet of public employees. But more often than not, good government workers are the scapegoats for vague and poorly designed statutes and policies, failed political and corporate leadership, insufficient resources, and other factors beyond the control of civil servants. It must also be recognized that occasional lapses in government administrative ethics often pale in comparison with frequent corporate corruption scandals, including recent ones involving defense contractors and mortgage banking and finance firms. An extensive analysis of published studies on characteristics of public- and private-sector employees debunks certain stereotypes.

TABLE 8.1	Comparing Public- and Private-Sector Employees	
CHARACTERISTIC	**ADVANTAGE**	
Motivation	Equal	
Work habits	Equal	
Competence	Equal	
Personal achievement	Private employees	
Concern for compensation	Private employees	
Educational achievement	Public employees	
Values of public service and civic duty	Public employees	
Ambition	Private employees	
Compassion and self-sacrifice	Public employees	
Ethics	Public employees	
Helping other people	Public employees	
Making a difference	Public employees	

SOURCE: Adapted from Alice H. Munnell et al., "Comparing Compensation: State-Local Versus Private Workers," Issue Brief, Center for State and Local Government Excellence, www.slge.org (April 21, 2010); Mary K. Feeney, "Sector Perceptions Among State-Level Public Managers," *Journal of Public Administration Research and Theory* 18, no. 3 (2008): 465–94; Richard W. Stackman, Patrick E. Connor, and Boris W. Becker, "Sectoral Ethos: An Investigation of the Personal Values Systems of Female and Male Managers In the Public and Private Sectors," *Journal of Public Administration Research and Theory* 16 (October 2006): 577–97; Norman Baldwin, "Public Versus Private Employees: Debunking Stereotypes," *Review of Public Personnel Administration 11* (Fall 1990–Spring 1991): 1–27; and Gene A. Brewer, Sally Coleman Selden, and Rex L. Facer II, "Individual Conceptions of Public Service Motivation," *Public Administration Review* 60 (May/June 2000): 254–64.

PUBLIC EMPLOYEES IN STATE AND LOCAL GOVERNMENT: WHO THEY ARE, WHAT THEY DO

More than 19.8 million employees work for states and localities. Until the onslaught of the Great Recession in 2008, their numbers had grown steadily since accurate counts were first compiled in 1929. Government work tends to be labor intensive. As a result of this fact and of inflation, personnel expenditures for states and localities have risen along with the number of workers. Total payroll costs for state and local governments exceed $278 million per month.[5]

Of course, the number of employees varies greatly among jurisdictions. Generally speaking, states and localities with large populations and high levels of per capita income provide more services and thus employ larger numbers of workers than do smaller, less affluent jurisdictions. Employment figures are further influenced by the distribution of functions and service responsibilities between states and their local jurisdictions. A state government may have hundreds of agencies, boards, and commissions. A municipality or county may have dozens of departments, boards, and commissions.

Public Management and Private Management: What Are the Distinctions?		TABLE 8.2
	PUBLIC MANAGEMENT	**PRIVATE MANAGEMENT**
CONSTRAINTS	Politics, public opinion, resources.	Markets, competitors, resources.
CLIENTS	Citizens, legislatures, chief executives, interest groups.	Customers who purchase products or services.
ACCOUNTABILITY	To citizens and elected and appointed officials.	To customers, boards of directors, and shareholders.
PURPOSE	To serve the public interest and the common good.	To make profits and grow the organization.

SOURCE: © Cengage Learning

Such figures do not adequately account for the real people who work for states, cities, counties, towns, townships, and school districts. These include the police officer on patrol, the welfare worker finding a foster home for an abandoned child, the eleventh-grade English teacher, the state trooper, and even your professor of state and local government (if you attend a public institution). Their tasks are as diverse as their titles: sanitation engineer, animal control officer, heavy-equipment operator, planner, epidemiologist, and so on. The diversity of state and local government work rivals that of the private sector, although there are important distinctions in the nature of the work (see Table 8.2). From the sewer-maintenance worker to the director of human services, all are public servants—often identified as bureaucrats. Approximately one of every six working Americans is employed by government at some level. If bureaucrats are the enemy, we have met them and they are us. Public- and private-sector management differ in terms of constraints, clients, accountability, and purpose.

BUDGETING IN STATE AND LOCAL GOVERNMENT

The budget is the very lifeblood of government and public administration. Without a budgetary appropriation, state and local organizations would cease to exist. The monies are allocated by legislative bodies, but the politics of the budgetary process involves all the familiar political and bureaucratic players: chief executives, interest groups, other government employees, the general public, firms and industries, and, of course, the recipients of legislative appropriations—the state highway department, the municipal police department, the county sanitation office, and so on. In a phrase, budget making is a highly charged political poker game with enormous stakes. To understand public administration, one must have a grasp of budgetary politics.

An often-quoted definition of politics is Harold Lasswell's famous line: "Politics is who gets what, when, where, and how."[6] The budget document provides hard dollars-and-cents data in answer to this question. It is a political manifesto—the most important one you will find in state and local government. The budget is a policy statement of what government intends to do (or not do), detailing the amount of the taxpayers' resources that will be dedicated to each program and activity. The outcomes of the budgetary process represent the results of a zero-sum game—for every winner there is a loser—because public resources are limited. An extra million dollars for corrections can mean that much less for higher education.

The Budget Cycle

The process of governmental budgeting is best understood as a cycle with overlapping stages, five of which can be identified: preparation, formulation, adoption, execution, and audit (see Figure 8.1). Several stages are simultaneously taking place at any given time. For example, while the 2014 budget is being executed and revenues and expenditures are being monitored to guard against an operating deficit, the governor and the legislature are developing the 2015 budget. Meanwhile, the 2013 budget is being audited to ensure that monies were properly spent and otherwise accounted for.

FIGURE 8.1   The Budget Process

PREPARATION	FORMULATION	ADOPTION	EXECUTION
Expression of citizen and group interests	Executive budget assembled	Passed by legislative body	Transfers of funds to government units
Revenue estimates by budget office	Public hearings	Signed by chief executive	Funds expended
Spending requests by agencies and departments	Legislative budget review		Financial management
	Legislative debate		Revenue or expenditure adjustments

AUDIT
Review and evaluation of financial records, program performance, operations, and management

SOURCE: © Cengage Learning

Budgets are normally based on a *fiscal* (financial) *year* rather than on the calendar year. Fiscal years for all but four states run from July 1 through June 30 (the exceptions are Alabama, Michigan, New York, and Texas). Twenty-four states, including Montana, Indiana, and Kentucky, have biennial (two-year) budget cycles. Most local governments' fiscal years also extend from July 1 to June 30.

The initial phase of the budget cycle involves demands for slices of the budget pie and estimates of available revenues for the next fiscal year. State and local agency heads join the chorus of interest groups and program beneficiaries seeking additional funding (with no concern for "profits," agencies have little incentive to ask for less funding instead of more). Large state agencies are typically represented by their own lobbyists, or "public information specialists." State and local financial administrators and analysts develop estimates of revenues based on past tax receipts and expected economic conditions, communicating them to their respective state agencies or municipal departments, which then develop their individual spending requests for the fiscal year. Such spending requests may be constrained by legislative and executive "guidance," such as agency or program dollar ceilings, program priorities, or performance-based budgeting considerations.

Formulation, or initial development, of the budget document is the responsibility of the chief executive in most states and localities. Exceptions include states in which the balance of power rests with the legislature (such as Arkansas, Mississippi, and South Carolina) and local governments in which budgeting is dominated by a council or commission. The executive budget of the governor or mayor is submitted to the appropriate legislative body for debate, review, and modification. The lengthy review process that follows allows agencies, departments, interest groups, citizens, and other stakeholders to express their points of view. Finally, sometimes following all-nighters as deadlines loom, the legislative body enacts the amended budget.[7]

The state legislature or city council ensures that the final document balances revenues with expenditures. Balanced-budget requirements are contained in the constitutions or statutes of forty-eight states and operate through precedent in Vermont and Indiana. These requirements usually apply to local governments as well. Balanced-budget requirements force state and local governments to weigh projected expenditures against expected revenues, but they may be circumvented to some extent. One popular device is the "off-budget," in which costs and revenues for public enterprises such as government corporations or for special projects are exempt from central review and are not included in budget documents and figures. Another accounting tactic is to borrow money from public employee pension funds or next year's anticipated revenues to cover the current year's deficit. Perhaps the simplest way to balance a problematic budget is to "assume" extra revenues or savings (fiscal realism may take a back seat to political necessity). Before the budget bill becomes law, the chief executive must sign it. Last-minute executive-legislative interactions may be needed to stave off executive vetoes or to override them. Once the chief executive's signature is on the document, the budget goes into effect as law, and the execution phase begins.

During budget execution, monies from the state or local general fund are periodically allocated to agencies and departments to meet payrolls, purchase goods and materials, help average citizens solve problems ranging from a rabid raccoon in the chimney to a car-swallowing sinkhole in the backyard, and generally to try to achieve program goals. If revenues have been overestimated, the chief executive or legislative body must make adjustments to keep the budget in the black. In a crisis, the governor may call the legislature into special session, or impose a variety of money-saving measures, including hiring and travel freezes, layoffs, furloughs, and across-the-board spending reductions. Rainy day funds are tapped as well (see Chapter 12). Local governments implement similar strategies, including spending reductions, tax or fee hikes, short-term borrowing, and delayed or canceled capital expenditures. Eventually, real pain is experienced by many organizations and individuals.

The final portion of the budget cycle involves several types of audits, each with a different objective. Fiscal audits seek to verify that expenditure records are accurate and that financial transactions have been made in accordance with the law. Performance audits examine agency or department activities in relation to goals, objectives, and outcomes. Operational and management audits review how specific programs are carried out and assess administrators' performance. A performance measurement and management trend has firm traction in state and local government today, reflecting these governments' genuine determination to improve service provision to citizens.[8]

The Actors in Budgeting

Four main actors participate in the budget process: interest groups, agencies, the chief executive, and the legislative body. Interest groups organize testimony at budget hearings and pressure the other three actors to pursue favored policies and programs. The role of the agency or department is to defend the base—the amount of the last fiscal year's appropriation—and to advocate spending for new or expanded programs. Agency and department heads are professionals who believe in the value of their organization and its programs, but they often find themselves playing Byzantine games to get the appropriations they want, as set forth in Table 8.3.

Political scientist Aaron Wildavsky described the basic quandary of agency and departmental representatives as follows:

> Life would be simple if they could just estimate the costs of their ever-expanding needs and submit the total as their request. But if they ask for amounts much larger than the appropriating bodies believe is reasonable, their credibility will suffer a drastic decline. . . . So the first decision rule for agencies is: do not come in too high. Yet the agencies must also not come in too low, for the assumption is that if the agency advocates do not ask for funds they do not need them.[9]

What agency heads usually do is carefully evaluate the fiscal-political environment. They take into consideration the previous year's events, current and estimated agency expenditures, the composition and inclinations of the

The Games Spenders Play		TABLE 8.3
MASSAGE THE CONSTITUENCY	Locate, cultivate, and utilize clientele groups to further the organization's objectives. Encourage them to offer committee testimony and contact legislative members on your behalf.	
ALWAYS ASK FOR MORE	If your agency or department doesn't claim its share of new revenues, someone else will. The more you seek, the more you will receive.	
WHINING FOR DOLLARS	Keep whining to your boss about the need for more money until his annoyance level is so high that he coughs it up to shut you up.	
SPEND ALL APPROPRIATED FUNDS BEFORE THE FISCAL YEAR EXPIRES	An end-of-year surplus indicates that the elected officials were too generous with you this year; they will cut your appropriation next time.	
CONCEAL NEW PROGRAMS BEHIND EXISTING ONES	Incrementalism means that existing program commitments are likely to receive cursory review, even if an expansion in the margin is substantial. An announced new program will undergo comprehensive examination. Related to this game is *camel's nose under the tent*, in which low program start-up costs are followed by ballooning expenses down the road.	
HERE'S A KNIFE; CUT OUT MY HEART WHILE YOU'RE AT IT	When told that you must cut your budget, place the most popular programs on the chopping block. Rely on your constituency to organize vigorous opposition. Alternatively, state that all your activities are critically important so the elected officials will have to decide what to cut (and answer for it to voters).	
A ROSE BY ANY OTHER NAME	Conceal unpopular or controversial programs within other program activities. And give them appealing names (for instance, call a sex education class "Teaching Family Values").	
LET'S STUDY IT FIRST (AND MAYBE YOU WON'T BE RE-ELECTED)	When told to cut or eliminate a program, argue that the consequences would be devastating and should be carefully studied before action is taken.	
SMOKE AND MIRRORS	Support your requests for budget increases with voluminous data and testimony. The data need not be especially persuasive or even factual, just overwhelming. Management writer James H. Boren calls this "bloatating" and "trashifying."	
A PIG IN A POKE	Place an unneeded item in your budget request so you can gracefully give it up while protecting more important items.	
END RUN	If the chief executive initiates a budget cut, scurry quickly to friends in the legislature.	
EVERY VEIN IS AN ARTERY	Claim that any program cut would so completely undermine effectiveness that the entire program would have to be abandoned.	

SOURCE: © Cengage Learning

legislature, policy statements by the chief executive, the strengths of clientele groups, and other factors. Then they put forward a figure somewhat larger than they expect to get. The following are tactics used by state and local officials to maximize their share of the budget during negotiations and hearings with governors, local chief executives, and the legislative body.

The chief executive has a much different role in the budget process. In addition to tailoring the budget to his program priorities as closely as possible, he acts as an economizer. Individual departmental requests must be reconciled, which means that they must be cut, since the sum total of requests will greatly exceed estimated revenues. Of course, an experienced governor or mayor recognizes the games played by administrators; she knows that budget requests are likely to be inflated in anticipation of cuts. In fact, various studies on state and local budgeting indicate that the single most influential participant is the chief executive.[10] Not surprisingly, astute administrators devote time and other resources to cultivating the chief executive's support for their agency's or department's activities.

The role of the legislative body in the initial stage of the budget cycle is essentially to respond to and modify the initiatives of the chief executive. The governor, mayor, or city manager proposes, and the legislature or council reacts. Later in the budget cycle, the legislative body performs another important function through its review of agency and department spending and its response to constituents' complaints.

What about the taxpayers? The traditional budgeting approach is essentially to exclude them from the process. But more and more states and localities offer budget transparency, encouraging citizens to attend and speak at budget hearings and focus groups or to participate in Web-based applications. Web access to revenues, expenditures, and budget proposals is increasingly being offered by state and local governments.[11] Unfortunately, few taxpayers avail themselves of the opportunity.

Pervasive Incrementalism

In a perfect world, budgeting would be a purely rational enterprise. Objectives would be identified, stated clearly, and prioritized; alternative means for accomplishing them would be considered; revenue and expenditure decisions would be coordinated within the context of a balanced budget.

That is how budgeting *should* be done. But state and local officials have to allocate huge sums of money each year in a budgetary environment where objectives are unclear or controversial and often conflict with one another. It is nearly impossible to prioritize the hundreds or thousands of policy items on the agenda. Financial resources, time, and the capacity of the human brain are severely stretched.

To cope with such complexity and minimize political conflict over scarce resources, decision makers "muddle through."[12] They simplify budget decision making by adopting decision rules. For example, instead of searching for the optimal means for addressing a public policy problem, they search only until they find a feasible solution. As a result, they sacrifice comprehensive analysis and rationality for **incrementalism** in which small adjustments (usually an increase) are made to the nature and funding base of existing programs. Thus the policy commitments and spending levels of ongoing programs are usually accepted as a given—they become the base for next year's funding. Decisions are made on a very small proportion of the total budget: the increments from one fiscal year to the next. If the budget has to be cut, as most were during the Great Recession years (2009–2012), it is done decrementally; small percentage adjustments are subtracted from the base. In this way, political conflict over values and objectives is held to a minimum.

The hallmarks of incremental budgeting are consistency and continuity: the future becomes an extension of the present, which is itself a continuation of the past. Long-range commitments tend to be made, then honored indefinitely. This is not to say that state and local budgeting is a simple affair. On the contrary: It is as tangled and intricate as the webs of a thousand spiders on methamphetamines.

incrementalism
A decision-making approach in the budgetary process in which the previous year's expenditures are used as a base for the current year's budget figures.

Types of Budgets

A budget document can be laid out in various ways, depending on the purposes one has in mind: control, management, and planning. Historically, *control*, or fiscal accountability, has been the primary purpose of budgeting, incrementalism the dominant process, and the line-item budget the standard document.

Control Through Line-Item Budgets The **line-item budget** facilitates control by specifying the amount of funds each agency or department receives and monitoring how those funds are spent. Each dollar can be accounted for with the line-item budget—which lists every object of expenditure, from police uniforms to toilet paper—on an individual line in the budget document. Line-item budgets show where the money goes, but they do not tell us how effectively the money was spent.

line-item budget
A budget that lists detailed expenditure items such as personal computers and paper, with no attention to the goals or objectives of spending.

Budgeting for Performance Budget formats that are intended to help budget makers move beyond the narrow constraints of line items and incrementalism toward more rational and flexible decision-making techniques that help attain program results are known as performance budgets. Chief executives and agency officials seek to ensure that priorities set out in the budget are carried out. Formal program and policy evaluations are necessary to ensure program performance and public accountability.

In **performance budgeting**, the major emphasis is on services provided and program results. The idea is to focus attention on how effectively goals are achieved rather than on what is spent or acquired. Whereas line-item budgets are input oriented, performance budgets are output and outcome oriented. Government managers decide what they want to accomplish and measure these accomplishments versus expenditures. For example, the performance of a fire department can be evaluated by response times to emergency calls and by how

performance budgeting
Budgeting that is organized to account for the outcomes of government programs.

quickly a fire is contained once firefighters arrive at the scene. Police departments can track crime rates, arrests, clearance rates, and citizen survey results. By focusing on program objectives and work performance, performance budgets can assist managers, elected officials, and citizens in improving the quality of government operations.[13]

Capital Budgets The budget formats described above apply to operating budgets whose funds are depleted within a year. Capital outlays are made over a longer period of time and are composed of big-ticket purchases such as hospitals, university buildings, libraries, new bridges, and new information systems. They represent one-time, nonrecurring expenditures that call for special funding procedures, or a **capital budget**. Because such items cannot be paid for within a single fiscal year, governments borrow the required funds, just as most individuals do when buying a house or an expensive automobile. The debt, with interest, is paid back in accordance with a predetermined schedule.

Capital projects are funded through the sale of general obligation or revenue bonds. *Bonds* are certificates of debt sold by a government to a purchaser, who eventually recovers the initial price of the bond plus interest. *General obligation bonds* are paid off with a jurisdiction's regular revenues (from taxes and other sources). In this instance, the "full faith and credit" of the government is pledged as security. *Revenue bonds* are usually paid off with user fees collected from use of the new facility (for example, a parking garage, auditorium, or toll road). Payments for both types of bonds are scheduled over a period of time that usually ranges from five to twenty years. The costs of operating a new facility, such as a school or sports arena, are met through the regular operating budget and/or user fees.

capital budget
A budget that plans large expenditures for long-term investments, such as buildings and bridges.

HUMAN RESOURCE POLICY IN STATE AND LOCAL GOVERNMENT: FROM PATRONAGE TO MERIT

Whether the tasks of state and local government are popular (fighting crime, educating children) or unpopular (imposing and collecting taxes and fees), serious (saving a helpless infant from an abusive parent), or mundane (maintaining the grass on municipal sports fields), they are usually performed by public employees. The 5.0 million state workers and 14.3 million city, county, and town employees are the critical links between public policy decisions and how those policies are implemented. Agencies and departments must be organized to solve problems and deliver services effectively, efficiently, and reliably. Human resource (personnel) rules and procedures must determine how public employees are recruited, hired, paid, and fired.

In the nation's first decades, public employees came mainly from the educated and wealthy upper class and, in theory, were hired on the basis of fitness for office. During the presidency of Andrew Jackson (1829–1837), who wanted to open up national government jobs to all segments of white, male society, the *patronage* system was adopted to fill many positions. Hiring could depend on party affiliation and other political alliances rather than on job-related qualifications.

Patronage became entrenched in many states and localities where jobs were awarded almost entirely on grounds of partisan politics, personal friendships, family ties, or financial contributions. This system made appointees accountable to the governor, mayor, or whoever appointed them, but it did nothing to ensure honesty and competence. By the beginning of the Civil War, the spoils system permeated U.S. governments at all levels. The quality of public service plummeted.

The Merit System

The concept of the **merit system** is usually associated with the national campaign for passage of the federal Pendleton Act of 1883. Two key factors led to its realization. First, Anglo-Saxon Protestants were losing political power to urban political machines dominated by "new" Americans of Catholic faith and Irish, Italian, and Polish descent. Second, scandals rocked the administration of President Ulysses S. Grant, and spawned a public backlash that peaked with the assassination of President James Garfield in 1881 by an insane attorney seeking a political appointment. The Pendleton Act set up an independent, bipartisan *civil service* commission to make objective, merit-based selections for federal job openings.

The *merit principle* was to determine all personnel-related decisions. Those individuals best qualified would receive a job or a promotion based on their knowledge, skill, and abilities. Far from perfect, the merit system was thoroughly overhauled by the Civil Service Reform Act of 1978. As a result of the Pendleton Act, the negative effects of patronage politics in national selection practices were mostly eliminated. **Neutral competence** became the primary criterion for obtaining a job, as public servants were expected to perform their work competently and in a politically neutral manner.

New York was the first state to enact a merit system, in 1883, and Massachusetts followed in 1884. The first municipal merit system was established in Albany, New York, in 1884; a year later, Cook County, Illinois, became the first county with a merit system. (Ironically, both Albany and Cook County, in Chicago, were later consumed once again by machine politics and spoils-ridden urban governance, a condition not entirely eradicated even today.[14])

Many states and numerous local governments followed with merit-based civil service systems of their own. Congressional passage of the 1939 amendments to the Social Security Act of 1935 gave additional impetus to such systems. This legislation obligated the states to set up merit systems for employees in social service and employment security agencies and departments that were at least partly funded by national grants-in-aid under the Social Security Act. Thus, all states are now required to establish a merit system for a sizable segment (around 20 percent) of their workforce; most of them have in fact

merit system

The organization of government personnel providing for hiring and promotion on the basis of knowledge, skills, and abilities rather than patronage or other influences.

neutral competence

The concept that public employees should perform their duties competently and without regard for political considerations.

developed comprehensive systems that encompass almost all state employees. Common elements of these modern personnel systems include recruitment, selection, and promotion according to knowledge, skills, and ability; regular performance appraisals; and employee incentive systems.

Some merit systems work better than others. In a handful of states and localities, they are mere formalities—lifeless skeletons around which a shadowy world of patronage, spoils, favoritism, and incompetence flourishes.[15] Such conditions came to public attention when terrorists boarded and hijacked two commercial aircraft at Boston's Logan Airport on September 11, 2001. For years, gubernatorial patronage appointees with little or no experience in security or law enforcement had run Logan's security operations.[16]

Rigid personnel rules, a lack of training programs, and inadequate salaries continue to plague some jurisdictions. Political control over merit-system employees is limited nearly everywhere because most cannot be fired without great difficulty. Georgia and Florida are exceptions: in these states, new employees are hired on contracts and not granted tenure in the job.

State and Local Advances

On balance, however, state and local personnel systems have been greatly improved, and the process continues. Nonnational governments are experimenting with recruitment and testing innovations, pay-for-performance plans and other incentive systems, participative management innovations, new performance-appraisal methods, Web-based training programs, and many other concepts. Virtually every state has reformed its civil service in some way.[17] General public dissatisfaction with government at all levels, combined with increasing needs for government to become more sophisticated and responsive to its clients, means that efforts to "reinvent" human resource management are certain to continue.

These reforms are designed to make the executive branch leaner and more responsive to the chief executive and more transparent to citizens; to improve service efficiency and effectiveness; to shift the overarching focus to outputs and outcomes instead of inputs and processes; and, through decentralization of authority, to enhance flexibility for chief executives, agency heads, city managers, and other officials. Reformers remain dedicated to the principle of protecting the civil service from unnecessary and gratuitous interference by politicians with patronage considerations in mind. But they also want to increase the capacity of government executives to manage programs and people in their organizations and to achieve desired results.

Merit-System Controversies

As we shall see, state and local governments have been leaders in addressing controversial questions that involve merit-system principles and practices, including representative bureaucracy, sexual harassment, and public employee collective bargaining.

Representative Bureaucracy The concept of representative bureaucracy—which is related to the concept of affirmative action—suggests that the structure of government employment should reflect major sexual, racial, socioeconomic, religious, geographic, and related components in society. The assumptions behind this idea are that (1) bureaucrats have discretion; (2) a workforce representative of the values, points of view, and interests of the people it governs will be responsive to their special problems and concerns; and (3) a representative bureaucracy provides strong symbolic evidence of a government "of the people, by the people, and for the people." In some situations representative bureaucracy has "active" implications. Empirical research indicates that although organizational socialization and professionalism are stronger predictors of public policy preferences than racial, sexual, and other personal characteristics, women and minority public workers sometimes use their discretion to improve the treatment of, and outcomes for, minority clients.[18] For instance, female employees tend to be more active in representing female child support recipients than male employees.[19] Blacks are more likely to perceive police interactions as legitimate when African American officers are present.[20] Black and white police officers tend to treat victims and suspects differently according to race.[21] And black local government administrators tend to be more supportive of governmental decisions that specifically serve African American communities.[22] The symbolic aspects of representative bureaucracy are important. A government that demonstrates the possibility of social and occupational mobility for all sorts of people gains legitimacy in the eyes of its citizens and expands the diversity of views taken into account in bureaucratic decisions.

A controversial question is how to *achieve* a representative workforce, particularly at the upper levels of government organizations, without sacrificing the merit principle. *Equal employment opportunity (EEO)*—the policy of prohibiting employment practices that discriminate for reasons of race, sex, color, religion, age, disability, or other factors not related to the job—is mandated by federal law. This policy has been the law for well over a century; yet progress was very slow until the past three decades or so, when **affirmative action** policies were adopted throughout government.

Affirmative action recognizes that equal opportunity has not been sufficient because employment discrimination persists. Governments must take proactive steps to hire and retain those categories of workers legally defined as "protected classes" who have suffered discrimination in the past. These measures may be adopted voluntarily, but they are required under certain conditions specified by the U.S. Equal Employment Opportunity Commission (EEOC), the regulatory body created to enforce EEO, and, in some instances, by the courts. These measures include goals, timetables, and other preferential selection and promotion devices intended to make the workforces of public and private organizations more representative of the racial, sexual, and other characteristics of the available labor pool.

Under affirmative action, the absence of overt discrimination in employment may not be sufficient; organizations can implement preferential hiring and promotion schemes to redress existing imbalances. The legitimacy of

affirmative action

Special efforts to recruit, hire, and promote members of disadvantaged groups to eliminate the effects of past discrimination.

affirmative action policies imposed on employers by the EEOC has been seriously questioned in a series of U.S. Supreme Court decisions during the past two decades and by state legislative actions and referendums.

Obviously, affirmative action is highly controversial. Establishing specific numerical goals and timetables for hiring and promoting minorities does not necessarily correspond with selection or promotion of the best person for the job. In other words, affirmative action appears to conflict with the merit principle. It has also alienated many white males, who feel that they have become victims of "reverse discrimination."

Legal clashes among the federal courts, the Congress, and the states and localities continue but have not produced a coherent interpretation of affirmative action's legal standing. Two examples illustrate the complexity of issues surrounding affirmative action policy. The first concerns the 1996 passage in California of Proposition 209, which amended the state constitution by prohibiting race and gender consideration in contracting decisions and in hiring for state and local jobs. The initiative was approved by nearly 55 percent of the voters. Soon, however, a federal judge blocked enforcement on the grounds that "Prop 209" was discriminatory and therefore unconstitutional. Judges for the Ninth Circuit Court of Appeals reinstated the judgment, an action that was upheld by the U.S. Supreme Court. Subsequently, Washington voters approved an antidiscrimination initiative, and Governor Jeb Bush of Florida eliminated racial preferences in his state through an executive order.

The second example of confusion and complexity involves a pair of U.S. Supreme Court rulings in 2003 on admissions procedures at the University of Michigan.[23] The Court invalidated a point system used to select undergraduates that awarded additional points for minority status, but it upheld the law school's consideration of race as a nonqualified "plus" in its admissions decisions. In 2006, Michigan voters approved a constitutional amendment banning affirmative action in college admissions. When a federal appeals court struck down the amendment in 2011, a return engagement of the U.S. Supreme Court in higher education seemed a strong possibility.[24] It occurred on June 24, 2013, when the Court rejected a race-conscious admissions policy for the University of Texas as being insufficiently "narrowly tailored."[25] Despite such confusion and ugly political invective, substantial progress toward representative bureaucracy has been made, especially in recruiting and hiring protected-class individuals for entry-level positions. Indeed, African Americans are *over*represented in relation to their presence in the workforce in most state governments. Latinos, however, have experienced much less success in securing public jobs.[26] Granted, some minorities and women continue to bump against a "glass ceiling" as they try to penetrate the upper levels of state and local agencies, as well as "glass walls" that restrict their access to certain occupations, agencies, or departments.[27] But substantial progress is being seen even with respect to these final barriers to representative bureaucracy. For example, the number of female, African American, and Latino city managers in state and local government has grown dramatically in recent years. Female and minority employment at all levels of state and local government exceeds that in the private sector.[28]

Indeed, state and local governments today widely recognize the need to recruit, motivate, and manage a work force that reflects an increasingly diverse general population. When employees working together differ in terms of gender, color, religion, customs, and other characteristics, misunderstandings and miscommunications are inevitable. The astute public manager helps employees recognize and accept such differences, leveraging diverse experiences, perspectives, and knowledge of the workforce to maintain and in many instances even raise levels of organizational productivity and effectiveness.[29]

Sexual Harassment Sexual harassment has long been a problem in public and private employment, but it has only recently gained widespread recognition. Sexual harassment can consist of various behaviors: unwanted touching or other physical contact of a sexual nature, implicit or overt sexual propositions, or (in one of its worst forms) extortion of a subordinate by a supervisor who demands sexual favors in return for a promotion or a raise. A "hostile working environment" that pervasively discriminates on the basis of gender also constitutes sexual harassment.[30] Examples in this category include repeated—and unwelcome—leering, sexual joking or teasing, and lewd calendars or photographs at the workplace. Isolated incidents of sexual teasing or innuendo do not constitute sexual harassment.[31] Sexual harassment is illegal according to federal and state law, and it is a form of punishable employee misconduct under civil service rules. It is also subject to prosecution in the courts.

Sexual harassment is common in the workplace: surveys of women reveal that at least half of the respondents report being a victim.[32] Approximately 15 percent of men have experienced sexual harassment. Such behavior subverts the merit principle when personnel decisions such as hiring or promotion are influenced by illegal or discriminatory considerations of a sexual nature, or when an employee cannot perform his or her assigned duties because of sexual harassment. Sexual harassment can exact a significant price on organizational productivity, not to mention the costs of monetary settlements with victims. Unfortunately for the recipient of unwanted sexual attention, there are seldom any witnesses. The matter becomes one person's word against another's. And when one of the parties is the supervisor of the second party, a formal complaint may be decided in favor of the boss.

Much of the official activity aimed at stopping sexual harassment has been concentrated in the states, with local governments following suit. In 1979, Michigan was the first to adopt a sexual harassment policy; since then, nearly every other state has adopted a statewide policy through legislation or executive order. States offer employee-training programs that help workers and supervisors identify acts of sexual harassment, establish procedures for effectively addressing it, and enforce prompt, appropriate disciplinary action against offenders.

The consequences of sexual harassment go well beyond the personal discomfort, stress, or injury suffered by victims. The problem also results in significant financial costs to organizations whose employees lose productive work time. Such misconduct is unacceptable today, particularly in a national workforce that is more than 50 percent female.

Unions and Collective Bargaining Nearly always controversial in government, *public-employee unions* present a potentially serious threat to the merit principle. They usually insist on seniority as the primary criterion in personnel decisions, often seek to effect changes in merit-system rules and procedures that benefit their membership, and regularly challenge management authority. Moreover, unions aggressively seek higher pay and benefits, threatening to drive up the costs of government and, in some instances, prompting tax increases.

Until the 1960s, unionization was largely a private-sector phenomenon. Federal legislation protected the rights of workers in industry to organize and engage in **collective bargaining** with their employers over wages, benefits, and working conditions. Workers then organized in record numbers. By the late 1950s, however, private-sector union growth began to decline for a number of reasons, including corporate opposition, the shift in the U.S. economy from manufacturing to services, and the globalization of labor markets.

Unionization in state and local government developed and flourished in the 1960s and 1970s, some thirty years after the heyday of private-sector unions, more than tripling during the 1960s alone. Why the sudden growth? In retrospect, several reasons are apparent.

First, the rise of unionism in government was spurred by the realization by state and local employees that they were underpaid and otherwise poorly treated in comparison to their private-sector counterparts, who had progressed so well with unionization and collective bargaining. Second, the bureaucratic and impersonal nature of work in large government organizations encouraged unionization to preserve the dignity of the workers. A third reason for the rise of state and local unionism was the employees' lack of confidence in many civil service systems. Not only were pay and benefits inadequate, but grievance processes were controlled by management, employees had little or no say in setting personnel policies, and merit selection, promotion, and pay were often fraught with management favoritism.

Perhaps most important, the growth of unions in government was facilitated by a significant change in the legal environment. The rights of state and local employees to join unions and bargain collectively with management were guaranteed by several U.S. Supreme Court rulings, state legislation, local ordinances, and various informal arrangements that became operative during the 1960s and 1970s. Wisconsin was the first state to permit collective bargaining for state workers, in 1959. Today, forty states specifically allow at least one category of state or local government employees to engage in some form of collective bargaining.

collective bargaining

A formal arrangement in which representatives of labor and management negotiate wages, benefits, and working conditions.

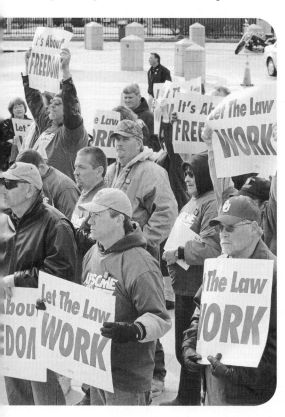

Picketing Public Workers
SOURCE: AP Photo/The Oklahoman, David McDaniel

Collective Bargaining Rights in the States

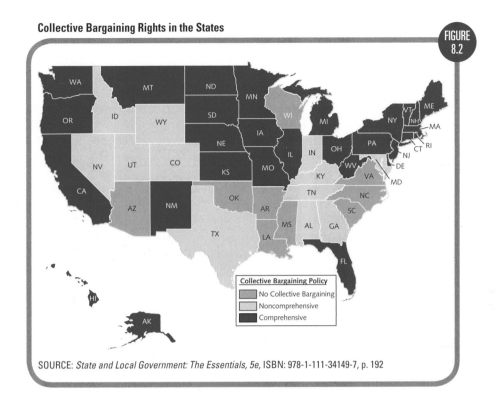

FIGURE
8.2

Collective Bargaining Policy
- No Collective Bargaining
- Noncomprehensive
- Comprehensive

SOURCE: *State and Local Government: The Essentials, 5e,* ISBN: 978-1-111-34149-7, p. 192

The extent of unionization and collective bargaining is greatest in the states of the Midwest and Northeast—the same areas so fertile for the growth of private-sector unions. A handful of traditionalistic states, including Arizona, Mississippi, Utah, Virginia, and North and South Carolina, continues to resist the incursion of state and local unions (see Figure 8.2). Public employees in these jurisdictions have the legal and constitutional right to join a union, but their government employers do not have a corresponding duty to bargain with them over wages, benefits, or conditions of work.

Approximately 31.3 percent of state and 41.7 percent of local government workers belong to unions, compared with only 6.6 percent of workers in private industry. The highest proportions of union workers are found in education, highways, public welfare, police and fire protection, and sanitation.[33]

The surge in the fortunes of state and local unions was partially arrested by the taxpayer revolt of the late 1970s and by President Ronald Reagan's successful effort to "bust" a federal air traffic controllers' union. Further resistance to unions developed in the 1990s and then stiffened in 2011 as a new, powerful crop of antiunion governors and legislators took control of traditionally union states such as Wisconsin, Michigan, and Ohio, and fueled public anger against unions. Wisconsin stripped public employees of their bargaining rights and cut pensions, health care, and other benefits. Wisconsin governor Scott Walker declared that "we can no longer live in a society where the public employees are the haves and the taxpayers who foot the bill are the have-nots."[34] In many states, budget-balancing meant extensive public employee layoffs, which also weakened the unions. Despite these attacks, unions remain an important and highly visible component of many state and local government personnel systems.

What is the impact of collective bargaining in state and local government? Market forces, such as profit levels and the supply and demand for labor, largely determine the outcomes of bargaining between a union and a firm in the private sector. In government, however, political factors are much more important. The technical process of negotiating over wages and other issues in government is very similar to that in business. But the setting makes government labor relations much more complex, mostly because the negotiating process culminates in the political allocation of *public* resources.

Four factors make government labor relations highly political. First, public officials are under greater pressure than private employers to settle labor disputes. Public services are highly visible and often monopolistic in nature; for example, there are no other convenient suppliers of police and fire protection. Accordingly, elected officials who confront a controversial labor dispute in an "essential service" may fear that negative developments will derail their opportunity for re-election.

Second, despite recent setbacks, public-employee unions continue to wield political clout. Their members can influence election outcomes, particularly at the local level. A recalcitrant mayor or city council member who opposes a generous wage or benefit increase may suffer the consequences at the polls in the next election if the municipal union members vote as a bloc. Unions actively engage in politics by raising money, writing letters to the editor about candidates, knocking on doors to get out the vote, formally endorsing candidates, or using any of the other electoral techniques employed by interest groups. Many unions have professional lobbyists to represent them at the state capitol or in city hall.

A third politicizing factor in government labor relations is the symbiotic relationship that can develop between unions and elected officials. In exchange for special consideration at the bargaining table and perhaps elsewhere, the unions can offer public officials two valued commodities: labor peace and electoral support.

Finally, a hard-pressed union can use the strike or a related job action (such as a slowdown or a picket line) as a political weapon. In the private sector, a strike is not likely to have widespread public repercussions unless it involves goods or services that the nation relies on for its economic well-being (such as air transportation or communications). In government, however, a strike can directly involve the health and safety of all the citizens of a jurisdiction. Striking workers shut down Minnesota state government for 20 days in July 2011. A 2005 strike by 33,700 subway and bus workers left millions of commuters in New York City on street corners and in snarled traffic. A general strike involving police officers, firefighters, and sanitation workers has the potential to turn a city into filthy, life-threatening anarchy. At a minimum, any strike leaves the public inconvenienced. Strikes and other job actions by public employees are illegal in most jurisdictions, although twelve states permit work stoppages by "nonessential" workers under strictly regulated conditions. Teachers, health care workers, firefighters, and others, however, sometimes walk off the job anyway.

Given these politicizing factors, one might expect unions in government to be extravagantly successful at the bargaining table, but quite the opposite is true. Public-employee unions have raised wages and salaries an average of 4 to 8 percent, depending on the service, place, and time period under consideration (for example, teachers earn around 5 percent more, and firefighters around 8 percent more, if represented by a union). These figures are much lower than those representing the union-associated wage impacts that have been identified in the private sector, and the union advantage in government has dissipated further since the Great Recession. Greater success has come in the form of better benefits, such as pensions and health care insurance, though these are being rolled back in many financially weakened jurisdictions. It should be noted that union-driven wage and benefit hikes in the private sector are absorbed through profits, layoffs, productivity gains, or higher product prices. In government, by contrast, the choices are to raise taxes or fees, cut services, increase productivity, or contract out to a nonprofit or private firm.

Certain personnel impacts also have been associated with collective bargaining in government. Clearly, unions have gained a stronger employee voice in management decision making. Many personnel-related issues are potentially negotiable, from employee promotion procedures to retention in the event of a reduction in force. As a result of collective bargaining, many government employers have altered civil service rules, regulations, and procedures. In heavily unionized jurisdictions, two personnel systems coexist uncomfortably—the traditional civil service system and the collective bargaining system. Certainly the rights of public employees have been strengthened by unions; but in the view of critics, collective bargaining damages the merit principle

Generally speaking, governments and collective bargaining have reached an uneasy accommodation. The principle of merit in making human resource management decisions is still largely in place; and it is usually supported strongly by the unions, so long as seniority is fully respected as an employment decision rule. In an increasing number of jurisdictions, unions are cooperating with management to boost productivity in government services through participative decision-making techniques, labor-management partnerships, and worker empowerment programs.

THE POLITICS OF BUREAUCRACY

In an ideal representative democracy, political officials popularly elected by the people would make all decisions regarding public policy. They would delegate to public administrators in the executive branch the duty of carrying out these decisions through the agencies of state and local government. In the real world of bureaucratic politics, however, the line dividing politics (policy) and administration is anything but clear. Politicians frequently interfere in administrative matters, as when a legislator calls an agency head to task for not hiring a favored constituent or a city council member intrudes into the affairs of a municipal department. Administrators practice politics at the state capitol and in city hall by participating in and influencing policy formulation decisions.

Joining Administration and Politics

Bureaucrats are intimately involved in making public policy, from the design of legislation to its implementation. Government workers often plant and tend the seedbed for policy ideas that grow to become law, in large part because they are more familiar with agency, departmental, and clientele problems and prospective solutions than anyone else in government. It is not unusual, for instance, for law enforcement policy to originate with police officers or administrators, or higher-education policy to be the brainchild of university officials.

Passage of a bill actually marks "not the end of the political story, but the start of another chapter."[35] State and local employees must interpret the language of the legislation to put it into effect. Because most legislation is written in very general terms, civil servants must apply a great deal of **bureaucratic discretion** in planning and delivering services, making rules for service delivery, adjudicating cases and complaints, and otherwise managing the affairs of government. All states have legal systems for hearing and acting on disputes over agency rules and regulations, such as environmental permits and social service eligibility. These administrative procedures permit individuals, firms, and local governments to challenge agency rules and regulations before an administrative law judge, who issues an order settling the dispute.

In a very real sense, the ultimate success or failure of a public policy depends on the administrators and "street-level bureaucrats" who are responsible for its implementation.[36] Experienced legislators and chief executives understand this, and they bring relevant administrators into the legislative process at a very early stage. The knowledge and expertise of these administrators are invaluable in developing an appropriate policy approach to a specific problem, and their cooperation is essential if a policy enacted into law is to be carried out as the lawmakers intend.

Thus, bureaucratic power derives from knowledge, expertise, information, and discretionary authority. It also comes from external sources of support for agency activities—that is, from the chief executive, legislators, and interest groups. Those who receive the benefits of government programs—the clientele, stakeholders, or customers—are also frequently organized into pressure groups. All government programs benefit some interest—agricultural policy for the farm community, tourism policy for the resort and hotel community, public assistance policy for the poor—and these **clientele groups** often are capable of exerting considerable influence in support of policies that benefit them. Their support is critical for securing the resources necessary to develop and operate a successful government program. They serve as significant political assets to state agencies and municipal and county departments that are seeking new programs or additional funding from legislative and executive bodies, and they can become fearsome political in-fighters when their program interests

bureaucratic discretion

The ability of public employees to make decisions interpreting law and administrative regulations.

clientele group

Groups that benefit from a specific government program, such as contractors and construction firms in state highway department spending programs.

are threatened.[37] Often, clientele and other concerned interest groups form ad hoc coalitions with relevant government agencies and legislative committees to dominate policymaking and implementation in a particular policy field.

The problem of politics and administration, then, has two dimensions. First, elected officials have the duty of holding administrators responsible for their decisions and accountable to the public interest, as defined by the constitution and by statute. Second, political oversight and intrusion into administrative activities should be minimized so that administrative decisions and actions are grounded in objective rules and procedures—not in the politics of favoritism. For example, legislators have the duty of ensuring that decisions by a state department of environmental protection guard the public from harmful effects of pollution while treating polluting companies fairly. Nevertheless, state representatives should not instruct agency employees to go easy on a favored business constituent. Most government agencies discharge their tasks competently and professionally, and therefore require little direct oversight. Occasionally, however, a rogue agency or department head may strike out in the wrong direction.

An example of the proper balance of politics and administration is the attempt to influence public administrators by legislative officials. This typically occurs when legislators and council members perform casework for members of their constituency. Although the legislator may occasionally seek favorable treatment that borders on illegality, the bulk of legislative casework comprises responses to citizens' inquiries or complaints, or requests for clarification of administrative regulations or decisions. Such legislative casework is useful because it promotes both feedback on the delivery of services and helpful exchanges of information between elected officials and administrators. If inquiries determine bias or error in the means by which services are being delivered, corrective political actions can be taken.

In sum, state and local politics are intricately joined with administration. Public policy is made and implemented through the interaction of elected officials, interest groups, and public administrators. Nonetheless, the vast majority of administrative decisions are based on the neutral competence and professionalism of public employees.

This is not to say that such decisions are never made on the basis of political favoritism. Sometimes powerful political pressures or personal interests influence bureaucratic discretion. On the whole, however, state and local services are provided in an unbiased fashion through the application of professional norms and standards.

NEW PUBLIC MANAGEMENT

State and local government employment has burgeoned at a rate much faster than that of population growth. In Texas, for instance, the number of state workers jumped from 223,000 in 1990 to 347,601 in 2009. The total state government payroll in the Lone Star State exceeds about $4.9 billion per year.

Explanations for this huge expansion in the size and costs of government are numerous, including federal mandates, expanding levels of services, partisan politics, and the power of incremental budgeting. The Great Recession, however, played havoc with state and local budgets and resulted in significant reductions in state jobs through attrition and layoffs. Some of the larger, more populated states experienced workforce reductions numbered in the tens of thousands of workers.

Moreover, state and local employees find little sympathy for their plight. Fueled by the economic fires over the states and burning conservative criticism, taxpayer ire and criticism of government are high at all levels. New strategies are being tried in an effort to solve this quite perplexing puzzle for public administrators, particularly those intended to improve the performance, productivity, responsiveness, and transparency of state and local governments.

new public management

An international movement to improve government efficiency and effectiveness through market-based solutions.

The most far-reaching approach is called **new public management** (NPM), based in the U.S. on a widely read book named *Reinventing Government* by David Osborne and Ted Gaebler.[38] According to NPM proponents, governments today are preoccupied with rules, regulations, and hierarchy; their bureaucracies are bloated, inefficient, and altogether poorly suited for meeting the demands made on them. The solution is for governments to free up managers to tap the powers of entrepreneurialism and market competition to design and provide efficient and effective services to state and local "customers." In short, governments should "steer, not row," by stressing a facilitative or cooperative approach to getting services to citizens rather than delivering all services directly. Among the alternative service-delivery systems are intergovernmental and public-private partnerships, volunteerism, voucher plans, and technical assistance. Once transformed, the governments would be enterprising, mission driven, outcome oriented, focused on their customers' needs, and prepared to "do more with less."

Among the formidable obstacles to such profound change in government activities and behavior are labor-intensive tasks such as teaching and policing that do not lend themselves readily to labor-saving technology; rule-bound civil service systems, which tend to discourage management entrepreneurialism and risk taking; the inevitable inertia that plagues public organizations having no bottom line and few market-driven incentives; the difficulties of innovating in organizations created essentially to regulate; the need for politicians to buy into and support the movement, which implies greater autonomy and discretion for administrative agencies, but more risks and more mistakes as well; and the certain opposition by vested interests, such as public-employee unions, that feel threatened by change.

Undeterred by the carping critics and maligning malcontents, many state and local governments have adopted a reinventing attitude in tackling various problems. Principally, they have placed their bets on (1) alternative service delivery mechanisms and (2) e-government. Two increasingly popular alternatives to traditional service delivery arrangements are intergovernmental cooperation and privatization.

Intergovernmental Cooperation Population growth and accompanying service delivery demands; deep cuts in state and federal financial support for municipalities, counties, and school districts; and citizen resistance to taxes and fees pressure local governments to seek efficiencies in service provision. One common means of achieving such efficiencies is coordination of services with neighboring jurisdictions.[39] Though intergovernmental cooperation in such areas as law enforcement, fire protection, and water and sewer service have long histories as shared services, cooperation is today being extended into new service functions. For example, a recent study of small municipalities in three states found that intergovernmental service arrangements are "quite common" in those areas mentioned above, as well as in programs for senior citizens, delinquent tax collection, animal shelters, and bill processing.[40] A comprehensive interstate service partnership between Minnesota and Wisconsin searches for efficiencies in joint purchasing, consolidated food services, child support payments across state lines, IT services, and many others.[41]

Privatization Privatization is service delivery through such arrangements as vouchers, franchises, public-private partnerships, and contracting out. *Privatization* garners much support today, especially among conservatives, Republicans, and others who want to see a "businesslike" approach to government. Virtually any government service is a candidate for contracting out (outsourcing), from jails to janitorial work, from teaching to trash collection. (In theory, most government facilities could even be sold to private interests and operated as businesses; airports and bridges are obvious examples.) The purported benefits of privatization include cost savings, higher-quality services, the acquisition of highly specialized skills, and more efficient service delivery. It is a popular strategy for reducing service costs. To date, privatization has been most frequently used to outsource vehicle towing, human resource management tasks, solid waste collection, building maintenance and security, street repair, ambulance services, printing, information technology, and social welfare services.[42]

In choosing the privatization route to reinventing government, Massachusetts has contracted out mental health care, prison health care, various highway maintenance functions, and operations of interstate highway rest stops, among many other functions. Florida has outsourced projects valued at $1.6 billion. Riverside, California, has privatized operations of its public libraries, while Chicago outsources window washing, sewer cleaning, compost processing, and parking garages. Privately built and operated toll roads and bridges operate in a growing number of states. Indiana leased a toll road to a foreign consortium, raising $3.85 billion (when tolls jumped a public backlash ensued).[43]

Privatization is not as easy as it sounds, and it does not guarantee savings.[44] It usually elicits virulent opposition from public-employee unions, who fear the loss of jobs or reductions in pay and benefits. Unless governments carefully negotiate contracts and then monitor the quality and effectiveness of privatized services, performance may decline, and costs may actually rise. Contracts that are vaguely worded or filled with loopholes, and insufficient contract over-sight on the part of some jurisdictions, have resulted in cost overruns, shoddy services, and fraud or corruption by the contractors. For example, Indiana's $1.34 billion contract with IBM to administer state welfare services met with so many complaints and delays that Governor Mitch Daniel was forced to cancel the contract, but at a cost of $10 million in legal bills and a $52 million court judgment.[45]

Successful outsourcing requires not only careful government planning, design, and analysis of what the jurisdiction and its citizens need and want to have done but also a recognition that government accountability cannot be negotiated. The state, county, or city must remember that ultimately *it* will be held accountable for successful, reliable delivery of a service. Successful contract monitoring requires careful inspections, comprehensive performance reports, and assiduous investigations of citizen complaints.[46]

To keep contractors honest, some governments use "managed competi-tion," wherein firms, government agencies, or nonprofit organizations compete to deliver the same service to different agencies or departments. In Phoenix, Arizona, for instance, garbage workers compete head to head with private trash collection firms. Such collaboration between governments, nonprofit organi-zations, and private firms saved Indianapolis some $100 million in four years through negotiated arrangements in wastewater treatment, recycling, sewer bill-ing, street sweeping, and many other services.[47]

Is privatization worthwhile? Local officials believe that outsourcing improves service delivery in most cases, and some research suggests that priva-tization saves cities up to 20 percent for some service categories but little or nothing in others. There are many notable failures of privatization, particularly those involving sweetheart deals and no-bid contracts.[48] It is not a cure-all for the problems besetting states and local governments, but privatization does represent one potentially useful alternative for reinventing government.

E-Government

e-government
The use of information technology to simplify and improve interactions between governments and citizens, firms, and other entities.

E-government involves reinventing, or reengineering, the way a variety of gov-ernment activities are conducted, and making the face of government more user-friendly. Some improvements are rather mundane and commonsensical. For instance, most states permit online tax filing and renewal of licenses and registrations. Chicago, Denver, Charlotte, and other cities have launched call centers for citizens to report service problems and relieve pressure on emer-gency 911 calls. San Francisco, Boston, Seattle, and other cities have launched apps for citizens to link their 311 systems to Twitter and Facebook.[49] Other improvements run the gamut. Arizonans can vote in primary elections on the Web and view live proceedings of the state legislature through "digital democracy." New York City, Baltimore, and Washington State have mounted computer-synchronized attacks on crime that electronically track incidents and suspects, detect emerging crime patterns, and coordinate some crime-fighting activities with other state and local jurisdictions. Many jurisdictions send mass alerts to citizens through their Blackberries and iPhones. Facebook, LinkedIn, and other social networks enable citizens to connect and interact with their governments in a timely and convenient way.

Unmistakably, we are well down the road to electronic government. "Virtual offices" operating through the Internet are establishing convenient, 24-7 connections among citizens, businesses, nonprofit organizations, and their governments. From a home or office computer or tablet, smart phone or a conveniently located PC in the neighborhood library or kiosk, citizens can obtain everything from critical information updates at IN.gov, to live chats about everything from what government does to specific services on Arkansas. gov. Citizens can use My.Seattle.gov to find customized web portals and blogs that push content on crime, fire calls, and other public safety updates to users. Massive filing systems for documents and other hard copy are no longer needed as paperless offices and cloud computing make virtual storage space available to store important records of marriages, births, deaths, business licenses, and a host of other documents. Despite great enthusiasm, various hurdles must be cleared for e-government to work as intended: substantial investments required to pay for the computer hardware and software and trained personnel; staff expertise may be lacking; unresolved legal questions of liability, privacy, and security are troublesome, like all users, governments are vulnerable to cyber attacks on sensitive data; it is difficult to integrate software across multiple agencies and departments; and there exists a "data paradox"—the explosion of data and information sometimes overwhelms public officials, leading to indecisiveness.[50] Nevertheless, the potential of e-government to make government more accessible, understandable, and efficient is virtually limitless.[51]

Is NPM simply a fad? Definitely not. Responsive states and localities have been reinventing their operations and services ever since they were created, and will continue to do so for as long as they exist. Now, state agencies and municipal departments can obtain instant citizen feedback and criticism on how good (or bad) a job they are doing through apps, blogs, texts, and other means.

In the short run, some governments will be reinvented, or at least changed in fundamental ways, but others continue to do things the old way. (Of course, sometimes "old ways" work just fine. When fast-growing kudzu vines threatened to choke access to city property, Chattanooga summoned a herd of goats to the rescue.) Change is politically risky, and inertia is a powerful force. Ultimately, it is the responsibility of citizens and the elected officials who represent them to bring about change and reforms.

THE QUALITY OF PUBLIC ADMINISTRATION

Despite the quantity of criticism and vitriol spewed at government agencies, departments, and workers by the media, elected officials, and others, the quality of public administration in state and local government has improved markedly. Of course, there is considerable variance among jurisdictions; that capacity is generally of a higher quality in affluent, highly educated, and urban environments.

Administrative quality is a critical factor in support of the revitalization and responsiveness of states and localities. State and local governments, particularly through partnerships with other governments and private and nonprofit organizations, have the capacity to accomplish more and on a grander scale than ever before; this trend is continuing. The basics of providing services, from disposing of dead animals to delivering healthy human babies, will continue to depend on government employees with high standards of performance and professionalism.

CHAPTER RECAP

- The quality and capacity of public administration have greatly improved in the vast majority of the states and local governments.

- State and local government employment has grown rapidly.

- State and local operating budgets must be balanced each year.

- Interest groups, agencies, the chief executive, and the legislative body are the four principal actors in the budgetary process.

- Budgets tend to expand (or contract) incrementally.

- The trend in accounting for revenues and expenditures is performance-based budgeting.

- Most state and local jobs are part of a merit system and are filled based on knowledge, skills, and experience.

- Affirmative action led to gains in advancement of minorities and women in state and local employment, but it is very controversial.

- States and localities are addressing the problem of sexual harassment in public agencies.

- Unions and collective bargaining present special challenges to many state and local governments.

- Bureaucratic discretion makes public employees important decision makers.

- The NPM movement, aimed at reinventing government through privatization, e-government, and other steps, is a long-term trend.

Key Terms

bureaucracy *(p. 174)*
incrementalism *(p. 183)*
line-item budget *(p. 183)*
performance budgeting *(p. 183)*

capital budget *(p. 184)*
merit system *(p. 185)*
neutral competence *(p. 185)*
affirmative action *(p. 187)*
collective bargaining *(p. 190)*

bureaucratic discretion *(p. 194)*
clientele group *(p. 194)*
new public management *(p. 196)*
e-government *(p. 198)*

Internet Resources

All major municipalities and states have websites. Many provide links to jobs, NPM initiatives, service-provision information, and other data.

Innovative, award-winning websites include Indianapolis's "Electronic City Hall" at **www.indygov.org;** Service Arizona at **www.servicearizona.com;** NC@YourService at **www.ncgov.com**; Delaware's at **www.Delaware.gov; and AccessWashington** at www.access.wa.gov.

An informative public-employee union website is that of the American Federation of State, County and Municipal Employees at **www.afscme.org**.

An interesting site on technology and e-government is **www.govtech.net**.

For a step-by-step illustration of a state budget process, see **www.budget.state.ny.us/citizen/process/process.html**.

You can play a budget simulation for New York City at **www.gothamgazette.com/ budget-game/budgetgame.html**.

To view streaming video of public meetings in Indiana, see **www.stream.hoosier.net/cats**.

9

The Judiciary

CHAPTER OUTLINE

- The Structure of State Court Systems
- How Judges Are Selected
- Judicial Decision Making
- Judicial Federalism
- Administrative and Organizational Improvements

FOCUS QUESTIONS

1. What are the various methods by which state judges are selected?
2. What are the trade-offs in terms of independence and accountability?
3. Judicial decision making is influenced by what factors?
4. How are states reforming their courts?

In the case of *Barnes* v. *Glen Theatre Inc.* (1991), a prudish U.S. Supreme Court ruled that nude dancing, being dangerous to "order and morality," is not protected as free expression under the First Amendment of the U.S. Constitution. This case, which arose in Indiana, was tried in the federal courts under national constitutional law. Under Ohio's "Eleventh Commandment" of 2007, patrons of strip clubs and the performers themselves are barred from touching "the naughty bits" at the risk of receiving six months in jail and a $1,000 fine.[1]

Yet in Boston, a city once known for banning all manner of objects and activities deemed to be immoral, totally naked women grind, bump, and pirouette at tacky cabarets and "gentleman's clubs," fully confident that their activities are legal. In Massachusetts, the voluntary display of a naked body has been protected under the state constitution as a form of expression since the state supreme court ruled it so in 1984.[2]

Even as the U.S. Supreme Court has evidenced a conservative majority for the past two decades, many of the state courts have become more open to individuals and groups advocating causes such as civil rights, free speech, and freedom of expression. All sorts of conflicts and problems find their way to state and local courts, from the profound (abortion rights) to the profane (nude dancing). And courts at this level are very busy; New York State's cases alone outnumber those filed in all federal courts by a ratio of 9 to 1. Many of the state courts are innovative in their decision making and administration; in addition, all are far more accessible to the people and responsive to their concerns than are the federal courts. Surveys have found that Americans have greater confidence in the courts than in the other two branches of state government.[3]

As the third branch of government, the judiciary is the final authority on the meaning of the language of laws and constitutions, as well as the ultimate arbiter of disputes between the executive and legislative branches. It also makes public policy through rulings on questions of political, social, and economic significance, and may serve as the last chance for minority interests to defend themselves from the decisions of the majority. As noted in Chapter 3, state courts have become more active policymakers in recent years and have increasingly based important decisions on state constitutions rather than on the national constitution. And as with the other branches of state government, their structures and processes have been greatly reformed and modernized. In our lifetimes, nearly all of us will personally experience the judicial branch in some role as direct participants. At times, the courts are more accessible to us than are the other branches of government. Disputes that cannot be resolved through ordinary legislative, executive, and political processes frequently wind up before a judge, as litigation.

The work of the fifty state court systems is divided into three major areas: civil, criminal, and administrative. In **civil cases**, one individual or corporation sues another over an alleged wrong. Occasionally, a governmental body is party to a civil action. Typical civil actions are divorces, property disputes, and suits for damages arising from automobile or other accidents. **Criminal cases** involve the breaking of a law by an individual or a corporation. The state is usually the plaintiff; the accused is the defendant. Murder, assault, embezzlement, and disorderly conduct are common examples. **Administrative cases** concern court actions such as probating wills, revoking driver's licenses, or determining custody of a child. Some administrative cases involve administrative law judges and quasi-judicial (less formal) proceedings.

State courts adjudicate (resolve disputes) by interpreting state statutes, the state and federal constitutions, and common law. In developing and deciphering the **common law**, courts are concerned with the legal rules and expectations that have developed historically in a state through the citizens' customs, culture, and habits, and that have been given standing through the courts. The most

civil case
A case that concerns a dispute involving individuals or organizations.

criminal case
A case brought by the state against persons accused of violating state law.

administrative case
A case in which a government agency applies rules to settle a legal dispute.

common law
Unwritten law based on tradition, custom, or court decisions.

important applications of common law today concern enforcing contracts (contract law), owning and selling property (property law), and establishing liability for death or injuries to people as well as damage to property (tort law).

THE STRUCTURE OF STATE COURT SYSTEMS

State courts have evolved in response to changes in their environment. In colonial days, they developed distinctly, influenced by local customs and beliefs. Owing to a shortage of trained lawyers and an abiding distrust of English law, the first judges were laymen who served on a part-time basis. It did not take long for the courts to become overwhelmed with cases: case overloads were reported as long ago as 1685.[4] More than three centuries later, case backlogs still plague our state judiciaries.

As the population and the economy grew, so did the amount of litigation. Courts expanded in number and in degree of specialization. Their development, however, was not carefully planned. Rather, new courts were added to existing structures. The results were predictably complex and confusing, with overlapping, independent jurisdictions and responsibilities. For instance, Chicago offered an astounding array of jurisdictions, estimated at one time to number 556.[5] State court systems were beset as well by a host of other serious problems, including underfunding, administrative inefficiency, congestion, and excessive delays. In short, the American system of justice left much to be desired.

original jurisdiction
The power of a court to hear a case first.

The organization of the state courts is important because it affects the quality and quantity of judicial decisions and the access of individuals and groups to the legal system. It also influences how legal decisions are made. An efficiently organized system, properly staffed and administered, can do a better job of deciding a larger number of cases than can a poorly organized system. Court structure is of great interest to those who make their living in the halls of justice—namely lawyers, judges, and court staff. It can also be an issue of concern to citizens who find themselves in court.

appellate jurisdiction
The power of a court to review cases previously decided by a lower court.

The Two Tiers of Courts

Most states today have a two-tiered court structure: trial courts and appellate courts. There are two types of trial courts: those of limited jurisdiction, and major trial courts. Each tier, or level, has a different *jurisdiction*, or range of authority. **Original jurisdiction** gives courts the power to hear certain types of cases first, in contrast to **appellate jurisdiction**, which gives the courts power to review cases on appeal after they have been tried elsewhere.

Trial courts, which comprise the lower tier, include (1) minor courts of limited jurisdiction and (2) major trial courts of general jurisdiction.

limited jurisdiction trial courts
Courts with original jurisdiction over specialized cases such as juvenile offenses and traffic violations.

Limited jurisdiction trial courts, also known as special trial courts, handle minor, specialized cases, such as those involving juveniles, traffic offenses, and small claims. Most states have three to five courts of limited jurisdiction, with names that reflect the type of specialized case: traffic court, police court, probate court, municipal court, and so on. Criminal cases here are usually restricted by law to misdemeanor violations of municipal or county ordinances that are punishable by a small fine, a short jail term, or both. Additional courts of limited jurisdiction, sometimes called boutique or "problem-solving" courts, have been created to deal with special types of cases or circumstances. For example, all states have created drug courts with the dual aims of processing drug-related offenses more efficiently and reducing the recidivism (return to jail or prison) rates of drug offenders on probation or parole. "Water courts" in Colorado and Montana hear disputes over water rights. Illinois, Wisconsin, and other states have recently established "veterans' courts" to hear cases involving Iraq and Afghanistan war vets who have had scrapes with the law.[6] In San Francisco, "neighborhood courts" grant individuals charged with minor crimes the option of accepting "restorative justice" in exchange for having their record erased. For instance, a graffiti "artist" might be required to clean up his artwork and apologize at a public meeting.[7]

Present in almost all states are *small-claims courts*, which offer a relatively simple and inexpensive way to settle minor civil disputes without either party having to incur the financial and temporal burdens of lawyers and legal procedures. Small-claims courts are usually divisions of county, city, or district trial courts. In the cases they hear, the plaintiff (the person bringing the suit) asks for monetary recompense from the defendant (the individual or firm being sued) for some harm or damage. Claims are limited to varying amounts, usually around $1,000.

The proceedings are informal. Each party presents to a judge the relevant facts and arguments to support her case. The party with the preponderance of evidence on his side wins. Most disputes involve tenant-landlord conflicts, property damage, or the purchase of goods (for example, shoddy merchandise or the failure of a customer to pay a bill).

The second type of trial court is the **major trial court**, which exercises general authority over civil and criminal cases. Most cases are filed initially under a major trial court's original jurisdiction. However, trial courts also hear cases on appeal from courts of limited jurisdiction. Major trial courts are often organized along county or district lines. Their names—circuit courts, superior courts, district courts, courts of common pleas—vary widely.

The upper tier of the two-tiered state court system consists of appellate courts: **supreme courts** (sometimes called courts of last resort) and, in most states, **intermediate appellate courts**. Oklahoma and Texas have two supreme courts, one for criminal cases and the other for civil disputes. Forty states have intermediate appellate courts. (Alabama, Oklahoma, Oregon, Texas, Pennsylvania, and Tennessee have two, typically one each for criminal and civil cases.) Most intermediate appellate courts are known as courts of appeals. Their work generally involves cases on appeal from lower courts. Thus, these courts exercise appellate jurisdiction. By contrast, state supreme courts have original jurisdiction in certain types of cases, such as those dealing with constitutional issues, as well as appellate jurisdiction.

Intermediate appellate courts represent the most notable change in the structure of the state court system during the past forty years. They are intended to increase the capability of supreme courts by reducing their caseload burden, speeding up the appellate process, and improving the quality of judicial

major trial court
Court of general jurisdiction that handles major criminal and civil cases.

supreme court
The highest state court, beyond which there is no appeal except in cases involving federal law.

intermediate appellate court
A state appellate court that relieves the case burden on the supreme court by hearing certain types of appeals.

decision making. The weight of the evidence points to moderate success in achieving each of these objectives. Appellate case backlogs and delays have been somewhat reduced, and supreme court justices are better able to spend an appropriate amount of time on significant cases. Counteracting this positive trend, however, is the growing number of mandatory appeals, such as those for death penalty cases, that make up more than 60 percent of the caseload.

If a state supreme court so chooses, it can have the final word on any state or local case except one involving a national constitutional question, such as First Amendment rights. Some cases can be filed in either federal or state court. For example, a person who assaults and abducts a victim and then transports him across a state line can be charged in state court with assault and in federal court with kidnapping. Some acts violate nearly identical federal and state laws; possession or sale of certain illegal drugs is a common example. Other cases fall entirely under federal court jurisdiction, such as those involving treason, mail theft, or currency-law violations.

Thus, there exists in the United States a *dual system* of courts that is sometimes referred to as *judicial federalism*. Generally, state courts adjudicate, or decide, matters of state law, whereas federal courts deal with national law. The systems are separate and distinct. In some instances, however, there is jurisdictional overlap and even competition for a case. Following the April 15, 2013, Boston Marathon bombings, one of the suspects, Tamerlan Tsarnaev, was killed and his brother, Dzhokhar, arrested. The State of Massachusetts first sought jurisdiction over the case, but because this was an act of terrorism, the U.S. Department of Justice brought the multiple murder case to trial first (three victims were killed in the bombings). A much more complicated case involved the "Beltway snipers," who killed people in Virginia, Maryland, and the District of Columbia. All wanted to bring the case to trial first. (Virginia was selected for the initial prosecution.)

Although state courts cannot overturn federal law, they can base certain rulings on the federal constitution. Recently, state courts have decided cases governed by both state and federal law in areas such as hate crimes, free speech, the right to die, and gay rights. It is very unusual for a case decided by a state supreme court to be heard by the U.S. Supreme Court or any other federal court. An important exception to the custom occurred in the aftermath of the 2000 presidential election, when the U.S. Supreme Court overturned a Florida Supreme Court decision that had ordered a recount of ballots in three counties. The intervention of the nation's highest court effectively awarded the presidency to George W. Bush.

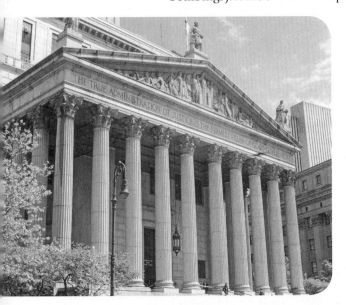

The New York State Courthouse
SOURCE: Patti McConville/Alamy

Structural Reforms

Although the two tiers of state courts appear to represent a hierarchy, in fact they do not. Courts in most states operate with a great deal of autonomy. They have their own budgets, hire their own staff, and use their own procedures. Moreover, the decisions of major and specialized trial courts usually stand unchallenged. Only around 5 percent of lower-court cases are appealed, mostly because great expense and years of waiting are certain to be involved.

Unified court systems consolidate the various trial courts with overlapping jurisdictions into a single administrative unit and clearly specify each court's purpose and jurisdiction. The aim of this arrangement, which includes centralized management and rule making, is to make the work of the courts more efficient, saving time and money and avoiding confusion. Instead of a system whereby each judge runs her own fiefdom, such responsibilities as rule making, record-keeping, budgeting, and personnel management are standardized and centralized, usually under the authority of the state supreme court or chief justice.

Centralization relieves judges from some of the mundane tasks of day-to-day court management so that they can concentrate on adjudication. Additional efficiencies are gained from *offices of court administration.* Court administration involves actively managing, monitoring, and planning the courts' resources and operations. Information technology is enabling tremendous improvements in how the courts manage criminal cases.

Responsiveness to the public is also growing. An increasing number of state courts are electronically disseminating court documents, judicial rulings, case processing speed and efficiency measures, and general information such as instructions for jury duty, maps showing directions to the courthouse, and answers to commonly asked questions about the courts.[8] Some display photographs and biographies of judges, many permit interested citizens to ask questions via e-mail, and others even provide performance evaluations of judges and broadcast cases live over the Internet.[9] (See "Internet Resources" at the end of the chapter.)

Despite consolidation and centralization, court structures and processes continue to vary widely among the states, as shown in Figure 9.1. Generally, the most modern systems are found in the "newer" states, including Alaska and Hawaii, while some of the most antiquated are situated in southern states, among them Arkansas and Georgia.

HOW JUDGES ARE SELECTED

In large part, the quality of a state court system depends on the selection of competent, well-trained judges. According to the American Bar Association (ABA), the leading professional organization for lawyers, judges should be chosen on the basis of solid professional and personal qualifications, regardless of their political views and party identification. Judges should have "superior

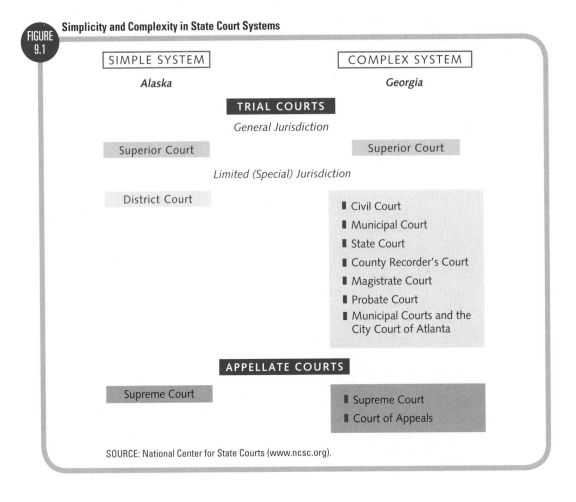

FIGURE 9.1 Simplicity and Complexity in State Court Systems

SIMPLE SYSTEM	COMPLEX SYSTEM
Alaska	*Georgia*

TRIAL COURTS

General Jurisdiction

| Superior Court | Superior Court |

Limited (Special) Jurisdiction

District Court

- Civil Court
- Municipal Court
- State Court
- County Recorder's Court
- Magistrate Court
- Probate Court
- Municipal Courts and the City Court of Atlanta

APPELLATE COURTS

Supreme Court	

- Supreme Court
- Court of Appeals

SOURCE: National Center for State Courts (www.ncsc.org).

self-discipline, moral courage, and sound judgment."[10] They should be good listeners, broadly educated, and professionally qualified as lawyers. (Though Arizona, New Mexico, New York, Texas, and Utah have large numbers of judges without law degrees.[11]) An appellate or general trial court judge should also have relevant experience in a lower court or as a courtroom attorney.

For a great many years, however, controversy has swirled over the selection of state judges. Should they be elected by popular vote? Should they be appointed by the governor? By the legislature? Many critics insist that judges should be free from politics and interest-group influences. Others claim that judges should regularly be held accountable to a majority of the voters or to elected officials for their decisions.

The conflict between judicial independence and accountability is manifest in the five types of selection systems used in the states: legislative selection, partisan popular election, nonpartisan popular election, the merit plan, and gubernatorial appointment. Most states use a single selection system for all

Appellate and Major Trial Court Selection Plans

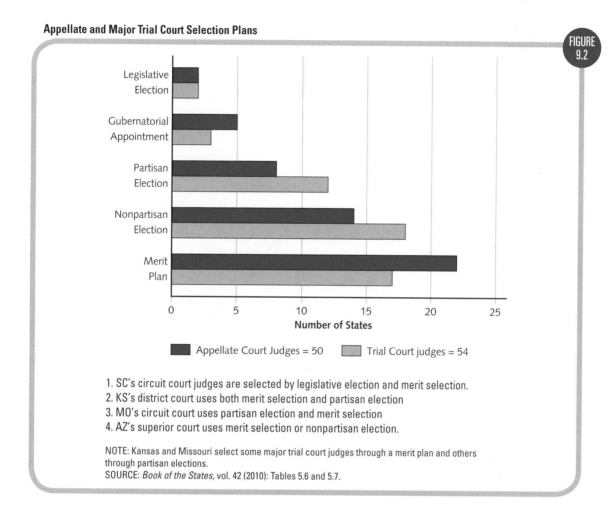

1. SC's circuit court judges are selected by legislative election and merit selection.
2. KS's district court uses both merit selection and partisan election
3. MO's circuit court uses partisan election and merit selection
4. AZ's superior court uses merit selection or nonpartisan election.

NOTE: Kansas and Missouri select some major trial court judges through a merit plan and others through partisan elections.
SOURCE: *Book of the States*, vol. 42 (2010): Tables 5.6 and 5.7.

appellate and major trial court judges. The others take separate approaches to selecting judges, depending on the tier. Figure 9.2 shows the presence of these selection techniques for appellate and major trial courts. Some states have rather elaborate systems.

Legislative Selection

In South Carolina and Virginia, the legislature elects judges by majority vote from among announced candidates. Not surprisingly, a sizable majority of judges selected under this plan have been former legislators (in South Carolina, the proportion once approximated 100 percent).[12] In these two states, a judge-ship is viewed as a highly valued reward for public service and a prestigious cherry on the top of a legislative career.

Few people other than legislators approve of legislative election. Indeed, the method is open to criticism. The public has no role in either choosing judges or reelecting them, so democratic accountability is minimal. The judges may be independent, but since the major criterion for selection is service as a legislator, they often lack other qualifications. Legislative service has little connection to the demands of a judgeship.

Popular Election

Judges on one or more courts face elections in thirty-eight states. Some are listed on the ballot by party identification; others are not. In theory, elections maximize the value of judicial accountability to the people. Judges must run for office on the same ticket as candidates for other state offices. Like other candidates, they must raise and spend money for their election campaigns and publicly engage political issues.

Partisan Popular Election This plan enjoyed widespread popularity during the Jacksonian era as a way to create a judiciary answerable to the voters. Most of the partisan election states are located in the South. In theory, partisan elections maximize the value of judicial accountability to the people.

Nonpartisan Popular Election This plan won favor during the first half of the twentieth century, when reformers sought to eliminate party identification in the election of judges and certain other officials in state and local government. Political parties are prohibited from openly taking sides in nonpartisan judicial elections. In reality, they play a covert role in such contests. The vast majority of judges have a political party preference. Most list it in the official biographies that are available to interested voters during campaigns. A disadvantage of nonpartisan popular elections is that they tend to depress voter participation because incumbent judges are less likely to be challenged. Another is that party identification is an important voting cue for many citizens.

The Problems with Popular Elections It is worth mentioning that electing judges is virtually unknown in the rest of the world. Voter turnout is very low in many judicial elections, whether partisan or nonpartisan. This fact is a major criticism of both methods of electing judges: the winners may not be truly accountable to the people, which is the principal advantage commonly associated with elections. Low rates of voter interest and participation frequently combine with low-key, unexciting, and issueless campaigns to keep many incumbent judges on the bench as long as they run for reelection. One study indicates that less than 10 percent are defeated.[13] Still, this is comparable to state legislative races involving incumbents. Recent research suggests that even nonpartisan judicial elections encourage state supreme court justices to follow public opinion in their decisions.[14] Research also finds that the electorate can be mobilized by candidates or circumstances in individual states.[15] On controversial issues, judges today seem increasingly vulnerable, particularly in partisan election states in which the voters' views have high emotional content and differ significantly from those of the incumbent judge.[16]

Two problems have become increasingly troublesome: the politicization of judicial races and the creeping realization that campaign donations influence decisions from the bench. The American Bar Association Code of Judicial Conduct forbids judicial campaigning on legal issues, but this prohibition is often ignored in close contests and in elections where crime-related concerns, such as the death penalty or an accused murderer freed on a legal technicality, claim voters' attention. Moreover, federal courts have ruled that judicial campaigning is protected free speech. As in other electoral contests, negative campaigning is on the rise in judicial elections. Judicial candidates today energetically sling mud at their opponents for allegedly letting drug dealers free, being corrupt, sympathizing with terrorists, favoring abortion or gay marriage, and acting soft on crime. Several states have tried to restrict aggressive judicial politicking through ethics rules and other limitations. When challenged in federal courts, however, such restrictions have been overturned as intrusions on the candidates' First Amendment rights to free speech.[17]

Even more serious is the problem that occurs when judges elected on a partisan ballot are accused of pandering to special interests during election campaigns and of paying back campaign support through favorable court decisions. In Texas, for instance, supreme court justices deciding a $10.5 billion judgment against Texaco in favor of Pennzoil were criticized for accepting huge campaign contributions from both parties. In some recent Ohio supreme court rulings all seven justices had accepted campaign money from lawyers for the plaintiffs or defendants.[18] Nonpartisan elected judges have been open to similar charges, especially because political action committees (PACs) have boosted their contributions to candidates for state court judgeships. Recent research has found systematic empirical evidence that judicial decisions have followed dollars. Similar conclusions have been drawn from research on judicial decision making in Alabama, Ohio, and Georgia.[19] Elected judges themselves are troubled by the role of money in judicial elections. As an Ohio Supreme Court justice remarked recently, "I never felt so much like a hooker down by the bus station … as I did in a judicial race.""[20]

In addition, popular elections are criticized for the growing amount of money necessary to win a state judgeship. As in other political contests, money talks. The candidate who spends the most is the likely winner.[21] In some cases, the implication is that judges have sacrificed their independence and professionalism for crass electoral politics. Following the trend set in executive and legislative contests, judicial campaign spending for state supreme court candidates for TV ads alone exceeded $16.1 million in 2009–2010, including $5 million just in Michigan.[22] In a heated 2004 race for an Illinois Supreme Court seat, two candidates spent about $4.5 million each. The geographical district in which they ran (it was not a statewide contest) had experienced high-profile personal injury and product liability litigation, including a $10.1 billion product liability award against Philip Morris Tobacco Company.

The largest campaign contributors are usually trial lawyers, corporations, and corporate lawyers, and other groups with an interest in judges' decisions, such as labor unions, business interests desiring to limit the amount of jury awards through tort reform, and various professions, such as insurance or medicine.[23] In some states, attorneys allege that judges "shake them down" for campaign contributions. A supreme court justice was brought down in West Virginia largely through the efforts of a CEO, who, with a pending lawsuit before the "unfriendly" judge, invested $2.3 million in that judge's opponent. The CEO in question, Don Blankenship of Massey Energy, had shamelessly vacationed in Monte Carlo with one sitting justice while the case was under appeal.[24]

It looks as though judges running for election are forfeiting their independence in certain legal disputes while offering accountability only to the highest bidders instead of to the general public. If indeed justice is for sale or rent, neither independence nor accountability is achieved and faith in the legal system is being eroded. According to the president of the Ohio State Bar Association, "The people with money to spend who are affected by court decisions have reached the conclusion that it's a lot cheaper to buy a judge than a governor or an entire legislature, and he can probably do a lot more for you."[25] The sentiment is supported by recent research showing a positive correlation between campaign contributions and judges' decisions.[26]

If it is unethical for a judge to rule on a case in which he or she has accepted money from one or more of the interested parties, then it would be difficult to bring together enough judges to hear cases in some states. Increasingly, the general sentiment is that judges should be both qualified and dignified, and that elections do not further either objective. In 2009, Wisconsin joined early adopters North Carolina and New Mexico to launch public financing for judges' campaigns to help contain spiraling costs. Other states are imposing spending restrictions and penalties for false campaign advertising. Meanwhile, the U.S. Supreme Court ruled in an important 2009 case involving the West Virginia race mentioned above that judges must recuse or exclude themselves from cases involving individuals or corporations that have given them large sums of campaign dollars.[27]

Merit Plan

Dissatisfaction with the other methods for selecting judges has led to the popularity of the so-called *merit plan*. Incorporating elements of gubernatorial appointment and elective systems, the merit plan attempts to provide a mechanism for appointing qualified candidates to the bench while permitting the public to evaluate a judge's performance through the ballot box.

Strongly supported today by virtually the entire legal community, the merit plan has been adopted by nearly all of the states that have changed their selection systems since Missouri became the initial adopter in 1940. Another twenty-one states have adopted the merit plan, and others are considering it.

Three Steps Commonly referred to as the Missouri Plan, the basic merit plan
involves three steps:

1. A judicial nominating commission meets and recommends three (or more)
   names of prospective judges to the governor. Members of this bipartisan
   commission usually include a sitting judge (often the chief justice), representatives chosen by the state bar association, and laypersons appointed
   by the governor. The nominating commission solicits names of candidates,
   investigates them, chooses those it believes to be the best-qualified individuals, and then forwards their names and files to the governor.
2. The governor appoints the preferred candidate to the vacant judgeship.
3. A retention election is held, usually after one or two years, in which the
   newly appointed judge's name is placed before the voters on a nonpartisan,
   noncompetitive ticket. The voters decide whether or not the judge should
   be retained in office. If he or she is rejected by a majority vote, the judicial
   nominating commission begins its work anew. Subsequent retention elections may be held every eight or twelve years, depending on the merit plan's
   provision.

Various hybrids of the basic plan are also in use. For example, the
California Plan for choosing appellate judges begins when the governor identifies a candidate for a vacancy on the bench and sends that person's name
to the Commission on Judicial Appointments. The commission, composed
of two judges and the attorney general, hears testimony regarding the nominee and votes to confirm or reject. The new judge is then accepted or rejected
in a retention election in the next regularly scheduled gubernatorial contest.
Thus, although the governor appoints, the new judge is subject to confirma-
tion by both the Commission on Judicial Appointments and the voters. In New
Mexico's multistage merit plan, a judge is nominated by a commission and
appointed by the governor. During the next general election the judge must
run in a partisan election. If he or she wins, the judge must run unopposed in
a nonpartisan retention election on the next general-election ballot.

The object of the merit plan is to permit the governor some appointive
discretion while removing politics from the selection of judges. If it works as
intended, election or direct gubernatorial appointment is replaced with a careful appraisal of candidates' professional qualifications by an objective commission. The process is intended to ensure both the basic independence of judges
and their accountability to the people.

The Politics of Merit Selection The merit plan looks great on paper, but
in practice it has not fulfilled its promise. First, it has not dislodged politics
from judicial selection. A judgeship is too important a political office in any
state ever to be immune from politics. It is a prized job and an important point
of judicial access for numerous individuals, firms, and interest groups, especially the powerful state bar association.

Studies of judicial nominating commissions show that politics—partisan
and otherwise—is rampant in the review and nomination of candidates.[28] For

better or worse, the legal profession often dominates the process. Counting the judge who presides over the nominating commission, lawyers make up a commission majority in most of the states. Bar association lobbying is often the prime reason that merit plans are adopted in the first place. The legal profession, however, is not monolithic in its politics, often dividing into two camps: plaintiff's attorneys and defendant's attorneys.

Furthermore, the governor's influence can be exceptionally strong. The laypersons he or she appoints to the nominating commission may hold the judge in awe, but they are there to represent the governor's point of view and sometimes to promote specific candidates or the agenda of the governor's political party. The member who is a judge may also respect the governor's preferences, particularly if he owes his appointment to that chief executive.

A second criticism of the merit plan is that the procedure intended to ensure judicial accountability to the people—the retention election—rarely generates voter interest and seldom results in the departure of an incumbent judge from office. Turnout in retention elections is normally very low and, on average, favors the incumbent by more than 70 percent.[29] Few incumbent judges have been voted out in retention elections. In most cases, then, merit selection essentially means a lifetime appointment.

Voter backlashes, however, have occurred against judges whose decisions are distinctly out of step with public opinion. In 1986, California Chief Justice Rose Bird and two associate justices were swept from the state supreme court by large margins in retention elections, as voters reacted negatively to a series of supreme court rulings that significantly expanded the rights of the accused and of convicted felons. Bird had voted to overturn all sixty-one capital punishment cases brought to the court during a period when polls showed 80 percent support for the death penalty in California.[30] Ten years later, Tennessee Supreme Court Justice Penny White was rejected in a retention election for failing to support the death penalty for the perpetrator of a particularly heinous crime.[31] In 2010, Iowa voters tossed three supreme court justices out of office, in retribution for ruling that a same-sex marriage ban violated the state constitution's equal protection guarantee.

The final charge leveled against the merit plan is that despite reformers' claims to the contrary, it does not result in the appointment of better-qualified judges or of more women and minorities. When background, education, experience, and decision making are taken into account, judges selected through the merit plan are comparable to those selected through other plans. A large majority are white males. Most leave private practice for the bench and stay there until retirement. And a substantial majority were born, raised, and educated in the state in which they serve.

Gubernatorial Appointment

All gubernatorial appointment states are former colonies, reflecting the early popularity of the plan. As a method per se, gubernatorial appointment rates fairly high on independence, since the judge is appointed and retained without an election; but it is weak on accountability because the judge is directly beholden to only one person for his or her job.

Although only a handful of states formally recognize it, gubernatorial appointment is in fact the most common method for selecting a majority of appellate and major trial court judges in the United States. Judges in states with popular elections or merit plans often resign or retire from office just before the end of their term.[32] Under most state legal systems, the governor has the power to make interim appointments to vacant seats until the next scheduled election or the commencement of merit-plan selection processes. The governor's temporary appointee then enjoys the tremendous advantage of running as an incumbent for the next full term. Gubernatorial appointment is also used to replace a judge who dies before the expiration of their term.

What criteria does a governor apply in making appointments to the bench? Political considerations usually come first. The governor can use the appointment to reward a faithful legislator, to shore up support in certain regions of the state, to satisfy the demands of party leaders and the state legal establishment, or to appeal to women's or minority groups.[33]

Which Selection Plan Is Best?

An ongoing debate is over which selection plan best achieves a healthy balance of (1) judicial independence from interest groups, attorney organizations, and other influences and (2) accountability to the people. It is unlikely ever to be settled. Legislative selection and gubernatorial appointment probably maximize the value of judicial independence, but may be the least desirable; judges selected under these systems tend to come from a rather specific political occupation (the legislature), and the general public has little opportunity to hold them accountable. Judicial accountability is maximized when judges and judicial candidates must face voters, but few incumbents are defeated in elections. Significant policy issues involving the courts, however, can rouse voters to the polls in certain instances, meaning that elected judges who want to stay on the bench must pay attention to public opinion.

None of the judicial selection systems produces "better" judges, although gubernatorial appointment is more likely to benefit women.[34] And minorities have not done well under any selection plan. African Americans fill about 8 percent of state court seats and Latinos only 4 percent.[35] Gubernatorial appointment and partisan election increases the selection opportunities for minority judges; more substantial gains await the development of a larger pool of Latino and black attorneys.

Politics, of course, is what raises all judges to the bench, regardless of the selection method. According to research by political scientists, what matters is the path a judge takes to the bench. Those chosen through elective systems tend to view the judiciary through a more political—as opposed to juridical—lens than do those who reach the bench through gubernatorial or merit appointment systems. Elected judges also tend to be more activist in their decision making, and they are more likely to dissent from other judges in their opinions than are appointed judges.[36] Voter preferences carry extra weight in the decision making of judges facing competitive elections, particularly with respect to issues of criminal justice, abortion rights, and same-sex marriage. Those in merit-plan states have less to fear from an angry minority in the electorate; they can be guided more by personal ideological preferences and their interpretation of the law.

In other words, judges who attain their jobs through electoral politics tend to behave similarly to other elected officials in state government by emphasizing political—rather than legal—factors in their decision making.[37] The irony is that voters prefer to elect their judges but they fear that campaign contributions influence what judges decide in court.[38]

Removal of Judges

Like anyone else, judges can (and do) break the law, go mad, suffer dementia, or become physically incapable of carrying out their responsibilities. If a judge displays serious deficiencies, he or she must be removed from the bench. Forty-five states provide for impeachment, wherein charges are filed in the state house of representatives and a trial is conducted in the senate. Other traditional means for removing justices include the legislative address and popular recall. In the legislative address, both houses of the legislature by two-thirds vote must ask the governor to dismiss a judge. Popular recall requires a specified number of registered voters to petition for a special election to recall the judge before the term has expired. Angry Nevada voters attempted to recall six supreme court justices in 2003 for ruling invalid a popular tax limitation initiative. But these traditional mechanisms are cumbersome and uncertain, and hence seldom successful.

Today, states generally use more practical methods to remove judges. Problems related to senility and old age are ameliorated in at least thirty-seven states by a mandatory retirement age (generally seventy years) or by the forfeiture of pensions for judges serving beyond the retirement age. Such measures have the added benefit of opening up the courtrooms to new, and younger, judges, even in situations where advancing age does not impair performance.

Most states have established special entities to address behavioral problems. *Courts of the judiciary*, whose members are all judges, and *judicial discipline and removal commissions*, composed of judges, lawyers, and laypersons, are authorized to investigate complaints about judges' qualifications, conduct, or fitness. These entities may reject allegations if they are unfounded, privately warn a judge if the charges are not serious, or hold formal hearings. Hearings may result in dismissal of the charges, recommendation for early retirement, or, in some states, outright suspension or removal.

The discipline, suspension, or removal of state court judges is uncommon, but it becomes necessary in all states at one time or another. Judges have been found guilty of drunkenness and drug abuse; sexual misconduct with witnesses and defendants; using state-paid staff members to work in their campaigns; soliciting and accepting bribes; buying and selling verdicts; and just about every other kind of misconduct imaginable, including choking a fellow supreme court justice.[39] Sometimes judicial ethics seems to be in seriously short supply. In Rhode Island, a state seldom celebrated as a paragon of political virtue, two consecutive supreme court chief justices vacated the bench when faced with impeachment. One resigned following allegations and testimony that he associated with criminals and had adulterous relations with two women in a Mafia-linked motel—among other things. Later, another pleaded guilty to fixing friends and relatives' speeding tickets, using court money to pay for personal expenses, and ordering his secretary to destroy financial records.[40] Alabama Chief Justice Roy Moore was removed by the Court of the Judiciary for defying federal court orders to remove a 2½-ton Ten Commandments monument he had installed in the state judicial building.

JUDICIAL DECISION MAKING

What factors influence the rulings of state court judges? Why are some courts widely recognized as liberal (California and Hawaii) and others as conservative (Arizona and Mississippi)? Why does a prosecutor "judge shop" and prefer to file a case before one judge rather than another? Isn't justice supposed to be blind, like its symbol of the woman holding the scales?

Judges, alas, are mere mortal beings just like the rest of us. The legal formalities and jargon of the courtroom tend to mask the fact that judges' decisions are no less discretionary and subjective than the decisions of a governor, legislator, or agency head. Before we examine the factors that affect judicial decision making, however, we must distinguish between the legal settings of appellate courts and trial courts.

In and Out of the Trial Court

Approximately 90 percent of all civil and criminal cases are actually resolved outside of the courtroom. In many civil cases, the defendant never appears in court to defend himself, thereby implicitly admitting guilt, and so loses the case by default. Other civil cases are settled in a pretrial conference between the defendant and the plaintiff (where, for instance, payments on an overdue debt might be rescheduled) or through voluntary dispute resolution procedures such as mediation or arbitration.

The process of settling criminal cases out of court at the discretion of the prosecutor and the judge is called **plea bargaining**. Although some defendants plead guilty as originally charged, acknowledging guilt for a lesser charge is more typical in criminal proceedings. With the possible exceptions of the

plea bargaining
Negotiation between a prosecutor and a criminal defendant's counsel that results in the defendant's pleading guilty to a lesser charge or pleading guilty in exchange for a reduced sentence.

victim and the general citizenry, everyone benefits from plea bargaining, a fact that accounts for its extensive use. The accused gets off with lighter punishment than she would face if the case went to trial and she lost. The defense attorney frees up time to take on additional legal work. The prosecuting attorney increases his conviction rate, which looks good if he has political ambitions. The judge helps cut back the number of cases awaiting trial. Even police officers benefit by not having to spend time testifying (and waiting to testify) and by raising the department's clearance rate (the number of cases solved and disposed of).

Out-of-court settlements through plea bargaining are negotiated in a very informal atmosphere in the judge's chamber, or between attorneys in the halls of the court building, or over drinks in a neighboring pub. This is a disturbingly casual way to dispense justice. The process is secretive and far removed from any notion of due process. The prosecuting (district) attorney enjoys enormous discretion in making deals. Often her propensity to settle depends on the length of her court docket or her professional relationship with the accused's attorney, not on the merits of the case. All too often, an innocent person pleads guilty to a lesser offense for fear of being wrongly convicted of a more serious offense, or because he cannot post bail and does not want to spend any unnecessary time behind bars. Equally disturbing—particularly to a victim—is the fact that plea bargaining can soon put a guilty person back on the streets.

Nonetheless, plea bargaining is widely practiced. It is almost inevitable when the prosecutor's case hinges on weak evidence, police errors, a questionable witness, or the possibility of catching a bigger fish. Negotiation of a guilty plea for a lesser offense can occur at any stage of the criminal justice process.

bench trial
A trial by a single judge, without a jury.

If the accused is unable to make a deal with the prosecuting attorney, he faces either a **bench trial** by a single judge or a **trial by jury**. Both involve a courtroom hearing with all the legal formalities. In some jurisdictions and for certain types of cases, the defendant has a choice. In other situations, state legal procedures specify which trial format will be utilized. A jury is always mandatory for murder cases.

trial by jury
A trial in which a jury decides the facts and makes a finding of guilty or not guilty.

In a bench trial, the judge alone hears all arguments, determines the facts, and makes rulings on questions of law. Jury trials depend on a panel of citizens who decide the facts of the case; the judge instructs the jury on the applicable law. Although juries and judges would usually come to identical decisions, the uncertainty introduced by twelve laypersons is usually great enough to convince a defendant to choose a bench trial or, if offered, alternative means of resolving the dispute such as mediation. Only about 2 percent of all cases are resolved by jury trial.

When jury trials do occur, attorneys seek to limit the unpredictable nature of juries by extensively questioning individuals in the jury pool. Each side in the dispute has the right to strike the names of a certain number of potential jurors without giving a specific reason. Others are eliminated for cause, such as personal knowledge of the case or its principals. In high-stakes cases, the jury selection process involves public opinion surveys, individual background investigations of potential jurors, and other costly techniques.

Inside the Appellate Court

Appellate courts are substantially different from trial courts. No plaintiffs, defendants, or witnesses are present. The appeal consists of a review of court records and arguments advanced by the attorneys, who frequently are not the same lawyers who originally represented the parties. Appellate court rulings are issued by a panel of at least three judges, who are tasked with deciding if legal errors have occurred. Unlike decisions in most trial courts, appellate court decisions are written and published. The majority vote prevails. Judges voting in the minority have the right to make a formal, written dissent that justifies their opinion.

State supreme courts vary dramatically in ideology. The supreme courts in Hawaii, Rhode Island, and Maryland are much more liberal than those in Arizona, Mississippi, and New Hampshire. There is marked variation in the dissent rates of state appellate courts. Some courts maintain a public aura of consensus on even the most controversial matters by almost always publishing unanimous opinions. Justices may disagree, but they do not necessarily dissent formally. Other courts are racked by public disputes over legal questions. Personal, professional, partisan, political, and other disagreements can escalate into open hostility over casework. As an Illinois chief justice has observed, "dissents are born not of doubt but of firm convictions."[41] Supreme courts in states such as California, New York, Michigan, and Mississippi have a history of contentiousness, whereas others, like those in Rhode Island and Maryland, are paragons of harmony. Dissent rates appear to be positively related to state socioeconomic and political complexity, such as urbanization and partisan competition. Judges with long tenures on the bench and who do not have to face the voters in elections are more likely to dissent.[42] More dissent also occurs in courts with a large number of justices and in states with intermediate appellate courts. The more time the justices have at their disposal, the more likely they are to find reasons to disagree.

Influence of the Legal System

In addition to the facts of the case itself, judicial decision making is influenced by factors associated with the legal system, including institutional arrangements, accepted legal procedures, caseload pressures, and the ease with which certain interested parties gain access to the legal process.

Institutional Arrangements The level, or tier, of court is a structural characteristic that influences decision making. Trial court judges enforce legal norms and routinely *apply* the law as it has been written and interpreted over the years. The trial court permits direct interpersonal contacts among the judge, the jury, and the parties. Divorce cases, personal injury cases, and minor criminal cases predominate in trial courts.

Appellate courts are more apt to *interpret* the law and create public policy. Cases typically involve governments and large corporations. State constitutional issues, state–local conflicts, and challenges to government regulation of business are the kinds of issues likely to be found in appellate courts. A particular case in a high court sometimes has an enormous impact on public policy, as judges depart from established precedent or offer new interpretations of the law. Recently, the supreme court of Wisconsin essentially overturned a 1998 constitutional amendment guaranteeing the right to carry a concealed weapon; the Massachusetts supreme court legalized same-sex marriages; and Nevada's highest court nullified a state constitutional provision that two-thirds of the legislature had to approve a tax increase. Florida's supreme court struck down an education voucher system, and Iowa's, New Jersey's, and New York's instructed the legislature to recognize civil unions.

Another important institutional arrangement is the selection procedures for judges. For instance, judicial decisions may be influenced by partisan electoral competition. Especially when a judge facing reelection votes on an issue highly salient to voters, public opinion can affect the judge's ruling.[43] Death penalty cases provide a good example of this point. A study of judicial decision making in Texas, North Carolina, Louisiana, and Kentucky found that judges seeking reelection tend to uphold death sentences.[44] In these traditionally conservative states, a decision in support of the death penalty helps to avoid preelection criticism from political opponents.[45]

precedent

The legal principle that previous court decisions should be applied to future decisions.

stare decisis

The legal doctrine that precedents should guide judges' rulings.

Legal Procedures and Precedent On the basis of **precedent**, under the doctrine of *stare decisis*, the principles and procedures of law applied in one situation are applied in any similar situation. In addition, lower courts are supposed to follow the precedents established by higher courts. An individual decision may seem unimportant, but when it is taken in the context of other, similar cases it helps judicial precedent evolve. Through this practice, the doctrine of equal treatment before the law is pursued. When lower-court judges refuse to follow precedent or are ignorant of it, their decisions can be overturned on appeal. Of course, conflicting precedents may relate to a case; in such instances, a judge will choose among them in justifying his ruling. A previous ruling may become obsolete, may be manifestly absurd, or may simply clash with a judge's values or points of view.

Where do judges look to find existing precedent? Within a state, supreme court decisions set the norms. Supreme courts themselves, however, must scan the legal landscape beyond state boundaries. In the past, decisions of the U.S. Supreme Court heavily influenced those of the state supreme courts. Increasingly, however, state supreme courts are practicing doctrinal diversity and looking to one another for precedent. State appellate judges borrow from the experiences of other states. They especially tend to rely on the more professional, prestigious supreme courts, such as those of California, Washington, and Colorado.[46] State courts also tend to "network" with courts in the same region of the country, where cultural and other environmental factors are similar.[47]

Caseload Pressures Caseload affects judges' decisions. The number of cases varies in accordance with crime rates, socioeconomic characteristics of the jurisdictions, state laws, the number of judges, and many other variables. It stands to reason that the quality of judicial decision making is inversely related to caseload. Judges burdened by too much litigation are hard-pressed to devote an adequate amount of time and attention to each case before them.

Access to the System The final legal-system characteristic affecting judicial decisions is the access of individuals, organizations, and groups to the court system. Wealthy people and corporations are better able to pay for resources (attorneys, legal research, alternative dispute settlement, etc.) and therefore enter the legal system with a great advantage over poorer litigants. (Perhaps this helps account for why African Americans and Latino defendants tend to receive harsher sentences than white defendants.) Such courts often have specialized knowledge in areas of litigation, such as environmental or business regulation. Lobbying by interest groups is much less prominent in the judicial branch than in the legislative and executive branches, but groups can affect outcomes by providing financial aid to litigants in important cases, by filing amicus curiae (friend of the court) briefs supporting one side or the other in a dispute, or, in popular election systems, making monetary contributions to a judge's reelection campaign.

The states have implemented several reforms to increase access to the judicial system for those who are disadvantaged. For example, court interpreters are available in states with large Latino populations. Physical and communication barriers are being removed so that persons with disabilities can fully participate in all aspects of the legal system. Racial, ethnic, and gender biases against attorneys, plaintiffs, defendants, witnesses, and other court participants are being addressed (although women still tend to receive less severe sentences than men who commit similar crimes).[48] Night courts remain open past closing hours for people who have difficulty getting off their day jobs to appear in court. And day care is being provided for children of plaintiffs, defendants, witnesses, and jurors. Gradually, the state courts are responding to changes in the nature of society.

Personal Values, Attitudes, and Characteristics of Judges

Simply put, judges do not think and act alike. Each is a product of his or her individual background and experiences, which in turn influence decisions made in the courtroom. Studies of state court justices have found that decisions are related to the judges' party identification, political ideology, prior careers, religion, color, age, and sex. In other words, personal characteristics predispose a judge to decide cases in certain ways.

For example, Democratic judges tend to favor the claimant in civil rights cases, the injured party in liability (tort) cases, the government in tax disputes, the employee in worker's compensation cases, the government in business regulation cases, the defendant in criminal contests, the union in disagreements with management, and the tenant in landlord–tenant cases. Republicans tend to support the opposite side on all these issues. Female judges, who presently occupy one of every four state supreme court seats, are more supportive of women on sex discrimination and other feminist issues, more likely to favor the accused in death penalty and obscenity cases, and, in general, are more liberal than their male colleagues.[49] And, finally, the judge's race appears to have little effect on the sentences handed down to black and white defendants,[50] although according to one study, African American judges tend to be tougher on defendants than Latino judges.[51] Obviously, these distinctions do not hold in all situations, but the point is that "justice" is an opaque concept.

JUDICIAL FEDERALISM

During the 1950s and 1960s, the U.S. Supreme Court was far and away the leading judicial actor in the land. Under the Chief Justiceship of Earl Warren (1953–1969) and his liberal majority, the Court handed down a long series of rulings that overturned racial segregation, mandated legislative reapportionment, extended voting rights, and expanded the rights of accused criminals. Significant reversals of state court decisions were commonplace.

judicial federalism
State constitutional and statutory law are consulted and applied before federal law.

Beginning with Chief Justice Warren Burger (1969–1986) and a growing proportion of conservative justices, however, the Supreme Court changed directions in the 1970s and 1980s. Since 1988, a conservative majority has been in control. The Court has been somewhat less intrusive in state and local affairs and has, through its own caution, flashed a green light to state courts inclined to activism (see Chapter 2). The result is **judicial federalism**, in which state courts look first to state constitutional and statutory law in rendering legal judgments on important state and local issues once addressed mostly by the federal courts.

Judicial Activism in the States

judicial activism
Judges' making of public policy through decisions that overturn existing law or effectively make new laws.

Judicial activism is a term with value-laden and ideological dimensions. When associated with politically liberal Court decisions, it is decried by conservatives. Some conservative judges (such as the majority on the U.S. Supreme Court), however, are also tagged as activists. Whether liberal or conservative, all tend to show strong ideological tendencies.

An objective definition of judicial activism, then, points to court-generated change in public policy that is perceived as illegitimate by opponents who favor the status quo.[52] Judicial activism is in the eye of the beholder. All too often an "activist" judge is one who does not decide a case the way one *thinks* she should.

Regardless of one's feelings on the matter, state supreme courts have clearly become *more* activist by expanding into new policy areas. They are more likely to be involved in the policymaking process by making decisions that affect policy in the executive branch, and they even appear to preempt the lawmaking responsibility of the legislature when the courts invalidate a statute based on constitutional grounds. Examples of new judicial federalism include the following:

- California, Connecticut, and Massachusetts courts have expanded a women's right to have an abortion on demand and the right to state financial aid for abortions. Although the U.S. Supreme Court has upheld state sodomy prohibitions, courts in New York, Pennsylvania, and other states have struck down sodomy laws as violations of the right to privacy, as spelled out in state constitutions.
- Washington's supreme court ruled that a popular initiative requiring a legislative supermajority to approve tax hikes violated the state constitution.[53]
- Oregon's supreme court rejected a U.S. Supreme Court decision that provided guidelines for declaring certain printed and visual materials to be obscene. The Oregon court noted that its state constitution had been authored "by rugged and robust individuals dedicated to founding a free society unfettered by the governmental imposition of some people's views of morality on the free expression of others." The court went on to declare, "In this state, any person can write, print, read, say, show or sell anything to a consenting adult even though that expression may be generally or universally considered 'obscene.'"[54]

How can the state courts override the decisions of the highest court in the land? The answer is that they are grounding their rulings in their own constitutions instead of in the national Constitution. In several decisions, the U.S. Supreme Court has upheld the right of the states to expand on the minimum rights and liberties guaranteed under the national document. Of course, when there is an irreconcilable conflict between state and federal law, the latter prevails.

Current Trends in State Courts

The new wave of state court activism is not carrying all the ships of state with it. Many state supreme courts remain caught in the doldrums, consistently endorsing—rather than repudiating—U.S. Supreme Court decisions. Some of them are so quiet, as one wag suggested, "that you can hear their arteries harden." But even traditionally inactive courts, such as those in Wisconsin and North Carolina, have been stirred into independent actions recently. The U.S. Supreme Court is likely to have a conservative majority for the foreseeable future, permitting the state courts to explore the legal landscape further. Meanwhile, state court activism seems to be contagious, as courts utilize their own information and case networks instead of those of the Supreme Court.

Of course, with rare exceptions, judges cannot seize issues as governors and legislators can; they must wait for litigants to bring them to the courthouse. And although judges can issue rulings, they must depend on the executive and legislative branches to comply with and enforce those rulings. Nonetheless, many state supreme courts are becoming more active in the policymaking process.[55] The reluctance of the federal courts to address important and controversial issues comprehensively has resulted in more cases for state supreme courts to decide.

State court activism does have some negative points. First, some courts may overstep their authority and try to go too far in policymaking, intruding into the proper domain of executive and legislative actors. The Nevada Supreme Court, for example, ruled that the legislative branch violated the state constitution by seizing local government funds to balance the state budget.[56] Courts in California, New Jersey, and elsewhere issued similar decisions that state budget actions violated constitutional obligations, notwithstanding the problems besetting them from the Great Recession. A related problem is that judges have little expertise in the substance of public policy or in the policymaking process. They have no specialized staff to perform in-depth policy research on particular policy issues, and they cannot realistically depend on lawyers to do policy research for them. After all, lawyers are trained and practiced in legal research and reasoning, not social science or political science. Second, state courts are increasingly issuing policy decisions that have significant budgetary implications. Court rulings on school finance, prison overcrowding, and treatment of the mentally ill have severely affected state budgets. Such court actions rarely take into account their related financial effects. A third problem is that in the context of state constitutional rights, geography is limiting. A state-by-state approach may not be appropriate for such policies as civil rights, clean air and water, business regulation, or safe food, which should be provided equally for all citizens.

ADMINISTRATIVE AND ORGANIZATIONAL IMPROVEMENTS

We have already discussed several important judicial reforms: intermediate appellate courts; court consolidation; merit selection plans for judges; more practical means for disciplining and removing judges; and administrative and organizational improvements, including those of a financial nature. This last category deserves further consideration.

Financial Improvements and Pressures

The exorbitant costs of some trials can bankrupt local jurisdictions if state financial assistance is not forthcoming. For example, one child molestation case in Los Angeles County lasted two and a half years and carried a tab of $15 million. (Neither of the two defendants was convicted.) The price tag for a murder trial and subsequent appeals can also be counted in the millions. A 2007 high-profile multimurder case in Georgia effectively drained the public defender's office of resources and halted proceedings in seventy-two other capital cases.[57] Given such contingencies, more than half of the states have assumed full financial responsibility for the operation of all state and local courts.

The Great Recession resulted in substantial cuts to state court budgets, with serious consequences for indigent defendants and all parties interested in justice and speedy trials. In 2011, judicial budgets in twenty-eight states experienced serious cuts, and more occurred in 2012.[58] The alarming results included staff reductions, suspension of jury trials, reduced court operating hours, and, in some cases, even court closings.[59] New Hampshire suspended jury trials for a month in 2009; Florida laid off 10 percent of its court employees; and caseloads for prosecutors, public defenders, and judges soared nationally with rising numbers of foreclosures, civil disputes, and other filings.[60] The Massachusetts Chief Justice warned that state courts had "reached the tipping point of dysfunction."[61]

Centralized budgeting, also referred to as *unified court budgeting*, consolidates the budget for all state and local courts and details all personnel, supplies, equipment, and other expenditures. It is intended to enhance financial management and help maintain judicial independence from the executive and legislative branches. A unified court system, centralized management and financing, and unified budgeting share the objective of bringing a state's entire court system under a single authoritative administrative structure, helping to avoid additional legislative underfunding.

Dealing with Growing Caseloads

Recently, court reformers have recognized the need to deal more effectively with case backlogs. State trial courts alone confront more than 100 million new cases each year.[62] Some judges hand down more than 300 opinions annually. Delays of two years or more are not uncommon for appellate court hearings, and the unprecedented pressure is growing. Calls for tort reform to reduce the number of personal injury cases and the size of jury awards are increasingly insistent. (**Torts** account for about two-thirds of all civil trials; the average award in a tort trial is around $30,000.[63])

Excessive caseloads are caused by numerous factors, including the greater propensity of losing parties to appeal lower-court decisions, the tremendous growth in litigation, heightened interest group activity, huge increases in drug-related and drunk-driving cases, and poor caseload management procedures. Exacerbating the problem is the demand for litigation encouraged by the sheer number of lawyers in the United States, which accounts for nearly two-thirds of all the lawyers in the world (approximately 728,000 in 2010).[64]

The larger concern is that long delays thwart the progress of justice. The quality of evidence deteriorates as witnesses disappear or forget what they saw, and victims suffer from delays that prevent them from collecting damages for injuries incurred during a crime or an accident. Increasingly, criminal cases are thwarted because of witness intimidation. Innocent defendants can be harmed by the experience of being held in prison for long periods while awaiting trial.

Reducing excessive caseloads is not a simple matter. Common sense dictates establishing intermediate appellate courts and adding new judgeships. But much as a new highway draws more traffic, intermediate appellate courts, by their very existence, tend to attract more appeals. And although additional judges can speed up the trial process in lower courts, they may also add to appellate backlogs. Expanding the number of judges in an appellate court is

Torts

Torts are civil wrongs resulting in injury or harm that are recognized by law as grounds for a lawsuit by the injured party.

also problematic; hearings may actually take longer because of more input or factional divisions among judges. And for better or worse, the nation's law schools continue to pump out new lawyers looking for something to do.

The stubborn persistence of case backlogs has led to some interesting and promising new approaches:

1. *Alternative dispute resolution.* Almost all states today use mediation, arbitration, or other techniques to help settle litigation prior to or in between formal courtroom proceedings. Mediation involves a neutral third party who tries to help the disputants reach a voluntary settlement. Arbitration consists of a binding ruling by a neutral party in favor of one disputant or the other. In a growing number of states, civil litigants in search of timely settlement hire private judges to arbitrate their disputes.

2. *Fines against lawyers and litigants.* New laws or court rules provide for judges to levy monetary fines against lawyers and litigants guilty of delaying tactics, frivolous litigation, or standards violations that require cases to be heard within a specified time period.

3. *Case management systems.* Judges can take charge of their dockets and impose an aggressive case management system. Although individual systems vary widely, a typical approach is multitracking, or differentiated case management. It distinguishes between simple and complex cases, as well as between frivolous and potentially significant cases, and treats them differently. Complex and significant cases are waved on down the traditional appellate track. Simple and frivolous cases take a shorter track, usually under the direction of staff attorneys. In Vermont, this case management system is called the "rocket docket." Experiments with multitracking have been successful in reducing case delays in Arizona, Maine, New Hampshire, and other states. As previously noted, another case management innovation designed to speed up the wheels of justice is boutique courts, in which environmental law disputes, drug cases, or others with special characteristics are heard by judges in specialized courts.

4. *New technology.* Technological innovations are also improving the quality and quantity of court operations. Electronic databases (for example, LEXIS and WESTLAW) store case information and legal research and transmit information from law offices to courts. Electronic filing of court documents helps track child support payments, store case data and research, and transmit data from law offices to courts. Arraignment procedures, during which suspects are formally charged, are videotaped to save time or to prevent potential problems from a disruptive defendant. Video courtrooms, in which trials are filmed, create a more accurate trial record and cost much less than a written transcript by a court stenographer. Lawyers in high-tech courtrooms speed up proceedings by using PowerPoint, video clips, and Internet sources, all displayed for jurors on individual flat screen monitors. Audiovisual technology permits hearings, motions, pleas, sentencing, and other proceedings to be conducted long-distance between jail and courthouse, thereby both saving money and enhancing security.

5. *Performance standards.* The National Center for State Courts has developed performance standards for state trial courts to aid self-assessment and improvement.[65] A growing number of states are not only adopting quantitative indicators of the speed with which cases are processed but also trying to measure broader concerns such as access to justice, fairness and integrity, public trust and confidence, and the quality of judges' decision making.

Compensating the Judges

At first glance, judicial salaries seem high enough. In 2011, state supreme court judges earned an average of $152,000.[66] The variation is great: California justices make $218,237; their counterparts in Mississippi are paid only $112,530. Trial court judges were paid 10 to 20 percent less. These amounts, however, are substantially below what an experienced, respected attorney can expect to make. A successful lawyer who gives up private practice and a partnership for the bench must be willing to take a considerable cut in income. Unlike legislators, state judges are permitted very little outside income. Therefore, it is reasonable to ask whether the best legal minds will be attracted to judgeships, given that judicial compensation is relatively low. This dilemma exists at all levels and in all branches of public service, from the municipal finance officer to the highway patrol officer, because most state and local government compensation lags behind pay for comparable jobs in the private sector. If we expect our judges, law enforcement officers, and other public employees to be honest, productive, and highly qualified, perhaps they should be compensated fairly. Recent salary increases for state judges seem to reflect this principle.

Judicial Performance Evaluation

Who judges the judges? In popular election and merit system states, the voters hold judges accountable.[67] But voters have no voice in gubernatorial and legislative selection states. And even when judicial elections are held, how much do the voters really know about the candidates?

Judicial performance evaluation (JPE) offers an objective process to assess the performance of judges. Voters are educated, and judges can use results of the evaluation for self-improvement. First adopted by Alaska in 1975, JPE programs are now mandated in eighteen other states and under active consideration in several others. JPE involves confidential surveys of attorneys, court professionals, witnesses, jurors, and other court participants. Respondents are questioned about how the judge interprets the law, manages his workload, and interacts with people in the courtroom, among other factors.[68]

Research indicates that JPE can contribute to judicial self-improvement and provide valuable, job-related information on judges' performance to the voters. Used appropriately, JPE helps preserve the hallmark characteristics of independence and accountability of the judiciary.[69]

State Courts Today

Like the other two branches of government, the state judiciary has been reformed significantly. Court systems have been modernized and simplified, intermediate appellate courts have been added, processes have been streamlined, and case delays are being addressed as limited resources permit. Disciplinary and removal commissions now make it easier to deal with problem judges, and JPE furnishes useful data on the performance of judges. Courts are still striving for adequate financial resources, greater independence from political pressures and favoritism, and more accountability for their actions. Justice may at times appear to be an ephemeral ideal, and an expensive one at that; but it is more likely to be approximated in state judicial decisions today than ever before. But the courts, like the rest of society, are participants in the technological age. New innovations and approaches will follow the recommendations of commissions in states now studying the needs of state judicial systems in the future.

Court modernization and reform have been accompanied by increased judicial activism. The newly assertive state courts have far surpassed the federal courts in public policy activism. They sometimes blatantly disagree with federal precedents and insist on decisions grounded in state constitutional law rather than in the national constitution. In short, the state courts are actively responding to public concern with the administration of justice and, by inference, to the perennial issues of crime and criminal justice.

CHAPTER RECAP

- State courts are organized into two tiers: appellate courts and trial courts.

- The five methods for selecting judges are legislative election, partisan election, nonpartisan election, the merit plan, and gubernatorial appointment. Each selection plan has certain advantages and disadvantages—there is no "one best way."

- Many factors influence judicial decision making, including institutional arrangements; legal procedures; case precedent; caseload pressures; access to the legal system; and personal values, attitudes, and characteristics of judges.

- Judicial federalism is related to increased capability and judicial activism in many state courts.

- Efforts to reform state courts are in full swing, including financial improvements, better caseload management, and improved compensation for judges.

Key Terms

civil case *(p. 203)*
criminal case *(p. 203)*
administrative case *(p. 203)*
common law *(p. 203)*
original jurisdiction *(p. 204)*
appellate jurisdiction *(p. 204)*

limited jurisdiction trial courts *(p. 204)*
major trial court *(p. 205)*
supreme court *(p. 205)*
intermediate appellate court *(p. 205)*
plea bargaining *(p. 217)*

bench trial *(p. 218)*
trial by jury *(p. 218)*
precedent *(p. 220)*
stare decisis (p. 220)
judicial federalism *(p. 222)*
judicial activism *(p. 222)*
Torts *(p. 225)*

Internet Resources

The National Center for State Courts maintains a list of courts and their Web addresses at **www. ncsc.org/information-and-resources/browse- by-state/statecourtwebsites.aspx**. This is a rich source of information on the courts, including state court decisions, court organization, and caseload statistics.

Interesting sites include the following: California at **www.courtinfo.ca.gov**/, Florida at **www. flcourts.org**, and Alaska at **www.courts.alaska. gov**/.

The American Bar Association's website provides an analysis of current controversial cases and other legal information. It is located at **www. abanet.org**.

The Law Forum Legal Resources site, located at **www.lawforum.net**, has links to all online state and local courts.

To watch live performances of Indiana's court proceedings, see **www.in.gov/judiciary/webcast/**.

10

State–Local Relations

CHAPTER OUTLINE

- The Distribution of Authority
- State–Local Organizations
- Metropolitics: A New Challenge for State Government
- States and Their Rural Communities
- The Interaction of States and Localities

FOCUS QUESTIONS

1. How would you characterize state–local government relationships, from the state perspective and from the local perspective?
2. What are the three types of common state–local organizations?
3. What are the causes and consequences of urban sprawl and smart growth?
4. Regionalism may be a solution to what major issues in state–local relations?

In 2013, the city council of Austin, Texas, adopted an ordinance that banned single-use plastic bags at retail establishments. Austin was following in the footsteps of several California cities that had enacted similar ordinances over the past several years. Later in 2013, a member of the Texas House of Representatives introduced legislation that would prohibit municipalities in the Lone Star state from adopting such an ordinance. That same year, a California state senator introduced a bill that would establish a statewide ban on plastic bags, thereby superseding local ordinances. Neither bill passed that year, but despite their opposite intentions (in Texas, to prevent cities from banning plastic bags and in California, to institute a bag ban statewide), the underlying theme was the same: the state's action would supplant local preferences.[1] Can state governments impose these types of limitations on their localities? The answer is an emphatic "yes." A state can supersede the local governments within its boundaries.

The relationship between states and their communities is often strained. On the one hand, state government gives local governments life. States create the rules for their localities. On the other hand, state governments historically have not treated their local governments very well. It appears, however, that states have realized that mistreating their governmental offspring is counter-productive, and many have launched a sometimes uncoordinated process of assistance and empowerment of local governments.

Capturing this evolution is the statement of the National Conference of State Legislatures (NCSL) Task Force on State–Local Relations: "Legislators should place a higher priority on state–local issues than has been done in the past. The time has come to change their attitude toward local governments—to stop considering them as just another special interest group and to start treating them as partners in our federal system."[2] Stronger, more competent local governments are an asset to state government.

THE DISTRIBUTION OF AUTHORITY

In essence, local governments are creatures of their states. In the terminology of Chapter 2, the relationship is that of a unitary system: The state holds all legal power. Federal and state courts have consistently upheld the dependency of localities on the state since Iowa judge John F. Dillon first laid down **Dillon's rule** in 1868. Dillon's rule established that local governments may exercise only those powers explicitly granted to them by the state, those clearly implied by these explicit powers, and those absolutely essential to the declared objectives and purposes of the local government. Any doubt regarding the legality of a specific local government power is resolved in favor of the state.[3] This perspective runs counter to the more Jeffersonian concept that local governments are imbued with inherent rights, an argument that was elaborated in a Michigan Supreme Court ruling in 1871.[4]

Dillon's rule

A rule that limits the powers of local government to those expressly granted by the state or those powers closely linked to the expressed powers.

In the words of the U.S. Advisory Commission on Intergovernmental Relations (ACIR), "State legislatures are the trustees of the basic rules of local governance in America. The laws and constitutions of each state are the basic legal instruments of local governance."[5] The ACIR statement denotes the essence of the distribution of authority between a state and its localities. In short, it is up to the state to determine the amount and type of authority a local government may possess. As specified by Dillon's rule, localities depend on the state to grant them sufficient power to operate effectively.

The Amount and Type of Authority

As the discussion indicates, states' regulatory reach is potentially extensive. For example, states may regulate local governments':

- finances (by establishing debt limits and requiring balanced budgets),
- personnel (by setting qualifications for certain positions and prescribing employee pension plans),

- structure (by establishing forms of government and outlawing particular electoral systems),
- processes (by requiring public hearings and open meetings and mandating financial disclosure),
- functions (by ordering the provision of public safety functions and proscribing the pursuit of enterprise activities),
- service standards (by adopting solid waste guidelines and setting acceptable water quality levels).

The preceding list makes the point: The state capitol casts a long shadow.

It is important to note that the amount and type of authority that states give their local governments vary widely. Some states grant their localities wideranging powers to restructure themselves, impose new taxes, and take on additional functions. Others, much more conservative with their power, force local governments to turn to the legislature for approval to act. Empowerment also depends on the type of local government. General-purpose governments such as counties, cities, and towns typically have wider latitude than special-purpose entities like school districts. (The concept of general-purpose governments is discussed in Chapter 11.) Even among general-purpose governments, there are different degrees of authority; counties tend to be more circumscribed than cities in their ability to modify their form of government and expand their service offerings.

Building codes offer an illustration of the variability in state–local authority. Several years ago, researcher Peter May examined all fifty states to determine the amount of discretion allowed local governments to adopt and enforce building codes.[6] He found several different patterns. Twelve states (Kentucky and Michigan among them) played an aggressive role, imposing mandatory building codes on their local governments and overseeing local compliance. Thirteen states (including Indiana and Wyoming) had mandatory local codes but stopped short of state review or oversight. The rest of the states gave their local governments more leeway. In eight states (Iowa and Nebraska among them), local governments themselves decided whether to enforce the state building code. And in seventeen states (including Delaware and Oklahoma), there were no comprehensive building codes; thus, local governments were free to design and enact their own **ordinances**. The building code example underscores a second important point: States vary in their treatment of local government.

ordinance

Enacted by the governing body, it is the local government equivalent of a law.

home rule

The legal ability of a local government to run its own affairs, subject to state oversight.

Many state constitutions set forth a provision for **home rule**, which, although it falls short of actual local self-government, is an important step in the direction of greater local decision making.[7] Home rule means that local officials can tailor their policies to fit their community, but it also means less uniformity from one jurisdiction to another. (In a few states, home rule provisions are statutory, not constitutional.) And local jurisdictions tend to be extremely protective of whatever power they have wrested from state government. For example, the beleaguered Baltimore school system resisted a state plan to take over the schools in 2004 because, in the words of one local official, "the solution to the problems in Baltimore city starts with Baltimore city."[8] An even more dramatic case is that of Detroit, where in 2013, over the fierce protests of the city's elected officials, the governor of Michigan appointed an emergency manager to take control of the city's troubled finances.

A State–Local Tug of War

Local governments want their states to provide them with adequate funding and ample policymaking discretion. Local officials are supremely confident of their abilities to govern, given sufficient state support. These same local officials express concern that neither their policymaking power nor their financial authority has kept pace with the increased administrative responsibilities placed on them by state government. This shift in power that they seek is known as **second-order devolution**. For example, in 2011, the Alabama legislature authorized its cities and counties to create public organizations to promote tourism; in Oklahoma, municipalities were given more leeway by the state to tear down abandoned buildings. In both cases, the state did not require local governments to act but rather gave them the authority to act if they so desired. What kinds of states tend to give their localities comparatively more power? On average, states that operate with traditional citizen-style, part-time legislative bodies are more likely to empower their local governments, as are states with slower rates of population growth and less robust economies.[9]

The diagram presented in Figure 10.1 reflects the two fundamental ways states can influence the authority of local governments. One way is through the vertical state–local government relationship—states can choose to retain power (centralize) or disperse power (decentralize). The other way is horizontal—the power relationships of local governments to each other. Combining the two dimensions, vertical and horizontal, produces the four square-shaped boxes on the right half of the diagram.[10] Box A reflects a state that centralizes vertically and horizontally; Box C is a state that decentralizes on both dimensions. In a metropolitan area in "A" states, there are few local governments, and they lack power. In states characterized by the pattern described in box "C," many local governments exist and they enjoy substantial power. The states depicted by boxes B and D have one centralizing feature and one decentralizing feature. A state's political history, its constitution, and actions of the legislature combine to determine where a state fits in this diagram. Too, some shifts can occur over time, especially as metropolitan areas develop.

The ability of states and localities to work together effectively has gotten a real test with the issue of homeland security. Concerned that state and local governments were ill-prepared to respond to a disaster in a comprehensive and cooperative way, the federal government funded several antiterrorism exercises. One simulation, a bomb and chemical weapon attack, took place in Connecticut; the other, a bioterror incident, was set in New Jersey.[11] The exercises exposed weaknesses in response capability, especially in communications among responders. The results of the mock disasters sent state and local officials throughout the nation back to the drawing boards to try to determine how to improve their response systems. One outcome has been the creation of "all

second-order devolution
A shift in power from state government to local government.

FIGURE 10.1

Typology of Governance Structure of Metropolitan Regions

SOURCE: David K. Hamilton, David Y. Miller, and Jerry Paytas, "Exploring Horizontal and Vertical Dimensions of the Governing of Metropolitan Regions," *Urban Affairs Review* 40 (November 2004): 152. Copyright 2004 by *Sage Publications Inc. Journals*. Reproduced with permission from *Sage Publications Inc. Journals* in the format Textbook via Copyright Clearance Center.

hazards" emergency operations plans that identify and assign responsibilities to state and local agencies—and to nonprofit organizations—in the event of a disaster. These plans are designed to improve coordination and communication not only vertically (between the state government and localities) but also horizontally (among local jurisdictions).

State Mandates

Although local governments generally want increased autonomy, state governments have shared their policymaking sphere with reluctance. Rather than let these "subgovernments" devise their own solutions to problems, states frequently prefer to impose a solution. For instance, when solid waste management became a concern in Florida, the state legislature's reaction was to require counties to establish recycling programs. Not only were counties required to initiate programs, they were ordered to achieve a recycling rate of 30 percent.[12] This kind of requirement or order is an example of a _mandate._ Unfunded mandates are a persistent source of friction between state and local levels of government.

From the perspective of state government, mandates are necessary to ensure that vital activities are performed and desirable goals are achieved. State mandates promote uniformity of policy from one jurisdiction to another (for instance,

POLICY AREA	AVERAGE FOR CITY MANAGERS	AVERAGE FOR STATE LEGISLATORS
The Impact of State Mandates: Comparing the Perceptions of City Managers and State Legislators		
Parks and Recreation	−0.29	−0.05
Health	−0.50	0.19
Hospitals	−0.60	−0.14
Police	−0.65	0.00
Economic Development	−0.62	0.25
Corrections	−0.67	0.00
Public Welfare	−0.69	0.05
Highways	−0.78	0.00
Natural Resources	−0.84	−0.05
Land Use and Planning	−1.05	0.00
Education	−1.21	0.09
Financial Administration	−1.25	0.05

TABLE 10.1

NOTE: Scores reflect each group's perceptions of the impact of state mandates (e.g., legislative enactments, regulatory actions, administrative actions, and court decisions) since 2000 on cities. Lowest possible score is −2 (state mandates have had a significant negative impact); highest possible score is +2 (state mandates have had a significant positive impact).

SOURCE: Adapted from Ann O'M. Bowman and Richard C. Kearney, "Second-Order Devolution: Data and Doubt," *Publius: The Journal of Federalism* 41 (Fall 2011): 573.

regarding the length of the public school year or the operating hours of precinct polling places). In addition, they promote coordination, especially among adjacent jurisdictions that provide services jointly (as with a regional hospital or a metropolitan transportation system).

Officials at the local level tend to see state mandates as unnecessary, and often costly, intrusions into local matters. A recent nationwide survey of city managers and state legislators captured the differing perspectives of the two groups.[13] When asked about the impact of state mandates in twelve policy areas, city managers judged them as negative across the board, while state legislators viewed nine of twelve as positive or neutral. Table 10.1 displays the average scores of the two groups. The range of possible scores runs from −2 (most negative) to +2 (most positive).

Local officials offer several suggestions for fixing the mandate problem. Three solutions supported by more than 80 percent of officials surveyed in a Minnesota study of state mandates are as follows:

- The state should provide a clear statement of the rationale behind the mandate; in other words, the state should justify its action.

- Localities should be given greater flexibility in implementing the provisions of the mandate.
- Financial aid to local governments should be increased so that they can deal with mandates effectively.[14]

As might be expected, these solutions are substantially less popular with state officials. But certainly, more communication between state policymakers and local officials, especially at the outset, would reduce some of the friction generated by mandates. Allowing local governments more leeway in implementation, either through extension of time or variation in rules, would lessen the punch that mandates pack. Even more central to any type of mandate reform is adequate state funding of mandates. This action would go a long way toward improving state–local relationships. Recognizing that funding is one of the key considerations, some states have adopted **mandate-reimbursement requirements**. These measures require states either to reimburse local governments for the costs of state mandates or to give local governments adequate revenue-raising capacity to pay for them.

mandate reimbursement requirements
Measures that take the financial sting out of state mandates.

State and Local Government Finances: An Uneasy Relationship

A conflicted relationship exists between states and local governments when it comes to money. Cities, counties, and other local governments will always live within the constitutional constraints of their states. Localities enjoy their own sources of revenue—property taxes, user fees, and business license fees—but depend on the states for much of their income. They suffer the frustration of having to cope with rising expenditure demands from their residents while their authority to raise new monies is highly circumscribed by state law. No wonder they turn to the national government to bail them out when times are tough.

But by far the single largest source of local revenues is the state. About 40 percent of all state expenditures goes to local governments. Like federal grants-in-aid, however, state grants come with lots of strings attached. Most state dollars are earmarked for public education and social welfare; other state assistance is targeted for roads, hospitals, public safety, and public health. The result is that local governments have little discretion in spending state-appropriated funds. And as noted, during bad economic times, states have a tendency to push a portion of their own budget shortfalls down to their already struggling local governments.

Naturally, great diversity characterizes the levels of encumbered (earmarked) and unencumbered state assistance to local jurisdictions, much of which is related to the distribution of functions between a state and its localities. Highly centralized states fund and administer at the state level many programs that are funded and administered locally in decentralized states. In states where taxation and expenditure limitations have hampered the ability of local jurisdictions to raise and spend revenues, the trend has been toward fiscal centralization at the state level. Greater centralization has also resulted from state efforts to reduce service disparities between wealthy and poor jurisdictions, and to lessen the dependence of local governments on the property tax.

What Local Governments Want from the States

Simply put, when it comes to state-local fiscal relations, what localities want most is *more money*. But they also want more control over how it is spent and the independent power to raise it. The Great Recession, taxpayer resistance, unfunded federal and state mandates, and pressing infrastructure needs have left many local jurisdictions in a financial bind. State governments know they must provide help. State aid for all local governments has grown over the past decades, though not as much as local governments would like. And during the recent economic troubles, many states cut funding to local governments and pulled back local governments' share of sales and other tax revenues, all while foisting new service delivery responsibilities on them.[15]

Most state aid is devoted to education, corrections, health care, and social services. But many states also distribute a portion of their tax revenues based on local fiscal need, thus tending to equalize or level economic disparities between local jurisdictions.

The specific means for sharing revenues takes many forms. Most of the states make special PILOTS (payments in lieu of taxes) transfers to local governments where state buildings or other facilities are located. These buildings or facilities are exempt from property taxes but cause a drain on local services. Such payments are of particular concern to capital cities, in which large plots of prime downtown property are occupied by state office buildings.

In addition, local governments want the *legal capacity to raise additional revenues themselves,* especially through local option sales and income taxes. A share of gasoline, tobacco, and other tax benefits is greatly appreciated, as is the authority to impose impact fees on developers of residential property. The key is local option, whereby jurisdictions and their voters can decide for themselves which, if any, of these additional taxes they will exact. More than two-thirds of the states have authorized an optional sales or income tax for various local governments, and some permit localities to adopt optional earmarked taxes. Local option taxes are attractive because they provide local jurisdictions with the flexibility to take action as they see fit in response to local needs. What protects citizens against "taxaholic" local legislative bodies is the state requirement that local tax hikes must be approved by the voters in a referendum.

As noted in the "State Mandates" section of this chapter, localities also want limitations on and reimbursements for state mandates. Local governments believe that they should not have to obey *and* pay, and that states should reimburse them for expenses incurred in carrying out mandates. Although some states have enacted mandate reimbursement requirements, most states have responded to this request by attaching fiscal notes to any proposed legislation or administrative regulation or rule that involves local governments; these notes estimate the local costs and fiscal impact of implementing the legislation.

More money, more power to spend it based on local preferences, and freedom from mandates would go a long way in addressing local governments' complaints about their state government. But at a time when dollars are tight and there is greater public scrutiny about how those dollars are spent by governments at all levels, local jurisdictions are unlikely to see their fiscal "wants" realized.

STATE–LOCAL ORGANIZATIONS

Legal, administrative, and financial ties link state and local governments. Additional interaction occurs when state governments establish organizations such as local government study commissions and advisory panels of local officials. Among the most prevalent structures are task forces, advisory commissions on intergovernmental relations, and departments of community affairs.

Task forces tend to be focused organizations set up by the governor or the state legislature in response to a perceived local-level problem. If a state wants to investigate the ramifications of changing its **annexation** statutes, the legislature might create a task force on annexation and boundary changes (or something similar), composed of state and local officials, community leaders, and experts on the subject of annexation. First, the task force would collect information on how other states handle the annexation question; next; it would conduct a series of public hearings to get input from individuals and groups interested in the issue; and, finally, it would compile a report that included recommendations suitable for legislative action. Its work completed, the task force would then disband, although individual members might turn up as advocates when the task force's recommendations receive legislative attention. Task forces are quick organizational responses to local problems that have become too prominent for state government to ignore. A task force is a low-cost, concentrated reaction that undertakes specific tasks and, in some instances, actually influences legislative deliberations.

In a more comprehensive effort at state–local cooperation, twenty-five states established state-level *advisory commissions on intergovernmental relations* (ACIRs), modeled after the commission, now defunct, created by the U.S. Congress in 1959. State-level ACIRs are designed to promote more harmonious, workable relations between the state and its governmental subdivisions. They are intended to offer a neutral forum for discussion of long-range state–local issues—a venue in which officials can engage in focused dialogue; conduct research on local developments and new state policies; promote experimentation in intergovernmental processes, both state–local and interlocal; and develop suggested solutions to state–local problems.[16]

Despite their promise, many state ACIRs met their demise in the 1990s and early 2000s, among them the ACIRs in Oklahoma and Virginia, victims of budget cuts and insufficient legislative support. (Kansas bucked the trend by creating an ACIR in 2002). By 2009, only ten state ACIRs remained viable.

annexation
The addition of unincorporated adjacent territory to a municipality.

Those that have survived have been able to demonstrate their utility and steer a nonpartisan path in a partisan environment.[17]

Another way in which states can generate closer formal ties with their local governments is through specialized administrative agencies. All fifty states have created *departments of community affairs* (DCAs) that are involved in local activities. They have different labels (Kentucky calls its DCA the Department for Local Government; Washington's is the Department of Community, Trade and Economic Development), but their function is similar: to offer a range of programs and services to local governments. DCAs are involved in housing, urban revitalization, antipoverty programs, and economic development; they also offer local governments such services as planning, management, and financial assistance. DCAs vary on several dimensions: their niche in state government, the sizes of their budget and staff, and whether they include an advisory board of local officials. Compared with state-level ACIRs, DCAs function much more as service deliverers and much less as policy initiators. Therefore, these two types of organizations tend to complement rather than compete with one another. Both function as advocates for local government, however, at the state level.

METROPOLITICS: A NEW CHALLENGE FOR STATE GOVERNMENT

State governments often find their dealings with local governments to be confounded by the side effects of urban change. Regardless of which state we examine, its urban areas show the effects of three waves of suburbanization. An early wave occurred during the 1920s, when automobiles facilitated the development of outlying residential areas. Although the dispersion slowed during the Great Depression and World War II, its resurgence in the 1950s triggered a second wave, during which retail stores followed the population exodus, the so-called malling of America. Now a third wave of suburbanization is upon us, one fueled by what has been called America's "exit ramp economy." Office, commercial, and retail facilities are increasingly located along suburban freeways.[18] This phenomenon is occurring nearly everywhere, from New York City to San Diego, from Milwaukee to Miami. This third wave has caught the attention of state governments.

As a result of the transformation of American **metropolitan areas**, central cities have lost some of their prominence as the social, economic, and political focal points. People have moved to surrounding **suburbs** and beyond; businesses and firms have sprung up in the hinterlands; communities have formed their own service and taxing districts. The outward flow of people and activities has fundamentally altered metropolitan areas, creating a multiplicity of local governments. Continued growth beyond the central city suggests the need for changes in outmoded state government policy toward metropolitan

metropolitan area

A central city of at least 50,000 people, the adjacent suburbs, and the surrounding county (or counties); often called an urban area.

suburbs

Populated areas, often residential in character, on the outskirts of a central city. Some suburbs have their own governments; some do not.

jurisdictions. A serious concern is that rapid, unplanned growth is producing sprawl. A logical question is: What is state government doing while all of this is occurring? The answer: more than it used to, as the next section of the chapter explains.

Urban Sprawl Versus Smart Growth

Population growth is, of course, something that states and localities desire. But the consequences of rapid and unplanned population growth test the capability of governments to provide services efficiently and effectively. As growth spills beyond city limits into unincorporated areas, as **edge cities** spring up along interstate highways, the result is often traffic congestion and overcrowded schools. Far from the central city, subdivisions and strip malls sprout up on land that was recently forests and farms. It costs a lot of money for government to provide infrastructure—streets, water and sewer lines, schools—to these new developments. Meanwhile, many inner cities, where the infrastructure is already in place, are plagued by empty storefronts, vacant lots, and abandoned factories. Many states and localities have struggled to balance the benefits of new growth against the attendant costs.

edge cities

New boom towns featuring retail shops and malls, restaurants, office buildings, and housing developments, far from the central city.

Sprawling Growth One of the hottest issues of the early twenty-first century is **urban sprawl**, a term that carries negative connotations. It refers to development beyond the central city that is characterized by low densities, rapid land consumption, and dependence on the automobile. It is often called leapfrog development because it jumps over established settlements. Exit ramp communities and edge cities are a manifestation of sprawl. Urban sprawl is resource-intensive and costly, and it is also the subject of much political debate.

urban sprawl

Development characterized by low population density, rapid land consumption, and dependence on the automobile.

Until the mortgage crisis in 2008 and the subsequent recession, Las Vegas, Nevada, offered perhaps the best contemporary example of a fast growing, sprawling city. According to the city's statistics, "two hundred new residents arrive in Las Vegas every day; a house is built every fifteen minutes."[19] Traffic congestion intensified as did concern over maintaining an adequate water supply in this desert city. As human settlement pushed ever outward to lower-cost land, local government was pressed to provide schools, parks, and roads. Growth quickly outstripped the infrastructure needed to support it. The mayor of Las Vegas proposed a $2,000 per house **impact fee** to mitigate the effects of growth, but the city lacked the authority to levy the fee. The Nevada legislature had to approve the proposal before it could take effect.

impact fee

A fee, levied by a government on developers, which is intended to shift some of the societal costs of growth to the developer.

Although the pace of growth has slowed in Las Vegas and the surrounding area, the issues related to planning and paying for new development remain. Even though revenues for local governments will increase as a result of development, costs of providing services will also rise and not necessarily commensurately. One study of Georgia counties found that for every $1.00 of revenue brought in by new housing developments, the cost of services was between $1.23 and $2.07.[20] Public education was the big-ticket item pushing up service costs. This is the primary explanation for the popularity of impact fees. Research on Florida counties found that rapid population growth stimulates the adoption of impact fees especially if nearby counties have adopted them already.[21] Only when commercial and industrial development complements subdivision growth do local governments typically enjoy a net revenue gain.

The relentless creep of urban sprawl has prompted reactions in many states and communities. In 2012, fifty-seven open space protection measures appeared on ballots throughout the country; forty-six of them passed. These measures committed more than $2 billion for land conservation; much of it in the form of tax increases.[22] In Alabama, for instance, more than 75 percent of voters supported the twenty-year extension of the state's Forever Wild land conservation program, funded by revenue collected from offshore drilling. In Houston voters overwhelmingly approved a $166 million park bond to complete the last sections of the city's bayou greenways network.

Smart Growth The majority of land use decisions occur at the local level. Many states have begun to provide localities with more tools to manage growth. Hawaii was a pioneer in this effort with its State Land Use Law, adopted in 1961; Vermont and Oregon got on board in 1970 and 1973, respectively, with growth management acts designed to control the pace of development and protect environmentally sensitive areas. The **smart growth** movement represents the new generation in state growth management. It is an effort to reduce the amount of sprawl and minimize its impact. Communities tend to define "smart growth" in ways that fit their own particular circumstances, but the basic principles of the movement are listed in Table 10.2.

smart growth
Government efforts to limit urban sprawl by managing growth.

The Principles of Smart Growth	TABLE 10.2
SMART GROWTH INVOLVES MANY OF THESE PRINCIPLES:	
• Create a range of housing opportunities and choices	
• Create walkable neighborhoods	
• Encourage community and stakeholder collaboration	
• Foster distinctive, attractive communities with a strong sense of place	
• Make development decisions predictable, fair, and cost-effective	
• Mix land uses	
• Preserve open space, farmland, natural beauty, and critical environmental areas	
• Provide a variety of transportation choices	
• Strengthen and direct development towards existing communities	
• Take advantage of compact building design	

SOURCE: Smart Growth Network, "Smart Growth Principles," www.smartgrowth.org/about/default.asp (August 26, 2010).

Maryland was one of the first states to take action to limit sprawl. Calling sprawl "a disease eating away at the heart of America," Governor Parris Glendening signed the Smart Growth Areas Act into law in 1997.[23] In effect, the state rewards local governments that target new growth to areas that already have infrastructure, and it denies state funding for infrastructure projects that encourage sprawl. Several other states moved quickly to follow Maryland's lead. The following year, Arizona adopted the Growing Smarter Act; by 2003, another twenty states had taken antisprawl actions of one sort or another.[24] A particularly ambitious plan was New Jersey's Blueprint for Intelligent Growth (BIG). Had BIG been adopted as originally drafted, huge portions of the Garden State would have been off limits to additional development, much to the dismay of many local officials and builders.[25] Although the far-reaching antisprawl proposal was eventually pared down, it was clear that in New Jersey, as in many other places, state governments are reestablishing themselves as major influences in local governments' land use decisions.

A word of caution is necessary. Not everyone thinks that sprawl is so bad. In fact, to some, sprawl is simply the consequence of the unfettered workings of a market economy.[26] Given a choice, they contend, Americans prefer a spread out, car-centered lifestyle. Obviously, there is some truth to that argument. Smart growth inevitably means higher density, that is, smaller lot sizes and taller buildings to accommodate more people. High-rise condominium complexes and soaring office towers appeal to some folks, but to most suburbanites, increased density is not something they want.[27]

Regional Governance

regional government
An area-wide structure for local governance, designed to replace multiple jurisdictions.

A **regional government** is a structure put in place because of the interdependence of proximate communities. A typical metropolitan area is fragmented, that is, it is comprised of many local governments. Under a regional government, local jurisdictions give up some of their power and authority to a larger government in exchange for area-wide solutions to local problems. State legislatures are important players in this process because, aside from the state constitution, they create the rules of the regional game. Their actions either facilitate or hinder local government reorganization into regional units.

city–county consolidation
The merger of city and county governments into a single jurisdiction.

City–County Consolidation In the United States, the closest thing to regional government is **city–county consolidation**, whereby area jurisdictions are absorbed into a single countywide government. Structure and function are unified. In a pure consolidation, one police department, one fire department, and one water and sewer system serve the entire area. The functions of local government—public safety, public works, health and human services, community and economic development, and recreation and arts programs—are provided by a single jurisdiction. Thirty-three city–county consolidated governments operate in the United States. Some of these consolidated governments reflect political decisions of the nineteenth century, such as the city–county governments of Philadelphia, San Francisco, and New Orleans. Among the most prominent mergers of the past forty years are those of Indianapolis–Marion County, Indiana; Jacksonville–Duval County, Florida; Nashville–Davidson County, Tennessee; and more recently, Louisville–Jefferson County, Kentucky.

Regional government seems so rational, yet it has proven to be quite difficult to achieve. Voters usually defeat proposals to consolidate city and county government. At various times, voters have rejected the mergers of Des Moines and Polk County, Iowa; Albuquerque and Bernalillo County, New Mexico; Topeka and Shawnee County, Kansas; Memphis and Shelby County, Tennessee, to name but a few. Opponents of jurisdictional consolidation often include city and county governing boards, city and county employees, and taxpayer organizations. Support for merging governments typically comes from the local Chamber of Commerce, real estate developers, local newspapers, and civic organizations.[28]

To reformers, this lack of success is perplexing. The logic is straightforward: If small local governments in a metropolitan area merge to form a larger local government, two positive outcomes will occur. First, stubborn public policy problems can be tackled from an area-wide perspective. For example, the pollution generated by city A but affecting city B can be handled as a regional problem rather than as a conflict between the two cities. Second, combining forces produces *economies of scale* in service delivery. Instead of a situation in which each jurisdiction constructs and operates jails, for example, one large regional facility can be maintained, providing jail service at a lower cost to each participating jurisdiction. These anticipated outcomes are persuasive arguments in favor of consolidation.

Regional government does not always perform as expected, however. Research has shown that city–county consolidation does not necessarily reduce the costs of government, and may even increase them.[29] Another criticism of regional government is that it can be inaccessible and destructive of the hard-won political gains of minorities. Compared with a city or town government, regional government is farther away, both literally and figuratively. Residents of small towns fear the loss of identity as their community gets swept into bigger government. The effect on minority political strength is no less troublesome. Because the proportionate number of minorities may be lessened when jurisdictions are combined, their voting strength can be diluted. For instance, African Americans comprised 34 percent of premerger Louisville, Kentucky, but only 19.5 percent of the consolidated Louisville–Jefferson County Metro Government.[30]

A competing perspective on regional government comes from **public choice theory**. According to this theory, the existence of many jurisdictions in a metropolitan area gives people options, that is, they can choose to live in the central city, in nearby suburbs, or in the county. Each of these jurisdictions offers a particular mix of tax rates, policies, and public services. In deciding where to reside or open a business, individuals seek places that are in line with their own tax, policy, and service preferences.[31] To public choice theorists, consolidating cities and counties or creating regional governments robs people of important choices and creates inefficiencies. The consolidation of

public choice theory

The theory that individuals shop around to find a local government whose taxes and services are in line with their own preferences.

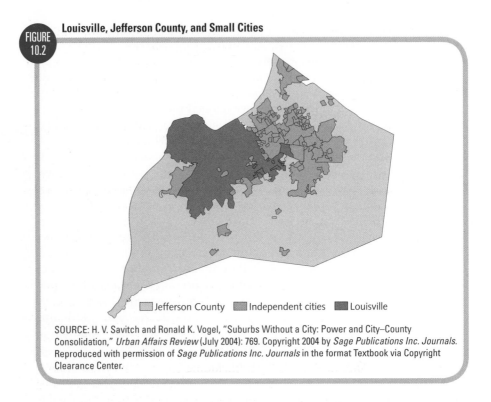

FIGURE 10.2 Louisville, Jefferson County, and Small Cities

Jefferson County ▢ Independent cities ▢ Louisville ▢

SOURCE: H. V. Savitch and Ronald K. Vogel, "Suburbs Without a City: Power and City–County Consolidation," *Urban Affairs Review* (July 2004): 769. Copyright 2004 by *Sage Publications Inc. Journals.* Reproduced with permission of *Sage Publications Inc. Journals* in the format Textbook via Copyright Clearance Center.

the city of Louisville and Jefferson County borrowed a page from public choice theory when, in a political compromise, it left 80 smaller jurisdictions in the county out of the merger. Figure 10.2 shows the boundaries of preconsolidated Louisville and Jefferson County, as well as the other jurisdictions.

A City and Its Suburbs The former mayor of Albuquerque, David Rusk, after thinking long and hard about the relationship between a central city and its suburbs, jumped into the regionalism debate with this statement: "The real city is the total metropolitan area—city and suburb."[32] He uses the concept of elasticity (and inelasticity) to signify the ability of a city to expand its city boundaries (or not) through annexation. In a sense, a city's elasticity is its destiny. Elastic cities are able to capture suburban growth; by adjusting their boundaries through annexation, they can keep pace with urban sprawl. Conversely, many inelastic cities trapped in existing boundaries suffer population loss and tax base erosion, resulting in higher levels of racial and class segregation.

The solution offered is a familiar one: metropolitan (or regional) government. But to be effective, the metropolitan government must include the central city and at least 60 percent of the area's population, according to Rusk. How to do this? It depends on the characteristics of the metropolitan area. In single-county metropolitan areas, empowerment of the urban county would effectively create metropolitan government, as would city–county consolidation. And in multicounty metropolitan areas, a single regional government could be created out of existing cities and counties. Obviously, the restructuring of local governments in these ways would engender substantial opposition; as Rusk acknowledges, however, there are few alternatives in areas with low elasticity.

The argument for a metropolitan-wide government is simple: Because economies are essentially regional in nature, governance can (and should) be, too. As discussed earlier, however, regional governance has never been a popular alternative in this country. Overcoming traditional antiregionalism sentiment will not be easy, but regional approaches may be necessary for effective competition in an increasingly global economy. And there is some evidence that thinking regionally is gaining favor. Maybe the mayor of Missoula, Montana, a college town, said it best when he commented: "It is not possible for Missoula to understand itself, or its future, except in a regional context. The city draws its strength from the region."[33]

It's Up to the States Both Portland, Oregon, and the Twin Cities area of Minnesota have embraced regionalism. In Oregon, Portland joined with its suburbs and outlying jurisdictions to develop a region-wide vision for the future. The 2040 Plan, as it is called, aims at accommodating orderly growth while maintaining a desirable quality of life in the region. The planning process involved extensive public participation, including citizen surveys and public forums. In addition, the plan's backers launched media campaigns and loaned videos to acquaint residents with the proposal. The 2040 Plan is enforced by an elected, region-wide council that works to secure the compliance of local governments. In addition, the council conducts periodic updates, "Portland's Progress," to gauge whether the implementation of the plan is on track.

In the Minneapolis–St. Paul area of Minnesota, jurisdictions contribute 40 percent of their new commercial and industrial tax base to a regional pool. The money in this pool is redistributed to communities throughout the region on the basis of financial need, thereby reducing fiscal disparities across jurisdictions. Thus, for instance, a new industry locating in one city becomes a benefit to neighboring cities as well. With regional tax base sharing as a start, Minnesota went even further in 1994, when the state legislature placed all regional sewer, transit, and land use planning in the hands of a regional organization—the Metropolitan Council of the Twin Cities.[34] This significantly empowered council makes crucial decisions about growth and development in the Twin Cities area from a regional perspective.

In the final analysis, it is up to state government to provide a sufficiently supportive environment in which regionalism can take root. It was Oregon and Minnesota that created the legal environment for Portland and the Twin Cities, respectively. As political scientists Margaret Weir, Harold Wolman, and Todd Swanstrom declared in their research on city–suburban coalitions, "states are critical players; they set the terms and conditions under which regionalism occurs."[35] They have to because the natural tendency for officials in cities and their suburbs is to see each other as rivals rather than allies or partners.

councils of governments (COGs)

Formal organizations of general-purpose governments in an area, intended to improve regional coordination.

Regional Coordination Councils of governments (COGs), or regional planning commissions, are examples of regional coordination. They do not involve a formal merger or combination of governments; instead, COGs are loose collections of local governments designed to increase communication and coordination in an area. They provide a neutral forum in which local leaders can come together to identify and discuss issues of common concern.[36] For instance, the Metropolitan Washington (D.C.) COG recently conducted a planning exercise organized around four "what if?" scenarios:

- an extended economic recession and massive government debt,
- low oil prices that derail strong climate change policies,
- the dispersal of many federal government agencies from the region,
- the advent of a green industrial revolution.[37]

The point of the scenario planning process was to get local leaders thinking about how large-scale events could affect the future.

State governments, in fact, were not active in the creation of COGs; national government programs spurred their development. For example, the federal government requires states to use planning organizations such as COGs to coordinate transportation programs in urban areas where a multitude of local governments exists.[38] Currently, there are more than 500 COGs active in the United States.

Although area-wide planning is the most common activity of councils of government, they also perform other tasks. Member governments can turn to these councils for technical assistance (such as help in writing federal grant applications), professional services (planning, budgeting, engineering, legal advice), and information (economic data for the region). For example, when city officials in Colorado Springs, Colorado, were developing their plans for a bicycle trail system in 2013, they decided to partner with the area COG. As a local reporter explained, "City officials could have gone it alone, but they figured it would be wiser to be part of a regional effort to leverage funding and brainpower" and work with the Pikes Peak Area Council of Governments.[39]

The impact of these councils has been less significant than their creators hoped, but they have had at least two positive effects. First, councils have elevated the concept of area-wide policy planning from a pipe dream to a reality. They have been heavily involved in criminal justice, water quality, housing, and especially transportation planning. Second, councils have substantially improved the operational capacity of rural local governments by providing expertise to small local jurisdictions that cannot afford to hire specialized staff.

Some localities have taken a more informal route to regional coordination through service sharing. In service sharing, jurisdictions agree to consolidate specific services, cooperate in their provision, or exchange them. For instance, recreational facilities may be provided jointly by several jurisdictions, one government may rent jail space from another, or county residents may use the city library in return for city residents' use of the county's solid waste landfill. Service sharing arrangements are popular because they hold the promise of greater efficiency in service delivery, *and* they do not threaten the power and autonomy of existing jurisdictions the way consolidation does. These agreements provide for a modicum of regional governance…without a regional government.

STATES AND THEIR RURAL COMMUNITIES

When the local Dairy Queen closes its doors, a small town in rural America knows that it is in trouble. The Dairy Queen, like the coffee shop on Main Street, serves as a gathering place for community residents. Its demise symbolizes the tough times that a lot of rural communities face. In fact, some analysts argue that the major distinctions in regional economics are no longer between the Sunbelt and Frostbelt, or the East Coast and West Coast, but between metropolitan America and the countryside.[40] People are leaving many rural areas, with the most relentless decline occurring in a broad swath stretching northward from west Texas through the Plains states.[41]

The decline of rural America has provoked a question: What can state governments do to encourage the right kind of growth in rural areas? Short of pumping enormous amounts of money into the local economy, they can encourage the expansion of local intergovernmental cooperation, whereby small rural governments join together to increase their administrative capacity to deliver services and achieve economies of scale. Two state actions facilitate such cooperation. One is the reforming of state tax codes so that jurisdictions can share locally generated tax revenues, similar to the Twin Cities example discussed earlier. Rather than competing with one another for a new manufacturing plant or a shopping mall, local governments can cooperate to bring the new facility to the area; regardless of where this facility is located, all jurisdictions can receive a portion of the tax revenue. A second useful state action is the promotion of statewide land use planning. As one observer has noted, "Currently too many rural local governments engage in wasteful intercommunity competition, mutually antagonistic zoning, and contradictory development plans."[42]

Twelve small towns in Kansas have embraced a new strategy to reverse population loss: offering free land to families who will build a home on the parcel. Before long, Marquette, a central Kansas town of 500 people a few years ago, had given away forty free residential lots and had seen its population reach nearly 700. Others of these proverbial one-stoplight towns offer additional inducements to new residents: free water and sewer hookups, no-cost building permits, and memberships at nearby golf courses. Still, even with the offer of free land, some of these Kansas towns have not been able to attract enough new residents to offset their population loss.[43]

In an effort to find new ways to compete, rural places are getting entrepreneurial. For instance, an action that may bear fruit is the attempt to foster business by installing high-speed Internet connections to isolated rural areas. Indiana created its I Light program to bring broadband to its farming communities; Alabama and Alaska give tax credits to broadband firms committed to investing in rural areas.[44] Nebraska developed its EDGE program ("Enhancing,

Developing and Growing Entrepreneurs") in an effort to boost business capacity in rural communities. Also, the abundance of wind in the Great Plains region has spurred talk of the possibilities of developing large-scale wind farms to provide an alternative energy source to other parts of the country. And music festivals—Wakarusa in the Arkansas hills; Dfest, Rocklahoma, and Country Fever in rural Oklahoma; and Bonnaroo in south central Tennessee—provide a significant shot in the arm to rural economies.

THE INTERACTION OF STATES AND LOCALITIES

Constitutionally, state governments are supreme in their dealings with local governments. New York City, Los Angeles, and Chicago are large, world-class cities, but even they have to follow the dictates of their respective state governments. Even so, power does not flow in only one direction. The political realities are such that these cities and their smaller counterparts influence what happens in their state capitols. Suffice it to say, the state–local relationship is subject to constant adjustment. A Governor's Task Force to Renew Montana Government, for instance, adopted several provisions aimed at diminishing the influence of the state in what are considered purely local issues. But in a different vein, when Philadelphia's mayor proposed closing some fire stations to cut costs, state legislators intervened, passing a bill to prevent the city from doing so.[45] (The governor of Pennsylvania, a former mayor of Philadelphia, vetoed the bill, saying it infringed on the city's home rule power.)

Some issues or problems require a statewide, uniform response, while others are the particular concern of a single local jurisdiction. Consider the problem of drought, a condition that has affected most of the western states since 2000. Some areas of Colorado, such as Denver, have been especially hard hit. A local agency, Denver Water, is responsible for water management in the city; a state agency, the Colorado Water Conservation Board, has statewide authority. To address the drought problem, both agencies had to work together. The comments of a hydrologist capture the situation, "There needs to be a state coordinating mechanism, but it needs to be sensitive to the local context."[46] Thus, even with the constitutional superiority of the state, the state–local relationship is much more nuanced.

When he was elected governor of New York, George Pataki said, "as a former mayor, I know firsthand the importance of freeing our cities, towns, and counties from the heavy hand of state government."[47] But as Governor Pataki quickly learned, a governor has to engage in big picture, statewide thinking, and it is awfully tempting to impose the state's will on those same localities. To make sure their voice is heard, many local governments do what those in California do: hire lobbyists to represent their interests in the state legislature. Localities in the Golden State spent nearly $40 million lobbying lawmakers in a single year.[48] Even so, cities and counties found themselves on the losing side of several key measures, including one that diverted funds for local transportation projects to the state. The state–local relationship can be rocky indeed.

CHAPTER RECAP

- States vary in the amount and type of authority they give their local governments. Although some states have increased their assistance to and empowerment of localities, other states continue to keep their local governments on a short leash.

- The issue of mandates is a particularly contentious state–local matter.

- Local governments want more money from the state, more power to generate revenues, and more control over how the revenues are spent.

- Three types of state–local organizations are common: task forces, advisory commissions on intergovernmental relations, and departments of community affairs.

- Urban sprawl has become a major issue in state–local relations. States have begun to adopt "smart growth" laws that are designed to help localities manage growth.

- Regionalism continues to be advocated as a solution to many local problems. More jurisdictions are creating regional organizations to link their local governments.

- With many rural communities in decline, states are seeking ways of revitalizing them.

- Even as the interaction of states and localities becomes more positive, the tug of war between the two levels continues.

Key Terms

Dillon's rule *(p. 231)*
ordinance *(p. 232)*
home rule *(p. 232)*
second-order devolution *(p. 233)*
mandate reimbursement requirements *(p. 236)*

annexation *(p. 238)*
metropolitan area *(p. 239)*
suburbs *(p. 239)*
edge cities *(p. 240)*
urban sprawl *(p. 240)*
impact fee *(p. 240)*
smart growth *(p. 241)*

regional government *(p. 242)*
city–county consolidation *(p. 242)*
public choice theory *(p. 243)*
councils of governments (COGs) *(p. 246)*

Internet Resources

The National Association of Regional Councils maintains a website at **www.narc.org/**. It shows the differences and similarities of regional councils across the country.

For information on the activities of a state level ACIR, see the Facebook page of the Tennessee ACIR at **www.facebook.com/TN.ACIR**.

The award-winning site of the Association of Bay Area Governments can be found at **www.abag.ca.gov**. Another noteworthy COG site is that of the Kansas City area's Mid-America Regional Council at **www.marc.org**.

The Urban Institute's site for research on economic and social policy can be found at **www.urban.org**. It is a useful source of information on states and localities.

The organization Smart Growth America leads a national coalition of state and local organizations dedicated to smart growth. The website is **www.smartgrowthamerica.org**.

Information about the Michigan Rural Council can be found at **www.rural.cedam.info**/. Georgia maintains an informative website at **www.ruralgeorgia.org**.

Local Government: Structure and Leadership

11

FOCUS QUESTIONS

1. What are the five types of local governments, and what is the primary role of each?
2. How does the structure of local government affect public policy?
3. How can leadership make a difference in the quality of local government?
4. What are some of the key changes in city governance?

In 2011, the governor of Illinois signed legislation creating a Local Government Consolidation Commission. The Commission's official task was to review the effectiveness and impact of local units of government in the state.[1] Advocates of the Commission hoped that it would come up with recommendations to reduce the number of local governments...and potentially save millions of dollars. With nearly 7,000 units of local government of various types and sizes—far more than any other state—Illinois is ripe for a rethinking of its local government landscape.

What do citizens expect of their local governments? They expect to be governed well. They want governmental structures that work and leaders who are effective. They want jurisdictions with adequate capacity to resolve the tough public problems of our times. But as this chapter demonstrates, the goal of being "governed well" is hard to achieve. Even with improved capacity, local governments confront a series of difficult challenges.

FIVE TYPES OF LOCAL GOVERNMENTS

general-purpose local government

A local government that performs a wide range of functions.

single-purpose local government

A local government, such as a school district, that performs a specific function.

Local government is the level of government that fights crime, extinguishes fires, paves streets, collects trash, maintains parks, provides water, and educates children. Some local governments provide all of these services; others, only some. A useful way of thinking about them is to distinguish between general-purpose and single-purpose local governments. **General-purpose local governments**—those that perform a wide range of governmental functions—include three types of local governments: counties, municipalities, and towns and townships. **Single-purpose local governments**, as the label implies, have a specific purpose and perform one function. School districts and special districts are single-purpose governments. The boundaries of single-purpose districts may or may not coincide with the general-purpose local governments covering the same territory. For example, the boundaries of a school district may be coterminous with the county, they may cover smaller portions of the county, or even extend over sections of two or more counties. (Note that Native American reservations are not a type of local government, even though tribal governments perform many local government functions.)

In the United States, the number of local governments exceeds 89,000. Figure 11.1 shows the number of each type of local government at two points in time: 1952 and 2012. The greatest change occurred among single-purpose local governments: Between 1952 and 2012, nearly 81 percent of America's school districts were abolished or consolidated with surrounding districts; in the same period, special districts tripled in number.

American local governments were not planned according to some grand design. Rather, they grew in response to a combination of citizen demand, interest-group pressure, and state government acquiescence. As a consequence, no rational system of local governments exists. What does exist is a collection of autonomous, frequently overlapping jurisdictional units. The number of local governments varies from state to state. Consider the case of Pennsylvania and its 4,905 local jurisdictions: 66 counties; 1,015 cities; 1,546 townships; 1,764 special districts; and 514 school districts.[2] Nevada, on the other hand, has a grand total of 190 local governments.

Being so close to the people offers special challenges to local governments. Citizens are well aware when trash has not been collected or when libraries do not carry current bestsellers. Moreover, they can contact local officials and attend public hearings—and they do. A recent survey asked a national sample of Americans about their interaction with government. More than 40 percent said that they had contacted an elected local official or attended a community meeting.[3] The interactive nature of local government makes the questions of capacity and responsiveness all the more critical.

Counties

State governments have carved up their territory into 3,031 discrete, general-purpose subunits called counties (except in Louisiana, where counties are called

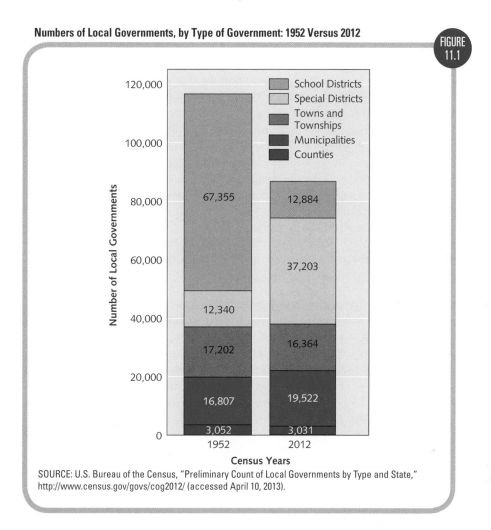

Numbers of Local Governments, by Type of Government: 1952 Versus 2012

FIGURE
11.1

SOURCE: U.S. Bureau of the Census, "Preliminary Count of Local Governments by Type and State," http://www.census.gov/govs/cog2012/ (accessed April 10, 2013).

parishes, and in Alaska, where they are called boroughs). Counties exist everywhere, with only a few exceptions. The exceptions include Connecticut and Rhode Island, where there are no functional county governments; Washington, D.C., which is a special case in itself; municipalities in Virginia that are independent jurisdictions and are not part of the counties that surround them; and cities such as Baltimore and St. Louis, which are not part of a county because of past political decisions. Also, there are jurisdictions—Philadelphia and San Francisco, for example—that are considered cities but are actually consolidated city-county government structures.

Counties vary dramatically in terms of size. At one extreme is Los Angeles County, California, which, with nearly 10 million residents, is larger than many states. Loving County, Texas, at the other extreme, has fewer than 100 people spread over its 673-square-mile territory.

Why We Have County Government Counties were created by states to function as their administrative appendages. In other words, counties were expected to manage activities of statewide concern at the local level. Their basic set of functions traditionally included property tax assessment and collection, law enforcement, elections, record keeping (land transactions, births, and deaths), and road maintenance.

The twin pressures of modernization and population growth have placed additional demands on county governments. As a result, their service offerings expanded and now include health care and hospitals, pollution control, mass transit, industrial development, social services, and consumer protection. The more new services that a county provides, the more it is delivering city-type services to its residents and businesses.[4] As a result, counties are increasingly regarded less as simple functionaries of state government than as important policymaking units of local government. Thirty-eight states have adopted home rule provisions for at least some of their counties.[5] This has made it easier for counties to change their organizational structure and reform their practices.

How County Governments Are Organized The traditional structure of county government is based on an elected governing body, usually called a board of commissioners or supervisors, that is the central policymaking apparatus in the county. The board enacts county ordinances, approves the county budget, and appoints other officials (such as the directors of the county public works department and the county parks department). One of the board members acts as presiding officer. Historically, this form of government has been the most popular; more than half of U.S. counties still use it, although its predominance is decreasing. A typical county commission has three or five members and meets in regular session twice a month.

The board is not omnipotent, however—several other county officials are elected, thereby forming a plural executive structure. In most places, these officials include the sheriff, the county prosecutor (or district attorney), the county clerk (or clerk of the court), the county treasurer (or auditor), the county tax assessor, and in some states even the coroner. These officials can become powerful political figures in their own right through their control of bureaucratic units. Figure 11.2 sketches the typical organizational pattern.

There are two primary criticisms of this type of organization. First, it has no elected central executive official, like the mayor of a city or the governor of a state. County government is run by a board. Second, it does not have a single professional administrator to manage county government, the way a city manager does in a municipality. Elected officials are responsible for administering major county functions.

These criticisms have led to calls for reform of the structure of county government. Two alternative county structures have grown in popularity over the past three decades. In one, called the *county council–elected executive plan*, the voters elect an executive officer in addition to the governing board. The result is a clearer separation between legislative and executive powers—in effect, a two-branch system of government. The board still has the power to set policy, adopt the budget,

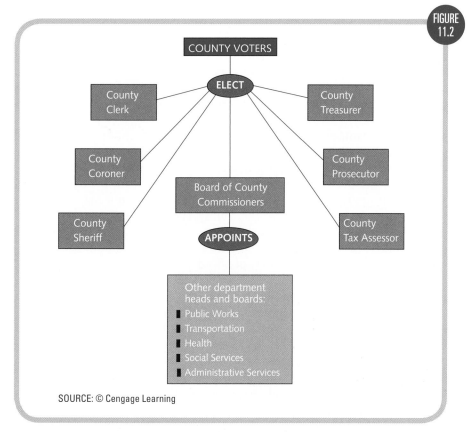

SOURCE: © Cengage Learning

FIGURE 11.2

Traditional Organization of County Government
The most common form of county government lacks a central executive.

and audit the financial performance of the county. The executive's role is to prepare the budget, administer county operations (in other words, implement the policies of the board), and appoint department heads. More than 400 counties have adopted this arrangement—among the most recent is Cuyahoga County, Ohio, where Cleveland is located. In the other alternative structure, the *council-administrator plan*, the county board hires a professional administrator (sometimes called a "county manager") to run the government. The advantage of this form of government is that it brings to the county a highly skilled manager with a professional commitment to efficient, effective government. Approximately 1,000 counties have variations of the council-administrator structure. One of the most recent large counties to adopt such a plan is Bexar County, Texas, population 1.8 million, where San Antonio is located.

Determining the most effective structural arrangements for county government is an ongoing issue. Defections from the long-standing commission form of county government and experimentation with alternatives continue, especially in the most populous counties. For example, Los Angeles County, which employs 100,000 people and has a budget of $20 billion, recently empowered its county administrator by giving him the power to hire and fire most department heads.[6]

Does structure matter? Research has shown that there are policy consequences attributable, at least in part, to structure. For example, among fast-growing counties in Florida, the adoption of a reformed structure led to an expansion of the counties' services to their residents.[7] A national study found a link between reformed structures and increased county spending on redistributive programs such as child welfare, homeless shelters, and mental health services.[8]

The Performance of County Government Counties are now more prominent than they were in the old days, when they were considered the shadowy backwaters of local governments. As urban populations spill beyond the suburbs into the unincorporated territory of counties, the pressure on local governments grows. A county and the cities located within it may find themselves at odds on myriad issues. The county–state relationship can be rocky, primarily because of spiraling costs of state-imposed mandates for programs such as indigent services and long-term health care. In addition, counties are expected to tackle tough dilemmas of affordable housing and land-use planning at the same time as they are expanding their services to include such matters as disaster preparedness and consumer protection.

The pressures on county government are many. One novel idea for relieving the burdens on counties was suggested in California a while back, when the legislature considered a proposal to divide the state into seven regions that would be governed by thirteen-member elected boards. These regional "supergovernments" would assume many of the development and infrastructure functions currently assigned to county governments. Although the bill did not pass, the performance of county government remains an issue in many parts of the nation. In Massachusetts, where cities and towns provide most local services, the state legislature has abolished several counties, contending that they were superfluous in the Bay State. Clearly, county governments must continue to modernize and focus on the big picture or run the risk of being bypassed. With that in mind, voters in Allegheny County, Pennsylvania (the Pittsburgh area), approved a restructuring plan in 2005 that merged several elected county positions and made some elective offices appointed.[9]

Municipalities

Municipalities are cities; the words are interchangeable, referring to a specific, populated territory, typically operating under a charter from the state government. Cities differ from counties in terms of how they were created and what they do. Historically, they have been the primary units of local government in most societies—the grand enclaves of human civilization.

incorporation

The creation of a municipality through the granting of a charter from the state.

Creating Cities A city is a legal recognition of settlement patterns in an area. In the most common procedure, residents of an area in a county petition the state for a charter of **incorporation**. The area slated for incorporation must meet certain criteria, such as population or density minimums. In Alabama, for instance, the population threshold required for incorporation is 300 people; in Arizona, the number is 1,500. In most cases, a referendum is required. The referendum enables citizens to vote on whether they wish to become an incorporated municipality. If the incorporation measure is successful, then a **charter** is granted by the state, and the newly created city has the legal authority to elect officials, levy taxes, and provide services to its residents. Not all cities have charters, however. Most California cities, for example, operate under general state law rather than a charter.

New cities are created every year. For instance, during a single six-year period, 145 places incorporated around the country (and 33 cities disincorporated, or ceased to exist as official locales).[10] Although most new cities tend to be small, some begin with sizable populations. For example, more than 86,000 people were living in Sandy Springs, Georgia, when the city incorporated in 2005.

Like counties, cities are general-purpose units of local government. But unlike counties, they typically have greater decision-making authority and discretion. Almost all states have enacted home rule provisions for cities, although in some states, only those cities that have attained a certain population size can exercise this option. (One of the few states without home rule for cities, New Hampshire, sought to provide it through a constitutional amendment in 2000, but the measure was defeated by voters.) In addition, cities generally offer a wider array of services to their citizenry than most counties do. Police and fire services, public works, and parks and recreation are standard features, supplemented in some cities by publicly maintained cemeteries, city-owned and operated housing, city-run docks, city-sponsored festivals, and city-constructed convention centers. City government picks up garbage and trash, sweeps streets, inspects restaurants, maintains traffic signals, and plants trees.

City Governmental Structure Nearly all city governments operate with one of three structures: a mayor-council form, a council-manager form, or a city commission form. In each structure, an elected governing body, typically called a city council, has policymaking authority. What differentiates the three structures is the manner in which the executive branch is organized:

1. *Mayor-council form.* In the mayor-council form of government, executive functions such as the appointment of department heads are performed by elected officials. This form of government can be subdivided into two types, depending on the formal powers held by the mayor. In a **strong-mayor-council structure**, the mayor is the source of executive leadership. As noted later in the chapter, strong mayors run city hall the way governors run the statehouse. They are responsible for daily administrative activities, the hiring and firing of top-level city officials, and budget preparation. They have a potential veto over council actions. The **weak-mayor-council structure** limits the mayor's role to that of executive figurehead. The council (of which the mayor may be a member) is the source of executive (and legislative) power. The council appoints city officials and develops the budget, and the mayor has no veto power. He or she performs ceremonial tasks such as speaking for the city, chairing council meetings, and attending ribbon-cutting festivities. A structurally weak mayor can emerge as a powerful political figure in the city, but only if he

charter
A document that sets out a city's structure, authority, and functions.

strong-mayor-council structure
The mayor is empowered to perform the executive functions of government and has a veto over city council actions.

weak-mayor-council structure
The mayor lacks formal executive power; the city council (of which the mayor may be a member) is the source of executive and legislative power.

Mayor-Council Form of Government
The primary difference between these two structures concerns the power and authority possessed by the mayor. Strong mayors are more ideally situated to exert influence and control.

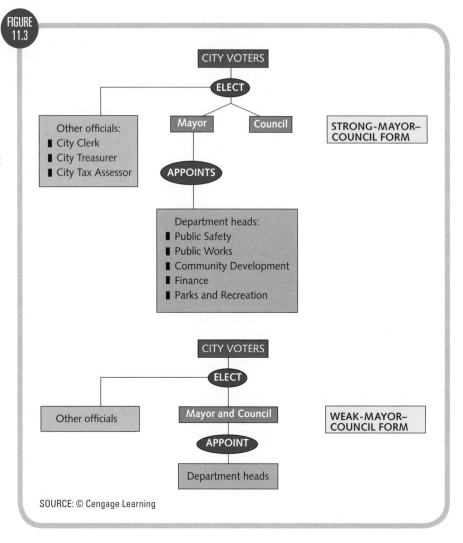

FIGURE 11.3

CITY VOTERS

ELECT

Other officials:
■ City Clerk
■ City Treasurer
■ City Tax Assessor

Mayor   Council

STRONG-MAYOR–COUNCIL FORM

APPOINTS

Department heads:
■ Public Safety
■ Public Works
■ Community Development
■ Finance
■ Parks and Recreation

CITY VOTERS

ELECT

Other officials

Mayor and Council

WEAK-MAYOR–COUNCIL FORM

APPOINT

Department heads

SOURCE: © Cengage Learning

or she possesses informal sources of power. Figure 11.3 highlights the structural differences between the strong- and weak-mayor-council forms of city government. Mayor-council systems are popular both in large cities (populations greater than 250,000) and in small cities (populations less than 10,000).

2. *Council-manager form.* The council-manager form of government emphasizes the separation of politics (the policymaking activities of the governing body) from administration (the execution of the policies enacted by the governing body). Theoretically, the city council makes policy, and administrators execute policy. Under this structure, the council hires a professional administrator to manage city government. Figure 11.4 sketches this structure. (An important variation within the council-manager form is whether the mayor is directly elected by the voters [in 63 percent of council-manager cities] or selected by the council from its membership [37 percent].[11])

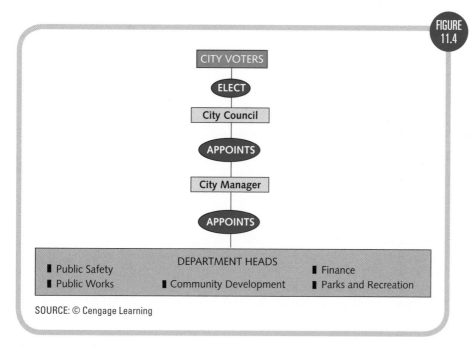

FIGURE 11.4

Council-Manager Form of Government
The council–manager form of government places administrative responsibility in the hands of a skilled professional. The intent is to make the operation of city government less political.

SOURCE: © Cengage Learning

The administrator (usually called a city manager) appoints and removes department heads, oversees service delivery, develops personnel policies, and prepares budget proposals for the council. These responsibilities alone make the manager an important figure in city government. But, add to them the power to make policy recommendations to the city council, and the position becomes even more powerful. In council-manager cities, the council and the manager typically have a working understanding about how far the manager can venture into the policymaking realm of city government.

More than half of U.S. cities use the council-manager form of city government. Among cities with populations of 25,000 to 75,000, the council-manager structure predominates; it is also popular in homogeneous suburban communities and in the newer cities of the Sunbelt region. Examples of large cities with a council-manager structure include Phoenix, San Antonio, and Dallas.

3. *City commission form.* Under the city commission form of government, illustrated in Figure 11.5, legislative and executive functions are merged. Commissioners not only make policy as members of the city's governing body, they also head the major departments of city government. They are both policymakers and policy executors. One of the commissioners is designated as mayor simply to preside over commission meetings.

The original appeal of the commission structure was its ostensible reduction of politics in city government. But almost as fast as the commission form of government appeared on the scene in the early 20th century, disillusionment set in. One problem stemmed from the predictable tendency of commissioners

City Commission Form of Government
Executive leadership is fragmented under a commission form of government. Each commissioner heads a department; together, they run city hall.

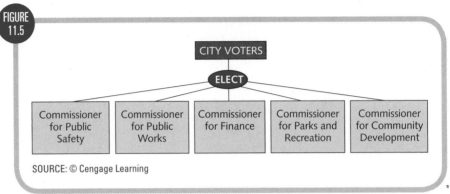

FIGURE 11.5

CITY VOTERS

ELECT

| Commissioner for Public Safety | Commissioner for Public Works | Commissioner for Finance | Commissioner for Parks and Recreation | Commissioner for Community Development |

SOURCE: © Cengage Learning

to act as advocates for their own departments. Each commissioner wanted a larger share of the city's budget allocated to her department. Another problem had to do with politicians acting as administrators: Elected officials do not always turn out to be good managers. The result was that public enthusiasm for the commission form declined. By 1990, when Tulsa, Oklahoma, replaced its commission system with a mayor-council form, only a few cities were operating with a commission structure. Notable among them is Portland, Oregon, with its modified commission form of government. And Portland likes its commission form: A measure to change to the council-manager form of government was handily defeated by voters in 2007. (A few council-manager cities such as Ft. Lauderdale, Florida, refer to their city council as a "commission" but they do not have a commission structure as described here.)

Which Form of City Government Is Best? Experts disagree about which city government structure is best. Most would probably agree that structures lacking a strong executive officer are generally less preferable than others. By that standard, the weak-mayor-council and the commission forms are less favorable. The strong-mayor-council form of government is extolled for fixing accountability firmly in the mayor's office, and the council-manager system is credited with professionalizing city government by bringing in skilled administrators to run things. Yet strong-mayor structures are criticized for concentrating power in the mayor's office; council-manager forms are taken to task for placing too much power in the hands of an unelected city manager. A recent study adds some clarity with its finding that cities lacking a professional administrator tend to have more conflict and less cooperation in formulating public policy.[12] Thus, it is up to community residents to decide which form of government they want, and they have been doing just that.

In 2004, Richmond, Virginia, switched from a weak-mayor structure to a strong-mayor form; in 2006, San Diego replaced its council-manager form of government, empowered the mayor, and added a chief operating officer who reports to the mayor. El Paso, Texas, however, moved in a different direction and abandoned its strong-mayor structure and joined the ranks of council-manager cities. For some cities, a hybrid form that combines features of several structures may be the answer. For instance, both Oakland, California, and Cincinnati, Ohio, amended their council-manager form of government by adding a strong-mayor position *and* retaining the position of city manager. In fact, the distinction between the mayor-council form and the council-manager form may be blurring as more cities tinker with their structures, designing entities that contain elements of both.[13] A recent study of Michigan cities found just such a pattern.[14]

Towns and Townships

Towns and townships are general-purpose units of local government, distinct from county and city governments. Only twenty states, primarily in the Northeast and Midwest, have official towns or townships. In some states these small jurisdictions have relatively broad powers; in others they have a more circumscribed role.

How Do We Know a Town When We See One? In New England, towns offer the kinds of services commonly associated with cities and counties in other states. Many New England towns continue their tradition of direct democracy through a **town meeting** form of government. At a yearly town assembly, residents make decisions on policy matters confronting the community. They elect town officials, pass local ordinances, levy taxes, and adopt a budget. In other words, the people who attend the town meeting function as a legislative body. Although the mechanism of the town meeting exemplifies democracy in action, it often falls short of the ideal, primarily due to the relatively low rate of citizen participation in meetings. Often, fewer than 10 percent of a town's voters actually attend the meeting. Those who do show up tend to be older and, not surprisingly, more engaged in politics in general. Some research has found that "some citizens are in fact turned off by the lack of civility of the face-to-face interactions at town meetings."[15] Larger towns in Connecticut and Massachusetts rely on representatives elected by residents to vote at the meetings.

Towns in New England, along with those in New Jersey, Pennsylvania, and to some degree Michigan, New York, and Wisconsin, enjoy fairly broad powers. In large measure, they act like other general-purpose units of government. In the remainder of the township states (Illinois, Indiana, Kansas, Minnesota, Missouri, Nebraska, North Dakota, Ohio, and South Dakota), the nature of township government is more rural. Rural townships tend to stretch across thirty-six square miles of land (conforming to the surveys done by the national government before the areas were settled), and their service offerings are often limited to roads and law enforcement. A part-time elected board of supervisors or trustees commonly rules the roost in townships. In addition, some of the jobs in government may be staffed by volunteers rather than salaried workers. The closer these rural townships are to large urban areas, however, the more likely they are to offer an expanded set of services to residents.

town meeting
An annual event at which a town's residents enact ordinances, elect officials, levy taxes, and adopt a budget.

The Future of Towns and Townships The demise of the township type of government has long been expected. As rural areas become more populated, they will eventually meet the population minimums necessary to become municipalities. For instance, residents of a Minnesota township decided to incorporate as a municipality to ward off annexation by a neighboring city.[16] Some towns face a different problem. Many are experiencing a substantial population exodus and, in the process, losing their reason for existence. These towns may die a natural death, with other types of government (perhaps counties or special districts) providing services to the remaining residents. Despite the dire predictions, towns and townships have proved to be remarkably resilient. The U.S. Census Bureau counted 16,364 towns and townships in 2012, down only 265 from the 1997 figure.

Towns and townships have not sat idly by as commentators speculated on their dim future. They formed an interest group, the National Association of Towns and Townships (NATaT), to lobby on their behalf in Washington, D.C. NATaT spawned a spinoff organization, the National Center for Small Communities, to provide training and technical assistance to towns. Many small towns have embarked on ambitious economic development strategies—industrial recruitment, tourism promotion, and amenity enhancement—in an attempt to stimulate new growth.

Special Districts

Special districts are supposed to do what other local governments cannot or will not do. They are created to meet service needs in a particular area. Special districts can be formed in three different ways:

- States can create them through special enabling legislation.
- General-purpose local governments may adopt a resolution establishing a special district.
- Citizens may initiate districts by petition, which is often followed by a referendum on the question.

public authority

A type of special district funded by nontax revenue and governed by an appointed board.

Some districts have the power to levy taxes; others rely on user fees, grants, and private revenue bonds for funding. Taxing districts typically have elected governing boards; nontaxing districts—called **public authorities**—ordinarily operate with appointed boards.[17] The United States has approximately 37,000 special districts, and that number is increasing (see Figure 11.1).

Not all special districts are organized alike. Ninety-two percent of them provide a single function, but the functions vary. Natural resource management, fire protection, housing and community development, and water and sewer service are the most common. Among the 2,309 special districts in Texas are drainage districts, utility districts, river authorities, emergency services districts, sports facility districts, community college districts, and hospital authorities. Most states have other, state-specific districts, such as Colorado's mine drainage districts and tunnel districts or Florida's beach and shore preservation districts and mobile home park recreation districts.

The budget and staff size of special districts range from minuscule to mammoth. Some of the more prominent include the Port Authority of New York and New Jersey, the Chicago Transit Authority, and the Los Angeles County Sanitation District.

Why Special Districts Are Needed Special districts overlay existing general-purpose local governments and address deficiencies in them. Three general categories of deficiencies are worth examining: technical conditions, financial constraints, and political explanations.

First are the *technical conditions* of a general-purpose local government. In some states, cities cannot extend their service districts beyond their boundaries, which is a challenge when the problem to be addressed does not fit neatly within a single jurisdiction. A river that runs through several counties may periodically overflow its banks in heavy spring rains—a problem affecting small portions of many jurisdictions. A flood control district covering only the affected areas of these jurisdictions may be a logical solution. Problems of scale must also be considered. A general-purpose local government simply may not be able to provide electric service to its residents as efficiently as a special utility district that covers a multitude of counties. Finally, some states prohibit jurisdictional co-venturing that would allow jurisdictions to offer services jointly. In that case, operation of a two-county library would require the establishment of a special two-county library district.

A second set of deficiencies has to do *with financial constraints*. Local general-purpose governments commonly operate under debt and tax limitations. Demands for additional services that exceed a jurisdiction's revenue-raising ceiling or lead to the assumption of excessive debt cannot be accommodated. By using special districts, existing jurisdictions can circumvent the debt and tax ceilings. (A new study of Indiana's special districts found that they accounted for 8 percent of local government expenditures, but carried approximately 38 percent of total local government debt in the state.[18]) Furthermore, special districts are better suited than general-purpose governments for service-charge or user-fee financing, whereby the cost of the service can be directly apportioned to the consumer (as with water or sewer charges).

Technical and financial deficiencies of general-purpose local governments help to explain the creation of special districts, but *political explanations* shed even more light. Restrictive annexation laws and county governments with limited authority are political facts of life that encourage the use of special districts. For residents of an urban fringe area, a public service district (which may provide more than one service) may be the only option. Some special districts owe their existence to a federal mandate. For example, national government policy has spurred the establishment of soil conservation and flood control districts throughout the country.

Once created, a special district may become a political power in its own right. In places where general-purpose governmental units are fully equipped legally, financially, and technically to provide a service, they may encounter resistance from special-district interests fighting to preserve the district.

Concerns About Special Districts The arguments in favor of special districts revolve around their potential for efficient service provision and the likelihood that they will be responsive to constituents whose demands are not otherwise being met.[19] But for the most part, scholarly observers look at special districts with a jaundiced eye. The most frequently heard complaint is that special districts lack accountability. The public is often unaware of their existence, so they function free of much scrutiny. A study of 100 airport and seaport districts found that those with an elected governing board were no more likely to be responsive to public preferences than were those with appointed boards.[20] And, as research by Nancy Burns reminds us, the establishment of special districts is a costly political act.[21] Well-placed groups such as businesses, developers, and homeowners' associations are among the beneficiaries of special-district creation.

One thing is certain: The proliferation of special districts complicates the development of comprehensive solutions to public problems. It is not uncommon for cities and counties to be locked in governmental combat with the special districts in their area. All of these governmental units tend to be turf-protecting, service-providing rivals. Moreover, special districts may actually drive up the costs of service delivery. Research on 300 metropolitan areas, which compared services provided by special districts with those provided by general-purpose governments, found districts had a higher per capita cost.[22]

Cognizant of these concerns, state governments are looking more closely at special districts and the role they play in service delivery. Several states have taken actions that give their general-purpose local governments more input into the state's decision to create special districts.

School Districts

School districts are a type of single-purpose local government. They are a distinct kind of special district and, as such, are considered one of the five types of local government. The trend in school districts follows the theory that fewer is better (see Figure 11.1). Despite serving as a source of community identity, small districts were so expensive to maintain that consolidations have occurred throughout the nation. Nebraska exemplifies the trend. In 1952, there were 6,392 school districts in the state; by 2012, the Cornhusker State had only 272. Currently, the states with the largest number of school districts by far are Texas (1,079) and California (1,025).

School Politics The school board is the formal source of power and authority in the district. It is typically composed of five to seven members, usually elected in nonpartisan, at-large elections. Their job is to make policy for the school district. One of the most important policy decisions involves the district budget—how the money will be spent.

School districts are governed by these boards and managed by trained, full-time educational administrators. Like city governments, school districts have invested heavily in the reform model of governance, and the average district has become more professional in operation in the past forty years. An appointed chief administrator (a superintendent) heads the school district staff, the size of which varies according to the size of the district.

Revamping public education has been a hot topic for the past two decades. Concern over mismanagement of funds and low student achievement has led some states to shift control of schools away from the school district itself and place it in the hands of city government, typically in the mayor's office, for a period of time. New York City, Chicago, Baltimore, Cleveland, and Detroit are among the most prominent examples. At the same time, other school districts have sought to decentralize, shifting power to the individual school level. This school-based management approach has meant greater involvement of the private sector in some schools; in others it has enhanced the role of parents.

Parental influence in school district policy is most clearly emerging in the matter of **school choice**. School districts around the country have begun to adopt measures that allow parents to decide whether their child will attend the neighborhood school or one elsewhere in the district, perhaps a charter school. In effect, schools are competing for students. Schools are anxious to attract students because district and state funds are allocated on a per-pupil basis. To increase their appeal, some schools specialize in a particular academic area, such as arts or sciences; others emphasize certain teaching styles. Advocates of parental choice claim that this approach offers poor families some of the options that wealthy families have always had with private schools. They argue that competition among schools will generate creativity and responsiveness among teachers and principals.

school choice
Market-based approach to education improvement that permits parents to choose which school their child will attend. Examples include charter schools and voucher programs.

School District Issues Among the myriad challenges faced by school districts is one persistent conundrum: how to secure sufficient funding for public education. Although the relationship is a bit more complex than "you get what you pay for," there is widespread agreement that children in well-funded school districts are better off educationally than those in poorly funded ones.

Serious disparities in school funding, caused by great differences in the available property taxes that provide most of the revenue, have led to the increasing financial involvement of state government in local school districts. State governments use an **equalization formula** to distribute funds to school districts in an effort to reduce financial disparities. Under this formula, poorer school districts receive a proportionately larger share of state funds than do wealthier districts. Although these programs have increased the amount of funding for education, they have not eliminated the interdistrict variation. Wealthier districts simply use the state guarantee as a foundation on which to heap their own resources. Poorer school districts continue to operate with less revenue. This situation prompted many state supreme courts around the country to declare their public-school finance systems unconstitutional. Legislatures have struggled to design new, more equitable financial arrangements. Michigan lowered property taxes for schools and substituted sales taxes and other revenues. Other states have established lotteries and earmarked the proceeds for education. The issue of money for schools is one that stays at the top of legislative agendas, year in and year out.

equalization formula
A means of distributing funds (primarily to school districts) to reduce financial disparities among districts.

LEADERSHIP IN LOCAL GOVERNMENT

In 2009, Antonio Villaraigosa was reelected mayor of America's second largest city, Los Angeles. When he was sworn in for his second term, he declared:

> I stand, hopefully a little bit wiser as well, chastened and enlightened both by our successes and failures over the last four years. I stand renewed and reinvigorated, re-committed to the task before us. Above all, I stand determined to finish what we started, determined to find a second wind in our second term. I intend to lead with everything I have![23]

Among the items on the mayor's agenda were job creation, economic development, crime fighting, renewable energy, and rail transit. By the time he left office in 2013, Mayor Villaraigosa had encountered plenty of opportunities to exercise leadership. Leadership goes hand in hand with governance. Regardless of the jurisdiction, leadership can make the difference between an effectively functioning government and one that lurches from one crisis to another. The terms that conjure up images of leadership in local government circles these days include *initiative, persistence, entrepreneurship, innovation,* and *vision.* These words share a common element: They denote activity and engagement. Leaders are people who "make a difference."[24]

Real questions about who is running the show in local government do arise. At the risk of being accused of naïveté, we might suggest that "the people" run government, local and otherwise. Unfortunately, there is much evidence to persuade us otherwise. But we should not become too cynical, either. Citizen preferences do have an impact on public policy decisions; recent research confirms that public opinion influences city governments' budget choices.[25] Can we assume, therefore, that those who occupy important positions in government, such as the mayor and the city council, are in fact in charge? Are they the leaders of the community?

In sorting through the issue of who's running the show, we find that several different theories have been advanced. In general, they revolve around the concentration of power and the influence of different groups. For instance, **elite theory** argues that a small group of leaders called an elite possesses power and rules society;[26] **pluralist theory**, conversely, posits that power is dispersed among competing groups, whose clash produces societal rule.[27] Another approach, **regime analysis**, contends that certain individuals and groups possess systemic power and enjoy a strategic advantage in influencing government decisions.[28] It is important to remember that not all communities are organized alike; furthermore, even within a single community, power arrangements shift as time passes and conditions change.

Mayors and Managers

Mayors tend to be the most prominent figures in city government primarily because their position automatically makes them the center of attention.

elite theory
A theory of government asserting that a small group possesses power and rules society.

pluralist theory
A theory of government asserting that multiple open, competing groups possess power and rule society.

regime analysis
An approach asserting that certain individuals and groups possess systemic power and enjoy a strategic advantage in influencing government decisions.

Successful mayors blend vision with communication skills and, even more important, an ability to get results.

Differences Between Strong and Weak Mayors As discussed earlier in the chapter, strong mayors are different from weak mayors. It is important to note that these labels refer to the *position*, not to the person who occupies it. Similarly, a structure creates opportunities for leadership, not the certainty of it. True leaders are those who can take what is structurally a weak-mayor position and transform it into a strong mayorship in practice.

A strong-mayor structure establishes the mayor as the sole chief executive who exercises substantive policy responsibilities. Directly elected by the voters rather than selected by the council, a strong mayor serves a four-year (not a two-year) term of office and has no limitations on reelection. She also has a central role in budget formulation, extensive appointment and removal powers, and veto power over council-enacted ordinances. The more of these powers a mayor has, the stronger her position is and the easier it is for her to become a leader.

A weak-mayor structure does not provide these elements. Its design is such that the mayor shares policy responsibilities with the council and perhaps a manager, and serves a limited amount of time in office. (In a system with an especially weak mayor, the job is passed around among the council members annually, each of whom takes a turn at being mayor.) A weak-mayor structure usually implies strong council involvement in budgetary and personnel matters.

Some observers argue that large, diverse communities grappling with complex problems are better served by a structure that fixes leadership and accountability in the mayor's office.[29] Others fear that a too-powerful mayor could run amok, building political machines based on the exchange of benefits. Structural differences can indeed have consequences, but the individuals who work within structures are the essential factor. As David Morgan and Sheilah Watson note, "Even in council-manager communities—where mayors have the fewest formal powers—by negotiating, networking, and facilitating the efforts of others, mayors clearly rise above the nominal figurehead role."[30] In the words of one politician: "It's your leader, not your form of government."[31]

African American Mayors, Women Mayors In the past, few African Americans or women were elected to the top job in America's largest cities. Like so many aspects of local politics, this too has changed. These days, it is not uncommon to find African Americans and women leading major U.S. cities.

Today's African American mayors have been called a new generation by some observers because they consider themselves problem solvers, not crusaders; political pragmatists, not ideologues.[32] For example, in his successful 2006 campaign for mayor of Newark, New Jersey, Cory Booker's message was about hard work...and hope. On his campaign website he proclaimed, "Working together we're going to make Newark's neighborhoods safe and our schools safe.... Bringing real change to Newark won't be easy."[33]

TABLE 11.1	African American Mayors in Big Cities, 2013	
CITY	**AFRICAN AMERICAN % OF POPULATION**	**MAYOR**
Philadelphia, PA	43.4	Michael Nutter
Jacksonville, FL	30.7	Alvin Brown
Columbus, OH	28.0	Michael Coleman
Charlotte, NC	35.0	Anthony Foxx
Detroit, MI	82.7	David Bing
Memphis, TN	63.3	A. C. Wharton Jr.
Baltimore, MD	63.7	Stephanie Rawlings-Blake
Denver, CO	10.2	Michael Hancock
Sacramento, CA	14.6	Kevin Johnson
Kansas City, MO	11.7	Sly James
Atlanta, GA	54.0	Kasim Reed
Cleveland, OH	53.3	Frank Jackson
Wichita, KS	11.5	Carl Brewer
Cincinnati, OH	44.8	Mark Mallory
Toledo, OH	27.2	Mike Bell
Newark, NJ	52.4	Cory Booker
Plano, TX	7.6	Harry LaRosiliere
Buffalo, NY	38.6	Byron Brown
Baton Rouge, LA	54.5	Melvin Holden
Durham, NC	41.0	William V. Bell
Birmingham, AL	73.4	William A. Bell Sr.
Richmond, VA	50.6	Dwight Jones

NOTE: Cities with populations of 200,000 or more, listed in descending order according to size.
SOURCE: Adapted from the U.S. Conference of Mayors, "Mayors at a Glance," http://www.usmayors.org/meetmayors/mayorsatglance.asp (accessed April 10, 2013); U.S. Bureau of the Census, "State and Local QuickFacts," http://quickfacts.census.gov/qfd/index.html (accessed on April 10, 2013).

Table 11.1 lists big-city African American mayors and the African American population percentage in the cities they lead. The increased success of blacks in mayoral elections has led some scholars to speak of deracialization, or the de-emphasis of race as a campaign issue for black candidates seeking white voter support.[34] Instead of making racial appeals, candidates offer a race-neutral platform that stresses their personal qualifications and political experience.[35]

In cities where the white electorate outnumbers the black electorate, such as Sacramento and Wichita, neither Kevin Johnson nor Carl Brewer could have been elected without the support of white voters. Deracialization works both ways. Baltimore, a majority African American city, had a black mayor from 1987 to 1999, a white mayor from 1999 to 2007, and a black mayor since then. The manner in which a mayor elected by a multiracial coalition governs once in office is a compelling subject for research. For example, a study of Houston found that when minority mayors run for reelection, evaluations of job performance are more important to voters than racial group affiliation is.[36]

More women, too, are running for and winning local elective offices. The data from cities with populations of 30,000 or more are instructive. In 1973, fewer than 2 percent of the cities in that population range had female mayors; a quarter century later, the proportion of cities with women mayors had increased to 21 percent, a level around which it has fluctuated. (In 2013, 17 percent of cities of 30,000 or more were governed by women.[37]) The list of female mayors leading cities with populations of 200,000 or more appears in Table 11.2.

The ranks of female mayors of major cities nearly increased by one in 2004 when Donna Frye, a member of San Diego's city council, ran against the incumbent mayor. Frye, competing as a write-in candidate, lost in a hotly disputed election. At issue were 5,547 ballots in which voters had written in Frye's name but neglected to fill in the small oval next to the write-in line. Election officials did not count these ballots because state law requires that the ovals be filled

TABLE 11.2 Woman Mayors in Big Cities, 2013		
CITY	**MAYOR**	**POPULATION**
Houston, TX	Annise D. Parker	2,099,451
Fort Worth, TX	Betsy Price	741,206
Baltimore, MD	Stephanie Rawlings-Blake	620,961
Las Vegas, NV	Carolyn Goodman	583,756
Fresno, CA	Ashley Swearengin	494,665
Raleigh, NC	Nancy McFarlane	403,892
Oakland, CA	Jean Quan	390,724
Corpus Christi, TX	Nelda Martinez	305,215
Chula Vista, CA	Cheryl Cox	243,916
North Las Vegas, NV	Shari L. Buck	216,961
Irving, TX	Beth Van Duyne	216,290

NOTE: Cities with populations of 200,000 or more, listed in descending order according to size.
SOURCE: Adapted from the U.S. Conference of Mayors, "Mayors at a Glance," http://www.usmayors.org/meetmayors/mayorsatglance.asp/ (accessed April 10, 2013).

in for a write-in vote to count. Frye's supporters contended that, regardless of the ovals, voter intent was clear: a vote for Frye. Had those ballots been counted, Frye would have won by 3,439 votes.[38] (Councilwoman Frye ran again for mayor in 2005, losing in the runoff election to the city's former police chief. She was reelected to the council in 2006.)

Studies of female mayoral candidates have dispelled several electoral myths.[39] For example, women do not appear to experience greater difficulty in raising money or gaining newspaper endorsements than men. Women mayors, however, do tend to be political novices. Few female mayors in Florida, for instance, had held elective office before their mayoral election; if they had, it was usually a city council seat. Other research indicates that mayors, regardless of gender, see their political environments similarly, which makes sense: Successful local politicians know their communities.

City Managers City managers (as well as county administrators and appointed school superintendents) exemplify the movement toward reformed local government. Local government reform was a **Progressive Era** movement that sought to depose the corrupt and inefficient partisan political machines that controlled many American cities. To the reformers, local government had become too political; what was needed, they believed, was a government designed along the lines of a business corporation. To achieve their goals, reformers advocated such fundamental structural changes in local government as the abolition of partisan local elections, the use of at-large electoral systems, and the installation of a professionally trained city manager. Altering the structure of local government has had profound consequences for local government leadership. City managers—the professional, neutral experts whose job it is to run the day-to-day affairs of the city—have become key leaders.

In the original conception, managers were to implement but not formulate policy. Administration and politics were to be kept separate. The managers' responsibility would be to administer the policies enacted by the elected officials—the city councils—by whom they were hired (and fired). But it is impossible to keep administration and politics completely separate. City managers are influenced not only by their training and by the councils that employ them but also by their own political ideologies.[40] When it comes to making choices, they balance professional norms, the politics of the issue, and their own predispositions. Hence city managers typically end up being far more influential on the local government scene than their neutral persona might suggest.

According to the International City/County Management Association, the city managers' professional association, the role of the manager is to help the governing body function more effectively. "Managers—and their staffs—need to build political capacity so they can assist the elected body in framing community issues."[41] Ways in which the manager can assume a larger role in policymaking include proposing community goals and service levels; structuring the budget preparation, review, and adoption process so that it is linked to goals and service levels; and orienting new council members to organizational processes and norms. The approach has had the intended effect. James Svara,

Progressive Era

A period in the early twentieth century that focused on reforming or cleaning up government.

who surveyed officials of large cities, concluded that managers have become "more assertive in attempting to focus the council on long-range concerns and in shaping the tone of the policymaking process."[42] Another indisputable role for the manager is as an information source for the busy, part-time city council.

A veteran city administrator in Missouri offered new managers this advice about dealing with elected officials:

- Don't substitute your political judgment for the judgments of the elected officials.
- Don't cut red ribbons, cut red tape . . . in other words, keep a low profile.
- Listen, count to three, and choose your words wisely.
- The council-manager relationship is not a game won on points.
- There's no great honor in being fired, but there's no shame in being fired for the right reason.[43]

Local Legislatures

Local legislatures include city councils, county commissions, town boards of aldermen or selectmen, special-district boards, and school boards. They are representative, deliberative, policymaking bodies. In this section we focus on city councils, because that is where most of the research has taken place; but many of the points made are applicable to the other local legislative bodies, especially county commissions and school boards. And although the ensuing discussion focuses on patterns across councils, it is important to remember that there may be significant variations from one city to another. For example, in some communities, council members receive high salaries, are assisted by clerical and research staff, and have no limits on the number of terms they can serve. In Chicago, for instance, city council members (called **aldermen**) earn more than $110,000 per year, have office staffs, and can serve an unlimited number of four-year terms. (To put it in perspective, the mayor of Chicago has an annual salary of $216,000.) But in Oklahoma City, a council-manager city, the council members receive a yearly salary of $12,000; the mayor earns $24,000. In many smaller places, council service is considered a volunteer activity, with members receiving virtually no compensation.

aldermen
A label used in some communities for members of a local legislative body, such as a city council.

City Council Members: Old and New A former member of the city council of Concord, California, defines "the good old days" on local governing boards with this comment: "When I first came on the city council, it was like a good-old-boys' club."[44] The standard view was that the city council was a part-time, low-paying haven for public-spirited white men who did not consider themselves politicians. Most councils used at-large electoral mechanisms, so individual council members had no specific territorially based constituency. Council members considered themselves volunteers. Research on city councils in the San Francisco Bay area in the 1960s found that these volunteer members were fairly unresponsive to public pressures and tended to vote their own preferences.[45] In other words, there was not much representation going on.

at-large elections

Citywide (or countywide) contests to determine the members of a city council (or county commission).

district (ward) elections

Elections in which the voters in one district or ward of a jurisdiction (city, county, school district) vote for a candidate to represent that district.

City Council Districts
Each council district contains approximately 81,000 people.

Today, the circumstances have changed. City councils are less white, less male, and less passive than they were in the past. City councilors are more engaged and active. Some of this change is due to modifications in the electoral mechanism, such as the switch from at-large or citywide elections to district (or ward) elections. In **at-large elections**, a city voter can vote for as many candidates as there are seats to be filled. In **district (ward) elections**, a city voter can vote only in the council race in her district. From the perspective of candidates, the at-large system means that a citywide campaign must be mounted; with districts, the candidate's campaign is limited to a specific area of the city. Figure 11.6 displays the district map for the El Paso city council, which uses the council-manager structure and elects eight councilors from districts. (The mayor is elected citywide and is a member of the council. Phoenix, San Antonio, Dallas, Fort Worth, and San Jose are examples of other large cities with similar structures.). Other cities have chosen to retain some at-large council seats while dividing the city into electoral districts. Houston, a strong-mayor city, is an example: Of the fourteen members of the Houston city council, five are elected at large, and nine are elected from districts. (Table 11.3 shows the wide variation both in council size and in number of members elected at

FIGURE 11.6

City Council Districts in El Paso, Texas, 2013

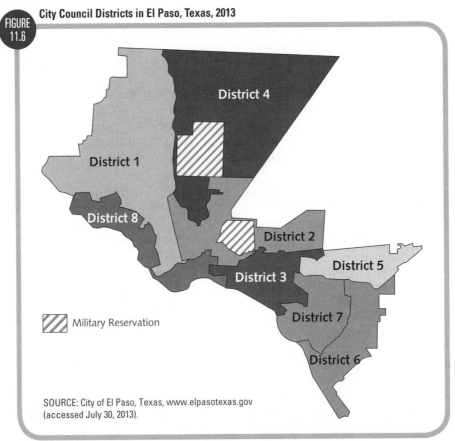

SOURCE: City of El Paso, Texas, www.elpasotexas.gov (accessed July 30, 2013).

City Councils of the Twenty Largest U.S. Cities				TABLE 11.3
CITY	**2011 ESTIMATED POPULATION**	**COUNCIL SIZE**	**NUMBER ELECTED AT-LARGE**	**NUMBER ELECTED FROM DISTRICTS**
New York, NY	8,244,910	51	0	51
Los Angeles, CA	3,819,702	15	0	15
Chicago, IL	2,707,120	50	0	50
Houston, TX	2,145,146	16	5	11
Philadelphia, PA	1,536,471	17	7	10
Phoenix, AZ	1,469,471	8	0	8
San Antonio, TX	1,359,758	10	0	10
San Diego, CA	1,326,179	9	0	9
Dallas, TX	1,223,229	14	0	14
San Jose, CA	967,487	10	0	10
Jacksonville, FL	827,908	19	5	14
Indianapolis, IN	827,609	29	4	25
Austin, TX	820,611	6	6	0
San Francisco, CA	812,826	11	0	11
Columbus, OH	797,434	7	7	0
Fort Worth, TX	758,738	8	0	8
Charlotte, NC	751,087	11	4	7
Detroit, MI	706,585	9	2	7
El Paso, TX	665,568	8	0	8
Memphis, TN	652,050	13	6	7

SOURCE: "Annual Estimates of the Resident Population for Incorporated Places over 50,000, Ranked by July 1, 2011 Population," U.S. Census Bureau, http://www.census.gov/popest/data/cities/totals/2011/index.html, (accessed April 9, 2013); individual city websites.

large and from districts.) Changes in election mechanisms signaled a change in council composition. There are more African Americans, Latinos, and women on city councils than ever before, and councils are taking their governance roles quite seriously.

Despite the rise in minority representation, the percentages remain relatively low. Much research has been done on the impact of structural considerations—for example, the at-large election format, the size of the council, and the use of nonpartisan elections—on minority council representation.[46] Other factors such as the size of the minority group, its geographical concentration, and its political cohesiveness affect electoral success. In general, a higher proportion of African American council members can be found in central cities that use a mayor-council structure and in southern cities with large black populations. Councils with higher-than-average Hispanic representation tend to be found in the West, particularly the Southwest, in larger central cities using council-manager structures. Thus far, Asian representation has been clustered primarily in the Pacific Coast area in larger council-manager central cities. And Native American representation is highest in very small communities using commission structures in the southwestern and Pacific Coast regions of the country. The increase in nonwhites on councils has policy consequences. Data from 351 city council members indicate that nonwhites pursue a more liberal policy agenda than whites.[47]

Given the finite number of council seats in any community and the fact that more groups are now clamoring for representation, two outcomes are possible: Minority groups may try to build coalitions, or they may opt for a more independent, competitive approach. Although temporary electoral coalitions have emerged in a few cities, it appears that interminority group competition is on the rise. Research in ninety-six cities demonstrates, for example, that an increase in the Latino population has a negative effect on black representation on city councils.[48] Another interesting question is the extent to which the concept of deracialization can be extended to Latinos and Asian Americans in their bids for local offices. Research on the Little Saigon area of Orange County, California, showed evidence of racial bloc voting in every election for city council or school board between 1998 and 2002 in which a Vietnamese American competed against a white candidate.[49]

Local governing boards in cities and counties are becoming more diverse in another way: The number of openly gay and lesbian elected officials is increasing. The Gay and Lesbian Victory Fund is a PAC that provides technical and financial support for openly gay and lesbian candidates, many of whom are seeking local offices. Christine Quinn, who in 2006 became speaker of New York City's council used that to launch her candidacy for the mayoralty in 2013, is one of the most prominent; so is Houston's recently reelected mayor, Annise Parker. A study focusing on cities and counties that had antidiscrimination ordinances in place revealed several findings about the election of gays and lesbians. Based on that sample of jurisdictions, gay and lesbian electoral success was more likely in larger cities; in jurisdictions with higher numbers of nonfamily households (such as university communities); and in places with partisan, district election of council members.[50] The limited nature of the sample makes it difficult to generalize to all localities, but the research yields interesting findings about council diversity.

Councils in Action: Increasing Conflict In earlier times, when members of the council came from the same socioeconomic stratum and when they shared a common political philosophy, governing was a lot easier. Members of the council could come together before the meeting and discuss the items on the agenda. That way, they could arrive at an informal resolution of any particularly troubling items and thereby transform the actual council meeting into a rubber-stamp exercise. No wonder that the majority of council votes were often unanimous; members were merely ratifying what they had already settled on. Nowadays, councils appear to be less collegial.

Council members elected by districts report more factionalism and less unanimity than do their counterparts elected at large.[51] The growing tendency of cities to move away from complete reliance on at-large electoral mechanisms suggests that council discord will be on the rise in the future. Whereas earlier studies had found about 33 percent of city council members reporting that intracouncil conflict was a serious source of frustration to them; ten years later, 55 percent voiced a similar concern.[52] High levels of council conflict have other consequences. Research on city managers has shown a link between council conflict and managerial burnout.[53] Burned-out city managers perform poorly and often leave the city or the profession itself. Conflict-management skills can assist novice managers in their dealings with the council.

Battles with the Mayor Relationships between a city council and the mayor can be conflictual, to say the least. In fact, they can be downright hostile. A former mayor of Philadelphia did not pull any punches when he referred to the city council as "the worst legislative body in the free world."[54] In Salt Lake City, the mayor who took office in 2000, Rocky Anderson, took several actions at odds with the city council. He vetoed several of the council's pet projects, and he took action unilaterally through executive orders when the council was indecisive on an issue. In the mayor's words, "You don't ask the council…you just do it."[55] And what did the city council in Salt Lake City think of the mayor's approach? One council member reacted this way: "It's not smart to treat us with such disdain."[56] The result for citizens of Utah's capital city was a tense political situation.

Council-mayor conflict is not necessarily unproductive. Conflict is expected in a political system that operates on the foundation of separation of powers. Clashes between the legislative branch and the executive branch can produce better government. But when the disagreements between the council and the mayor escalate to the point of gridlock, effective governance is stymied.

Nonprofit Organizations in the Community

Nonprofit organizations have become fully integrated into the government and politics of most communities. Four types of governmentally active nonprofit organizations can be identified:

- Civic nonprofits
- Policy advocates
- Policy implementers
- Governing nonprofits[57]

The first type, the civic nonprofit organization, plays a watchdog role, monitoring government and educating the public. A local citizen's league acts in

nonprofit organizations
Private sector groups that carry out charitable, educational, religious, literary, or scientific functions.

this way, attending city council meetings and publicizing council decisions. Policy advocates, the second type, move beyond the provision of information to become active supporters of particular policies or programs. For instance, if an education advocacy group endorses year-round schools, it would lobby the school board vigorously in support of such a policy change. The third type of nonprofit organization, the policy implementer, actually delivers services, often through a contract with a local government. For example, homeless shelters in many communities are operated by nonprofit groups supported by city funds, federal grants, and charitable contributions. Governing nonprofits, the fourth type, are different because they may work through or with local government but they also act independently. These nonprofits are the most powerful of the four types because they offer an alternative venue for decision making.

Nonprofit organizations of all types have become omnipresent in localities throughout the nation. In Detroit, for example, groups such as New Detroit and Detroit Renaissance have become important players in the city's politics.[58] New Detroit has more of a social agenda, focusing on race relations and education reform. Detroit Renaissance, a smaller organization made up of the corporate elite from the Detroit area, has concentrated its energies on economic renewal. For more than thirty years, these organizations have advocated ambitious reforms and new policies, and while not always successful, they have influenced local decisions.

COMMUNITIES AND GOVERNANCE

Let us return to the governance issue that was raised early in this chapter and has been alluded to throughout it: How do we know when a community is well governed? This chapter is full of examples of communities that have restructured their governments in hopes of improving governance. Voters oust incumbents and elect new council members in a similar effort. Once in office, many big-city mayors adopt a pragmatic approach, an orientation that is independent of race or ethnicity. It is a back-to-basics approach to governing, one that emphasizes service delivery, balanced budgets, and working with the private sector to cure the city's ills. Jurisdictions with workable structures and effective leaders have an advantage, to be sure.

Although there is no set of universally accepted criteria for evaluating the quality of governance, several organizations have come up with proxy measures. For example, the National Municipal League annually bestows its "All-America City" designation on jurisdictions (both cities and counties) that successfully tackle community problems in a collaborative way. Among the All-America Cities in 2013 were Birmingham, Alabama; Peoria, Illinois; Dubuque, Iowa; and Norfolk, Virginia .[59]

The governance question goes back to Plato and Aristotle, and we are unlikely to resolve it here. Local governments and their leaders are confronting their problems and challenges by trying new ideas, exploring alternatives, and reaching out for solutions. No doubt about it: this can be a tough task. Consider the case of Philadelphia. In 2007, voters elected a new mayor to take control of a city plagued by high rates of violent crime, pervasive poverty, and persistent unemployment; in addition, its school system had been taken over by state government. Not only that, a budget crisis loomed, and the contracts with public employee unions were due to be renegotiated. Despite the circumstances, the new mayor was optimistic, stating, "What I'm hoping to lead is literally the renaissance of Philadelphia."[60] Mayor Michael Nutter, reelected in 2011, would be the first to admit it has not been easy. But he—and leaders of many other local jurisdictions—remain undeterred.

CHAPTER RECAP

- There are five types of local governments: counties, municipalities, towns and townships, special districts, and school districts. There are more than 89,000 local governments in the United States.

- Counties were created by states to serve as their local administrative arms, while cities operate with a charter of incorporation, and typically have more power than counties.

- Special districts are both the most prevalent and the least understood of the five types of local government.

- School districts have many concerns, but one persistent issue is the availability of sufficient funding for public education.

- The public wants well-governed communities. Local governments redesign their structures in hopes of improving governance. A primary issue in redesigning structures is the role of the executive.

- Mayors tend to be the central figures in city politics and government, even if they operate in formally weak-mayor structures.

- City managers, as top-level appointed officials, have become policy leaders.

- City councils have changed from the good-old-boy clubs of the past. They are more active, they are more diverse, and there is more conflict on the council.

- Nonprofit organizations have become increasingly important in communities.

Key Terms

general-purpose local government (p. 252)
single-purpose local government (p. 252)
incorporation (p. 256)
charter (p. 257)
strong-mayor-council structure, (p. 257)

weak-mayor-council structure (p. 257)
town meeting (p. 261)
public authority (p. 262)
school choice (p. 265)
equalization formula (p. 265)
elite theory (p. 266)
pluralist theory (p. 266)

regime analysis (p. 266)
Progressive Era (p. 270)
aldermen (p. 271)
at-large elections (p. 272)
district (ward) elections (p. 272)
nonprofit organizations (p. 275)

Internet Resources

Most of the five types of government are represented by national associations, which have useful websites: **www.naco.org** (National Association of Counties), **www.nlc.org** (National League of Cities), **www.natat.org** (National Association of Towns and Townships), **www.nsba.org** (for school districts, the relevant website is that of the National School Boards Association).

To explore a specific school district, such as the City of Philadelphia's school district, see **www.phila.k12.pa.us**.

Special districts, by virtue of their specialized nature, tend to have function-specific national organizations. For example, to learn about the National Association of Conservation Districts, see **www.nacdnet.org**. A fifteen-county district, The Colorado River Water Conservation District, whose website can be found at **www.crwcd.org**, is an example of an individual special district. One of the most famous special districts is the Port Authority of New York and New Jersey; its website is **www.panynj.gov**.

The U.S. Conference of Mayors, the association of mayors of cities with populations of 30,000 or more, has a Web presence: **www.usmayors.org**.

Specialized constituency groups often have their own organizations and websites, as does the National Conference of Black Mayors at **www.ncbm.org**.

Over time, cities and counties have found that maintaining websites is a good way to connect with the public. See, for example, the website for Miami-Dade County at **www.miamidade.gov**. The website for the city of Los Angeles can be found at **www.lacity.org**; the website for the county is at **www.lacounty.gov**. To learn more about the largest county in Michigan, go to **www.waynecounty.com**. You can find information about the Big Apple at **www.nyc.gov**; while **www.houstontx.gov** and **www.cityofboston.gov** are the websites for the cities of Houston and Boston, respectively.

The website for the Center for American Women and Politics at Rutgers University, **www.cawp.rutgers.edu**, contains a wealth of data on women and politics.

Information about the city and county management profession can be found at the International City/County Management Association's website: **www.icma.org**.

Important outlets for the latest scholarly research on local politics are *Urban Affairs Review* at **http://uar.sagepub.com/**, and the *Journal of Urban Affairs* at **http://onlinelibrary.wiley.com/journal/10.1111/(ISSN)1467-9906**

Taxing and Spending

12

CHAPTER OUTLINE

- The Principles of Finance
- Revenues
- The Political Economy of Taxation
- Managing Money
- State and Local Spending
- Current Issues in State and Local Finance

FOCUS QUESTIONS

1. What are the two basic principles of state and local financial systems?
2. Among the variety of state and local taxes, what are the three major ones and what are some of the primary criteria for evaluating them?
3. What are some of the consequences of taxpayer resistance?
4. How would you characterize state and local financial relationships?

Stockton, California, a city of 292,000 situated east of San Francisco, shook the municipal finance world when it declared Chapter 9 bankruptcy on June 27, 2012. As the largest U.S. city in history to declare bankruptcy at that time (a much larger city, Detroit, filed for bankruptcy on July 18, 2013), Stockton's fall from financial grace was the result of several factors, including expensive new civic projects developed during the good times in the early 2000s and costly wage and benefits agreements with current and retired city workers. As property tax revenues collapsed during the housing crisis and Great Recession, the city cut the general fund substantially; reduced the police and fire forces by up to 30 percent, the general city staff by 40 percent; and took other steps to try to get its financial house in order. But the city found itself with a $26 million deficit, and mediation efforts with debt holders failed.

By declaring Chapter 9 bankruptcy, Stockton gained the ability to maintain basic services while engineering a "do-over" of its finance system, including a good possibility that the bankruptcy judge would void the city's union contracts. The hope, of course, was that the city would steady itself sufficiently to emerge from bankruptcy financially stronger. The neighboring city of Vallejo used bankruptcy to reinvent itself for the better, and Stockton pledged to do the same.[1] Bankruptcy comes with harsh consequences, however, including extremely low bond ratings, making future borrowing very difficult and expensive, leading to a possible exit of concerned homeowners, creating lengthy legal proceedings that could take several years and millions of dollars to conclude, and causing long-term damage to the standing and reputation of the jurisdiction. Across the country, similarly challenged municipalities and counties were watching closely, particularly Detroit, Michigan.

Such fiscal drama was not unusual in state capitals during and after the Great Recession. Budget shortfalls were astonishingly high and widely spread across the United States. Indeed, it has increasingly been the norm whenever revenues do not equal expenditures over the fiscal year. Sometimes budget problems are relatively isolated in a handful of states. At other times, such as 2009–2013, serious problems sweep across the states, forcing nearly all of them to make difficult choices.

This chapter deals with state and local finance: the politics and policies of taxing and spending. It is a topic of continuing, visceral interest in state and local jurisdictions, and an activity characterized by much change and experimentation. From taxpayer revolts to spending mandates, the fiscal landscape has changed profoundly. More change is certain as state and local governments strive to meet taxpayer service demands both economically and creatively.

THE PRINCIPLES OF FINANCE

A major purpose of government is to provide essential services to citizens. But this costs money: equipment must be purchased and employees must be paid. Governments raise needed funds through taxes, fees, and borrowing. In a democracy, the voters decide what range and quality of services they desire and register those opinions through elected representatives. Sometimes, when elected officials do not listen, voters revolt and take matters directly into their own hands.

Two basic principles describe state and local financial systems: *interdependence* and *diversity*. State and local fiscal systems are closely interlinked and heavily influenced by national financial activities. Intergovernmental sharing of revenues is a pronounced feature of our interdependent federal fiscal system. Yet our state financial structures and processes are also highly diverse. Though affected by national activities, their own economic health, and competitive pressures from one another, the states enjoy substantial autonomy in designing individual revenue systems in response to citizens' policy preferences.

Interdependence

State governments raise huge amounts of money. In 2012, the states and localities garnered about $2.7 trillion. Most of this money is **own-source revenue**, gathered from taxes, charges, and fees applied to people, services, and products within the jurisdiction of each level of government. Nonnational governments also benefit from **intergovernmental transfers**. The national government contributes about 25 percent of all state and local expenditures; however, more than 60 percent of this federal money is passed through to *individual* recipients such as those receiving Medicaid. For their part, states pass on more than $470 billion to their cities, counties, and special-purpose governments, though about half the states reduced aid to local governments in 2011.[2] Some of the states are economic powerhouses. California's beleaguered economy still exceeds $2 trillion, making it the ninth largest in the world.

Local governments rely heavily on the states, and to a lesser degree on the national government, for financial authority and assistance. Only the states can authorize localities to levy taxes and fees, incur debt, and spend money. State constitutions and laws place many conditions on local government taxing and spending. States provide monetary support of local governments through state grants-in-aid and revenue sharing; they also assume financial responsibility for activities previously carried out by localities—in particular, education and social welfare costs. Most local governments are fine with this arrangement. But the role of states as senior financial partners is criticized in some local government arenas as being both inadequate and unduly restrictive of local financial flexibility.

State–local finances are linked very closely to activities of the national government. For instance, when the federal government changes the tax code, it can wreak havoc on those thirty-five states that base their own income tax on that of the federal government. Congress's phase-out of the estate tax in 2011 was projected to cost the states billions of dollars. The 2013 federal budget sequester (approximately $1 trillion in budget cuts) threatened to cost states up to $6 billion in federal support for education and other programs.[3]

When the national economy falls into a recession, state and local governments suffer most. They cannot, after all, print money or run operating budget deficits like the federal government. This fact is sometimes recognized by Congress, which sent substantial amounts of **countercyclical aid** to the states and localities to help them recover from the ravages of the Great

own-source revenue
Monies derived by a government from its own taxable resources.

intergovernmental transfers
The movement of money or other resources from one level of government to another.

countercyclical aid
A transfer of federal dollars to states and localities to counteract a downturn in the economic cycle.

Recession. Special aid is also targeted to states suffering from natural disasters, including hurricanes, floods, and fires.

Diversity

The second basic principle of state and local finance systems is diversity of revenue sources. Each level of government depends on one type of revenue device more than others. For the national government it is the income tax; for the states, the sales tax; and for local governments, the property tax. But diversity triumphs among the states. Differences in **tax capacity (wealth)**, **tax effort (burden)**, and tax choices are obvious even to the casual traveler. Most states tax personal income and merchandise sales, but a handful of them do not; some tax services such as auto repair and attorney fees. A majority of states operate lotteries and pari-mutuel betting facilities.

Some states tax with a heavy hand. Others are relative tax havens. Most fall somewhere in the middle. If the basic objective of taxing is to pluck the maximum number of feathers from the goose with the minimum amount of hissing, the wealthy states hold a great advantage, since they can reap high tax revenues with much less effort than poor states, which must tax at high rates just to pull in enough money to pay for the basics. Per-capita state and local tax revenues vary from $9,098 in Alaska to $2,806 in Alabama. The U.S. average is $4,144 (see Table 12.1).

There is a close relationship between state wealth (as measured by personal income) and tax effort, which can be measured by *tax burden*. Table 12.1 shows how the states compare in state and local tax burden (taxes, controlling for personal income). New Jersey, New York, and Connecticut lay on their residents relatively high tax burdens compared to South Dakota, Nevada, and Alaska. Tax burden can also reflect such factors as citizen attitudes, population characteristics and trends, business climate, taxing and spending limitations, and the quality as well as quantity of government services. And taxing is only one means of plucking the public goose. State and local governments increasingly rely on fees and charges for services rendered. Examples include entrance fees for parks and recreation facilities, sewer and garbage fees, and motor vehicle fees.

tax capacity (wealth)

The taxable resources of a government jurisdiction.

tax effort (burden)

The extent to which a jurisdiction exploits its taxable resources.

REVENUES

Although the state and local finance systems have their own strengths, weaknesses, and peculiarities, certain trends can be found in all of them. The property tax is always unpopular. It is no longer a significant source of state revenue; its contribution to total *local* own-source local revenues, however, remains very important. User fees and other miscellaneous charges are gradually increasing.

State/Local and Total Taxes by State, as a Percentage of Personal Income, Per Capita, 2010						TABLE 12.1

STATE	STATE/LOCAL TAXES AS A % OF INCOME	STATE/LOCAL TAX COLLECTIONS PER CAPITA RANK	STATE	STATE/LOCAL TAXES AS A % OF INCOME	STATE/LOCAL TAX COLLECTIONS PER CAPITA RANK
U.S. Average	9.8				
New Jersey	12.2	1	North Dakota	9.5	26
New York	12.1	2	West Virginia	9.4	27
Connecticut	12.0	3	Idaho	9.4	28
Wisconsin	11.0	4	Washington	9.3	29
Rhode Island	10.7	5	Kentucky	9.3	30
California	10.6	6	Florida	9.2	31
Minnesota	10.3	7	Georgia	9.1	32
Vermont	10.2	8	Virginia	9.1	33
Maine	10.1	9	Missouri	9.0	34
Pennsylvania	10.1	10	Montana	8.7	35
Massachusetts	10.0	11	Mississippi	8.7	36
Maryland	10.0	12	Oklahoma	8.7	37
Illinois	10.0	13	Arizona	8.7	38
Arkansas	9.9	14	Colorado	8.5	39
Nebraska	9.8	16	Alabama	8.5	40
North Carolina	9.8	16	New Mexico	8.4	41
Oregon	9.8	17	Louisiana	8.2	42
Ohio	9.7	18	South Carolina	8.1	43
Kansas	9.7	19	New Hampshire	8.0	44
Utah	9.7	20	Texas	7.9	45
Michigan	9.7	21	Wyoming	7.8	46
Hawaii	9.6	22	Tennessee	7.6	47
Delaware	9.6	23	South Dakota	7.6	48
Iowa	9.5	24	Nevada	7.5	49
Indiana	9.5	25	Alaska	6.3	50

SOURCE: www.taxfoundation.org. Copyright © Tax Foundation. All Rights Reserved. Reprinted by permission.

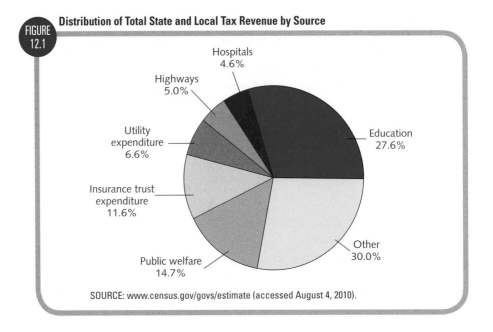

FIGURE 12.1

Distribution of Total State and Local Tax Revenue by Source

Hospitals 4.6%

Highways 5.0%

Utility expenditure 6.6%

Insurance trust expenditure 11.6%

Public welfare 14.7%

Education 27.6%

Other 30.0%

SOURCE: www.census.gov/govs/estimate (accessed August 4, 2010).

States continue to depend heavily on the sales tax, but alternatives are being used more widely. Revenues from the federal government make up almost one quarter of the total. In fact, revenue diversification is an important trend in all state and local tax systems (see Figure 12.1).

Criteria for Evaluating Taxes

Numerous criteria can be used to evaluate taxes. What one person or interest group likes about a tax may be what another detests. Nevertheless, most political scientists and economists agree that among the most important criteria are equity, yield, elasticity, ease of administration, political accountability, and acceptability.

Equity If citizens or firms are expected to pay a tax, they should view it as fair. In the context of taxation, equity usually refers to the distribution of the tax burden in accordance with ability to pay: high income means greater ability to pay and, therefore, a larger tax burden. Equity has other dimensions as well, such as the relative tax burden on individuals versus firms and the impact of various types of taxes on income, age, and social class. It is interesting to observe that despite the constant complaints about taxes, the typical American pays much less in total taxes today (as a percentage of income) than he or she did 30 years ago.[4] Taxes may be regressive, progressive, or proportional. A **regressive tax** places a greater burden on low-income citizens than on high-income citizens. Thus, the ability-to-pay principle is violated, with the result that upper-income groups contribute a smaller portion of their incomes

regressive tax

A tax in which the rate falls as the base (taxable income) rises.

than lower-income groups do. Most state and local levies, including property and sales taxes, are regressive. For example, both low-income and high-income people would pay, say, a 7 percent sales tax. The latter will likely make more purchases and contribute more total dollars in sales tax, but at a lower percentage of their total income than would the low-income individuals.

A **progressive tax** increases as a percentage of a person's income as that income rises. The more you make, the greater proportion of your income is extracted by the progressive tax. Thus, those who are better able to pay carry a heavier tax burden than the poor. Hawaii's personal income tax is most progressive, varying from 1.4 to 11.0 percent of taxable income. The more you earn, the higher your income tax bracket.

A **proportional tax**, sometimes called a **flat tax**, burdens everyone equally, at least in theory. For instance, a tax on income of, say, 10 percent that is applied across the board is a proportional tax. Whether you earn $100,000 or $10,000, you pay a flat 10 percent of the total in taxes. Of course, it can be argued that a low-income person is more burdened by a proportional tax than is a high-income person (as in the case of the sales tax).

In place of ability to pay, some people advocate the **benefit principle**. Under this principle, those who reap more benefits from government services should shoulder more of the tax burden than people who do not avail themselves of service opportunities to the same degree. As a hypothetical example, it might be argued that parents whose children attend public schools should pay higher taxes for education than should senior citizens, childless couples, or single people without children. The benefit principle is the theoretical underpinning for user fees, which charge a taxpayer directly for services received. The unfortunate downside is that it disadvantages those who have the least ability to pay.

progressive tax
A tax in which the rate rises as the base (taxable income) rises.

proportional (flat) tax
A tax in which people pay an identical rate regardless of income or economic transaction.

benefit principle
The principle that taxes should be levied on those who benefit directly from a government service.

Yield Taxes can also be evaluated on the basis of efficiency, or how much money they contribute to government coffers compared to the effort expended to administer and collect them. The administrative and other costs of applying a tax must be taken into consideration when determining yield. Taxes that return substantial sums of money at minimal costs to the government are preferred to taxes that require large outlays for moderate revenues. Income and sales taxes have high yields because they raise large sums of money at low expense. They are simple to understand and fairly easy to collect. Property taxes, however, have lower yields because they are more expensive to assess and collect. Property values must be regularly appraised, which involves a certain degree of subjectivity.

Yield depends on base and rate: the broader the tax base and the higher the rate, the higher the yield. As a simple example, a sales tax applied to all purchases yields much more than a sales tax on cigarette purchases, and a $1-per-pack tax produces more money than a 25¢ tax.

Elasticity This criterion is related to yield. Tax yields should be automatically responsive to changes in economic conditions, and revenue devices should expand or contract their yields as government expenditure needs change. Specifically, as per capita income grows within the state and its localities, revenues should keep pace without increases in the tax rate. Tax reductions should accompany economic recession and declines in per capita income, so that citizens' tax burdens are not increased during hard times. The progressive income tax is considered to be elastic because revenues increase as individuals earn more money and move into higher tax brackets and decline as income falls. User fees, for example, generally do not move in tandem with economic conditions and are therefore considered to be inelastic.

Political Accountability Tax increases should not be hidden. Instead, state and local legislative bodies should have to approve them deliberately—and publicly. Citizens should know how much they owe and when it must be paid. For example, some state income taxes are silently hiked as wages rise in response to cost-of-living increases. After inflation is accounted for, taxpayers make the same income as they did before, but they are driven into a higher income bracket for tax purposes. This phenomenon, known as bracket creep, can be eliminated by **indexing** income tax brackets to changes in the cost of living.

indexing

A system in which tax brackets are automatically adjusted to account for inflation.

Acceptability The type and mix of taxes imposed should be congruent with citizen preferences. No tax commands wild enthusiasm (and a portion of the good citizenry will *always* oppose *any* tax), but some are less disagreeable than others. Tax acceptability varies from place to place depending on numerous factors, including equity implications and the perceived pain of paying. Large, one-time payments, such as the annual property tax, inflict greater pain than small, frequently paid sales taxes. And a tax on someone else is always preferable. As Senator Russell Long of Louisiana put it many years ago, "Don't tax me, don't tax thee; tax that man behind the tree."

Major State and Local Taxes

The principal types of taxes are those on property, sales, and income. Various other miscellaneous taxes also provide revenue for state and local governments.

Property Tax Taxes on personal and corporate property account for 29 percent of all local government tax revenues. States hardly utilize the property tax at all today—about 2 percent of their total revenues—but local governments continue to depend on this fiscal workhorse for three-quarters of all their own-source revenues. Other revenue sources have augmented the property tax so that overall, its proportionate contribution has diminished. As always, there is considerable state-by-state variation, but more than three out of every four dollars in local revenues are derived from the property tax.

Property taxes are widely reviled. Assessments of value may seem to change suddenly or appear to stack up unfavorably against similar properties, and, when appealed, such taxes involve a frustrating process. Acceptability and accountability rank low in relation to other taxes. The best feature of the property tax is that it is certain; owners of property must pay it or the government may seize and sell their land, buildings, or other taxable possessions. But it has lost acceptability in recent years because it tends to be regressive, and sometimes must be paid in a large lump sum. At first thought, it seems that property taxes cannot be truly regressive, because only those people who own property pay taxes on it directly; however, renters pay property taxes indirectly through their monthly rent checks to the landlord. When property tax assessments climb, so do rental charges. Property taxes can also violate the ability-to-pay principle when housing values spiral upward. Retirees and other homeowners on fixed incomes may discover with alarm that their annual property tax bills are doubling or tripling as housing values escalate. Alternatively, as property values plummet as they did during the Great Recession, tax values remain the same until the next scheduled reassessment.

Just this sort of situation helped precipitate California's Proposition 13, which was credited with kicking off a taxpayer revolt across the United States. In the Los Angeles and San Francisco Bay areas during the 1970s, property taxes doubled and then tripled in only a few years. Some senior citizens were forced to sell their homes to pay their property taxes. Proposition 13 reduced property tax bills by approximately $7 billion in the first year; and it imposed strict limitations on the ability of local governments to raise property and other taxes in the future. California quickly dropped from being the eighth-highest property tax state to the twenty-eighth. This example illustrates the importance of political accountability.

Property taxes are difficult to administer and are somewhat arbitrary. The process of levying an annual fee on "real property" (land and buildings) begins with an assessor making a formal appraisal of the market value of the land and the buildings on it. Then property values are "equalized" so that similarly valued real estate is taxed at the same level. Next, an assessment ratio is applied to the property. For instance, houses might be assessed for tax purposes at 80 percent of market value. A rate is placed on the assessed value to calculate the annual tax amount. (Assessed at $100,000, taxed at a ratio of .80 and a rate of $3 per $100 [30 mils], a house would produce a tax due of $2,400.) Determining market value may seem fairly straightforward, but ultimately the appraised value depends on the findings of the assessor, who may or may not be biased, properly trained for the job, or fully aware of conditions in the local housing market. Property can thus be underappraised or overappraised. For the sake of equity, property should be appraised regularly (for example, every five years). Otherwise, property that does not change ownership may become increasingly over- or undervalued, depending on the local real estate market.

Property tax systems are further criticized for exempting certain types of real estate and buildings. Government buildings such as hospitals and state and federal offices are not taxed, even though they utilize police and fire protection, trash collection, and other local government services. Churches, synagogues, mosques, and related property used for religious purposes are also partly or wholly exempted in the vast majority of jurisdictions, as is property owned by charitable and nonprofit organizations. The amount of tax-exempt property in the most populous cities has been growing as more land and buildings are being acquired by nonprofit organizations, particularly in education and health care. Thirty percent of Baltimore's entire tax base escapes property taxation.[5] A relatively small proportion of this "lost" revenue is captured through payments in lieu of taxes (PILOTS), which are agreements negotiated by the state or municipality and the nonprofit owner. In addition, some state and local governments are sharpening the definition of what organizations qualify for tax exempt status.

In an effort to make property taxation more equitable and more in keeping with ability to pay, most states have enacted some form of **circuit breaker**. For instance, the property of low-income individuals is excluded from taxation in some states; others assign lower assessment ratios to the homes of senior citizens or set a top limit on the tax according to the owner's income (for example, 4 percent of net income). Many states have "truth in taxation" laws that roll back property taxes as appraised values rise rapidly. Most also offer homestead exemptions, in which owner-occupied homes are taxed at lower rates or assessed at lower values than rental homes or business properties. Several provide tax breaks to veterans. Massachusetts municipalities permit seniors to earn credits against their tax bills through public service activities.

circuit breaker

A limit on taxes applied to certain categories of people, such as the poor or the elderly.

Despite such attempts to make property taxes fairer, differences in property values among cities, counties, and school districts have important implications for the quality and distribution of services. Jurisdictions with many wealthy families, capital-intensive industries, or rapid construction growth can provide high levels of services with low tax rates, whereas areas with weak property tax bases must tax at high rates merely to yield enough revenues to maintain minimal services. Residential property tax rates vary widely in individual cities. For example, the rate is $29.30 per $1,000 of assessed value in Indianapolis, Indiana, but only $3.30 in Honolulu, Hawaii.[6] Altering the unequal distribution of property values is essentially beyond the control of local governments. As a result, "wealthy suburbs remain wealthy, poor communities remain poor, and services remain unequal."[7] Inequity in school funding has been the target of litigation in nearly every state.

Sales Tax States currently collect more of their revenues from the general sales and gross receipts tax than from any other source. It accounts for nearly one quarter of total state general revenues (again, see Figure 12.1). Only five states do not levy a general sales tax: Alaska, Delaware, Montana, New Hampshire, and Oregon. State sales tax rates vary from 7 percent in Indiana, Mississippi, and three other states to 2.9 percent in Colorado. Some states, particularly those that do not have personal income taxes, are exceptionally dependent on the sales tax: Florida, Washington, and Tennessee derive approximately 60 percent of their own-source revenues from the sales tax.

The sales tax has remained in favor for two major reasons. First, citizen surveys have consistently shown that when a tax must be raised, voters reluctantly prefer the sales tax. Although the reasons are not entirely clear, this tax is perceived to be fairer than other forms of taxation. Second, there is an abiding belief that high state income taxes depress economic development.[8] Moreover, the property tax is widely detested.

Thirty-six states authorize at least some of their municipalities and counties to levy local sales taxes. When state and local sales taxes are combined, the total tax bite can be painful. In Alabama and Tennessee cities, the purchase of a $1 item requires up to 9.43¢ in sales tax. Sales taxes are usually optional for the local jurisdiction, but may require legislative authorization. Typically, states impose ceilings on how many pennies the localities can attach to the state sales tax; states also specify which sizes and types of local governments are permitted to exercise this option.

When applied to all merchandise, the sales tax is clearly regressive. Poor folks must spend a larger portion of their incomes than rich people on basics such as food and clothing. Therefore, the sales tax places a much heavier burden on low-income people. Most of the forty-five states with a sales tax alleviate its regressivity by excluding certain necessities. Thirty-one states do not tax food purchased from the grocery store, only a handful tax prescription drugs and clothing, most exempt consumer electric and gas utilities.[9] New Jersey excludes paper products. When the sales tax was extended to paper products in 1990, enraged Jerseyites mailed wads of toilet paper—some of it used—to legislators, who quickly rescinded the tax. In 2010, Washington began applying the sales tax to candy, soda, and bottled water, deciding that these were not "food items" deserving of exemptions but voters vetoed the taxes in a later referendum.

States can improve the yield of the sales tax by broadening the base to include services. In this way, more of the burden is passed on to upper-income individuals, who are heavier users of services. More than half of the states' tax services including household, automobile, and appliance repairs; barber and beauty shop treatments; printing; rentals; dry cleaning; and interior decorating. Hawaii, Texas, and South Dakota tax virtually all professional and personal services. New Jersey taxes hair transplants and tummy tucks, while Arkansas taps into tattoos and nose rings. Colorado and Washington are anticipating new money from taxing recreational marijuana sales. Maryland residents must pay a "flush tax" of $30 on their sewer and septic bills to help clean up Chesapeake Bay. States can move too far and too fast, however, with taxes on services. Florida, Massachusetts, and Michigan broadened the base of their sales tax to services, only to have it repealed shortly afterward through aggressive lobbying efforts by the business community. Sweeping proposals to tax services are typically defeated by vested interests.

These setbacks may be temporary. Services are the largest and fastest-growing segment of the U.S. economy. Eighty-five percent of new jobs are in services. As one political journalist asked, "How can one rationalize taxing autos, videocassettes, and toothpaste, but not piped-in music, cable TV, parking lot services, or $100 beauty salon treatments?"[10] Pet grooming services, financial services, and many others from landscaping to legal work have lost their tax-favored status as states extend sales taxes to services incrementally, fighting industry and lobbyists one at a time.

Whatever form the sales tax takes, elasticity is not a strong point—although its productivity falls when consumer purchases slow and rises as consumers boost their spending. Broadening the base helps. States sometimes attempt to make the sales tax more responsive to short-term economic conditions by increasing it on a temporary basis, to make up lower-than-anticipated revenues, then reducing it when needed monies are collected. A problem with these tactics, however, is that consumers tend to postpone major purchases until the tax rate falls.

A big battle has been joined over state and local governments' right to tax an enormously promising revenue stream—electronic commerce on the Internet. Pressures from Internet interests, including servers (for example, Google), media companies, and retail businesses, led Congress to pass the Internet Tax Freedom Act, which imposed a moratorium on taxation of online sales. State and local officials strongly oppose such limitation, estimating that it costs them as much as $23 billion in annual revenues because more and more goods are purchased on the Internet. Already states estimate that they forfeit $5 billion a year in uncollected taxes from interstate catalog sales. Only Internet and catalog sales to citizens living in a state in which the firm has a physical presence are now taxed. Many states require citizens to declare and pay such sales taxes in their annual state income tax returns, usually to no avail because of the difficulty of enforcement.

Internet taxation is both complicated and controversial, and it has become a compelling issue for the states. A 1992 U.S. Supreme Court ruling blocked taxation of catalog sales on the grounds that it violated the Commerce Clause—a ruling that has obvious applicability to taxing Internet commerce today.[11] Predictably, Congress has been tied in knots over the issue, but no less than the fiscal integrity of state revenue systems is at stake. If states lose billions of dollars to a tax-free Internet, how will the gaping budget holes be filled? What about Main Street "brick and mortar" retailers whose prices are made less competitive by the amount of the sales tax? But would it not also lay a heavy burden on vendors to comply with the tax laws of 7,600 taxing jurisdictions in the United States?

A compromise is the streamlined sales tax (SST), wherein states collapse all their local sales tax rates into one (or just a few) statewide rates, resulting in a manageable number of Internet tax jurisdictions. This approach has the added value of laying the foundation for taxing mail-order catalog sales.

Twenty-four states have passed the SST model legislation. Sixteen additional states have adopted a sales tax on online purchases of music, games, ringtones, and other video entertainment. Venders are required to apply the state sales tax when the product is sold and remit it to the state.[12] Perhaps in anticipation of congressional action, as well as state arguments that many Internet retailers utilize "affiliate sellers" located within their states, huge online retailers such as Amazon have begun collecting sales taxes in sixteen states. The "Amazon tax" brought in an estimated $107 million in "e-taxes" in California in 2012.[13] Hope for a national solution to taxing Internet and catalog sales rests on Congress's disposition of the Marketplace Fairness Act, which grants states the power to compel online and catalog retailers to collect sales tax for each transaction. The Act passed the Senate on May 6, 2013 by a vote of 69-27, but was stalled in the House as of September 2013.

The sales tax is relatively simple for governments to administer. Sellers of merchandise and services are required to collect it and remit it to the state on a regular basis. Political accountability is also an advantage because legislative bodies must enact laws or ordinances to increase the sales tax rate. And, as we have observed, the sales tax is the least unpopular of the major taxes.

Income Tax Most states tax personal and corporate income. Wisconsin was the first, in 1911, two years before the national government enacted its own personal income tax. Forty-one states have broad-based taxes on personal income; two (Tennessee and New Hampshire) limit theirs to capital gains, interest, and dividends. Only Alaska, South Dakota, Florida, Texas, Nevada, Washington, and Wyoming leave *all* personal income untaxed. Texas, Nevada, Washington, and Wyoming abstain from taxing corporate income. Personal income taxes garner 21.3 percent of all state and local own-source taxes (see Figure 12.1), and the corporate tax brings in 3.6 percent.[14] Fifteen states permit designated cities, counties, or school districts to levy taxes on personal income.

State and local income taxes are equitable when they are progressive. Progressivity normally entails a sliding scale, so that high-income filers pay a greater percentage of their income in taxes than low-income filers. Most of the states do not levy a personal income tax on people whose earnings fall below a certain floor—say, $10,000. Overall, state personal income taxes are moderately progressive. Seven states, however, tax income at a flat rate varying from 3.07 percent in Pennsylvania to 6 percent in Tennessee.

Personal and corporate income taxes are superior to other taxes on the criteria of yield and elasticity. By tapping virtually all sources of income, they draw in large sums of money and respond fairly well to short-term economic conditions. Through payroll withholding, income taxes are fairly simple to collect. Also, many states periodically adjust income tax rates in response to annual revenue needs.

As mentioned earlier, political accountability can be problematic with respect to income taxes during periods of rising prices. Unless income tax rates are indexed to inflation, as they are in seventeen states, cost-of-living increases push salaries and corporate earnings into higher tax brackets.

Miscellaneous Taxes A wide variety of miscellaneous taxes are assessed by state and local governments. "Sin taxes" raise a small but rapidly growing percentage of all state revenues. Online gambling is the latest device; three states have authorized Internet gambling and placed a tax on it. All states tax cigarettes, and many have hiked this tax during the past few years. New York's $4.35 cigarette tax boosts the average price per pack to $9.20 ($11 in New York City, which levies an additional tax). Missouri charges only 17¢ per pack. This startling disparity in prices has led to a flourishing trade in Internet vending, cigarette smuggling, and sales on Indian reservations (where tobacco is not taxed at all).

In 1998, the states experienced the equivalent of winning the lottery. A court settlement with tobacco companies is sending an estimated total of $246 billion into state coffers over a period of years. The payments, however, are based on cigarette sales in each state, and this quantity has been declining as prices have risen. Ideally, states would spend their shares on smoking prevention and health care services. But few strings are attached, and many states have spent their windfall on economic development initiatives and balancing the budget. Some states have taken the fiscally unsound step of selling bonds to be paid off with future tobacco settlement funds.

Alcoholic beverages are also taxed in all fifty states, with rates varying according to classification: beer, wine, or spirits. Beer guzzlers should steer clear of Alaska, where the tax per gallon of beer is $1.07. Frequent imbibers are invited to visit Wyoming, where the tax is only 2¢ per gallon.

Though not a "sin," gasoline falls under taxation's shadow as well. The highest state tax on driving is found in New York (49¢ per gallon). The lowest is in Alaska (8.0¢). All states also tax vehicles and vehicle licenses. Alas, the gas tax is running toward empty as motorists purchase more fuel-efficient vehicles. The result is depletion of road maintenance and improvement funds for which gasoline taxes are earmarked.

Most states tax death in one form or another. Estate taxes must be paid on the money and property of a deceased person before the remainder is disbursed to the survivors. Sixteen states tax those who inherit substantial assets (typically valued at more than $1 million). Rates are generally staggered according to the value of the estate and the relationship to the deceased. A reduction of the federal estate tax has resulted in a decline for some such state taxes as well, unless a state acts to amend its own estate tax laws.

Other miscellaneous sources of revenue include hunting and fishing licenses, business licenses, auto license fees, parking tickets, and traffic violation fines. Utah imposes a 10 percent "pole tax" on strip clubs and escort services. One interesting instrument is the jock tax. Some twenty states and several cities require professional athletes to file a tax return and pay a prorated income tax for games played in their jurisdiction. Players and their associations object strongly to the jock tax.

User Fees

Setting specific prices on goods and services provided by state and local governments is one time-proven method that clearly pursues the *benefit principle*: Only those who use the goods and services should pay. Examples include college tuition, water and sewer charges, and trash collection assessments. Toll roads and bridges are coming back in fashion as well. Building fees, inspection fees, food truck licenses, and even fire service charges are assessed in some local jurisdictions. Today, user fees are being applied broadly as state and especially local officials attempt to tie services to their true costs. Such fees are increasingly being levied on "nonessential" local government services, such as parks and recreation, libraries, and airports. User fees make up about 40 percent of local governments' own-source revenues.

User fees offer several advantages. If priced accurately, they are perfectly appropriate under the benefit principle, and they enjoy a relatively high level of political acceptability. But those people who do not have enough money to purchase the goods and services may have to do without—a circumstance that violates the ability-to-pay principle. A good case in point is higher education, which is shifting increasingly from state funding to tuition and fee funding. (Rebates, scholarships, fee waivers, and reduced-fee schedules mitigate ability-to-pay difficulties among low-income residents.)

User fees are structured to yield whatever is needed to finance a particular service. An added benefit is that service users who do not live in the taxing jurisdiction must also pay the price, say, for a day in the state park. Elasticity may be achieved if the amount of the charge is varied so that it always covers service costs. In many instances user fees can be levied without the specific permission of the state.

Because service users must be identified and charged, some user fees can be difficult to administer. Political accountability is low because the charges can be increased without legislative action. However, a special advantage of user fees is that they can be employed to ration certain goods or services. For instance, entrance charges can be increased to reduce attendance at an overcrowded public facility, or varied according to the day of the week in order to encourage more efficient utilization. If the municipal zoo has few visitors on Mondays, it can cut the entrance fee on that day of the week by one-half.

An increasingly popular and specialized form of user charge is the local impact fee, or exaction, requiring private land developers to contribute roads, sewers, and other infrastructure as a price for local regulatory approval for development projects, such as subdivisions or industrial facilities. The cost of infrastructure is shifted to private firms and, ultimately, to those who purchase or use their buildings or facilities. A related concept is applied through a special sales tax on travel and tourism-related services. Here, taxes on lodging, rental cars, and other services paid largely by out-of-towners are imposed at rates averaging 12 percent. Table 12.2 rates major taxes and fees based on the five criteria discussed at the beginning of this section.

Rating State and Local Taxes According to Five Criteria — TABLE 12.2

TAX	EQUITY	YIELD	ELASTICITY	POLITICAL ACCOUNTABILITY	ACCEPTABILITY
Property	C	C	C	D	D
Sales	D	B	B	A	B
Personal and corporate income	B	A	B	C	C
User fees	C	B	A	C	B

SOURCE: © Cengage Learning

Severance Tax

States blessed with petroleum, coal, natural gas, and minerals have for many years taxed these natural resources as they are taken from the land and sold. A fortunate few are able to "export" a substantial portion of their tax bite to people living in other states. In-staters, however, must pay the same tax rate as out-of-staters.

A large majority of states (thirty-eight) place a severance tax on some form of natural resources, but just ten states collect 90 percent of all severance tax revenues. Taxes on oil and natural gas account for around 50 percent of total state revenues in Alaska. Wyoming and Alaska bring in about $4 billion in revenues from severance taxes on coal, oil, and gas. (Perhaps this explains why these states are able to forgo personal income taxes). Several states are rather creative in applying the severance tax. Washington levies the tax on oysters, salmon, and other food fish; Louisiana, on freshwater mussels.[15]

Severance taxes are popular in states rich in natural resources, because they help keep income, property, and sales taxes relatively low. Severance tax revenues also help to pay for environmental damage resulting from resource extraction operations, such as strip mining and "fracking." The major disadvantage is that a state economy too dependent on severance taxes can be damaged badly when the price of its natural resources declines, as Alaska experience from time to time with depressed crude oilprices. Even so, natural resources have been individually enriching for Alaskans. For more than twenty years every man, woman, and child resident of Alaska has received a rebate from the state's Permanent Fund. Checks totaled $878 per person in 2012. Established primarily with severance taxes on petroleum, the Permanent Fund's $40 billion reserves are diversified through investments in office buildings, industrial complexes, stocks, and bonds.[16]

Gambling: Lotteries and Casinos

The lottery is an old American tradition; initially established in the 1600s, it was popular from the colonial days until the late 1800s. Lotteries flourished throughout the country as a means of raising money for such good causes as new schools, highways, canals, and bridges. But scandals and mismanagement led every state and the national government to ban "looteries." From 1895 to 1963, no legal lotteries were operated. Then New Hampshire established a new one, followed in 1967 by New York. Since then forty-three additional states have created lotteries.

Several factors account for the rebirth of "bettor government." First, lotteries can bring in large sums of money—some $59 billion in "profits" in 2010.[17] Second, they are popular and entertaining. And they are voluntary—you do not have to participate. In addition, lotteries help relieve pressure on major taxes. In some states, net lottery earnings take the place of a 1¢ increase in the sales tax.

But lotteries also have disadvantages. They are costly to administer and have low yields. Prize awards must be great enough to encourage future ticket sales; the higher the payout, the more people play. New games must be created to retain enthusiasm. Ticket vendors must be paid commissions. And tight (as well as expensive) security precautions are required to guarantee the game's integrity. As a result, lotteries generate only a small percentage of most states' total revenues. The average yield for players is low as well: about 50 percent of the total revenue is returned to players in prize money. This is far below the returns of other games of chance, such as slot machines, roulette, or craps. Although many states earmark lottery proceeds for popular programs, especially education, the result is often a shell game. For instance, Florida's lottery officially benefits schools and colleges, but in reality lottery money simply *replaces* general-fund revenues, rather than actually enhancing education funding.

Lotteries can also be attacked on the grounds of equity and elasticity. Although the purchase of a ticket is voluntary and thus seemingly fair, studies indicate that low-income individuals are more likely to play. Participation is also higher among African Americans, Latinos, older people, and those with low levels of education.[18] The lottery, then, is a regressive way to raise revenues.[19] Furthermore, lotteries tend to encourage compulsive gambling. In recognition of this problem, some states earmark a portion of lottery proceeds for treatment programs. Lotteries are considered inelastic because earnings are cyclical and generally unstable. Sales depend on such factors as the legalized gambling activities in neighboring states, the size of jackpots, and the effectiveness of marketing efforts.

As interstate lottery competition has saturated markets and depressed profits, states have adopted other forms of legalized gambling, such as pari-mutuel betting on horse and dog races, racinos with slots at the track, as well as gambling on riverboats, Indian reservations, and at Old West historical sites like mining towns. In a persistent quest for more revenues, many states have legalized casino gambling. Once restricted to Atlantic City and Las Vegas, casino gambling and Internet betting parlors are now offered in forty states, including operations on about 440 Native American reservations. Gambling establishments virtually blanket Minnesota and Mississippi. Touted as producers of jobs, tourist dollars, and state revenues, casinos and slot parlors share many of the same disadvantages as lotteries, including diminishing returns as new casinos open across the country. Yet they do rake in a significant amount of revenues, approximately $8.6 billion in casino taxes and about $1.5 billion in Pennsylvania alone in 2012.[20]

Now, get ready for legal Internet gambling, including online poker. Previously forbidden by the federal government under the 1961 Federal Wire act, Internet gambling (other than sports wagering) was approved in a U.S. Justice Department ruling in 2011. Nevada was the first state to proceed with "Ultimate Poker," followed soon by Delaware and New Jersey; several other states were seriously considering Internet gambling in 2013. Although Congress will probably need to regulate Internet gaming, the potential take for the states is substantial, estimated to be $2–4 billion in tax revenues.[21]

THE POLITICAL ECONOMY OF TAXATION

Decisions to raise or lower taxes and fees are inherently political. There are winners and losers, payers and receivers, both in the taxing and in the spending that follows.

Spending

Taxes lead to spending. The principle of diversity in state and local finance is evident given what nonnational governments choose to do with their revenues. First, these governments spend a great deal of money. State and local spending has been ascending much faster than the gross national product and the level of inflation. The functional distribution of spending varies from state to state. As indicated in Figure 12.2, education consumes the largest proportion of total state spending.

Within each of these functional categories lies a wide range of financial commitments. For instance, higher-education expenditures in a recent year ran from 24.4 percent of total state and local spending in Iowa to only 2.2 percent in Maine. Utah dedicated 25.9 percent of its spending to transportation, whereas Maryland and Colorado set aside only 4.6 percent for the same purpose.[22] Such differences represent historical trends, local economic circumstances, and citizens' willingness to incur debt to pay for services. Demographic factors also play a role. For instance, states with high populations of children invest more money in schools than do states with large proportions of senior citizens. State population growth also drives up expenditures for such services

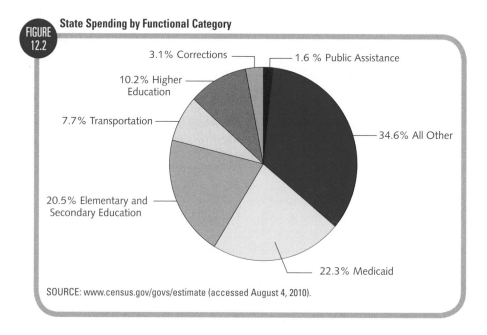

FIGURE 12.2

State Spending by Functional Category

3.1% Corrections

1.6 % Public Assistance

10.2% Higher Education

7.7% Transportation

34.6% All Other

20.5% Elementary and Secondary Education

22.3% Medicaid

SOURCE: www.census.gov/govs/estimate (accessed August 4, 2010).

as schools, law enforcement, water and sewer systems, and street maintenance. The largest expenditure gains in recent years have been registered in Medicaid as populations of the medically indigent have swelled.

One of the most difficult decisions for an elected official is to go on record in favor of raising taxes. The political heat can scorch even the coolest incumbent. But when revenues do not equal service costs and citizens do not want to cut services, raising taxes may be the only answer. Most people, however, do not want higher taxes. This is the familiar **tax-service paradox**: people demand new, improved, or at least the same level of government services, but do not want to pay for them through taxes. For instance, the people of Washington State, in their collective wisdom, voted in a 1999 constitutional referendum to slice taxes. But the very next year they passed another initiative to reduce class size and hike teachers' pay—without providing any new money. Voters in a dozen other states have taken similar action. As a former legislator put it, "I wouldn't say voters are stupid. But the same voter who wants unlimited services also does not want to pay for it. There is a disconnect."[23] Is it any wonder that user charges have become a popular option?

The tax-service paradox reflects a growing alienation between government and its citizens. The widespread belief that government at all levels has become too big and wasteful undoubtedly has some basis in fact. The size and responsibilities of state and local governments have grown dramatically, and waste and inefficiency have sometimes accompanied this growth. But the unwillingness of citizens to accept the inevitable reductions in services that follow tax cuts borders on mass schizophrenia.

Helping promote the tax-service paradox are the news media, which "commonly paint government with the broad brush of incompetence."[24] Prime-time television news capsules on "how government wastes your money" and typical reporting on actions of states and localities focuses on the negative while ignoring the positive. Government-bashing is a popular conservative blog and talk show sport. Meanwhile, state and local government functions have become much more complex and technical, tending to make government more difficult to understand, interact with, and communicate with.

State and local governments are responding with outreach efforts designed to educate citizens about what their governments are doing for them and where their tax dollars are going. Local governments send annual notices showing taxpayers what their money goes to pay for. In several recent cases, most notably in 2012 in California, state voters have repealed or loosened up the restrictions of taxing and spending limitations, indicating the ability of state leaders to get their "dollars and sense" messages across to voters.

Thus, the **political economy**—the set of political choices that frames economic policy—has become enormously perplexing for state and local officials. Several features of the political economy merit additional discussion: the tax revolt, fiscal stress, limited discretion in raising new revenues, and unfunded retiree pension and health care benefits.

tax-service paradox
A situation in which people demand government services but do not want to pay for them through taxes.

political economy
Political choices that have economic outcomes.

Tax Revolt

Taxpayer resentment of property taxes, and the general perception of government as too big, too costly, and too wasteful, first took on a tangible form in 1978 with the passage of Proposition 13 in California. Its most Draconian form was enacted by initiative and referendum in 1992 in Colorado as the Taxpayer's Bill of Rights (TABOR). (TABOR's severity was lessened in another referendum adopted in 2005.) Today, nearly every state has put into place statutory or constitutional limitations on taxing and spending by restricting personal or corporate income tax increases, indexing their income taxes to the cost of living, limiting expenditures to increases in the cost of living, and other measures. In most instances, voters took tax matters into their own hands through the initiative process. In other cases, state legislators jumped in front of the parade and cut taxes and spending themselves. The taxpayer revolt continues at a slower pace today. Its legacy, however, remains enormously important. Watchdog organizations such as Americans for Tax Reform, led by famous taxophobe Grover Norquist, insist that candidates for public office sign "no-tax" pledges. Public officials must work hard to justify tax increases; otherwise, they risk a citizen uprising and perhaps political death.

Indeed, the stirrings of new tax revolts are constantly in evidence. Oklahomans approved a 2012 ballot measure that limited property tax increases to 3 percent a year, and four other states endorsed their own property tax cuts. Coloradans voted in November 2010 on a monumental cut in property taxes and various fees and a prohibition severely restricting local government debt. In Maine, voters in 2010 retracted a law that would have expanded the state sales tax to various services.

taxation and expenditure limitations (TELs)

Restrictions on state and/or local government taxing and spending.

Taxation and expenditure limitations (TELs) are restrictions on government taxing and spending, such as Oklahoma's. Forty-six states have some sort of property tax restriction in effect, and many place limitations on other forms of taxation as well. Raising taxes now requires a constitutional amendment, voter approval, or an extraordinary legislative majority in quite a few states. States and localities usually resist reducing service levels, opting instead to shift tax burdens or to find new sources of revenues, such as user charges.

Political and economic consequences of the tax revolt have been much studied. In many cases, TELs have made state and local finance an extraordinarily difficult undertaking: voters insist on passing spending mandates for education, law enforcement, or other popular programs while at the same time tying the hands of legislatures with restrictions on new revenue raising, spawning bureaucratic legerdemain and new fees to garner sufficient revenues to pay for essential services.[25] So far, TELs have not significantly reduced the size in addition to greater cost of government as advertised.[26] TELs, however, have caused local governments to depend more on the states and led to greater recognition by public officials of the continuing need to consult with the taxpaying public on tax issues.[27]

Fiscal Stress

During national and regional economic downturns, many state and local juris-dictions experience severe **fiscal stress**: they struggle to pay for programs and provide services that citizens want and need without taxing the citizens at unacceptably high levels. Many factors contribute to fiscal stress. Typically, adverse social and economic conditions, mostly beyond state and local gov-ernment control, establish an environment conducive to financial problems. The unwinding of the national economy in 2008–2011 was due to the deregu-lation of the financial industry, corporate greed, personal irresponsibility, and many other factors beyond state and local government control (though some jurisdictions incurred unrealistic spending obligations even as tax income lessened). Yet it was they—the states and localities—that paid the greatest financial price.

Older industrial cities are particularly vulnerable. Many jobs and manu-facturing industries have been lost because of the gradual but compelling shift to a service- and information-based economy and to company relocations to Sunbelt and foreign sites. In cities such as Detroit and Philadelphia, the exodus of jobs and firms has eroded the value of taxable resources (mostly property); yet citizens left behind have growing service demands. In New Orleans and other Gulf Coast communities, the local tax base was essentially destroyed by Hurricane Katrina in 2005, and badly damaged again as a result of the 2010 BP oil spill.

Concentration of the poor and minorities in deteriorating housing, the shortage of jobs, high levels of crime, the illegal drug trade, homelessness, large expanses of blighted property, and related factors have produced crisis-level situations. Declining infrastructure also plagues older cities: water and sewer lines, treatment plants, streets, bridges, sidewalks, and other components of the urban physical landscape are in dire need of restoration or replacement. The estimated amount needed to repair Atlanta's crumbling transportation infrastructure alone is a shocking $922 million.[28] Most of these problems, it should be noted, will require national government attention if they are to be addressed effectively.

Political sources of fiscal stress typically compound the economic problems of cities. Mismanagement of resources and inefficient procedures and activities are common complaints. Pressures from city workers and their unions have also driven up service provision costs in some localities. Thus, service demands and the costs of providing services grow while taxes and other revenues decline. This is a well-tested recipe for fiscal stress that evokes fears of bond defaults and even bankruptcy.

New York City offers a forty-year saga of fiscal stress. People, jobs, and industry fled the city for the suburbs and the Sunbelt in the early 1970s, thereby reducing fiscal capacity. Yet public employees' pay and pensions grew to some of the highest levels in the United States, and welfare payments to the poor and a growing number of unemployed were generous. The City University of

fiscal stress
Financial pressure on a government from such factors as revenue shortfalls and taxing and spending limitations.

New York (CUNY), which was tuition-free at this time, had an enrollment of 265,000 students.

As revenues increasingly lagged behind expenditures, the city government played fiscal roulette with the budget and borrowed huge sums through municipal notes and bonds. Eventually it was poised on the brink of bankruptcy. Defaults on the city's bonds, notes, and other debt instruments seemed imminent. City officials cried out to the national government and New York State for help, but some people had little sympathy for a city that had lived beyond its means for so long.

Aided by national guarantees of new long-term loans, New York State and other large holders of New York City debt finally agreed to a bailout. Had this immense urban financial edifice collapsed, the fiscal shocks would have threatened New York State's economic stability and even resulted in serious fiscal repercussions for other states and localities throughout the United States.

Unfortunately, the Big Apple once again risked being reduced to a seedy core in 1992. It faced a budget deficit of $3.5 billion, a mass exodus of jobs, and the enormous cost of thousands of AIDS and crack babies. New York City's fiscal problems cannot be solved overnight. Its 250,000 employees and $66 billion operating budget serve 8.4 million people spread throughout five boroughs. The city itself is the area's biggest landlord. It owns television and radio stations, a huge higher-education system, and four hospitals.

New York City continues today to struggle with its vast fiscal problems. As the ashes of the Twin Towers cooled in 2001, the new mayor, Michael Bloomberg, wrestling with a deficit of approximately $4 billion in his $43 billion budget, entertained the idea of a state takeover of city finances.[29] His "doomsday budget" included tens of thousands of layoffs, significant service cuts, and large property tax increases. Distressingly, the debts the City is still paying off from the 1970s had to be refinanced. The good news is that New York City's budget deficit had been turned into a surplus by 2007.[30] Spending restraints helped to buffer New York City during the Great Recession and enabled the city to recover more quickly than most other large cities.

Recessions notwithstanding, a growing number of states and localities face chronic fiscal shortfalls because of structural problems deeply embedded in their revenue systems. Structural imbalances result from tax systems developed for radically different state and local economies of more than half a century past.[31]

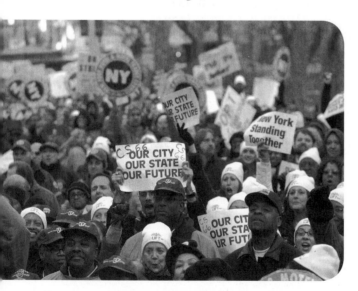

Protestors rally against New York State budget cuts.
SOURCE: Frances Roberts/Alamy

Limited Discretion

TELs have placed ceilings on rates and amounts of taxation and spending, thus limiting the discretion of the nonnational governments. Other constraining factors, too, keep state and local governments from falling prey to the temptation of taxing and spending orgies. One important factor is interstate competition for jobs and economic development. High-tax states run a risk of having jobs, firms, and investments "stolen" by low-tax states.

Earmarking taxes for popular programs also limits state and local taxing and spending discretion. Earmarking is well established: fuel taxes have been set aside for road and highway programs ever since automobiles first left ruts in muddy cow pastures. What differs today are the levels of specificity and creativity in earmarking. Approximately 25 percent of state tax revenues are earmarked. Surpluses may accumulate in some dedicated funds, such as highways, whereas other important needs such as education or law enforcement are not sufficiently met. The hands of government officials are tied, however, because they cannot move the funds around. Cigarette buyers in Washington cough up millions of dollars each year to help clean up Puget Sound. Several states earmark a penny of the sales tax for public education.

Financial discretion is partly determined by one's position on the fiscal food chain. The national government can essentially tax and spend as it wishes, subject only to citizen resistance and its highly underdeveloped capacity for self-discipline. States must meet federal spending mandates for Medicaid, corrections, and other services while somehow balancing their budgets each year. Local governments, in addition to suffering reductions in state aid during tough times in this game of "shift and shaft federalism," must comply with an increasing number of state spending mandates even as their legal authority to raise revenues remains highly circumscribed in most states. In some ways, then, local governments are not masters of their own fiscal fate.[32]

Pensions and OPEB

When the Governmental Accounting Standards Board (GASB) issued standards requiring state and local governments to publicly report the funding status of employee pensions and health care benefits, most respondents were caught with their financial pants down. As noted previously, for years most states and many local governments have been underfunding the future liabilities of employee retirement benefits. The estimated gap between promised health care and retirement benefits and what states have available to pay for them is estimated to be $1.38 trillion. California's unfunded pension liability is $516 billion and Illinois's is $139 billion.[33]

Equally serious are the estimated unfunded future liabilities of health care for retirees and their families. California is in the red for $77 billion, New Jersey for $71 billion, and Texas for $56 billion.[34] The larger the state employment numbers, the higher the future debt in most cases. But on a per capita basis, such states as Connecticut and Hawaii are hard hit. Connecticut is underfunded at more than $5,800 per person and Hawaii for nearly $7,640 per resident.

There are several reasons for these huge future retirement and health care obligations. The baby boom bulge in the government workforce has now reached retirement age. Unwise state borrowing from pension funds during difficult economic times is a major cause in some jurisdictions. Overly optimistic assumptions about health care cost inflation have been common. And, of course, legislators have a tendency to spend today and worry about the future later (or let the next generation of legislators worry about it).

Addressing the problem will require innovative thinking as well as aggressive prefunding of the future liabilities. The good thing about the GASB standards is that states and localities are being pressed to account for these future liabilities. The bad thing is that in some cases tax increases and reductions in promised benefits for government employees will have to be implemented to bring retiree pension and health care liabilities to sustainable levels.

MANAGING MONEY

Every state except Vermont is constitutionally or statutorily mandated to balance its budget each fiscal year. In turn, the states require their local governments to balance *their* budgets. These requirements, however, apply only to *operating budgets*, which are used for daily financial receipts and disbursements. Capital budgets, used for big purchases that must be paid for over time (for example, a new bridge or school building), typically run substantial deficits. Operating budgets may also run in the red during the fiscal year, so long as expenditures equal revenues at the end of the year. Consequently, the reliability of revenue estimates is a vital consideration.

Estimating Revenues

Not so long ago, state and local governments estimated their annual revenues simply by extrapolating from past trends. This incremental approach was simple, inexpensive, and worked well during periods of steady economic growth, but it failed miserably during years of boom or bust. The finance officers of states and most larger cities and counties are much more sophisticated today. Using computer software, they employ econometric modeling to derive mathematical estimates of future revenues. Economic forecasting firms and/or academics assist or provide independent projections.

Econometric modeling places key variables in equations to predict the fiscal-year yield of each major tax. A wide variety of variables are used, including employment levels, food prices, housing costs, oil and gas prices, consumer savings levels, interest rates, intergovernmental aid projections, and state and local debt obligations. Because state and local economies are increasingly linked to national and international factors, estimates often include measures for the value of the dollar, international trade and investment, and national fiscal policy. Despite sophisticated economic modeling and financial software, predictions can be wildly off the mark. State revenue estimates fell short by an average of more than 10 percent in 2009.[35]

Two critical factors determine the accuracy of revenue estimates: the quality of the data and the validity of the economic assumptions. Indeed, econometric modeling of state and local economies can be a voyage into the unknown. Data problems include difficulty in measuring key variables; periodic revisions of historical economic data, which require new calculations; and modifications in tax laws or fee schedules. But the major sources of error are the economic assumptions built into the models. Examples are legion. The national economy may not perform as expected; credit or housing markets can collapse; states with budget shortfalls may retract funds promised to local governments; credit and housing markets can collapse; energy prices may plummet or soar; natural or human disasters may disrupt state or local economic growth. Recessions are particularly damaging to fiscal stability because state and local sales and income tax revenues are highly sensitive to economic downturns.

Rainy Day Funds

Because a balanced budget is mandatory but estimation errors are inevitable, forty-eight states and many localities establish contingency, budget stabilization, or reserve funds. Popularly known as "rainy day funds," these savings accounts help insulate budgets from fiscal distortions caused by inaccurate data or faulty economic assumptions; they are also available to alleviate revenue shortfalls. In years of economic health, the funds accumulate principal and interest. When the economy falters, governments can tap their savings accounts to balance the budget and avoid imposing tax and fee increases.

During sunny days, the states typically fill up their contingency funds to as much as 10 percent of total spending. Amid the recessionary storms of 2009–2011, they were forced to dig deeply simply to retain essential services. By fall 2010, for instance, seventeen states had completely drained their rainy day funds.[36] The task of balancing the budget is especially daunting in local governments, given their lack of economic diversity, dependency on state taxes and financial aid, and sensitivity to economic dislocations. The departure of a single large employer can disrupt a local economy for years. So the potential advantages of such funds are numerous in the fragile fiscal context of cities and counties.

Other Financial Management Practices

State and local governments, of necessity, are becoming more knowledgeable about how to manage cash and investments. Cash reserves that once sat idly in non-interest-bearing accounts or a desk drawer are now invested in money market accounts, U.S. Treasury bills, certificates of deposit, and other financial instruments so that governments can maximize interest earnings. Most states have local government investment pools that manage billions of dollars in short-term assets. The process of spending and collecting monies is also manipulated to advantage. For example, large checks are deposited on the day they are received; conversely, payable checks are drawn on the latest date possible. In general, state and local financial management today resembles that of a large corporation instead of the mom-and-pop approach of years ago. After all, the nonnational governments spend and invest more than $3 trillion annually.

The most important state or local investment is usually the public-employee pension fund. In the past, they were conservatively managed and politically untouchable. Today, however, they tend to be invested in more aggressive instruments such as corporate stock. They also represent a tempting honey pot for financially suffering states whose governors have dipped their hands in the funds and pulled out billions to balance the budget. And as described previously, most retirement plans have very large unfunded liabilities.

State and local investments must not be managed too aggressively, as the case of Orange County, California, demonstrates. One of the nation's largest and wealthiest local jurisdictions, Orange County filed for federal bankruptcy in 1994. The county's financial nightmare commenced when its investment pool manager, Robert L. Citron, placed millions of dollars in financial instruments called derivatives. These instruments "derive" their value from underlying assets such as stocks, bonds, or mortgages. The derivatives' value changes when the price of the underlying assets changes. Orange County lost $1.5 billion when its derivatives, which were tied to interest rates, declined precipitously in value. In effect, Citron was borrowing money from stocks, bonds, and other assets to bet on the direction of interest rates. He lost, and so did Orange County's taxpayers.[37]

Long-Term Borrowing Like corporations, state and local governments issue long-term debt obligations, typically for five to twenty-five years. Bonds are the most common form of long-term borrowing. Because of federal and state tax breaks for investors, the nonnational governments are able to finance bonded indebtedness at significantly lower rates than corporations. There are three conventional types of bonds: general obligation bonds, revenue bonds, and industrial development bonds.

general obligation bond
A debt instrument supported by the full financial resources of the issuing jurisdiction.

The principal and interest payments on **general obligation bonds** are secured by the "full faith, credit, and taxing power" of the state or local jurisdiction issuing them. General obligation bonds are used to finance public projects such as highways, schools, and hospitals. Lenders are guaranteed repayment so long as the bond-issuing government is solvent; defaults are nearly nonexistent, but downgrades of cities' credit worthiness occur from time to time. A new credit vehicle, the Build America Bonds (BABs), was created in 2009 as part of the federal stimulus plan to boost the economy. Unlike tax-free bonds, BABs are subject to federal taxes. Their interest rate is higher than that for a conventional municipal bond, however, making it attractive to investors. The federal government subsidizes the interest rate by 35 percent, making BABs attractive to the issuers as well as the purchasers. $90 billion in BABs were issued to finance infrastructure and other capital projects in 2009.[38]

Revenue bonds are backed up by expected income from a specific project or service; examples include a toll bridge, a municipal sewer system, or a sports complex. Revenue bonds are payable only from the revenues derived from the specified source, not from general tax revenues. Because they typically represent a riskier investment than general obligation bonds, they command a higher rate of interest.

The **industrial development bond (IDB)** is a type of revenue bond. The payment of principal and interest on IDBs depends solely on the ability of the industry using the facilities financed by the bond to meet its financial obligation. If the user fails to make payments, creditors can seize and sell any real or personal property associated with the facility. Private interests, such as developers and retailers, are the primary beneficiaries of IDBs. Conventionally, these private-purpose bonds are issued by local governments to attract economic activity and investments; in fact, they are frequently used to furnish loans at highly favorable interest rates to small- or medium-size firms.

The **qualified private activity bond** is a municipal security that enables a firm to finance certain projects with bonds exempt from federal taxes. These financial instruments have been criticized for favoring businesses with government subsidies. Among the questionable uses have been for a Pakistani company's fertilizer plant in Indiana whose chemicals appeared in improvised explosive devices in Afghanistan, and financial offices for large and powerful firms such as Goldman Sachs Group and the Bank of America.[39] Any "public purpose" for such private activity bonds is difficult to discern.

Short-term borrowing is available to state and local governments that just need temporary funds to help tide them over or to meet unexpected circumstances. To borrow money on a short-term loan (e.g., one to six months), governments may access capital markets or even secure a loan from a bank or credit union.

Limits on Borrowing Almost all states place constitutional or statutory restrictions on their own and local government borrowing. Some set maximum levels of indebtedness; others require popular referenda to create debt or to exceed specified debt limits. They tightly restrict local government debt, especially general obligation bonds. (State-imposed constraints normally do not apply to revenue bonds.)

The bond market places its own informal limitations on debt by assessing the quality of bonds, notes, and other debt instruments. Investors in government

revenue bond
A bond that is paid off from income derived from the facility built with the bond proceeds.

industrial development bond (IDB)
A bond issued to fund the construction of a facility to be used by a private firm.

qualified private activity bond
A tax-exempt state or municipal security issued to a private firm used to finance a project or facility.

bonds rely on Moody's Investors Service, Standard & Poor's Corporation, Fitch Ratings, and other investment services for ratings of a jurisdiction's capacity to repay its obligations. Criteria taken into consideration in bond ratings include existing debt levels, unfunded future liabilities, rainy day funds, market value of real estate, population growth, per capita income, employment levels, and other measures of financial health and solvency. Highly rated bond issues receive ratings of *Aaa*, *Aa*, and *A*. Variations of *B* indicate medium to high risk. A rating of *C* is reserved for bonds in immediate danger of default. The average interest rate on risky low-rated bonds usually exceeds that of top-rated ones by one and a half to two percentage points; this translates into a considerable difference in interest payments. Bond ratings tend to rise during periods of economic growth but can drop rapidly during recessions, driving up borrowing costs. Four downgrades in general obligation bond ratings cost Illinois an extra $551 million in 2010. Other states suffering rating declines included Rhode Island, New Jersey, California, and Michigan.[40]

CURRENT ISSUES IN STATE AND LOCAL FINANCE

Rapid and severe deterioration in revenues slammed the state and local governments during the Great Recession and posed a monumental challenge to balanced budgets. Jurisdictions took a variety of actions, both large and small. Across-the-board cuts, hiring freezes, employee furloughs, and lay-offs were common. All told, some 535,000 public sector workers were laid off during 2008–2011. Some governments eliminated certain corporate tax breaks. California cut 17,500 state jobs and hacked K-12 and higher education budgets. Hawaii put into effect a four-day school week. Colorado and Virginia closed highway rest stops. Michigan canceled the state fair. Arizona sold its capitol buildings. The town of Maywood, California, disbanded its local government and contracted out essential services to neighboring jurisdictions. Some governors, in a desperate hunt for new revenues and budget fixes, proposed selling off state assets, including toll roads and bridges, parking lots, Interstate service plazas, and state buildings. California actually considered selling the Los Angeles Coliseum, San Quentin State Prison, the Orange County Fairgrounds, and scores of other assets. Arizona legislators considered selling the State Department of Public Safety Headquarters buildings, the state fairgrounds, prisons, and even the very buildings that the House and Senate meet in, and then leasing them back over a lengthy period of time. Minnesota essentially shut down state government over a lack of a 2011 budget, temporarily laying off 22,000 employees.

Harrisburg, Pennsylvania, won the "honor "of becoming first state capital to file for bankruptcy on October 12, 2011, attributing the action to a failed plan to finance and construct an incinerator and to "cash flow problems."

In 2013, Harrisburg was charged with securities fraud by the federal government for making misleading statements about the city's financial condition. On November 9, 2011, Jefferson County, Alabama, won the dubious distinction of becoming the largest local government to file a bankruptcy declaration in history, seeking relief from a debt of more than $4 billion. Jefferson County, home of Birmingham, ran up its huge debt thanks to political corruption, a bad investment in a sewer system, and dumb spending decisions.[41]

State and local governments are experiencing significant long-term problems in political economy. Tax systems designed for a primitive industrial age are badly out of step with today's service- and information-based global economy. Beset with its own chronic, self-inflicted financial travails and a record high budget deficit from wars and other spending, the budget-impaired federal government is not a consistently reliable fiscal partner. Indeed, the federal government threatened to revoke the tax exempt status of municipal bonds during the "sequestration" in 2013. The keys to surviving the inevitable financial problems in states and localities are intergovernmental cooperation, burden sharing, capacity building, and citizen comprehension of the basic tax-service relationship.

The spiraling costs of Medicaid and public education are burdens that cannot be shouldered by any single level of government. Mandates without money are certainly no help. When mandates and program responsibilities are pushed to a different rung of the federal ladder, funds should follow. Local governments in particular need more revenue-raising authority and broader tax bases to pay for the services they deliver. Most states have been receptive to these principles, but during the Great Recession many states cut funding to local governments, pulled back local governments' share of sales and other tax revenues, while foisting even more service delivery responsibilities on them.

The need to increase state and local capability and responsiveness by reinventing and reinvigorating government has perhaps never been greater. The financial structures and processes of state and local governments must be made more appropriate to the social and economic environment in which they operate, which includes a service-based economy; global markets; aging baby boomers; and the changing gender, racial, and ethnic composition of the labor force. State tax codes are littered with tax expenditures, commonly known as tax breaks or preferences, which benefit favored industries, firms, and individuals, costing hundreds of millions of dollars in tax revenues annually. Contemporary challenges to state and local governments are not being met sufficiently by present revenue systems.

Education is also needed for taxpayers, who do not always grasp the relationship between taxes paid and services rendered. Resistance to new or existing taxes is to be expected, but campaigns can educate citizens that the result of reducing or eliminating taxes will be fewer or lower quality services.

CHAPTER RECAP

- The two basic principles of state and local financial systems are interdependence of the three levels of government and diversity of revenue sources.

- Among the criteria for evaluating taxes are equity, yield, elasticity, ease of administration, political accountability, and acceptability.

- The major state and local taxes are those that are assessed on property, sales, and income. A variety of other taxes and fees are also imposed.

- Legalized gambling and gaming also raise money.

- Taxpayer resistance has produced tax and expenditure limitations in many states; increased sensitivity of state and local officials to taxpayer preferences; and, in some cases, caused fiscal stress for governments.

- State and local governments estimate annual revenues and set aside money in rainy day funds for emergencies and future contingencies.

- State and local financial relationships are characterized by sharing and cooperation, but also by conflict over mandates and limited local discretion.

Key Terms

own-source revenue *(p. 281)*
intergovernmental transfers *(p. 281)*
countercyclical aid *(p. 281)*
tax capacity (wealth) *(p. 282)*
tax effort (burden) *(p. 282)*
regressive tax *(p. 284)*
progressive tax *(p. 285)*

proportional (flat) tax *(p. 285)*
benefit principle *(p. 285)*
indexing *(p. 286)*
circuit breaker *(p. 288)*
tax-service paradox *(p. 297)*
political economy *(p. 297)*
taxation and expenditure limitations (TELs) *(p. 298)*

fiscal stress *(p. 299)*
general obligation bond *(p. 304)*
revenue bond *(p. 305)*
industrial development bond (IDB) *(p. 305)*
qualified private activity bond *(p. 305)*

Internet Resources

The National Conference of State Legislatures' Principles of a High Quality Tax System are available at **www.ncsl.org**.

One of the best individual sites on state tax and budget information, including an up-to-date look at "where the money goes," is that of the Texas State Comptroller at **www.window.state.tx.us**.

For current reports in developments, trends, and policy changes in state government finances, see the website of the Nelson A. Rockefeller Institute of Government at SUNY–Albany: **www.rockinst.org**.

Comparative state and local revenue, tax, and expenditure data may be found at the U.S. Census Bureau's website, **www.census.gov**, and at the Tax Foundation's website, **www.taxfoundation.org**.

See **www.taxsites.com** for a directory of general tax information and official state tax sites.

References

Chapter 1 New Directions for State and Local Governments pp. 1–20

1. Governor Maggie Hassan, "New Hampshire State of the State Address 2013," www.pewstates.org/projects/stateline/headlines/new-hampshire-state-of-the-state-address-2013.
2. Bruce Wallin, "State and Local Governments Are American, Too," *The Political Science Teacher* 1 (Fall 1988): 1–3.
3. Mike Sullivan, as quoted in "Wyoming's Governor Signs Law to Restructure State Government," *Denver Post* (March 5, 1989), 8B.
4. Council of State Governments, "Capitol Ideas," www.csg.org/pubs/capitolideas/index.aspx (February 20, 2012).
5. Beth Walter Honadle, "Defining and Doing Capacity Building: Perspective and Experiences," in Beth Walter Honadle and Arnold M. Howitt, eds., *Perspectives on Management Capacity Building* (Albany: State University of New York Press, 1986), 9–23.
6. Katherine Barrett and Richard Greene, "Grading the States '08," *Governing* 21 (March 2008): 24–95.
7. Julie Bund and Gene M. Lutz, "Connecting State Government Reform with Public Priorities: The Iowa Test," *State and Local Government Review* 31 (Spring 1999): 73–90.
8. David M. Hedge, *Governance and the Changing American States* (Boulder, CO: Westview, 1998).
9. "No Child Left Behind Act to Be Waived in 10 States, Official Says," *Politico* www.politico.com/news/stories/0212/72672.html (February 9, 2012).
10. Terry Sanford, *The Storm Over the States* (New York: McGraw-Hill, 1967), 21.
11. Quoted in ibid.
12. John Herbers, "The New Federalism: Unplanned, Innovative and Here to Stay," *Governing* 1 (October 1987): 28.
13. Sheryl Gay Stolbert, "As Congress Stalls, States Pursue Cloning Debate," *New York Times*, www.nytimes.com (May 26, 2002).
14. Ann O'M. Bowman and Richard C. Kearney, *The Resurgence of the States* (Englewood Cliffs, NJ: Prentice-Hall, 1986).
15. Sanford, *Storm Over the States*.
16. Ann O'M. Bowman and Richard C. Kearney, "Dimensions of State Government Capability," *Western Political Quarterly* 41 (June 1988): 341–62.
17. Donald P. Haider-Markel, "Policy Diffusion as a Geographical Expansion of the Scope of Political Conflict: Same Sex Marriage Bans in the 1990s," *State Politics and Policy Quarterly* 1 (Winter 2001): 5–26.
18. Craig Savoye, "States Spare Residents from Tele-marketers," *Christian Science Monitor* (December 22, 2000), 8.
19. Chris Hamby, "'Fire-Safe' Cigarette Laws Spread Quickly," www.stateline.org/live (August 7, 2007).
20. "Map of Participating Mayors," www.usmayors.org/climateprotection/map/ (April 30, 2013).
21. Lawrence J. Grossback, Sean Nicholson-Crotty, and David A. M. Peterson, "Ideology and Learning in Policy Diffusion," *American Politics Research* 32 (September 2004): 521–45.
22. David Winder and James T. LaPlant, "State Lawsuits Against Big Tobacco: A Test of Diffusion Theory," *State and Local Government Review* 32 (Spring 2000): 132–41.
23. Keith Loria, "Thirty-Three States Settle Computer Chip Suit," *Legal Newsline*, www.legalnewsline.com (June 25, 2010). See also Colin Provost, "An Integrated Model of U.S. State Attorney General Behavior in Multi-State Litigation," *State Politics and Policy Quarterly* 10 (Spring 2010): 1–24.
24. Ann O'M. Bowman, "Trends and Issues in Interstate Cooperation," in *The Book of the States 2004* (Lexington, KY: Council of State Governments, 2004), 34–40.
25. Governor George Voinovich, as quoted in "Reassessing Mandates," *State Policy Reports* 11 (October 1993): 16.
26. Brad Knickerbocker, "States Take the Lead on Global Warming," *Christian Science Monitor* (October 10, 2003), 1, 12; N. C. Aizenman, "Opponents Present Case Against Obama's Health-Care Law in 20-State Lawsuit," *Washington Post*, www.washingtonpost.com (September 14, 2010).
27. As quoted in "It's Scary: State of the States 2009," *State News* 52 (May 2009): 9.
28. National Conference of State Legislatures, *State Budget Update: Summer 2011*. Denver, CO: NCSL.
29. Pamela M. Prah, "Reports: State Income Levels Plunge," www.stateline.org/live (June 19, 2009).
30. Rudolph Bush, "Dallas City Council Knows 'Brutal' Budget Cuts Coming," *Dallas Morning News*, www.dallasnews.com (June 18, 2009).
31. Michael Johnston, "Right and Wrong in American Politics: Popular Conceptions of Corruption," in Arnold Heidenheimer and Michael Johnston, eds., *Political Corruption: Concepts and Contexts* (New Brunswick, NJ: Transaction, 2002), 173–91; see also Richard T. Boylan and Cheryl X. Long, "Measuring Public Corruption in the American States," *State Politics and Policy Quarterly* 3 (Winter 2003): 420–38.
32. Kenneth R. Gosselin and Christopher Keating, "Corruption Costs Jobs, Study Says," *Hartford Courant*, www.ctnow.com/news.local (February 25, 2004).
33. Boylan and Long, "Measuring Public Corruption in the American States."
34. Dick Simpson et al., "Chicago and Illinois, Leading the Pack in Corruption," Anti-Corruption Report Number 5 (Chicago: University of Illinois at Chicago: February 15, 2012).

35. U.S. Census Bureau, "Overview of Race and Hispanic Origin: 2010," www.census.gov/prod/cen2010/briefs/c2010br-02.pdf (Accessed May 1, 2013).

36. Michael Hoefer, Nancy Rytina, and Bryan C. Baker, "Estimates of the Unauthorized Immigrant Population Residing in the United States: January 2011," U.S. Department of Homeland Security, Office of Immigration Statistics, (March 2012).

37. Randal C. Archibold, "Arizona Enacts Stringent Law on Immigration," *New York Times*, www.nytimes.com (April 23, 2010).

38. Rodney E. Hero and Caroline J. Tolbert, "A Racial/Ethnic Diversity Interpretation of Politics and Policy in the States of the U.S.," *American Journal of Political Science* 40 (August 1996): 851–71.

39. U.S. Census Bureau, "The Next Four Decades: The Older Population in the United States: 2010 to 2050," www.census.gov/prod/2010pubs/p25-1138.pdf (Accessed May 1, 2013).

40. U.S. Census Bureau, "State and County Quick Facts," http://quickfacts.census.gov/qfd/index.html (April 15, 2013).

41. U.S. Census Bureau, "Table 7. Cumulative Estimates of Population Change for Metropolitan Statistical Areas and Rankings: April 1, 2010 to July 1, 2012," http://www.census.gov/popest/data/metro/totals/2012/. (Accessed May 1, 2013).

42. Daniel J. Elazar, *American Federalism: A View from the States*, 3d ed. (New York: Harper & Row, 1984).

43. Jody L. Fitzpatrick and Rodney E. Hero, "Political Culture and Political Characteristics of the American States: A Consideration of Some Old and New Questions," *Western Political Quarterly* 41 (March 1988): 145–53.

44. Keith Boeckelman, "Political Culture and State Development Policy," *Publius: The Journal of Federalism* 21 (Spring 1991): 49–62; Russell L. Hanson, "Political Culture Variations in State Economic Development Policy," *Publius: The Journal of Federalism* 21 (Spring 1991): 63–80.

45. James P. Lester, "A New Federalism: Environmental Policy in the States," in Norman Vig and Michael Kraft, eds., *Environmental Policy in the 1990s* (Washington, DC: Congressional Quarterly Press, 1994), 51–68; Lawrence M. Mead, "State Political Culture and Welfare Reform," *Policy Studies Journal* 32 (May 2004): 271–96.

46. Joel Lieske, "Regional Subcultures of the United States," *Journal of Politics* 55 (November 1993): 888–913; Joel Lieske, "The Changing Regional Subcultures of the American States and the Utility of a New Cultural Measure," *Political Research Quarterly* 63 (September 2010): 538–52.

47. Frederick M. Wirt, "'Soft' Concepts and 'Hard' Data: A Research Review of Elazar's Political Culture," *Publius: The Journal of Federalism* 21 (Spring 1991): 1–13.

48. Emily Van Dunk, "Public Opinion, Gender and Handgun Safety Policy Across the States," paper presented at the annual meeting of the Midwest Political Science Association, Chicago, April 2000.

49. Michael S. Lewis-Beck and Peverill Squire, "Iowa: The Most Representative State?" *PS: Political Science and Politics* 42 (January 2009): 39–44.

50. Elaine B. Sharp, "Introduction," in Elaine B. Sharp, ed., *Culture Wars and Local Politics* (Lawrence: University Press of Kansas, 1999), 1–20.

51. John Shannon, "The Return to Fend-for-Yourself Federalism: The Reagan Mark," *Intergovernmental Perspective* 13 (Spring 1987): 34–37; David R. Morgan and Kenneth Kickham, "Modernization Among the U.S. States: Change and Continuity From 1960 to 1990," *Publius: The Journal of Federalism* 27 (Summer 1997): 23–39. See also Peter Harkness, "Federalism From the Bottom Up," *Governing*, www.governing.com (March 2013).

52. Alan Ehrenhalt, "The Increasing Irrelevance of Congress," *Governing* 11 (January 1998): 6–7.

53. Kate Brown, as quoted in Rob Gurwitt, "Cookie-Jar Clampdown," *Governing* 20 (April 2007): 36.

Chapter 2 Federalism and the States pp. 21–46

1. James B. Stewart, "In Obama's Victory, a Loss for Congress," *New York Times*, www.nytimes.com (June 29, 2012).

2. Adam Liptak, "Blocking Parts of Arizona Law, Justices Allow Its Centerpiece," *New York Times*, www.nytimes.com (June 25, 2012).

3. Quoted in Richard Hofstadter, *The American Political Tradition* (New York: Vintage Books, 1948), 9.

4. Quoted in Richard H. Leach, *American Federalism*, No. 45 (New York: W.W. Norton, 1970), 1.

5. Charles S. McCoy, "Federalism: The Lost Tradition?" *Publius: The Journal of Federalism* 31 (Spring): 1–14.

6. Forrest McDonald, *States' Rights and The Union: Imperium in Imperio, 1776–1876* (Lawrence: University Press of Kansas, 2000).

7. Quoted in ibid., 1788.

8. Walter Berns, "The Meaning of the Tenth Amendment," in Robert A. Goldwin, ed., *A Nation of States* (Chicago: Rand McNally, 1961), 130.

9. David B. Walker, *Toward a Functioning Federalism* (Cambridge, MA: Winthrop, 1981), 47–48; McDonald, *States' Rights and the Union.*

10. Hofstadter, *American Political Tradition*, 72.

11. Manny Fernandez, "White House Rejects Petitions to Secede, but Texans Fight On," New York Times, www.nytimes.com (January 15, 2013); Jake Grovum, "Nullification: Old Arguments Against Feds Get New Life," www.pewstates.org (March 14, 2013).

12. *McCulloch v. Maryland,* 4 Wheaton 316 (1819).

13. *Gibbons v. Ogden,* 9 Wheaton 316 (1819).

14. Eric Kelderman, "Real ID Showdown Averted," Stateline.org (April 4, 2008).

15. Daniel C. Vock, "Federal Government Gives States More Time on Real ID," www.pewstates.org (January 9, 2013).

16. *National League of Cities v. Usery,* 426 U.S. 833 (1976).

17. *Garcia v. San Antonio Metropolitan Transit Authority,* 105 S. Ct. 1007, 1011 (1985).

18. Ibid. (O'Connor, dissenting).

19. John C. Pittenger, "Garcia and the Political Safeguards of Federalism: Is There a Better Solution to the Conundrum of the Tenth Amendment?" *Publius: The Journal of Federalism* 22 (Winter 1992).

20. *United States v. Lopez,* 115 S. Ct. 1424 (1995). See Kenneth T. Palmer and Edward B. Laverty, "The Impact of *U.S. v. Lopez* on Intergovernmental Relations," *Publius: The Journal of Federalism* 26 (Summer 1996): 109–26.

21. *Kansas v. Hendricks,* 117 S. Ct. 2072 (1997).

22. *Printz* v. *U.S.*, 521 S. Ct. 98 (1997).
23. *Kelo* v. *New London*, 545 U.S. 469 (2005).
24. *Seminole Tribe of Florida* v. *Florida*, 116 S. Ct. 1114 (1996).
25. *College Savings Bank* v. *Florida Prepaid Postsecondary Education Expense Board et al.*, 98 S. Ct. 149 (1999).
26. *Nevada Department of Human Resources* v. *Hibbs*, S. Ct. 631 (2000).
27. *Federal Maritime Commission* v. *South Carolina Ports Authority*, No. 01–46 (2002).
28. *Florida Prepaid* v. *College Savings Bank*, No. 98-531 (1999).
29. *Lorillard Tobacco* v. *Reilly*, No. 00–596 (2000).
30. *Bush* v. *Gore et al.*, 00 S. Ct. 949 (2000).
31. *Citizens United* v. *FEC*, 558 U.S. 50 (2010).
32. *American Electric Power Co.* v. *Connecticut*, U.S.10-174 (2011).
33. John Kincaid, "State-Federal Relations: Civil War Redux?" *Book of the States* 43 (2011): 21–28.
34. Deil S. Wright, *Understanding Intergovernmental Relations*, 3rd ed. (New York: Wadsworth, 1988); McDonald, *States Rights and the Union*.
35. Timothy J. Conlon, "Federalism and Competing Values in the Reagan Administration," *Publius: The Journal of Federalism* 16 (Winter 1986): 29–47.
36. John Kincaid and Richard L. Cole, "Public Opinion on Federalism in Canada, Mexico, and USA in 2003," *Publius: The Journal of Federalism* 33, no. 3 (Summer 2003): 142–62.
37. Quoted in U.S. Advisory Commission on Intergovernmental Relations, *State Constitutions in the Federal System* (Washington, DC: Author, 1989), 37.
38. Alan Greenblat, "The Washington Offensive," *Governing* (January 2005): 26–29.
39. Peter Harkness, "Shift-and-Shaft Federalism," *Governing .com* (March 9, 2008).
40. Kincaid, "State-Federal Relations: Civil War Redux?"
41. W. Dale Mason, *Indian Gaming: Tribal Sovereignty and American Politics* (Norman: University of Oklahoma Press, 2000).
42. Erich Steinman, "American Federalism and Intergovernmental Innovation in State-Tribal Relations," *Publius: The Journal of Federalism* 34 (Spring 2004): 95–115.
43. See Ann O'M. Bowman and Neal D. Woods, "Strength in Numbers: Why States Join Interstate Compacts," *State Politics and Policy Quarterly* 7 (Winter 2007): 347–68.
44. *National Federation of Independent Business, et al.* v. *Sebelius*, U.S. 11-393 (2012).
45. "Mandate Monitor," *National Conference of State Legislatures* (July 2010), 1, accessed at www.ncsl.org/print/ standcomm/scbudg/mandate monitor.
46. USGAO, *Unfunded Mandates: Views Vary About Reform Act's Strengths, Weaknesses, and Options for Improvement*, GAO-05-454 (March 31, 2005).
47. National Conference of State Legislatures. www.ncsl.org (accessed April 10, 2013).
48. Donald F. Kettl, "10th Amendment Turf War," *Governing* (October 1998), 13.
49. Martha Derthick, "American Federalism: Half-Full or Half-Empty?" *Brookings Review* (Winter 2000): 24.

Chapter 3 State Constitutions pp. 47–68

1. G. Alan Tarr, *Understanding State Constitutions* (Princeton, NJ: Princeton University Press, 1999).
2. U.S. Advisory Commission on Intergovernmental Relations (ACIR), *State Constitutions in the Federal System*, A-113 (Washington, D.C.: Author, 1989).
3. Robert F. Williams, *The Law of American State Constitutions* (New York: Oxford University Press, 2009).
4. Donald S. Lutz, "The United States Constitution as an Incomplete Text," *Annals of the American Academy of Political and Social Science* 496 (March 1989): 23–32.
5. Quoting James Quale Dealey, *Growth of American State Constitutions*, in Robert Williams, *The Law of American State Constitutions*.
6. G. Alan Tarr and Mary Cornelia Porter, "Introduction: State Constitutionalism and State Constitutional Law," *Publius: The Journal of Federalism* 17 (Winter 1987): 5.
7. Donald S. Lutz, "Toward a Theory of Constitutional Amendment," *American Political Science Review* 88 (June 1994): 356; G. Alan Tarr, ed., *Constitutional Politics in the States* (Westport, CT: Greenwood Press, 1996), xv.
8. Donald S. Lutz, "The Iroquois Confederation Constitution: An Analysis," *Publius: The Journal of Federalism* 28 (Spring 1998): 99–127.
9. Daniel J. Elazar, "The Principles and Traditions Underlying State Constitutions," *Publius: The Journal of Federalism* 12 (Winter 1982): 11.
10. Quoted in Perry Gilbert Miller, "Thomas Hooker and the Democracy of Early Connecticut," *New England Quarterly* 4 (1931): 695.
11. Bruce Fraser, *The Land of Steady Habits: A Brief History of Connecticut* (Hartford: Connecticut Historical Commission, 1986), 10.
12. John Estill Reeves, *Kentucky Government* (Lexington: University of Kentucky, 1966), 7. As quoted in Penny M. Miller, *Kentucky Government and Politics* (Lincoln: University of Nebraska Press, 1994), 82.
13. Albert L. Sturm, "The Development of American State Constitutions," *Publius: The Journal of Federalism* 12 (Winter 1982): 61.
14. Ibid., 62–63.
15. Paul G. Reardon, "The Massachusetts Constitution Makes a Milestone," *Publius: The Journal of Federalism* 12 (Winter 1982): 45–55.
16. David McCullough, *John Adams* (New York: Touchstone Books, 2001).
17. Quoted in Thomas Parrish, "Kentucky's Fourth Constitution Is a Product of Its 1980 Times," in Thad L. Beyle, ed., *State Government: CQ's Guide to Current Issues and Activities, 1991–92* (Washington, D.C.: Congressional Quarterly Press, 1991), 46.
18. U.S. Advisory Commission on Intergovernmental Relations (ACIR), *The Question of State Government Capability* (Washington, D.C.: Author, 1985), 36.
19. David Fellman, "What Should a State Constitution Contain?" in W. Brooke Graves, ed., *Major Problems in State Constitutional Revision* (Chicago: Public Administration Service, 1960), 146.
20. Sturm, "American State Constitutions," 64.
21. David C. Nice, "Interest Groups and State Constitutions: Another Look," *State and Local Government Review* 20 (Winter 1988): 22.
22. Donald S. Lutz, "Patterns in the Amending of American State Constitutions," in G. Alan Tarr, ed., *Constitutional Politics in the States* (Westport, CT: Greenwood Press, 1996), 24–27.

23. U.S. Advisory Commission on Intergovernmental Relations (ACIR), *A Report to the President for Transmittal to the Congress* (Washington, D.C.: U.S. Government Printing Office, 1955).

24. National Municipal League, *Model State Constitution*, 6th ed., rev. (New York: National Municipal League, 1968).

25. John J. Carroll and Arthur English, "Traditions of State Constitution Making," *State and Local Government Review* 23 (Fall 1991): 103–109.

26. *Gitlow v. New York*, 26 U.S. 652 (1925).

27. Ibid., 38.

28. Ibid., 38–42.

29. Thomas Jefferson to James Madison, "Popular Basis of Political Authority." In Philip B. Kurland and Ralph Lerner, eds., *The Founders' Constitution*, Web edition, http://press-pubs.uchicago.edu/founders (1987).

30. Aaron Deslatte, "Critics Call Failed Constitutional Amendments Too Conservative, Too Controversial," *Orlando Sentinel*, www.OrlandoSentinel.com (November 12, 2012).

31. Council of State Governments, *The Book of the States*, 42 (Lexington, KY: Council of State Governments, 2010), Table 1.3.

32. Josh Goodman, "Seizing the Initiative," *Governing* (October 2008): 32.

33. Vladimir Kogan, "Lessons from Recent State Constitutional Conventions," *California Journal of Politics and Policy* 2 (2010): 1–24.

34. Janice C. May, "State Constitutions and Constitutional Revision: 1988–89 and the 1980s," *The Book of the States, 1990–91* (Washington, D.C.: Council of State Governments, 1991), 25.

35. Quoted in U.S. Advisory Commission on Intergovernmental Relations (ACIR), *State Constitutions in the Federal System* (Washington, D.C.: Author, 1989), 37.

36. Sturm, "American State Constitutions," 104.

37. W. Brooke Graves, "State Constitutional Law: A Twenty-Five Year Summary," *William and Mary Law Review* 8 (Fall 1966): 12.

38. ACIR, *State Government Capability*, 60.

39. Richard H. Leach, "A Quiet Revolution: 1933–1976," in *The Book of the States, 1975–76* (Lexington, KY: Council of State Governments, 1976), 25.

Chapter 4 Citizen Participation and Elections pp. 69–92

1. Lindsay A. Powers, "Takoma Park Grants 16-Year-Olds Right to Vote," *Washington Post*, www.washingtonpost.com/local (May 14, 2013).

2. Robert D. Putnam, *Bowling Alone: The Collapse and Revival of American Community* (New York: Simon and Schuster, 2000).

3. John D. Griffin and Brian Newman, "Are Voters Better Represented?" *Journal of Politics* 67 (November 2005): 1206–27.

4. William E. Lyons, David Lowery, and Ruth Hoogland DeHoog, *The Politics of Dissatisfaction* (Armonk, NY: M. E. Sharpe, 1992).

5. Nicholas A. Valentino et al., "Election Night's Alright for Fighting: The Role of Emotions in Political Participation," *Journal of Politics* 73 (January 2011): 156–70.

6. Henry E. Brady, Sidney Verba, and Kay Lehman Schlozman, "Beyond SES: A Resource Model of Political Participation," *American Political Science Review* 89 (June 1995): 271–94; see also Jennifer Jerit, Jason Barabas, and Toby Bolsen, "Citizens, Knowledge, and the Information Environment," *American Journal of Political Science* 50 (April 2006): 266–82.

7. Richard Murray and Arnold Vedlitz, "Race, Socioeconomic Status, and Voting Participation in Large Southern Cities," *Journal of Politics* 39 (November 1977): 1064–72; Fredrick C. Harris, Valeria Sinclair-Chapman, and Brian D. McKenzie, "Macrodynamics of Black Political Participation in the Post-Civil Rights Era," *Journal of Politics* 67 (November 2005): 1143–63.

8. Virginia Sapiro, *The Political Integration of Women* (Urbana: University of Illinois Press, 1983).

9. Any Linomon and Mark R. Joslyn, "Trickle Up Political Socialization: The Impact of Kids Voting USA on Voter Turnout in Kansas," *State Politics and Policy Quarterly* 2 (Spring 2002): 24–36.

10. J. Eric Oliver, "City Size and Civic Involvement in Metropolitan America," *American Political Science Review* 94 (June 2000): 361–73.

11. Michael R. Alvarez et al., "2008 Survey of the Performance of American Elections," www.pewcenter on thestates.org (March 26, 2009).

12. Kim Quaile Hill and Jan E. Leighley, "Party Ideology, Organization, and Competitiveness as Mobilizing Forces in Gubernatorial Elections," *American Journal of Political Science* 37 (November 1993): 1158–78.

13. Alan S. Gerber and Todd Rogers, "Descriptive Social Norms and Motivation to Vote: Everybody's Voting and So Should You," *Journal of Politics; 71* (January 2009): 178–91.

14. Peter L. Francia and Paul S. Herrnson, "The Synergistic Effect of Campaign Effort and Election Reform on Voter Turnout in State Legislative Elections," *State Politics and Policy Quarterly* 4 (Spring 2004): 74–93.

15. Council of State Governments, "Election-Day Registration Considered in Illinois, its End Mulled in Wisconsin," http://knowledgecenter.csg.org/ (April 1, 2013).

16. Michael McDonald, "2012 General Election Turnout Rates," United States Election Project, http://elections.gmu.edu/Turnout_2012G.html (February 9, 2013).

17. "Absentee and Early Voting," National Conference on State Legislatures, www.ncsl.org/legislatures-elections/elections/absentee-and-early-voting.aspx (July 22, 2011).

18. Robert M. Stein and Greg Vonnahme, "Engaging the Unengaged Voter: Vote Centers and Voter Turnout," *Journal of Politics* 70 (April 2008): 487–97.

19. Priscilla Southwell and Justin Burchett, "The Effect of Vote-by-Mail Elections on Voter Turnout," *American Politics Quarterly* 29 (February 2000): 72–80; see also Cynthia Rugeley and Robert A. Jackson, "Getting on the Rolls: Analyzing the Effects of Lowered Barriers on Voter Registration," *State Politics and Policy Quarterly* 9 (Spring 2009): 56–78.

20. Michael J. Hanmer et al., "Losing Fewer Votes: The Impact of Changing Voting Systems on Residual Votes," *Political Research Quarterly* 63 (March 2010): 129–42.

21. Methods of Nominating Candidates for State Offices," *The Book of the States, 2010* (Lexington, KY: Council of State Governments, 2010), 334–35.

22. National Conference of State Legislatures, "State Primary Election Types," www.ncsl.org (September 28, 2011).

23. Charles S. Bullock III, Ronald Keith Gaddie, and Anders Ferrington, "System Structure, Campaign Stimuli and Voter Falloff in Runoff Primaries," *Journal of Politics* 64 (November 2002): 1210–24.

24. Kentucky Legislative Research Commission, "Election Filing Dates and Runoff Primary," www.lrc.ky.gov/record/08RS/SB3/SCS1LM.doc (July 1, 2009).

25. "Instant Runoff Voting," www.instantrunoff.com (September 20, 2010).

26. Randall W. Partin, "Economic Conditions and Gubernatorial Elections," *American Politics Quarterly* 23 (January 1995): 81–95.

27. Brian F. Schaffner, Gerald Wright, and Matthew Streb, "Teams Without Uniforms: The Nonpartisan Ballot in State and Local Elections," *Political Research Quarterly* 54 (March 2001): 7–30.

28. Zoltan Hajnal and Jessica Trounstine, "When Turnout Matters: The Consequences of Uneven Turnout in City Elections," *Journal of Politics* 67 (May 2005): 515–36.

29. Arnold Fleischmann and Lana Stein, "Campaign Contributions in Local Elections," *Political Research Quarterly* 51 (September 1998): 673–89. See also Jessica Trounstine, "Turnout and Incumbency in Local Elections," *Urban Affairs Review* 49 (March 2013): 167–89.

30. Luis Ricardo Fraga, "Domination Through Democratic Means: Nonpartisan Slating Groups in City Electoral Politics," *Urban Affairs Quarterly* 23 (June 1988): 528–55; Christopher A. Cooper and Anthony J. Nownes, "Citizen Groups in Big City Politics," *State and Local Government Review* 35 (Spring 2003): 102–11.

31. David B. Magleby, "Taking the Initiative: Direct Legislation and Direct Democracy in the 1980s," *PS: Political Science and Politics* 21 (Summer 1988): 600.

32. Elisabeth R. Gerber et al., *Stealing the Initiative* (Upper Saddle River, NJ: Prentice-Hall, 2001).

33. Initiative and Referendum Institute, "Election Results 2012: Breakthrough Wins for Marijuana and Same-Sex Marriage," www.iandrinstitute.org/BW%202012-3%20Election%20results%20v1.pdf (November 8, 2012).

34. John A. Grummel, "Morality Politics, Direct Democracy, and Turnout," *State Politics and Policy Quarterly* 8 (Fall 2008): 282–92; Joshua J. Dyck, "Initiated Distrust: Direct Democracy and Turnout," *American Politics Research* 37 (July 2009): 539–68.

35. Alana S. Jeydel and Brent S. Steel, "Public Attitudes Toward the Initiative Process in Oregon," *State and Local Government Review* 34 (Fall 2002): 173–82.

36. Valentina A. Bali, "Implementing Popular Initiatives: What Matters for Compliance?" *Journal of Politics* 66 (November 2003): 1141.

37. Government Accountability Board, State of Wisconsin, "Letter to Representative Vos," http://gab.wi.gov/sites/default/files/publication/65/letter_to_representative_vos_estimated_cost_of_a__17993.pdf (January 2012).

38. Nathan Dickerson, "Electronic Communications and Public Records," *Council of State Governments* (February 2012): 3.

39. Neal D. Woods, "Promoting Participation: An Examination of Rulemaking Notification and Access Procedures," *Public Administration Review* 69 (May/June 2009): 518–30.

40. Jonathan Walters, "Polling the Populace," *Governing* 20 (April 2007): 66–68.

41. Backseat Budgeter, www.backseatbudgeter.com/budgets/Colorado2011/default.apsx (Accessed March 7, 2012).

42. Stephen Knack, "Social Capital and the Quality of Government: Evidence From the States," *American Journal of Political Science* 46 (October 2002): 772–85.

43. Ericka Harney, "State of Volunteers," *State News* 52 (May 2009): 16–18.

44. Markus Prior, "News vs. Entertainment: How Increasing Media Choice Widens Gaps in Political Knowledge and Turnout," *American Journal of Political Science* 49 (July 2005): 577–92.

45. Evan J. Ringquist, Kim Quaile Hill, Jan E. Leighley, and Angela Hinton-Andersson, "Lower-Class Mobilization and Policy Linkage in the U.S. States: A Correction," *American Journal of Political Science* 41 (January 1997): 339–44.

46. Jonathan Walters, "O Citizen, Where Art Thou?" *Governing* 22 (April 2009): 60–62.

Chapter 5 Political Parties, Interest Groups, and Campaigns pp. 93–117

1. Gail Collins, "Alabama Goes Viral," *New York Times*, www.nytimes.com (May 26, 2010).

2. The Pew Research Center for the People and the Press, "Trend in Party Identification," www.people-press.org/2012/06/01/trend-in-party-identification-1939-2012/ (June 1, 2012).

3. Sarah M. Morehouse and Malcolm E. Jewell, "State Parties: Independent Partners in the Money Relationship," in John C. Green and Rick Farmer, eds., *The State of the Parties* (Lanham, MD: Rowman & Littlefield, 2003), 151–68.

4. Marjorie Randon Hershey, *Party Politics in America*, 11th ed. (New York: Pearson Longman, 2005).

5. Pew Research Center, "Trend in Party Identification."

6. James G. Gimpel and Jason E. Schuknecht, "Reconsidering Political Regionalism in the American States," *State Politics and Policy Quarterly* 2 (Winter 2002): 325–52.

7. Malcolm E. Jewell and Sarah M. Morehouse, *Political Parties and Elections in American States*, 4th ed. (Washington, D.C.: Congressional Quarterly Press, 2001).

8. John H. Aldrich, "Southern Parties in State and Nation," *Journal of Politics* 62 (August 2000): 643–70.

9. Robert E. Hogan, "Candidate Perceptions of Political Party Campaign Activity in State Legislative Elections," *State Politics and Policy Quarterly* 2 (Spring 2002): 66–85.

10. Ibid.

11. Shanna Pearson-Merkowitz and John Michael McTigue, "Partisan Mountains and Molehills: The Geography of U.S. State Intraparty Factionalism," *State Politics and Policy Quarterly* 8 (Spring 2008): 7–31.

12. James Dao, "Churches in Ohio Flex Political Muscle," *New York Times* (March 27, 2005), 12.

13. Libertarian Party, "Elected Officials," www.lp.org/candidates/elected-officials; Green Party of the United States, "Green Officeholders," www.gp.org/elections/officeholders/index.php (March 16, 2012).

14. Stephen C. Craig, "The Decay of Mass Partisanship," *Polity* 20 (Summer 1988): 705–13.

15. Michael Slackman, "Voters Choosing None of the Above, and Parties Scramble," *New York Times*, www.nytimes.com (April 13, 2004).

16. Justin H. Phillips, "Does the Citizen Initiative Weaken Party Government in the U.S. States?" *State Politics and Policy Quarterly* 8 (Summer 2008): 127–49.

17. Anthony J. Nownes, Clive S. Thomas, and Ronald J. Hrebnar, "Interest Groups in the States," in Virginia Gray and Russell L. Hanson, eds., *Politics in the American States: A Comparative Approach*, 9th ed. (Washington, D.C.: Congressional Quarterly Press, 2008), 98–126.

18. David H. Folz and P. Edward French, *Managing America's Small Communities* (Lanham, MD: Rowman & Littlefield, 2005).

19. Christopher A. Cooper and Anthony J. Nownes, "Perceptions of Power: Interest Groups in Local Politics," *State and Local Government Review* 37 (Fall 2005): 201–16. See also Paul Schumaker, "Group Involvements in City Politics and Pluralist Theory," *Urban Affairs Review* 49 (March 2013): 254–81.

20. Brian E. Adams, *Citizen Lobbyists: Local Efforts to Influence Public Policy* (Philadelphia, PA: Temple University Press, 2007).

21. Christopher A. Cooper and Anthony J. Nownes, "Citizen Groups in Big City Politics," *State and Local Government Review* 35 (Spring 2003): 102–11.

22. Virginia Gray and David Lowery, "A Niche Theory of Interest Representation," *Journal of Politics* 58 (February 1996): 91–111; Michael T. Heaney, "Issue Networks, Information, and Interest Group Alliances: The Case of Wisconsin Welfare Politics, 1993–99," *State Politics and Policy Quarterly* 34 (Fall 2004): 237–70.

23. Donald P. Haider-Markel, "Interest Group Survival: Shared Interests Versus Competition for Resources," *Journal of Politics* 59 (August 1997): 903–12.

24. Clive S. Thomas, Ronald J. Hrebnar, and Anthony Nownes "Interest Groups in the States," in *The Book of the States, 2008* (Lexington, KY: Council of State Governments, 2008), 327.

25. Alan Rosenthal, *The Third House* (Washington, D.C.: Congressional Quarterly Press, 1993).

26. National Conference of State Legislatures, "Ethics: Legislator Gift Restrictions Overview," www.ncsl.org/ legislatures-elections/ethicshome/50-state-table-gift-laws .aspx#ia (February 2012).

27. Joshua Ozymy, "Assessing the Impact of Legislative Lobbying Regulations on Interest Group Influence in U.S. State Legislatures," *State Politics and Policy Quarterly* 10 (Winter 2010): 397–420.

28. Chris Joyner, "Lobbyist Spending Jumps While Lawmakers Dine," *Atlanta Journal and Constitution*, www.ajc.com (February 8, 2012).

29. Anthony J. Nownes and Krissy Walker DeAlejandro, "Lobbying in the New Millennium: Evidence of Continuity and Change in Three States," *State Politics and Policy Quarterly* 9 (Winter 2009): 429–55.

30. Anthony J. Nownes and Patricia Freeman, "Interest Group Activity in the States," *Journal of Politics* 60 (February 1998): 86–112.

31. Daniel E. Bergan, "Does Grassroots Lobbying Work?" *American Politics Research* 37 (March 2009): 327–52.

32. William P. Browne and Delbert J. Ringquist, *Michigan Interests: The Politics of Diversification*, paper presented at the annual meeting of the Midwest Political Science Association, Chicago, 1987, 24.

33. Fred Monardi and Stanton A. Glantz, "Are Tobacco Industry Campaign Contributions Influencing State Legislative Behavior?" *American Journal of Public Health* 88, no. 6: 920.

34. Louay M. Constant, "When Money Matters: Campaign Contributions, Roll Call Votes, and School Choice in Florida," *State Politics and Policy Quarterly* 6 (Summer 2006): 195–219.

35. National Conference on State Legislatures, "State Limits on Contributions to Candidates," www.ncsl.org/Portals/1/ documents/legismgt/Limits_to_Candidates_2011-2012.pdf (September 30, 2011).

36. Daniel M. Shea and Michael John Burton, *Campaign Craft: The Strategies, Tactics, and Art of Political Campaign Management* (Westport, CT: Praeger, 2000), 75–98.

37. R. Michael Alvarez, Asa Hopkins, and Betsy Sinclair, "Mobilizing Pasadena Democrats: Measuring the Effects of Partisan Campaign Contacts," *Journal of Politics* 72 (January 2010): 31–44.

38. Jerry Hagstrom and Robert Guskind, "Selling the Candidate," *National Journal* 18 (November 1, 1986): 2619–26.

39. Michael Hurta, "Houston Mayoral Candidates Rake in the Cash," *Burnt Orange Report*, www.burntorangereport.com/ diary/8996/houston-mayoral-candidates-rake-in-the-cash (July 15, 2009).

40. Cleveland Ferguson III, "The Politics of Ethics and Elections," *Florida State University Law Review* 25 (Fall 1997): 463–503.

41. Ted Braden, "Striking a Responsive Chord: How Political Ads Motivate and Persuade Voters by Appealing to Emotions," *American Journal of Political Science* 49 (April 2005): 388–405.

42. L. Marvin Overby and Jay Barth, "Radio Advertising in American Political Campaigns," *American Politics Research* 34 (July 2006): 451–78.

43. Owen G. Abbe and Paul S. Hernnson, "Campaign Professionalism in State Legislative Elections," *State Politics and Policy Quarterly* 3 (Fall 2003): 223–45.

44. Donald A. Gross and Robert K. Goidel, "The Impact of State Campaign Finance Laws," *State Politics and Policy Quarterly* 1 (Summer 2001): 80–195. See also Nicholas R. Seabrook, "Money and State Legislative Elections: The Conditional Impact of Political Context," *American Politics Research* 38 (May 2010): 399–424.

45. Robert E. Hogan, "Campaign and Contextual Influences on Voter Participation in State Legislative Elections," *American Politics Quarterly* 27 (October 1999): 403–33.

46. Zach Patton, "Chasing the Shadow," *Governing* 19 (June 2006): 43–45.

47. Center for Responsive Politics, "527s: Advocacy Group Spending 2012," www.opensecrets.org/527s/index.php (April 30, 2013).

48. National Conference of State Legislatures, "State Limits on Contributions to Candidates," www.ncsl.org/Portals/1/ documents/legismgt/limits_candidates_2011-2012v2.pdf (May 20, 2013).

49. National Conference of State Legislatures, "Public Financing of Campaigns: An Overview," www.ncsl.org/ legislatures-elections/elections/public-financing-of- campaigns-overview.aspx (May 20, 2013).

50. Neil Malhotra, "The Impact of Public Financing on Electoral Competition: Evidence from Arizona and Maine," *State Politics and Policy Quarterly* 8 (Fall 2008): 263–81.

51. Kedron Bardwell, "Campaign Finance Laws and the Competition for Spending in Gubernatorial Elections," *Social Science Quarterly* 84 (December 2003): 811–25.

52. General Assembly of North Carolina, http://ssl.csg.org/dockets/29cycle/29B/2009bdocketbills/1629b01nc.pdf (July 16, 2009).

Chapter 6 State Legislatures pp. 118–143

1. Morgan Cullen, "New Alaska iPhone App," www.typepad.com/the_thicket/2012/02 (accessed March 4, 2012).

2. Mark C. Ellickson and Donald E. Whistler, "Explaining State Legislators' Casework and Public Resource Allocations," *Political Research Quarterly* 54 (September 2001): 553–69.

3. Ellen Perlman, "The 'Gold-Plated' Legislature," *Governing* 11 (February 1998): 36–40.

4. National Conference of State Legislatures, "Legislator Demographics: State-by-State," www.ncsl.org (Accessed April 15, 2013).

5. Lilliard E. Richardson Jr., Brian E. Russell, and Christopher A. Cooper, "Legislative Representation in Single-Member Versus Multiple-Member District System: The Arizona State Legislature," *Political Research Quarterly* 57 (June 2004): 337–44.

6. *Reynolds v. Sims*, 84 S.Ct. 1362 (1964).

7. Michael P. McDonald, "A Comparative Analysis of Redistricting Institutions in the U.S., 2001–02," *State Politics and Policy Quarterly* 4 (Winter 2004): 371–95.

8. Andrew J. Karch, Corrine M McConnaughy, and Sean M. Theriault, "The Legislative Politics of Congressional Redistricting Commission Proposals," *American Politics Research* 35 (November 2007): 808–25.

9. Ronald E. Weber, "Emerging Trends in State Legislative Redistricting," *Spectrum* 75 (Winter 2002): 13–15. See also Caroline J. Tolbert, Daniel A. Smith, and John C. Green, "Strategic Voting and Legislative Redistricting Reform: District and Statewide Representational Winners and Losers," *Political Research Quarterly* 62 (March 2009): 92–109.

10. National Conference of State Legislatures, "2013 State Legislator Compensation," www.ncsl.org/legislatures-elections/legisdata/2013-ncsl-legislator-salary-and-per-diem.aspx (May 21, 2013).

11. Peverill Squire and Gary Moncrief, *State Legislatures Today: Politics Under the Domes* (Boston: Longman, 2010).

12. Peverill Squire, "Member Career Opportunities and the Internal Organization of Legislatures," *Journal of Politics* 50 (August 1988): 726–44.

13. "Women in State Legislative Leadership Positions 2011," Center for American Women and Politics, http://www.cawp.rutgers.edu/fast_facts/levels_of_office/documents/LegLead11.pdf (May 21, 2013).

14. Henry A. Kim and Justin H. Phillips, "Dividing the Spoils of Power: How Are the Benefits of Majority Party Status Distributed in U.S. State Legislatures?" *State Politics and Policy Quarterly* 9 (Summer 2009): 125–50. See also Kristin Kanthak, "U.S. State Legislative Committee Assignments and Encouragement of Party Loyalty: An Exploratory Analysis," *State Politics and Policy Quarterly* 9 (Fall 2009): 284–303.

15. Keith E. Hamm, Ronald D. Hedlund, and Stephanie S. Post, *Committee Specialization in State Legislatures During the Twentieth Century*, paper presented at the annual meeting of the American Political Science Association, Washington, D.C., 1997.

16. Ralph G. Wright, *Inside the Statehouse: Lessons from the Speaker* (Washington, D.C.: Congressional Quarterly Press, 2005).

17. Alan Rosenthal, *Heavy Lifting: The Job of the American Legislature* (Washington, D.C.: Congressional Quarterly Press, 2004).

18. L. Marvin Overby, Thomas A. Kazee, and David W. Prince, "Committee Outliers in State Legislatures," *Legislative Studies Quarterly* 29 (February 2004): 81–107; David W. Prince and L. Marvin Overby, "Legislative Organization Theory and Committee Preference Outliers in State Senates," *State Politics and Policy Quarterly* 5 (Spring 2005): 68–87.

19. Christopher A. Cooper and Lilliard E. Richardson, Jr., "Institutions and Representational Roles in American State Legislatures," *State Politics and Policy Quarterly* 6 (Summer 2006): 174–94. See also Shannon Jenkins, "The Impact of Party and Ideology on Roll-Call Voting in State Legislatures," *Legislative Studies Quarterly* 31 (May 2006): 205–34.

20. Eric M. Uslaner and Ronald E. Weber, "U.S. State Legislators' Opinions and Perceptions of Constituency Attitudes," *Legislative Studies Quarterly* 4 (November 1979): 563–85.

21. "Bill and Resolution Introductions and Enactments, 2011 Regular Sessions," *The Book of the States 2012* (Lexington, KY: Council of State Governments), 163.

22. "Bill and Resolution Introductions and Enactments, 2011 Special Sessions," *The Book of the States 2012* (Lexington, KY: Council of State Governments), 165.

23. Alan Rosenthal, "The Legislature as Sausage Factory," *State Legislatures* 27 (September 2001): 12–15.

24. Tom Loftus, *The Art of Legislative Politics* (Washington, D.C.: Congressional Quarterly Press, 1994), 76.

25. Ibid., 77.

26. David C. Saffell, "School Funding in Ohio: Courts, Politicians, and Newspapers," *Comparative State Politics* 18 (October 1997): 9–25.

27. Citizens' Conference on State Legislatures, *The Sometimes Governments: A Critical Study of the 50 American Legislatures*, 2d ed. (Kansas City, MO: Author, 1973), 41–42.

28. Karl Kurtz and Brian Weberg, "What Legislatures Need Now," *State Legislatures* 36 (July/August 2010): 47–50.

29. Alan Rosenthal, "The New Legislature: Better or Worse and for Whom?" *State Legislatures* 12 (July 1986): 5. See also Alan Rosenthal, *Engines of Democracy: Politics and Policymaking in State Legislatures* (Washington, D.C.: Congressional Quarterly Press, 2009).

30. Charles W. Wiggins, as quoted in "Is the Citizen Legislator Becoming Extinct," *State Legislatures* 12 (July 1986): 22–25.

31. Representative Vic Krouse, as quoted in ibid., 24.

32. Rosenthal, *Heavy Lifting*; James D. King, "Changes in Professionalism in U.S. State Legislatures," *Legislative Studies Quarterly* 25 (May 2000): 327–43.

33. National Conference of State Legislatures, "Full and Part-Time Legislatures," www.ncsl.org/legislatures-elections/legislatures/full-and-part-time-legislatures.aspx (June 2009).

34. Richard Nathan, as cited in Kathe Callahan and Marc Holzer, "Rethinking Governmental Change," *Public Productivity Management and Review* 17 (Spring 1994): 202.

35. Brad Bumsted, "Rendell Jumps on Reform Bandwagon," *Pittsburgh Tribune-Review*, www.pittsburghlive.com (Accessed March 22, 2007).

36. Stuart Rothenberg, "How Term Limits Became a National Phenomenon," *State Legislatures* 18 (January 1992): 35–39.

37. National Conference of State Legislatures, "Legislators Termed Out: 1996–2010," www.ncsl.org/Default.aspx?TabId=14842 (June 23, 2010).

38. Joel A. Thompson and Gary F. Moncrief, "The Implications of Term Limits for Women and Minorities: Some Evidence from the States," *Social Science Quarterly* 74 (June 1993): 300–9.

39. John Gramlich, "Term Limits Will Create Rookie League in Some Legislatures," www.stateline.org (June 11, 2010).

40. Karen Hansen, "The Third Revolution," *State Legislatures* 23 (September 1997): 20–26; Thad Kousser, "The Limited Impact of Term Limits: Contingent Effects on the Complexity and Breadth of Laws," *State Politics and Policy Quarterly* 6 (Winter 2006): 410–29.

41. Gary Moncrief and Joel A. Thompson, "On the Outside Looking In: Lobbyists Perspectives on the Effects of State Legislative Term Limits," *State Politics and Policy Quarterly* (Winter 2001): 394–411; Joel Thompson and Gary Moncrief, "Lobbying Under Limits: Interest Group Perspectives on the Effects of Term Limits in State Legislatures," in Rick Farmer, John David Rausch Jr., and John C. Green, eds., *The Test of Time: Coping with Legislative Term Limits* (Lanham, MD: Lexington Books, 2003), 211–24. See also, Travis J. Baker and David M. Hedge, "Term Limits and Legislative-Executive Conflict in the American States," *Legislative Studies Quarterly* 38 (May 2013): 237–58.

42. Robert A. Bernstein and Anita Chadha, "The Effects of Term Limits on Representation: Why So Few Women?" in Farmer, Rausch, and Green, eds., *The Test of Time*, 147–58; Stanley M. Caress et al., "Effect of Term Limits on the Election of Minority *State Legislators*," *State and Local Government Review* 35 (Fall 2003): 183–95.

43. John M. Carey, Richard G. Niemi, Lynda W. Powell, and Gary F. Moncrief, "The Effects of Term Limits on State Legislatures: A New Survey of the 50 States," *Legislative Studies Quarterly* 31: (February 2006): 105–34.

44. Daniel C. Lewis, "Legislative Term Limits and Fiscal Policy Performance," *Legislative Studies Quarterly* 37 (August 2012): 305–28. For a different view, see Luke Keele, Neil Malhotra, and Colin H. McCubbins, "Do Term Limits Restrain State Fiscal Policy?" *Legislative Studies Quarterly* 38 (August 2013): 291–326.

45. Carol S. Weissert and Karen Halperin, "The Paradox of Term Limit Support: To Know Them Is Not to Love Them," *Political Research Quarterly* 60 (September 2007): 516–30.

46. Daniel A. Smith, "Overturning Term Limits: The Legislature's Own Private Idaho?" *PS: Political Science and Politics* (April 2003): 215–20.

47. Governor Haley Barbour, State of the State Address (January 26, 2004).

48. Travis J. Baker and David M. Hedge, "Term Limits and Legislative-Executive Conflict in the American States," *Legislative Studies Quarterly* 38 (May 2013): 237–58.

49. Thad Kousser and Justin H. Phillips, "Who Blinks First? Legislative Patience and Bargaining With Governors," *Legislative Studies Quarterly* 34 (February 2009): 55–86.

50. Brian J. Gerber, Cherie Maestas, and Nelson C. Dometrius, "State Legislative Influence Over Agency Rulemaking," *State Politics and Policy Quarterly* 5 (Spring 2005): 24–46; Sarah J. Poggione and Christopher Reenock, "Political Insulation and Legislative Interventions: The Impact of Rule Review," *State Politics and Policy Quarterly* 9 (Winter 2009): 456–85.

51. Dave McNeely, "Is the Sun Setting on the Texas Sunset Law?" *State Legislatures* 20 (May 1994): 17–20.

52. William M. Pearson and Van A. Wigginton, "Effectiveness of Administrative Controls: Some Perceptions of State Legislators," *Public Administration Review* 46 (July/August 1986): 328–31.

53. Rosenthal, "The New Legislature," 5.

54. Alan Rosenthal, *The Decline of Representative Democracy* (Washington, D.C.: Congressional Quarterly Press, 1998), 85.

55. Lilliard E. Richardson Jr., David M. Konisky, and Jeffrey Milyo, "Public Approval of U.S. State Legislatures," *Legislative Studies Quarterly* 37 (February 2012): 99–116.

56. Kurtz and Weberg, "What Legislatures Need Now," p. 47.

Chapter 7 Governors pp. 144–173

1. Matt Friedman, "Gov. Christie's Favorability Rating Skyrockets in Wake of Hurricane Sandy, Poll Shows," blog.nj.com/politics (November 21, 2012).

2. For a more detailed discussion of the processes and results of the state government reform movement, see Ann O'M. Bowman and Richard C. Kearney, *The Resurgence of the States* (Englewood Cliffs, NJ: Prentice-Hall, 1986).

3. Larry Sabato, *Goodbye to Goodtime Charlie: The American Governorship Transformed* (Lexington, MA: Lexington Books, 1978), 13.

4. Alan Rosenthal, *The Best Job in State Politics* (Washington, D.C.: CQ Press, 2012).

5. Thad L. Beyle, "Gubernatorial Elections, Campaign Costs and Powers," in *The Book of the States*, vol. 39 (Lexington, KY: Council of State Governments, 2007), 154–162.

6. Council of State Governments, *The Book of the States 2012* http://knowledgecenter.csg.org/drupal/view-content-type/1502 (Accessed April 15, 2013).

7. Randall W. Partin, "Assessing the Impact of Campaign Spending in Governors' Races," *Political Research Quarterly* 55 (March 2002): 213–24.

8. John R. Wright, "Unemployment and the Democratic Electoral Advantage," *American Political Science Review* 106 (4, 2012): 685–702; Malcolm E. Jewell and David M. Olson, *Political Parties and Elections in the American States*, 3d ed. (Chicago: Dorsey Press, 1988).

9. Peverill Squire, "Challenger Profile and Gubernatorial Elections," *Western Politics Quarterly* 45 (1992): 125–42.

10. Robert C. Lowry, James E. Alt, and Karen E. Feree, "Fiscal Policy Outcomes and Accountability in American States," *American Political Science Review* 92 (December 1998): 759–72; Jason A. MacDonald and Lee Sigelman, "Public Assessments of Gubernatorial Performance: A Comparative State Analysis," *American Politics Quarterly* 27 (April 1999): 201–15.

11. Sharon Sherman, "Powersplit: When Legislatures and Governors Are of Opposing Parties," *State Legislatures* 10 (May/June 1984): 9–12.
12. Sander M. Polster, "Maine's King Makes Independence a Virtue," www.stateline.org (November 30, 1999).
13. *New York Daily News* as reported by governing.com (September 11, 2008).
14. Josh Goodman, "The Christie Way," *Governing* (August 2010): 29–32.
15. Michael Dukakis, as quoted in Thad L. Beyle and Lynn Muchmore, eds., *Reflections on Being Governor* (Washington, D.C.: National Governors Association, 1978): 45.
16. Josh Goodman, "Politics, Kentucky Style," *Governing* (December 2009): 15.
17. Lizette Alvarez, "Facing Flurry of Lawsuits, a Governor Loses a Round," *New York Times*, www.nytimes.com (August 17, 2011).
18. *Book of the States*, vol. 43, pp 146–47.
19. *The Book of the States*, 2012.
20. Thad L. Beyle and Lynn R. Muchmore, "The Governor and the Public," in Beyle and Muchmore, eds., *Reflections on Being Governor*, 24.
21. Adam R. Brown, "Are Governors Responsible for the State Economy? Partisanship, Blame, and Divided Federalism," *The Journal of Politics* 72 (July 2010): 605–15; Jeffrey E. Cohen and James D. King, "Relative Unemployment and Gubernatorial Popularity," *Journal of Politics* 66 (November, 2004): 1267–82.
22. Thad L. Beyle and Lynn R. Muchmore, "The Governor as Party Leader," in Beyle and Muchmore, eds., *Reflections on Being Governor*, 44–51.
23. John Wagner, "Hunt," *News and Observer* (April 1, 2000), 1A, 18A.
24. As quoted in Samuel R. Soloman, "Governors: 1960–1970," *National Civic Review* (March 1971): 126–46.
25. As quoted in Coleman B. Ransome, Jr., *The American Governorship* (Westport, CT: Greenwood Press, 1982), 121.
26. *Rutan et al. v. Republican Party of Illinois*, 1110 S.Ct. 2229, 1990.
27. Beyle, "The Governors . . . ," 216.
28. Matthew Yi, "Governor Sets Record for Vetoing Bills," *San Francisco Chronicle* www.sfgate.com (October 2, 2008).
29. Daniel C. Vock, "Govs Enjoy Quirky Veto Power," *stateline.org* (April 24, 2007).
30. Nelson C. Dometrius and Deil S. Wright, "Governors, Legislatures, and State Budgets Across Time," *Political Research Quarterly* 63, no. 4 (2010): 409–17.
31. James Conant, "Executive Branch Reorganization: Can It Be an Antidote for Fiscal Stress in the States?" *State and Local Government Review* 24 (Winter 1992): 3–11.
32. Dan Durning, "Governors and Administrative Reform in the 1990s," *State and Local Government Review* 27 (Winter 1995): 36–54.
33. James Conant, "State Reorganization: A New Model?" *State Government* 58 (April 1985): 130–38.
34. As quoted in Flentje, "The Governor as Manager: A Political Assessment," *State Government* 1981: 70. For a description of failure in reorganization in Florida, see also Less Garner, "Managing Change Through Organization Structure," *State Government* 60 (July/ August 1987): 191–95.
35. Ibid.; Michael B. Berkman and Christopher Reenock, "Incremental Consolidation and Comprehensive

Reorganization of American State Executive Branches," *American Journal of Political Science* 48 (October 2004): 796–812.
36. Beyle, "The Governors . . . ," 206.
37. Alan Greenblat, "The Job of a Lifetime," *Governing* (June 2009): 24–30.
38. Ransome, *The American Governorship*, 156.
39. Pamela M. Prah, "Some Rookie Governors Fumble," *stateline.org* (March 23, 2007), accessed at www.stateline.org.; Jennifer Steinhauer, "A Rocky Start for Nevada's Governor," *New York Times*, www.nytimes.com (May 30, 2007).
40. Brendon Buhler, "How Did the Ferret Weasel Into This Mess?" *Las Vegas Sun* (April 9, 2009).
41. Alan Greenblatt, "The Job of a Lifetime.".
42. Scott M. Matheson, with James Edwin Kee, *Out of Balance* (Salt Lake City: Peregrine Smith Books, 1986), 186.
43. See Paul West, "They're Everywhere! For Today's Governors, Life Is a Never-Ending Campaign," *Governing* 3 (March 1990): 51–55.
44. Beyle, "Enhancing Executive Leadership in the States," *State and Local Government Review* 27 (Winter 1995): 33.
45. Alan Greenblatt, "Private Investigator," *governing.com* (January 2008); Josh Goodman, "Major Mover," *governing.com* (November 2008).
46. Julia Hurst, "The Constant Evolution of the Office of Lieutenant Governor,"
47. *The Book of the States* 43 (2011): 152–55.
48. Ronald Brownstein and Stephanie Czekalinski, "How Washington Ruined Governors," *National Journal.com* (April 11, 2013).

Chapter 8 Public Administration: Budgeting and Service Delivery pp. 174–201

1. H. George Frederickson, "Can Bureaucracy Be Beautiful?" *Public Administration Review* 60 (January/February 2000): 47–53.
2. Richard W. Stackman, Patrick E. Connor, and Boris W. Becker, "Sectoral Ethos: An Investigation of the Personal Values Systems of Female and Male Managers in the Public and Private Sectors," *Journal of Public Administration Research and Theory* 16 (October 2006): 577–97.
3. See, for example, Theodore H. Poister and Gary T. Henry, "Citizen Ratings of Public and Private Service Quality: A Comparative Perspective," *Public Administration Review* 54 (March/April 1994): 155–59.
4. Mary E. Guy, Meredith A. Newman, and Sharon H. Mastracci, *Emotional Labor: Putting the Service in Public Service* (Armonk, NY: M.E. Sharpe, 2008).
5. www.census.gov/compendia/statab/cats/state_local_govt_finances_employment.html
6. Harold D. Lasswell, *Politics: Who Gets What, When, Where, How?* (Cleveland: World, 1958).
7. See Kurt M. Thurmaier and Katherine G. Willoughby, *Policy and Politics in State Budgeting* (Armonk, NY: M. E. Sharpe, 2000); Dall W. Forsythe, *Memos to the Governor*, 2d ed. (Washington, D.C.: Georgetown University Press, 2004).
8. Ellen Perlman, "'Stat' Fever," *Governing* (January 2007): 48–49.

9. Aaron Wildavsky, "Toward a Radical Incrementalism," in Alfred De Grazia, ed., *Congress: The First Branch of Government* (Washington, D.C.: American Enterprise Institute, 1966).

10. Thurmaier and Willoughby, *Policy and Politics in State Budgeting;* Janet M. Kelly and William C. Rivenbark, *Performance Budgeting for State and Local Government* (Armonk, NY: M. E. Sharpe, 2003).

11. Ellen Perlman, "See Thru Government," *Governing* (May 2009): 34–37; Katherine Barrett and Richard Greene, "The Big Picture on Budgeting," *Governing* (November 2010): 60–62.

12. Charles E. Lindblom, "The Science of Muddling Through," *Public Administrative Review* 19 (Spring 1959): 79–88.

13. Kelly and Rivenbark, *Performance Budgeting.*

14. Jessica Trounstine, *Political Monopolies in American Cities: The Rise and Fall of Bosses and Reformers* (Chicago: University of Chicago Press, 2008).

15. Jay Shafritz, "The Cancer Eroding Public Personnel Professionalism," *Public Personnel Management* 3 (November/December 1974): 486–92; David K. Hamilton, "The Staffing Function in Illinois State Government After Rutan," *Public Administration Review* 53 (July/August 1993): 381–86.

16. H. George Frederickson, "The Airport That Reforms Forgot," *PA Times* (January 2000): 11.

17. Steven W. Hays and Richard C. Kearney, "Anticipated Changes in Human Resource Management: Surveying the Field," *Public Administration Review* 61 (September/October, 2001): 585–97; J. Edward Kellough and Sally Coleman Selden, "The Reinvention of Public Personnel Administration: An Analysis of the Diffusion of Public Personnel Management Reforms in the States," *Public Administration Review* 61 (November/December 2003): 165–76.

18. See, for example, Kenneth J. Meier, "Representative Bureaucracy: An Empirical Analysis," *American Political Science Review* 69 (June 1975): 526–42; and Samuel Krislow and David H. Rosenbloom, *Representative Bureaucracy and the American Political System* (New York: Praeger, 1981), 31–73, 75–107. But see also Judity Sadel and Karyn Loscocco, "Agency Leaders, Gendered Institutions, and Representative Bureaucracy," *Public Administration Review* 65 (March/April 2005): 158–170; and Norman Baldwin, "Predictors of African-American Representation in Municipal Government," *Review of Public Personnel Administration* 25 (March 2005): 29–55.

19. Vicky M. Wilkins, "Exploring the Causal Story: Gender, Active Representation, and Bureaucratic Priorities," *Journal of Public Administration Research and Theory* 17 (2006): 77–94.

20. Nick A. Theobald and Donald P. Haider-Markel, "Race, Bureaucracy, and Symbolic Representation: Interactions Between Citizens and Police," *Journal of Public Administration Research and Theory* 19, no. 2 (2008): 409–26.

21. J. Edward Kellough, "Affirmative Action and Diversity in the Public Sector," in Steven W. Hays, Richard C. Kearney, and Jerrell D. Coggburn, eds., *Public Human Resource Management: Problems and Prospects,* 5th ed. (New York: Pearson Education, 2009), 219–35; Mark Bradbury and J. Edward Kellough, "Representative Bureaucracy: Assessing the Evidence on Active Representation," *American Review of Public Administration* 40, no. 5 (2010): 1–11.

22. Mark D. Bradbury and J. Edward Kellough, "Representative Bureaucracy: Exploring the Potential for Active Representation in Local Government," *Journal of Public Administration Research and Theory* 18 (2011): 697–714; See also Kellough, "Affirmative Action and Diversity in the Public Sector."

23. *Gratz v . Bollinger,* No. 97–75321 (E.D. Mich.) (June 22, 2003); *Grutter* v. *Bollinger,* No. 02–241 F.3d 732 (June 23, 2003).

24. David Ashenfelter, Dawson Bell, and Lori Higgins, "Appeals Court Panel Strikes Down Michigan Affirmative Action Plan," www.freep.com (July 2, 2011); Also see *Ricci* v. *DeStafano,* (No.07-1428, 2009).

25. *Fisher v. University of Texas* No. 11-345 (2013).

26. Jared J. Llorens, Jeffrey B. Wenger, and J. Edward Kellough, "Choosing Public Sector Employment: The Impact of Wages on the Representation of Women and Minorities in State Government," *Journal of Public Administration Research and Theory* 18, no. 3 (2008): 397–413; See also Antonio Cisneros, "Hispanics in the Public Service in the Late Twentieth Century," *Public Administration Review* 53 (January/February 1993):

27. Mary E. Guy, "The Difference That Gender Makes," in Steven W. Hays and Richard C. Kearney, eds. *Public Personnel Administration: Problems and Prospects,* 4th ed. (New York: Pearson Education, 2003), 256–70; Norma Riccucci and Judith R. Seidel, "The Representativeness of State-Level Bureaucratic Leaders: A Missing Piece of the Representative Bureaucracy Puzzle," *Public Administration Review* 57 (September/October 1997): 423–30; Norma M. Riccucci, *Managing Diversity in Public Sector Workforces* (Boulder, CO: Westview Press, 2002).

28. www.bls.gov/bls/cpswomendata.htm (Accessed April 19, 2013).

29. Sonia Ospina and James F. O'Sullivan, "Working Together: Meeting the Challenge of Workplace Diversity," in Hays and Kearney, *Public Personnel Administration,* 2003, 238–55; Riccucci, *Managing Diversity;* Daniel N. Lipson, "Where's the Justice? Affirmative Action's Severed Roots in the Age of Diversity," *Perspectives on Politics* 6 (December 2008): 691–705.

30. *Meritor Savings Bank* v. *Vinson,* 477 U.S. 57 (1986); *Teresa Harris* v. *Forklift Systems, Inc.,* 510 U.S. 17 (1993).

31. *Clark County School District* v. *Breeden,* 532 U.S. 268 (2001).

32. Sally Coleman Selden, "Sexual Harassment in the Workplace," in Hays and Kearney, *Public Personnel Administration,* 2003, 225–37.

33. www.bls.gov/news.release/union2.nr0.htm (January 23, 2013); Steven Greenhouse, "Strained States Turning to Laws to Curb Labor Unions," *New York Times,* www.nytimes.com (January 3, 2011).

34. Richard C. Kearney, *Labor Relations in the Public Sector,* 5th ed. (New York: CRC Press, 2014) Chapter 3.

35. Eric M. Patashnik, *Reforms at Risk* (Princeton, N.J.: Princeton University Press, 2008): 161.

36. Michael Lipsky, *Street-Level Bureaucrats: The Dilemmas of the Individuals in Public Service* (New York: Sage, 1980).

37. Jeffrey S. Banks and Barry R. Weingast, "The Political Control of Bureaucracies Under Asymmetric Information," *American Journal of Political Science* 36 (May 1992): 509–24; Gerald T. Gabris and Douglas M. Ihrke, "Unanticipated Failures of Well-Intentioned Reforms: Some Lessons Learned From Federal and Local Sectors,"

International Journal of Organization Theory and Behavior 6 (February 2003): 195–225.

38. David Osborne and Ted Gaebler, *Reinventing Government* (New York: Penguin Books, 1993).

39. Robert Mohr and Steven C. Delier, "Alternative Methods of Service Delivery in Small and Rural Municipalities," *Public Administration Review* (November/December 2010): 894–905.

40. Ibid., 87.

41. Heather Kerrigan, "The Minnesota-Wisconsin Partnership," www.governing.com (August 2010); Heather Kerrigan, "Making Performance a Priority," *Governing* (April 2011): 54–55.

42. E. S. Savas, *Privatization in the City: Successes, Failures, Lessons* (Washington, D.C.: CQ Press, 2005); Keon S. Chi, Kelley A. Arnold, and Heather M. Perkins, "Privatization in State Government: Trends and Issues," *Spectrum: The Journal of State Government* (Fall 2003): 1.

43. Stephen C. Fehr, "Why Pa. Turnpike Plan Failed," www.stateline.org (March 24, 2009).

44. Gabris and Ihrke, "Unanticipated Failures of Well-intentioned Reforms"; George A. Boyne, "Bureaucratic Theory Meets Reality: Public Choice and Service Contracting in U.S. Local Government," *Public Administration Review* 58 (November/December 1998): 474–84.

45. Tony Cook, "Indiana Gov. Mitch Daniels' Legacy: Privatization," www.indystar.com (January 1, 2013).

46. Katherine Barrett and Richard Greene, "Bidding Wars," *Governing* (November 2012): 62–63.

47. Lawrence L. Martin, "Public-Private Competition: A Public Employee Alternative to Privatization," *Review of Public Personnel Administration* 19 (Winter 1999): 59–70.

48. See Eliot Sclar, *You Don't Always Get What You Pay For* (Ithaca, NY: Cornell University Press, 2000);Katherine Barrett and Richard Greene, "A Balancing Act," *Governing* (March 2005): 59.

49. Tina Trenker, "Apps and the City," *Governing* (January 2011): 38–39; Andy Opsahl, "San Francisco and Partnering Cities Launch 311 Open Source," *Government Technology* (March 3, 2010).

50. "IBM Survey: Too Much Data in Public Sector Stymies Effective Analysis," www.govtech.com (May16, 2011); Sharon S. Dawes, "The Evolution and Continuing Challenges of E-Governance," *Public Administration Review* 68 (December 2008): S86–S102.

51. Donald Norris and Jae Moon, "Advancing E-Government at the Grassroots: Tortoise or Hare?" *Public Administration Review* 65, no. 1 (2005): 64–75.

Chapter 9 The Judiciary pp. 202–229

1. W. John Moore, "In Whose Court?" *National Journal* (October 15, 1991): 2396.

2. Aaron Marshall, "Ohio House Makes 'Don't Touch' the Rule in Strip Clubs," www.Cleveland.com (accessed September 22, 2007).

3. National Center for State Courts poll, cited in David Rottman and Jesse Rutledge, "Facing Down a Budget Crisis: Rising Workloads, Two Judicial Elections and Living With Facebook: The State Courts in 2009," *Book of the States*, vol. 42 (Lexington, KY: 2010), 285.

4. Henry Robert Glick and Kenneth N. Vines, *State Court Systems* (Englewood Cliffs, NJ: Prentice Hall, 1973), 19.

5. Ibid., 21.

6. Kevin Sack, "Where the Bench Orders Some Southern Comfort," *New York Times*, www.nytimes.com (January 29, 2002).

7. Caroline Cournoyer, "'Neighborhood Courts' to Reduce Crowding, Cut Costs," www.governing.com (May 2, 2011).

8. See www.courts.MO.gov/casenet/base/welcome (October 1, 2011).

9. Kathering Barrett and Richard Greene, "Swift Justice," *Governing* (August 2011): 50–51.

10. American Bar Association, *Standards Relating to Court Organization* (New York: ABA, 1974), 43–44.

11. *Book of the States*, vol. 44 (2012), Chapter 5.3.

12. See Charles H. Sheldon and Linda S. Maule, *Choosing Judges: The Recruitment of State and Federal Judges* (Pullman: Washington State University Press, 1997).

13. Melinda Gann Hall, "State Supreme Courts in American Democracy: Probing the Myths of Judicial Reform," *American Political Science Review* 95 (June 2001): 315–30.

14. Richard P. Calderone, Brandice Canes-Wrone, and Tom S. Clark, "Partisan Labels and Democratic Accountability: An Analysis of State Supreme Court Abortion Decisions," *Journal of Politics* 71 (April 2009): 560–73.

15. Melinda Gann Hall and Chris W. Bonneau, "Mobilizing Interest: The Effects of Money on Citizen Participation in State Supreme Court Elections," *American Journal of Political Science* 52, no. 3 (2008): 457–70.

16. Paul Brace and Brent D. Boyea, "State Public Opinion, the Death Penalty, and the Practice of Electing Judges," *American Journal of Political Science* 52, no. 2 (2008): 360–72.

17. *Citizens United v. Federal Election Commission*, No. 08-205 U.S. Supreme Court (January 21, 2010).

18. Adam Liptak and Janet Roberts, "Campaign Cash Mirrors a High Court's Rulings," *New York Times* (October 1, 2006), 1, 10.

19. American Constitutional Society, *Justice at Risk: An Empirical Examination of Campaign Contributions and Judicial Decisions*, accessed August 9, 2013 in www.followthemoney.org/Research/special_topics.phtml; Damon M. Cann, "Justice for Sale? Campaign Contributions and Judicial Decisionmaking," *State Politics and Policy Quarterly* 7 (Fall 2007): 281–97; Stephen Ware, "Money, Politics, and Judicial Decisions: A Case Study of Arbitration Law in Alabama," *Journal of Law and Politics* 15 (Fall 1999): 645–86; Madhavi McCall, "The Politics of Judicial Elections: The Influence of Campaign Contributions on the Voting Patterns of Texas Supreme Court Judges," *Politics and Policy* 31 (June 2003): 314–33.

20. Maggie Clark, "Do Campaign Donations in Judicial Races Influence Court Decisions?" www.pewstates.org (accessed June 11, 2013).

21. Adam Liptak, "Justices Tell Judges Not to Rule on Major Backers," *New York Times*, www.nytimes.com (June 9, 2009); Len Boselovic, "W. Va. Chief Justice Accused of Bias," www.post-gazette.com (January 15, 2008).

22. Monica Youn, ed. *Money, Politics, and the Constitution: Beyond Citizens United* (New York: Brennan Center for Justice and the Century Foundation, 2011).

23. Damon M. Cann, "Justice for Sale?"; Chris W. Bonneau, "Campaign Fundraising in State Supreme Court Elections," *Social Science Quarterly* 88 (March 2007).

24. Adam Liptak, "Justices Tell Judges Not to Rule on Major Backers."

25. Sheila Kaplan, "Justice for Sale," in Thad Beyle, *State Government: CQ's Guide to Current Issues and Activities, 1986–87* (Washington, D.C.: Congressional Quarterly Press, 1987), 151–57.

26. Damon M. Cann, "Justice for Sale?"; Chris W. Bonneau, "Campaign Fundraising in State Supreme Court Elections," *Social Science Quarterly* 88 (March 2007).

27. American Constitutional Society, Justice at Risk: An Empirical Examination of Campaign Contributions and Judicial Decisions, accessed August 9, 2013 in www.followthemoney.org/Research/special_topics.phtml; *Caperton v. A. T. Massey Coal,* No. 08-22 U.S. Supreme Court (2009).

28. See, for example, Henry R. Glick and Craig Emmert, "Selection Systems and Judicial Characteristics: The Recruitment of State Supreme Court Justices," *Judicature* 70 (December/January 1987): 228–35.

29. Melinda Gann Hall, "Electoral Politics and Strategic Voting in State Supreme Courts," *Journal of Politics* 54 (1992): 427–46.

30. John Culver, "California Supreme Court Election: 'Rose Bird and the Supremes,'" *Comparative State Politics Newsletter* (February 1987), 13.

31. Steven D. Williams, "The 1996 Retention Election of Justice White," *Comparative State Politics* 17 (October 1996): 28–30.

32. Hall, "State Supreme Courts," 319.

33. Kathleen A. Bratton and Rorie L. Spill, "Existing Diversity and Judicial Selection: The Role of the Appointment Method in Establishing Gender Diversity in State Supreme Courts," *Social Science Quarterly* 83 (June 2002): 508–18; Kathleen A. Bratton and Rorie L. Spill, "Existing Diversity and Judicial Selection: The Role of the Appointment Method in Establishing Gender Diversity in State Supreme Courts," *Social Science Quarterly* 83 (June 2002): 504–18.

34. American Bar Association, *National Database on Judicial Diversity in State Courts,* www.abanet.org (April 24, 2013).

35. Melinda Gann Hall, "Electoral Politics and Strategic Voting in State Supreme Courts," *Journal of Politics* 54 (1992): 427–46; Melinda Gann Hall, "Toward an Integrated Model of Judicial Voting Behavior," *American Politics Quarterly* 20 (1992): 147–68.

36. Hall, "State Judicial Politics."

37. James P. Wenzel, Shaun Bowler, and David J. Lanoue, "Legislating from the State Bench: A Comparative Analysis of Judicial Activism," *American Politics Quarterly* 25 (July 1997): 363–79.

38. David Rottman and Roy Schotland, "2004 Judicial Elections," In *Book of the States 2005* (Lexington, KY: Council of State Governments, 2005), 37; Chris W. Bonneau, "The Effects of Campaign Spending in State Supreme Court Elections," *Political Research Quarterly* 60 (September 2007): 489–99.

39. Todd Justice, "Supreme Court Flap Between Justice Ann Bradley and Justice David Prosser Leads to Investigation," www.postcrescent.com (June 28, 2011).

40. "New Questions About Rhode Island Chief Justice," *New York Times* (October 3, 1993), sec. 1, 22; "Ex-Top Judge Ends Rhode Island Appeal With a Guilty Plea," *New York Times* (April 30, 1994), sec. 1, 12; "Justice in Impeachment Inquiry Quits in Rhode Island," *New York Times* (May 29, 1986), A14.

41. Brent D. Boyea, "Does Seniority Matter? The Conditional Influence of State Methods of Judicial Retention," *Social Science Quarterly* 91 (1) (2010): 209–27.

42. Ibid.

43. Hall, "Electoral Politics and Strategic Voting."

44. Melinda Gann Hall, "Justices as Representatives: Elections and Judicial Politics in the American States," *American Politics Quarterly* 23 (October 1995).

45. Jake Dear and Edward W. Jessen, "Followed Rates and Leading State Cases," *Davis Law Review* 41 (2007): 683.

46. Gregory A. Caldeira, "Legal Precedent: Structures of Communication Between State Supreme Courts," *Social Networks* 10 (1988): 29–55.

47. Walter V. Schaefer, "Precedent and Policy: Judicial Opinions and Decision Making," in David M. O'Brien, ed., *Judges on Judging: Views from the Bench* (Washington, D.C.: CQ Press, 2004), 108.

48. S. Fernando Rodriguez, Theodore R. Curry, and Gand Lee, "Gender Differences in Criminal Sentencing: Do Effects Vary Across Violent, Property, and Drug Offenses? *Social Science Quarterly* 87 (June 2006): 318–39.

49. Gerald S. Gryski, Eleanor C. Main, and William J. Dixon, "Models of State High Court Decision Making in Sex Discrimination Cases," *Journal of Politics* 48 (February 1986), 140–55; Donald R. Songer and Kelley A. Crews-Meyer, "Does Judge Gender Matter?" *Social Science Quarterly* 81 (September 2000): 750–62.

50. Chris W. Bonneau and Heather Marie Rice, "Impartial Judges? Institutional Context and U.S. State Supreme Courts," *State Politics and Policy Quarterly* 9, no. 4 (2009): 381–403.

51. S. Fernando Rodriguez, Theodore R. Curry, and Gand Lee, "Gender Differences in Criminal Sentencing: Do Effects Vary Across Violent, Property, and Drug Offenses? Social Science Quarterly 87 (June 2006): 318–39.

52. Stephanie Lindquist and Frank B. Cross, *Measuring Judicial Activism* (New York: Oxford University Press, 2010).

53. http://www.theolympian.com/2013/02/28/2441472/washington-state-supreme-court.html (February 28, 2013).

54. Scheb, Bowen, and Anderson, "Ideology, Role Orientations, and Behavior in the State Courts of Last Resort."

55. Bradley C. Canon, "Defining the Dimensions of Judicial Activism," *Judicature* 66 (6) (1983): 238–39.

56. Michael Cooper, "Courts Upend Budgets as States Look for Savings," *New York Times,* www.nytimes.com (June 6, 2011).

57. Laura Langer and Paul Brace, "The Preemptive Power of State Supreme Courts: Adoption of Abortion and Death Penalty Legislation," *Policy Studies Journal* 33 (2005): 317–39.

58. Adam Skaggs and Maria da Silva, "America's Judiciary: Courting Disaster," *LA Times,* www.latimes.com (July 8, 2011).

59. Ibid.

60. John Gramlich, "Court Cuts Trigger Blunt Warning," www.stateline.org (February 18, 2009).

61. Rottman and Rutledge, "Facing Down a Budget Crisis," 283.

62. National Center for State Courts, *Examining the Work of State Courts: An Analysis of 2009 State Caseload Statistics,* www.courtstatistics.org (accessed April 16, 2012); also see Melinda Gann Hall, "State Courts: Politics and the Judicial Process," in Virginia Gray, Russell L. Hanson, and Thad Kousser, eds., *Politics in the American States,* 10th edition (Thousand Oaks, CA: CQ Press, 2013), 229–55.

63. Melinda Gann Hall, "State Courts: Politics and the Judicial Process," 242.

64. http://www.bls.gov/ooh/legal/lawyers.htm (Accessed April 24, 2013).

65. George F. Cole, "Performance Measures for the Trial Courts, Prosecution, and Public Defense," in U.S. Department of Justice, *Performance Measures for the Criminal Justice System* (October 1993), 87–108.

66. National Center for State Courts, *Survey of Judicial Salaries,* www.ncsc.org (accessed April 17, 2012).

67. Council of State Governments, *The Book of the States,* vol. 42 (Lexington, KY: Author, 2010), Table 5.4.

68. Sharon Paynter and Richard C. Kearney, "Who Watches the Watchmen? Evaluating Judicial Performance in the States," *Administration and Society* 41 (8): 923–53.

69. Ibid.

Chapter 10 State–Local Relations pp. 230–250

1. "Rep. Springer Files HB 2416 'The Shopping Bag Freedom Act'," www.house.state.tx.us/news/press-releases/?id=4372& session=83&district=68&bill_code=2745 (March 5, 2013).

2. Steven D. Gold, "NCSL State-Local Task Force: The First Year," *Intergovernmental Perspective* 13 (Winter 1987): 11.

3. *Merriam* v. *Moody's Executors,* 25 Iowa 163, 170 (1868). Dillon's rule was first written in the case of *City of Clinton* v. *Cedar Rapids and Missouri Railroad Co.* (1868).

4. Jeffrey I. Chapman, "Local Government Autonomy and Fiscal Stress: The Case of California Counties," *State and Local Government Review* 35 (Winter 2003): 15–25.

5. U.S. Advisory Commission on Intergovernmental Relations, *The Organization of Local Public Economies* (Washington, D.C.: ACIR, December 1987), 54. See also Jesse J. Richardson Jr., "Dillon's Rule Is From Mars, Home Rule Is From Venus: Local Government Autonomy and the Rules of Statutory Construction," *Publius: The Journal of Federalism* 41 (Fall 2011): 662–85.

6. Peter J. May, *Policy Design and Discretion: State Oversight of Local Building Regulation,* paper presented at the annual meeting of the American Political Science Association, San Francisco, 1996.

7. Dale Krane, Platon N. Rigos, and Melvin B. Hill Jr., *Home Rule in America: A Fifty State Handbook* (Washington, D.C.: Congressional Quarterly Press, 2001).

8. As quoted in Laura Vozzella and David Nitkin, "City Rejects State Plan, Offers Own School Loan," *Baltimore Sun* (March 9, 2004), 1.

9. Ann O'M. Bowman and Richard C. Kearney, *Second Order Devolution: Who's Got the Power?* paper presented at the annual meeting of the Midwest Political Science Association, Chicago, 2010.

10. David K. Hamilton, David Y. Miller, and Jerry Paytas, "Exploring Horizontal and Vertical Dimensions of the Governing of Metropolitan Regions," *Urban Affairs Review* 40 (November 2004): 147–82.

11. David Kocieniewski and Eric Lipton, "Two States Get High Marks for Five-Day Antiterrorism Exercise," *New York Times,* www.nytimes.com (April 9, 2005).

12. Renu Khator, "Coping with Coercion: Florida Counties and the State's Recycling Law," *State and Local Government Review* 26 (Fall 1994): 181–91.

13. Ann O'M. Bowman and Richard C. Kearney, "Second-Order Devolution: Data and Doubt," *Publius: The Journal of Federalism* 41 (Fall 2011): 573.

14. Lawrence J. Grossback, "The Problem of State-Imposed Mandates: Lessons from Minnesota's Local Governments," *State and Local Government Review* 34 (Fall 2002): 191.

15. Tony Romm, "Cities, States Wrangle Over Cuts to Local Aid," www.stateline.org (August 26, 2009).

16. Andree E. Reeves, "State ACIRs: Elements of Success," *Intergovernmental Perspective* 17 (Summer 1991): 13.

17. Richard L. Cole, "The Current Status and Roles of State Advisory Commissions on Intergovernmental Relations in the U.S. Federal System," *Public Administration Review* 71 (March/April 2011): 190–95.

18. Bruce Katz, "Smart Growth: The Future of the American Metropolis?" (Washington, D.C.: Brookings Institution, 2002), 2.

19. William Fulton and Paul Shigley, "Operation Desert Sprawl," *Governing* 12 (August 1999): 16.

20. Christina McCarroll, "Measuring the Cost of Growth," *Christian Science Monitor* (February 6, 2002): 13.

21. Moon-Gi Jeong, "Local Choices for Development Impact Fees," *Urban Affairs Review* 41 (2006): 338–57.

22. Land Trust Alliance, "Voters Approve 81% of Land Conservation Ballot Measures," www.landtrustalliance.org (November 8, 2012).

23. Jayson T. Blair, "Maryland Draws Line Against Sprawl," *Boston Globe* (December 7, 1997), A26.

24. Christopher Swope, "McGreevey's Magic Map," *Governing* 16 (May 2003): 45–48.

25. Iver Peterson, "War on Sprawl in New Jersey Hits a Wall," *New York Times* (October 21, 2003), A15.

26. Christopher R. Conte, "The Boys of Sprawl," *Governing* 13 (May 2000): 28–33; Peter Gordon and Harry W. Richardson, "The Sprawl Debate: Let Markets Plan," *Publius: The Journal of Federalism* 31 (Summer 2001): 131–49.

27. Alan Ehrenhalt, "Breaking the Density Deadlock," *Governing* 20 (March 2007): 11–12.

28. Jered B. Carr and Richard C. Feiock, "Who Becomes Involved in City-County Consolidation?" *State and Local Government Review* 34 (Spring 2002): 78–94.

29. H. V. Savitch and Ronald K. Vogel, "Suburbs Without a City: Power and City-County Consolidation," *Urban Affairs Review* 39 (July 2004): 758–90; Dagney Faulk and Georg Grassmueck, "City-county Consolidation and Local Government Expenditures," *State and Local Government Review* 44 (December 2012): 196–205..

30. Alan Greenblatt, "Anatomy of a Merger," *Governing* 16 (December 2002): 20–25.

31. Ronald J. Oakerson, *Governing Local Political Economies: Creating the Civic Metropolis* (Oakland, CA: Institute for Contemporary Studies, 1999).

32. David Rusk, *Cities Without Suburbs* (Washington, D.C.: Woodrow Wilson Center Press, 1993), 5.

33. Daniel Kemmis, as quoted in Neal R. Peirce, "Missoula's 'Citistate' Claim Marks a New Way to Define Regions," *The News & Observer* (July 1, 1993), 14A.

34. Myron Orfield, *American Metropolitics: The New Suburban Reality* (Washington, D.C.: Brookings, 2002).

35. Margaret Weir, Harold Wolman, and Todd Swanstrom, "The Calculus of Coalitions: Cities, Suburbs, and the Metropolitan Agenda," *Urban Affairs Review* 40 (July 2005): 730–60. See also Annette Steinacker, "Metropolitan Governance: Voter Support and State Legislative Prospects," *Publius: The Journal of Federalism* (Spring 2004): 69–93.

36. James F. Wolf and Tara Kolar Bryan, "Identifying the Capacities of Regional Councils of Government," *State and Local Government Review* 41 (2009): 61–68.

37. Arnab Chakraborty, "Scenario Planning for Effective Regional Governance: Promises and Limitations," *State and Local Government Review* 42 (2010): 156–67.

38. James F. Wolf and Margaret Fenwick, "How Metropolitan Planning Organizations Incorporate Land Use Issues in Regional Transportation Planning," *State and Local Government Review* 35 (Spring 2003): 123–31.

39. Barbara Cotter, "City to Work with PPACG on Regional Bike Trail Plan," http://ppacg.org/news/ppacg-in-the-news/981-qcity-to-work-with-ppacg-onregional-bike-trail-planq-the-gazettte (February 13, 2013).

40. DeWitt John, as cited in William K. Stevens, "Struggle for Recovery Altering Rural America," *New York Times* (February 5, 1988), 8.

41. "The Great Plains Drain," *The Economist* (January 19, 2007): 35.

42. Jim Seroka, "Community Growth and Administrative Capacity," *National Civic Review* 77 (Jan/Feb 1988): 45.

43. Linda Bauer, "Free Land Fails to Draw New Homesteaders to Kansas Towns," www.mcclatchydc.com/2010/03/30/91343/free-land-in-kansas-towns-fails.html#.UaDe3dLBOQg# (March 30, 2010).

44. Patrik Jonsson, "North Carolina's Gambit to Bring Internet Age to Rural Areas," *Christian Science Monitor* (July 1, 2004): 2–3.

45. Arthur Holst, "Review of Local Government and the States: Autonomy, Politics, and Policy," *Publius: The Journal of Federalism* 35 (Fall 2005): 644–45.

46. Christopher Conte, "Dry Spell," *Governing* 16 (March 2003): 20–24.

47. George Pataki, "Governor Pataki Offers $1 Billion Plan to Help Local Governments," Press Release, January 10, 1997.

48. Patrick McGreevy, "Cities, Counties Pay Price for Capital Clout," *Los Angeles Times*, www.latimes.com/news/local (September 12, 2007).

Chapter 11 Local Government: Structure and Leadership
pp. 251–278

1. "Illinois' Local Governments to Get Review," *Chicago Tribune*, www.chicagotribune.com (Accessed August 15, 2011).

2. U.S. Census Bureau, 2012 Census of Governments: Organization Component Preliminary Estimates, "Table 2. Local Governments by Type and State: 2012," www2.census.gov/govs/cog/2012/formatted_prelim_counts_23jul2012_2.pdf (June 1, 2013).

3. Council for Excellence in Government 2000, www.excelgov.org (July 9, 2003).

4. Christopher Hoene, Mark Baldassare, and Michael Shires, "The Development of Counties as Municipal Governments," *Urban Affairs Review* 37 (March 2002): 575–91.

5. Dale Krane, Platon N. Rigos, and Melvin B. Hill Jr., *Home Rule in America: A Fifty State Handbook* (Washington, D.C.: Congressional Quarterly Press, 2001).

6. Alan Greenblatt, "New Clout in a Big County," *Governing* 20 (May 2007): 22–23.

7. J. Edwin Benton, "The Impact of Structural Reform on County Government Service Provision," *Social Science Quarterly* 84 (December 2003): 858–74.

8. Jayce L. Farmer, "County Government Choices for Redistributive Services," *Urban Affairs Review* 47 (January 2011): 60–83.

9. Jerome I. Sherman, "6 Elected Row Officers Become 3 Appointed," *Pittsburgh Post-Gazette*, www.post-gazette.com (May 18, 2005).

10. See Olesva Tkacheva, "New Cities, Local Officials, and Municipal Incorporation Laws: A Supply-Side Model of City Formation," *Journal of Urban Affairs* 20 (2008): 155–74.

11. Kimberly L. Nelson and James H. Svara, "Adaptation of Models Versus Variations in Form: Classifying Structures of City Government," *Urban Affairs Review* 45 (March 2010): 544–62.

12. Kimberly L. Nelson and Karl Nollenberger, "Conflict and Cooperation in Municipalities: Do Variations in Form of Government Have an Effect?" *Urban Affairs Review* 47 (September 2011): 696–720.

13. H. George Frederickson, Gary A. Johnson, and Curtis Wood, *The Adapted City: Institutional Dynamics and Structural Change* (Armonk, NY: M.E. Sharpe, 2004); Megan Mullin, Gillian Peele, and Bruce E. Cain, "City Caesars? Institutional Structure and Mayoral Success in Three California Cities," *Urban Affairs Review* 40 (2004): 19–43.

14. Jered Carr and Shanthi Karuppusamy, "Beyond Ideal Types of Municipal Structure," *American Review of Public Administration* 39 (2009): 304–21.

15. Victor S. DeSantis and David Hill, "Citizen Participation in Local Politics: Evidence From New England Town Meetings," *State and Local Government Review* 36 (2004): 172.

16. Melissa Conradi, "But Definitely Not St. Ventura," *Governing* 14 (January 2001): 16.

17. Kathryn A. Foster, *The Political Economy of Special Purpose Government* (Washington, D.C.: Georgetown University Press, 1997).

18. Larita Killian and Dagney Faulk, "Policy Brief: Special Districts and Local Government Reform," Center for Business and Economic Research, http://cms.bsu.edu/-/media/WWW/DepartmentalContent/MillerCollegeofBusiness/BBR/Publications/SpecialDistricts2012.pdf (March 2012).

19. Barbara Coyle McCabe, "Special District Formation Among the States," *State and Local Government Review* 32 (Spring 2000): 121–31.

20. Michael A. Molloy, *Local Special Districts and Public Accountability*, paper presented at the annual meeting of the Midwest Political Science Association, Chicago, 2000.

21. Nancy Burns, *The Formation of American Local Governments* (New York: Oxford University Press, 1994).

22. Foster, *The Political Economy of Special Purpose Government*.

23. "LA Mayor Villaraigosa Sworn in to 2nd Term," *Mercury News*, www.mercurynews/com/breakingnews/ (July 1, 2009).

24. Jameson W. Doig and Erwin C. Hargrove, eds., *Leadership and Innovation* (Baltimore: Johns Hopkins University Press, 1987).

25. Christine Kelleher Palus, "Responsiveness in American Local Governments," *State and Local Government Review* 42 (2010): 133–50.

26. Floyd Hunter, *Community Power Structure* (Chapel Hill: University of North Carolina Press, 1953) and *Community Power Succession* (Chapel Hill: University of North Carolina Press, 1980).

27. Robert Dahl, *Who Governs?* (New Haven, CT: Yale University Press, 1961).

28. Clarence N. Stone, *Regime Politics: Governing Atlanta, 1948–1988* (Lawrence: University Press of Kansas, 1989).

29. Rob Gurwitt, "The Lure of the Strong Mayor," *Governing* 6 (July 1993): 36–41; Terrell Blodgett, "Beware the Lure of the 'Strong' Mayor," *Public Management* 76 (January 1994): 6–11.

30. David R. Morgan and Sheilah S. Watson, *The Effects of Mayoral Power on Urban Fiscal Policy*, paper presented at the annual meeting of the American Political Science Association, New York City, September 1994.

31. Thomas P. Ryan Jr., as quoted in Jane Mobley, "Politician or Professional? The Debate Over Who Should Run Our Cities Continues," *Governing* 1 (February 1988): 42–48.

32. W. John Moore, "From Dreamers to Doers," *National Journal* (February 13, 1988): 372–77.

33. Cory Booker, "Fighting for Newark's Future," (audio) www.corybooker.com/main/cfm (July 5, 2006).

34. Huey L. Perry, "Deracialization as an Analytical Construct in American Urban Politics," *Urban Affairs Quarterly* 27 (December 1991): 181–91; Nicholas O. Alonzie, "The Promise of Urban Democracy: Big-City Black Mayoral Service in the Early 1990s," *Urban Affairs Review* 35 (January 2000): 422–34.

35. Mary E. Summers and Philip A. Klinkner, "The Daniels Election in New Haven and the Failure of the Deracialization Hypothesis," *Urban Affairs Quarterly* 27 (December 1991): 202–15.

36. Robert M. Stein, Stacy G. Ulbig, and Stephanie Shirley Post, "Voting for Minority Candidates in Multiracial/Multiethnic Communities," *Urban Affairs Review* 41 (November 2005): 157–81.

37. Center for American Women and Politics, "Women in Elective Office 2012," www.cawp.rutgers.edu/fast_facts/levels_of_office/documents/elective.pdf (August 25, 2010).

38. Philip J. LaVelle, "S.D. Political Hounds Catch First Scent of Recall Bid," *San Diego Union-Tribune*, www.signonsandiego.com (January 4, 2005).

39. Several of these studies are summarized in Susan A. MacManus and Charles S. Bullock III, "Women and Racial/Ethnic Minorities in Mayoral and Council Positions," in International City/County Management Association, *The Municipal Year Book 1993* (Washington, D.C.: International City/County Management Association, 1993), 70–84.

40. Clifford J. Wirth and Michael L. Vasu, "Ideology and Decision Making for American City Managers," *Urban Affairs Quarterly* 22 (March 1987): 454–74.

41. Martin Vanacour, "Promoting the Community's Future," in Charldean Newell, ed., *The Effective Local Government Manager*, 3d ed. (Washington, D.C.: International City/County Management Association, 2004), 84–85. See also Timothy B. Krebs and John P. Pelissero, "Urban Managers and Public Policy: Do Institutional Arrangements Influence Decisions to Initiate Policy?" *Urban Affairs Review* 45 (2010): 391–411.

42. James H. Svara, "Conflict and Cooperation in Elected-Administrative Relations in Large Council-Manager Cities," *State and Local Government Review* 31 (Fall 1999): 173–89. See also James H. Svara, "Exploring Structures

and Institutions in City Government," *Public Administration Review* 65 (2005): 500–506.

43. Mark M. Levin, "How to Work with Elected Officials," *Public Management* (December 2008): 4–5.

44. Larry Azevedo, as quoted in Alan Ehrenhalt, "How a Liberal Government Came to Power in a Conservative Suburb," *Governing* 1 (March 1988): 51–56.

45. Kenneth Prewitt, *The Recruitment of Political Leaders: A Study of Citizen-Politicians* (Indianapolis: Bobbs-Merrill, 1970).

46. MacManus and Bullock, "Women and Racial/Ethnic Minorities in Mayoral and Council Positions," 70–84; Joshua G. Behr, *Race, Ethnicity and the Politics of Redistricting* (Albany, NY: SUNY Press, 2004).

47. Bari Anhalt, *Minority Representation and the Substantive Representation of Interests*, paper presented at the annual meeting of the American Political Science Association, San Francisco, 1996.

48. Paula D. McClain and Steven C. Tauber, "Racial Minority Group Relations in a Multiracial Society," in Michael Jones-Correa, ed., *Governing American Cities: Immigrants and Inter-Ethnic Coalitions, Competition, and Conflict* (New York: Russell Sage Foundation, 2001),pp. 111–36.

49. Christian Collett, "Bloc Voting, Polarization, and the Panethnic Hypothesis: The Case of Little Saigon," *Political Research Quarterly* 67 (August 2005): 907–33.

50. James W. Button, Kenneth D. Wald, and Barbara A. Rienzo, "The Election of Openly Gay Public Officials in American Communities," *Urban Affairs Review* 35 (November 1999): 188–209.

51. Kimberly L. Nelson and Karl Nollenberger, "Conflict and Cooperation in Municipalities: Do Variations in Form of Government Have an Effect?" *Urban Affairs Review* 47 (September 2011): 696–720; see also Brianne Heidbreder et al., "Determinants of Policy Conflict in Michigan Municipalities," *State and Local Government Review* 43 (April 2011): 32–45.

52. James H. Svara, "Council Profile: More Diversity, Demands, Frustration," *Nation's Cities Weekly* 14 (November 18, 1991): 4. See also James H. Svara, "The Roles of City Councils and Implications for the Structure of Government," *National Civic Review* 91 (2002): 5, 23.

53. James B. Kaatz, P. Edward French, and Hazel Prentiss-Cooper, "City Council Conflict as a Cause of Psychological Burnout and Voluntary Turnover Among City Managers," *State and Local Government Review* 31 (Fall 1999): 162–72; see also Robert J. Tekniepe and Christopher Stream, "You're Fired: County Manager Turnover in Large American Counties," *American Review of Public Administration* 42 (2012): 715–29.

54. Rob Gurwitt, "Are City Councils a Relic of the Past? *Governing* 16 (April 2003): 20–24.

55. Alan Ehrenhalt, "Boldness Without Bluster," *Governing* 14 (December 2000): 8.

56. Ibid., 6.

57. J. M. Ferris, "The Role of the Nonprofit Sector in a Self-Governing Society," *Voluntas* 9 (1998): 137–51.

58. Richard C. Hula and Cynthia Jackson-Elmoore, "Governing Nonprofits and Local Political Processes," *Urban Affairs Review* 36 (January 2001): 324–58.

59. "All-America Cities Named," www.allamericacityaward.com (June 17, 2013).

60. Josh Goodman, "Out of the Blue," *Governing* 20 (October 2007): 40.

Chapter 12 Taxing and Spending pp. 279–308

1. Keith Fagan, "Cash-Strapped Stockton Set to Vote for Bankruptcy," www.SFGate.com (June 27, 2012).
2. Data obtained from U.S. Bureau of the Census, www.census.gov, May 15, 2013.
3. Pamela M. Prah, "Price Tag of Sequester to States: $6 Billion," www.stateline.org (March 1, 2013).
4. Binyamin Applebaum and Robert Febeloff, "Tax Burden for Most Americans Is Lower Than in the 1980s," *New York Times*, www.nytimes.com (November 29, 2012).
5. Mike Machiag, "Tax Exempt Properties Rise as Cities Cope With Shrinking Tax Bases," *Governing* (November 2012): 54–58.
6. U.S. Bureau of the Census, *Statistical Abstract 2011*, www.census.gov.
7. Mark Schneider, "Local Budgets and the Maximization of Local Property Wealth in the System of Suburban Government," *Journal of Politics* 49 (November 1987): 1114.
8. Thomas R. Dye and Richard C. Feiock, "State Income Tax Adoption and Economic Growth," *Social Science Quarterly* 76 (September 1995): 648–54.
9. *The Book of the States*, vol. 43 (Lexington, KY: Council of State Governments, 2011).
10. Neal R. Peirce, "Service Tax May Rise Again," *Public Administration Times* 11 (August 12, 1988): 2.
11. *Quill* v. *North Dakota*, 504 U.S. 298 (1992).
12. Penelope Lemov, "States Look to Collect Internet sales Taxes," *Governing*, www.governing.com (May 18, 2011); David C. Powell, "Internet Taxation and U.S. Intergovernmental Relations: From Quill to the Present," *Publius* 30 (Winter 2000): 39–51.
13. Nanette Byrnes, "Amazon Tax Payoff Starts to Arrive in Some U.S. States," www.reuters.com (February 20, 2013); Daniel C. Vock, "States Rack Up Victories in Bids to Collect Online Sales Taxes," www.pewstates.org (accessed April 20, 2013).
14. www.TaxFoundation.org (accessed May 5, 2013).
15. *Book of the States*, vol. 43 (2011): Table 7.15.
16. Alaska Permanent Fund, www.apfc.org (accessed May 8, 2013).
17. Lucy Dadayan and Robert B. Ward, "Back in the Black," www.rockinst.org (June 13, 2011).
18. Donald E. Miller and Patrick A. Pierce, "Lotteries for Education: Windfall or Hoax?" *State and Local Government Review* 29 (Winter 1997): 43–52.
19. Elizabeth A. Freund and Irwin L. Morris, "The Lottery and Income Inequality in the States," *Social Science Quarterly* 86 (2005): 996–1012.
20. Pamela M. Prah, "Kansas Has Biggest Jump in Casino Tax Revenue, New Jersey Has Largest Drop," www.pewstates.org (accessed May 12, 2013).
21. Pamela M. Prah, "Nevada Has Head Start as States React to Federal Gambling Decision," www.stateline.org (January 6, 2012); Ray Hagar, "Boon or Bust: Nevada Looks to Future With Online Poker," www.rgj.com (March 3, 2013).

22. National Association of State Budget Officers, www.nasbo.org (accessed May 12, 2013).
23. Timothy Egan, "They Give But They Also Take: Voters Muddle States' Finance," *New York Times* (March 2, 2001), 1, 4.
24. Mark A. Glaser and W. Bartley Hildreth, "A Profile of Discontinuity Between Citizen Demand and Willingness to Pay Taxes: Comprehensive Planning for Park and Recreation Investment," *Public Budgeting and Finance* 16 (Winter 1996): 97.
25. Chanhoon Jung and Suho Bae, "Changing Revenue and Expenditure Structure and the Reliance on User Charges and Fees in American Counties, 1972–2002," *American Review of Public Administration* (Spring 2010): 1–19.
26. Christine R. Martell and Paul Teske, "Fiscal Management Implications of the TABOR Bind," *Public Administration Review* (July/August 2007): 673–86.
27. Daniel R. Mullins and Bruce A. Wallin, "Tax and Expenditure Limitations: Introduction and Overview," *Public Budgeting and Finance* 24 (Winter 2004): 2–15.
28. http://www.atlantaregional.com/transportation/financing-transportation.
29. David W. Chen, "Mayor Bloomberg and Council Agree on Budget," *New York Times*, www.nytimes.com (June 16, 2009).
30. Pew Center on the States, *The Trillion Dollar Gap* (Washington, D.C.: Pew Center on the States, 2010): 4.
31. Ibid.
32. Michael A. Pagano and Jocelyn M. Johnson, "Life at the Bottom of the Fiscal Food Chain: Examining City and Council Revenue Decisions," *Publius* 30 (Winter 2000): 159–70.
33. Pew Center on the States, *The Trillion Dollar Gap Unfunded State Retirement Systems and the Road to Reform* (Washington, D.C.: Pew Center on the States, February 2010. http://www.pewstates.org/issues/pensions (Accessed May 13, 2013).
34. Pew Center on the States, http://www.pewstates.org/research/data-visualizations/the-widening-gap (accessed May 15, 2013).
35. Stephen C. Fehr, "States Get Off Revenue Roller Coaster," *Stateline*, www.stateline.org (March 1, 2011).
36. John Gramlich, "As State Budgets, Payroll Shrink, So Do Ambitions," *Stateline*, www.stateline.org (January 10, 2011).
37. Sallie Hofmeister, "Fund Head Resigns in California" and "Many Questions, But Too Late," *New York Times* (December 6, 1994), D1, D2.
38. John E. Petersen, "Happy Birthday, BABS," *Governing* (June 2010): 28–29.
39. Mary Williams Walsh and Louise Story, "A Stealth Tax Subsidy for Business Faces New Scrutiny," *New York Times*, www.nytimes.com (March 4, 2013).
40. Securities Industry and Financial Markets Association, *Municipal Bond Credit Report* (New York: 2011).
41. Mary Walsh Williams, "In Alabama, a County That Fell Off a Financial Cliff," *New York Times*, www.nytimes.com (February 18, 2012).

Index